PLATO AND THE
MYTHIC TRADITION IN
POLITICAL THOUGHT

PLATO AND THE
MYTHIC TRADITION IN
POLITICAL THOUGHT

TAE-YEOUN KEUM

THE BELKNAP PRESS OF HARVARD UNIVERSITY PRESS

Cambridge, Massachusetts   London, England

2020

First printing

LIBRARY OF CONGRESS CATALOGING-IN-PUBLICATION DATA

Names: Keum, Tae-Yeoun, 1986– author.
Title: Plato and the mythic tradition in political thought / Tae-Yeoun Keum.
Description: Cambridge, Massachusetts : The Belknap Press of Harvard
University Press, 2020. | Includes bibliographical references and index.
Identifiers: LCCN 2020014658 | ISBN 9780674984646 (cloth)
Subjects: LCSH: Plato—Influence. | Rationalism—Political aspects—History. |
Mythology—Political aspects—History. | Political science—Philosophy.
Classification: LCC B395 .K43 2020 | DDC 184—dc23
LC record available at https://lccn.loc.gov/2020014658

For Dong-Yeoun Lee and In-Ho Keum

CONTENTS

PLATO AND THE
MYTHIC TRADITION IN
POLITICAL THOUGHT

INTRODUCTION

Plato's Legacy and the Problem of Myth in Political Thought

"MYTH" IS HARDLY A WELCOME WORD in the discourse of political theory, where it is often understood in opposition to our most cherished political and philosophical ideals. As symbolically fraught narratives that resist critical scrutiny, myths are more readily associated with collective passions than with the autonomy of individuals to think and judge for themselves, with obscurity and irrationality rather than with clarity and reason, with social backwardness rather than with social progress. At the same time, such narratives abound in contemporary politics and culture. And, especially in times of polarization and political uncertainty, their enduring power suggests that they may be much more deeply entrenched in our way of life than we might think.

What follows is a study of myth through Platonic eyes. The endeavor may seem surprising to students of Plato and the Platonic tradition; Plato's legacy, often equated with the history of Western philosophy itself, is conventionally taken to be a rational and critical enterprise divorced from myth. But the well-known fact that Plato deliberately interlaced his philosophical writings with his own myths suggests a portrait of Plato in tension with his canonical reputation, and suggests, in turn, that the ramifications of this friction have not yet been fully drawn out in political theory.

Against the grain of predominant portrayals of Plato's legacy, both in the popular and in the philosophical imagination, the chapters that follow chart a tradition of authors for whom Plato's myths were a vital resource for investigating the role of myth in philosophy and political thought. Plato's myths helped teach the authors of this tradition to make myth a subject of philosophical inquiry, and to treat it as a medium through which to explore the full range of functions that unconditioned narratives can serve in the formation and maintenance of our world-views. Thus conceived, constructing a more complete account of Plato's legacy is also a way of confronting broader questions regarding the place of myth in political thought.

In the summer of 1952, a British family of three was murdered on a road-side while on holiday in France. One of the victims was a prominent scientist who had been knighted for his work with the Ministry of Food during the Second World War; the others were his wife and their daughter, who was only ten years old. The child's head had been smashed in so badly that handling her skull, according to the autopsy, "was like moving a bag of nuts."[1]

The man accused of the triple murder was Gaston Dominici, an il-literate seventy-five-year-old farmer who owned La Grand'Terre, the land adjacent to the site of the crime. His trial, which took place in No-vember 1954, was one of the greatest public scandals of 1950s France. It was allegedly remarked at the time that, in comparison to the drama that unfolded at court, "the theaters of Paris are dull."[2]

There were many things about the trial that were unusual, including, among them, a hopelessly botched body of forensic evidence and a con-spicuous communicative barrier between the legal language of the mag-istrates and the rural dialect of the accused. But perhaps the most striking feature of the trial was the naturalness with which, in the ab-sence of any concrete evidence or an identifiable motive, a fantastical narrative began to settle around the events in question. This narrative painted an intricate picture of a rough and uncouth farmer who presided over his clan and his land with a kind of raw brutality and who, upon discovering the hapless tourists on his property, simply disposed of them as he willed. In lurid detail, the prosecution kept going over a confession that Dominici had made during police interrogation, apparently under duress, in which he admitted to having initiated an erotic encounter with the wife and subsequently doing away with her husband and child the moment he deemed them a nuisance.[3]

For all its absurdity, the story forced onto the case of Gaston Dominici wasn't at all an unfamiliar one. It might easily recall, for instance, a scene from any number of films in which a farmer with a gun threatens to administer his own law on anyone who wanders onto his property. Or even if the echoes of such popular tropes in the prosecutor's account could be dismissed as merely one of several embarrassments in an exceptionally dysfunctional trial, there was still no way of denying the familiarity of another, more general pattern in that narrative, one that was endemic to the language of the courts. This was the story of a criminal who is single-mindedly fixated on one motive to the point of losing all hold on reason in its pursuit, as though overcome by a kind of animal or "monstrous" passion.[4] According to this sort of story, crimes are committed for specific reasons, and criminals are individuals who sacrifice their higher cognitive faculties to certain identifiable objects of obsession.

To this day, many consider the murder unresolved. However, it was clear, even at the time, that the case was being understood in unusually grand, symbolic terms. When the French philosopher and cultural critic Roland Barthes wrote about the so-called Dominici Affair two months later, he did so with the conviction that the sensationalist story spun by the court was no accident, but instead the determined product of a greater network of "mythologies" pervading our society.[5] By this he meant that the stories we end up telling about our world are conditioned by a tangle of assumptions, frames of mind, and narrative patterns that have already been made familiar to us.

Such frameworks were both insidious and pervasive: while they might find incidental expression in any one story that happens to be told at a given time, like the one told about Gaston Dominici at his trial, they would by and large form the implicit background to our social norms and expectations, a tissue of cognitive habits so basic to the way we make sense of things that we don't even notice their existence, or the extent to which they influence our thinking. Though they might seem to be an amorphous assemblage of subconscious biases, symbolic associations, and wishful thinking, they would often cluster around a narrative mold—like the one about a brute with a gun, or the one about a single-minded criminal; the story of the cheating villain who will eventually get his comeuppance and the hero who survives the fight; or the one about the conspiracy of an overeducated elite encroaching on the livelihood of the common folk.[6]

And, strangely, for Barthes, when such hidden narratives would surface in our courts, our political rhetoric, our films, and our advertisements, they would often seem to evoke the fabulous qualities of certain fantastical tales. The Dominici trial, for example, felt to him like the failed staging of a "rustic tale" in which "shepherds converse with judges without embarrassment."[7] The prosecution, for its part, was quick to depict the old goat-farmer as a lecherous half-beast, a kind of modern-day Pan. He was a "crafty trickster" perpetually "juggling with human souls and bestial thoughts," and it was this enchanted figure, rather than Gaston Dominici, who was being condemned at court: "He has not a few faces, this false patriarch of the Grand'Terre, he has a hundred!"[8]

Critically, these evocative and fantastical narratives, which were embedded everywhere in our culture and which could be dismissed so innocuously, were in fact immensely consequential. To the extent that such prevailing symbolic patterns undergirded the things that feel normal or natural to us, they controlled our expectations, and in turn helped determine what we see and don't see. Had society not already been predisposed to finding certain kinds of stories coherent, plausible, or worth imagining, the Dominici court could not have viewed the case through those lenses; instead, the account that it came up with would have been altogether unimaginable.

At their most powerful, these commonplace templates could dictate the course of justice, and they could change lives. At the end of the eleven-day trial, Dominici was sentenced to execution by guillotine. Eventually, as his health deteriorated to the point where it was deemed inhumane for him to remain in prison, he was released by Charles de Gaulle to live out his last years in a local hospice, where he died in 1965.[9]

DEEP MYTHS AND LITERARY MYTHS

Barthes's insight was that our social and political world is full of those deeply embedded narratives that we take for granted, and which condition our perception of our environment and the events that take place in it. Those tacit frameworks that Barthes associated with "mythology" might go by other names. To the extent that they are implicit lenses through which we view reality—and have the effect of determining what is natural and to be taken for granted in everyday life—they might resemble those irrefutably deep-seated worldviews that Pierre Bourdieu calls *doxa,* or the schematic medium of the symbol in the philosophy of Ernst Cassirer.[10] To the extent that they help constitute the rich cultural background shaping our views of the world and its possibilities, such frameworks might also be an alternative way of thinking about aspects of the broader web of tacitly shared understandings and representations that Charles Taylor calls a social imaginary.[11]

But Barthes was hardly alone in reaching for the category of "mythology" to make this observation about the frameworks forming the tacit background to our worldviews.[12] In both theoretical discourse as well as in common usage, "myth" is a ubiquitous term designating a particularly dense and pervasive form of thought that does not stand up to rational scrutiny.[13]

Theorists of myth tend to refer to something as a myth when it can be described as a narrative about conditions or events in our world that is taken for granted, and is not readily available for critical examination.[14] In that regard the theoretical understanding of the word "myth" retains a substantial share of the connotations it carries in common usage. That is, when we call something a myth, we don't simply mean that it is a piece of false information. Myths, rather, are tacit imaginative frameworks that circulate widely and are made familiar to us—in the way hearing a phrase like "the myth of the lone genius" might evoke in us a surprisingly precise array of images and story lines for envisioning the career, the personality, and even the physical attributes of such a figure. But despite their familiarity, these narratives are not grounded in reasons or verifiable facts—like the myths invoked in any number of newspaper headlines broadcasting the need to expose and debunk them.[15] Indeed, they are especially impervious to facts and arguments—much like the way so many of the myths exposed in those same newspaper headlines keep resurfacing, no matter how many times they are debunked.

This broad definition of myth encompasses a sprawling constellation of concepts understood to operate at the level of deep culture. They range from mundane and relatively undertheorized phenomena—like tropes, stereotypes, superstition, urban legends, conspiracy theories, and the everyday narrative patterns that exercised Barthes—to issues of more immediate political consequence, such as false consciousness, institutions, belief systems, and ideology, especially in relation to discussions of nationalism.[16]

It may seem unconvincing, if not odd, that theoretical discourse brings this vast and eclectic collection of concepts under the same category, let alone under the category of myth. But the motivation driving the line of thought is broadly intuitive. We might understand it as a theoretical effort to identify a set of unusually dense thought patterns, which tend toward the figurative and narrative, and which elude ordinary channels of rational scrutiny. In the most general instance, the contemporary study of myth is a way of acknowledging that people's worldviews are conditioned by arational frameworks fraught with symbolic meanings.

In this book, I am not so much intent on contesting the definitional boundaries of what can and cannot be brought under the broad theoretical heading of "myth," as I am concerned with examining a particular aspect of this effort. Namely, I explore the notion that the category that we use to identify a certain set of elusive background phenomena in modern politics and culture is the category of *myth* in particular. This move circumvents a more general definitional problem in existing theoretical work on myth, which scholars tend to conceptualize in terms that are at once too broad and too narrow. By examining the various ways in which a tradition of thinkers has ascribed wider significance to a narrow literary genre, in particular as it has been appropriated for philosophical use in Plato's writings, I hope to keep the focus of this study on a specific meaning and use of myth without losing sight of the larger stakes surrounding the concept.

So far I have been discussing a more contemporary, elusive understanding of myth as a kind of deep, tacit framework in the background of our worldviews. But this broad conception of myth also bears a close association to an older, more tangible meaning of the word: not of a tacit imaginative formula in deep cultural circulation, but of a narrated tale conforming to the conventions of a distinct literary genre. This is the definition of myth as a unique form of orally transmitted narrative fiction, featuring fantastical or supernatural elements, which we tend to encounter as the cultural artifacts of ancient or otherwise remote civilizations. Myths of this kind are not evocative templates for stories, but elaborated stories whose details have already been more or less filled out—with specific, often recurring, casts of fantastic characters or settings, sometimes with complex, interconnected plots.

There are, then, two distinct ideas of myth that figure in the discourse around myth. The first meaning, we might call *deep myths,* to refer to the broad conceptual collection formed around the elusive frameworks we find embedded in the background of contemporary culture. The second, by contrast, we might call *literary myths,* to indicate the traditional narrative genre of fantastical tales.

What is the proper relationship between these two understandings of myth? The two ideas—one a kind of tacit substratum, the other a cultural relic of a narrated form—are often mixed up together for reasons both intuitive and historically contingent. At one level, they share an entwined history: the concept of myth in the former sense was a modern construction, one that grew out of the study of pagan mythologies.[17] It wasn't until the seventeenth and eighteenth centuries—with the discovery and proliferation of literary myths from indigenous cultures outside of western Europe, and the interest that intellectuals took in comparing them both to the Greco-Roman myths pervading their own cultural heritage as well as to superstitious beliefs found in contemporary European society—that literary myths came to be associated with a distinct mode of thinking that opposed critical and scientific reasoning. On this view, deep myths would constitute a kind of dense and fraught cognitive habit that is formed in that uncritical mode, a tendency to approach any given aspect of reality one way.

At the same time, more intuitive connections can be drawn between the two ideas of myth. Literary myths are just-so stories, which characteristically portray certain states of affairs as part of the natural order of things, as though they already hold the status of those deeper aspects of one's worldview that are most taken for granted and rarely come up for questioning. Moreover, the realities presented in such traditional tales are presented fantastically, often featuring deities, magic, and other supernatural or fanciful elements. When stories wear fantasy so prominently on their surface, they do not readily invite critical scrutiny; rather, it would seem beside the point to take apart such tales using the rules of logic and facts. And so it can be said of the two concepts of myth that they share a structural parallel. Even though deep myths refer to that which is latent in societies more generally, and literary myths to the distinct cultural products of societies considered remote, those socially embedded frameworks that constitute myth in the first sense are narratives that are similarly resistant to scrutiny as that specific genre of fantastic tales that constitutes myth in the second sense.

It may be possible, at this point, to write off the traditional tales of distant civilizations as otherwise irrelevant to the issues confronting contemporary societies. If literary myths are a distinctly pervasive feature of non-modern cultures, where they appear to permeate not only aesthetic content but cosmological accounts and norms of social organization, they occupy a comparatively marginal place in contemporary culture, where we tend to encounter them as an inherited vocabulary of images, figures, and stories that are occasionally appropriated or alluded to in art and discourse. As Bernard de Fontenelle, writing at the end of the seventeenth century, observed about the status of such stories in his time: modern society produces no new myths, and is "satisfied with preserving the old ones."[18] Although some theorists of myth have since sought to identify contemporary counterparts to the literary myths of remote civilizations, their efforts have largely failed to dislodge a prevailing suspicion that myths of this kind are effectively obsolete in modernity—if not in form, then at least in the sense that the genre itself commands a radically diminished role in contemporary culture, to the point of being extremely difficult to recognize if we were to look for it using only its traditional markers.[19] By contrast, deep myths, as tacit and opaque substrates conditioning our worldviews, do manifest today in myriad everyday situations like the ones that exercised Barthes; but this phenomenon seems to share with the literary genre of myth little more than a name, a genealogy, and a loose, potential parallel in the structure of its psychological operation.

And yet, while only one of these two concepts of myth might properly bear contemporary relevance, contemporary discussions of myth as a consequential force in modern social life continue to make reference to both meanings. Though arguably obsolete, literary myths remain pertinent because such discussions use them to talk about the other, deep forms of myth that permeate the modern landscape. And as much as there is theoretical resistance to wholly separating them from one another, these two meanings of myth have been compounded together, and posed as a unified problem in philosophy and politics.

THE PROBLEM OF MYTH IN PHILOSOPHY AND POLITICS

The problem rests on the presupposition that deep myths—those tacit, deeply entrenched imaginative frames that persist in contemporary society—are modern analogues for that which was expressed in the literary myths of ancient or otherwise non-modern cultures. In turn, the analogy suggests that, even if contemporary cultures do not generate new literary myths, those deep myths that do endure today are being discharged in poorly delineated expressive outlets—in political rhetoric, in popular media, and in everyday speech—that nonetheless retain the characteristic impenetrability of the traditional genre of literary myths.

At the same time, such expressions can be said to run counter to a contemporary set of norms held about the structure of theoretical knowledge and rational discourse. For something to qualify as knowledge, we tend to expect that it shares in the grammar of rational argumentation: we must be able to formulate it in the form of a claim that advances a proposition, which in turn allows it to be examined critically and, should it prove inadequate to our experience of reality, replaced with a better proposition. The literary myths of distant cultures, on the other hand, do not do this—and, if the original analogy holds, neither do

Table 1. The problem of myth for contemporary political theory

	Non-modern societies	Contemporary society	
Tacit frameworks governing worldviews	Deep myths, as dense imaginative frames that are taken for granted in culture	Deep myths, as dense imaginative frames that are taken for granted in culture	Paradigms, norms, and ideas amenable to criticism and revision
Form of expression	Literary myths, as orally transmitted tales of a fantastic nature	Circulation in stunted or poorly delineated expressive outlets, such as popular media, political rhetoric, and everyday speech	Validity claims amenable to criticism and logical argumentation

$\rightarrow$
Direction of modernization

contemporary expressions of deep figurative content latent in society (see Table 1).

This linguistic differentiation, between what can and cannot be expressed in a mode that opens an idea to criticism and revision, is central to understanding why contemporary political theory continues to have a stake in the peculiar, effectively obsolete literary genre of myth. The particular conditions of contemporary culture—which might be considered devoid of those traditional literary myths that often pervade non-modern societies, but which is at the same time steeped in the arational deep myths thought to engender them—open up two broad ways of thinking about the status of myth in politics and philosophy.

Myth as a Problem of Modernization

The first, mainstream perspective poses the problem of myth as a problem of progress toward the ideals and expectations of the modern age. According to this account, the effective absence, in modern society, of fanciful fictions that fall readily into the traditional genre of literary myths, speaks to a process of modernization that is only half complete. In order to see that process through, contemporary society ought to eliminate the deep myths that it takes for granted—just as it has found a way to shed its strange, magical tales—and replace these residual structures with paradigms and ideas that can be expressed in a corresponding language that makes them available for critical examination.[20]

In turn, it is problematic for narratives that are not grounded in reasons to be making their way into circulation in the various and amorphous discursive outlets of contemporary life, because expressed forms of such narratives pull us further away from the goal of transforming the background to our worldviews into systems that are open rather than closed to critical scrutiny. Lending expression to these narratives neither dismantles them nor brings them into the light of reason, but instead has the effect of pushing them deeper into the mystifying realm of the opaque and unchallenged. Modern manifestations of such embedded frameworks, then, are in fact perpetuating expressions. They reinforce certain narrative patterns and harden their hold on our capacity to imagine things any other way.

For theorists who designate such modern phenomena as "myths," the opacity of these expressions appear to be sustained, fundamentally, through the same mechanisms behind the trappings of the old fantastic stories. Just as Barthes saw echoes of certain arcane tropes and images in the drama that unfolded at the Dominici trial, it is a telltale sign of the regressive status of these modern expressions that they periodically contain evocative elements that seem to appeal to the magical or otherworldly. The most prominent and shocking examples materialized in the twentieth century, with the rise of fascism and its distinctive reliance on propaganda that made explicit reference to national mythological traditions—such as the adoption of runic signs in Nazi symbolism—or otherwise recalled mystical tropes and patterns common to the genre of such stories, such as the appeal to the destiny of a chosen race of people, and the thousand-year kingdom it was to inherit.[21] As contemporary commentators repeatedly drew comparisons between fascist propaganda and the literary myths of remote cultures, they made a case for conceptualizing the former in terms of the latter, and in turn, for seeing the elements of fascism as belonging to a more primitive society than to the modern industrialized nations in which they did appear.[22]

If these examples and the efforts of concerned theorists helped to lend urgency to the study of myth for better understanding aspects of contemporary culture, they were also issuing, on the one hand, a grave warning against the drastic consequences of cultural regression, and, on the other, affirming the prescriptive account of progress that tends to motivate contemporary theoretic interest in myth. Here the fantastic tales of remote civilizations remain entangled in the problem of myth to the extent that they serve as the most tangible model for thinking about contemporary expressions of the uncritically held frameworks undergirding modern culture. As contemporary society progresses toward more rational institutions, we would expect not only that it would abandon all such deep myths that repel critical scrutiny, but also that it would in turn control the outlets in which they might find expression and harden over our worldviews. And so, according to this line of reasoning, a commitment to rational progress entails combating two kinds of contemporary phenomena associated with myth: the persistence of a tacit cultural substratum of undemonstrable imaginative templates, and their expression in forms that are analogous in their inscrutability to the literary myths of non-modern societies. The former is what contemporary societies must seek to eradicate, and the circulation of the latter is what hinders that goal.

This teleological argument against myth is a contemporary descendant of an evolutionary account of culture that goes back at least to Greek antiquity, but was most fully articulated in eighteenth-century theories of social progress that sought to distinguish modern European civilization from societies deemed primitive by comparison.[23] These theories presented a linear picture of cultural progress, whereby societies that possessed a coherent body of mythology, like Greco-Roman antiquity or indigenous tribes in the New World, represented an earlier stage of cultural development than that inhabited by modern European society. The process by which a society transitions from a more primitive to a more advanced stage of development, in turn, was conceived in terms of an epistemic transition in the character of thought itself, in which the confused and superstitious thinking that gives rise to literary myths comes to be replaced by the rigor of scientific reason. Where the arc of societal progress from barbarism to civilization is envisioned as an escape from myth, philosophy, too, becomes an act of purification and a shedding of its mythic beginnings—a conceit most memorably captured in a formulation coined by the twentieth-century classicist Wilhelm Nestle, who proposed that the advent of Greek philosophy supplied the pivotal turning point at which Western thought began to advance "from *mythos* to *logos*."[24]

There was also a religious dimension to this linear vision of progress. If eighteenth-century theories of social progress had looked to myth as a way of differentiating more developed societies from less developed ones, they were also preoccupied with distinguishing Christianity from the religious, often polytheistic, content of pagan mythology. When combined, however, with the evolutionary view of social development, the difference between Christianity and pagan religion lent itself to the extended logic that religion, too, is subject to the same processes of change that drove modern European civilization toward increased rationalization. For the intellectual heirs of the eighteenth-century preoccupation with myth, the trajectory of progress also aligned with increased secularization—as seen, for instance, in Auguste Comte's proposal that societies pass through stages of development beginning in an age of fetishism and polytheism that eventually gives rise to monotheism, then to metaphysical philosophy, and finally to an age governed by scientific principles. To live in modern society was to live, as Weber put it, in a disenchanted world.

It would be naive and reductive to claim these things today: that there is just one way societies come to be modern, or that cultural transformation occurs along a single axis with primitivism, myth, and religion on one end, and civilization, science, and secularism on the other. But it nonetheless bears emphasizing that contemporary political theorists are still very much working with inherited notions about what constitutes progress, the distinctiveness of modernity, and the extent to which a conception of scientific reason is bound up in both of these ideals. In particular, the theoretical discourse on myth has always been dominated by a concern for rational progress and the threat that myth poses to its various incarnations. As such, the general contours of the argument against myth have remained largely unchanged since the eighteenth century: whenever theorists subscribed to the premise that the form and content of myth are out of place in a modern society, they have appealed to the ideals of rationality and progress in order to call for its eradication.

Perhaps the most enduring legacy of the teleological account of social progress is an optimism around the possibility that the deep mythic frameworks that persist in contemporary society can in fact be dismantled rationally. This is true of the account of myth in Hegel's philosophy of history, which famously tracks a trajectory of increasing rationalization and freedom. For Hegel, earlier and less developed forms of human thought relied on the devices of myth for expression; accordingly, he equated myth with "the powerlessness of Thought which does not know yet how to hold itself for its own self and is not self-sufficient."[25] But in a modern landscape, advances in knowledge allowed for humans to think at increasingly higher and clearer levels of abstraction without leaning on the crutches of sensory expression, and both the cognitive powerlessness Hegel associated with myth, and the fantastic forms it assumed when it manifested in culture, were things that were in the process of being traded for superior modes of thought and representation.

Even after the Second World War, when the advent of new ideologies had intensified theoretical interest in the topic of myth, the basic shape of this argument continued to dominate debates, and those who declared a renewed urgency to eliminating myth from contemporary civilization did so because they accepted the premise that deep mythic frameworks can in fact be eradicated, or demystified and converted into ideas that can be expressed in a form that lends itself to criticism and scrutiny. Karl Popper, for whom myth and scientific knowledge existed on the same spectrum, called for the conversion of the former into the latter through critical refutation; Jürgen Habermas, who, unlike Popper, set aside myth into a special category of thought, was nonetheless optimistic that their modern counterparts would still be made more transparent and open to rational examination.[26]

In turn, a specific set of political prescriptions follows from construing myth as a premodern form of thought and expression that demands, but has not yet achieved, conversion into more rational forms. If a goal of philosophy and culture is to make the background to our worldviews increasingly available for critical dissection, politics must similarly aid that process by aspiring to norms of discourse that have more in common with logical propositions than with the strange, whimsical tales of remote civilizations. It must, in particular, guard against the thoughtless reinforcement of existing deep myths in the political sphere by a naive and uncritical public, as well the mobilization of new ones by an opportunistic elite looking to usurp the psychological power of such stories. In turn, working to diminish the activation of these mythic frameworks in political life is not only a means of assisting in their eradication from contemporary society; it is also a way of affirming a democratic vision organized around a philosophical ideal of the autonomous rational subject.

One aspect of this political vision is epistemic. Appeals to narratives that resist further scrutiny repel both criticism and the diversity of alternate opinions that are crucial to a democracy marked by the free exchange of—and competition between—ideas. Hence, the deep aversion to myth in political theory is in large part rooted in the position that the promulgation of such stories amounts to the obscuring of truths that might be otherwise reached through channels both democratic and rational. By a similar logic, myth also carries associations that are antidemocratic on deliberative grounds, because perpetuating, rather than dismantling, these stories obstructs deliberative discourse and debate.[27] From a liberal perspective, this would also seem to erode the integrity and autonomy of the individual citizen, who ought to be free to reason against the grain of that which is merely taken for granted in collective culture. Similarly, whenever a society tolerates or perpetuates narratives beyond questioning, this would seem to oppose an ideal of political participation, insofar as it encourages passive rather than active citizenship. And whenever stories of this kind are mobilized by particular political actors, they make us vulnerable to the kind of inequality built into the relationship between the elite creators and promulgators of myth, and their unsuspecting public.[28]

For all of these reasons, conceiving of myth as a problem of incomplete modernization entails, above all, committing to a vision of political progress devoid of myth. As we continue to dream of building political communities that are more democratic, more egalitarian, more conducive to participation and effective deliberation, and better at conveying respect for its individual members—it seems we should also hope to eliminate from political life both the deep narrative patterns and the modes of expression we associate with myth.

Myth as a Problem of the Human Condition

Against the predominant account of myth as a problem of modernization, there is a second strand of thought that rejects the thesis that liberation from myth is a defining feature of modernity. This view suggests instead that all societies, ancient and modern alike, are characteristically imbued with imaginative frameworks resistant to critical scrutiny; and it rejects in particular the premise that such deep myths are capable of being distilled into logical content without injury to the coherence of our social world and systems of thought. If the enduring presence of deeply held mythic frameworks in modernity had been the puzzle motivating the mainstream argument against myth, it may be said that, for theorists who take this second approach, the relative absence of literary myths in modernity is the more unusual puzzle.

There are two broad reasons for believing that deep myths that do not lend themselves to critical examination are an indelible and irreducible component of modern society. The first emphasizes their social function; the second, the ways in which they are prefigured into the psychological or linguistic structure of thought itself.

Accounts that attribute an important social function to those deep myths entrenched in contemporary society are rooted, on the one hand, in early romantic ideas of myth as expressions of national character, and, on the other, in the work of early twentieth-century anthropologists who linked the traditional literary myths of non-modern societies with collective rituals and ceremonies that seemed to cement social bonds and hierarchies in the group.[29] Though both the romantic and the early anthropological accounts of myth had largely kept to the view that myth belonged to a primitive age that modern civilization had already left behind, the respective intellectual heirs to both traditions have extended to contemporary contexts their hypotheses on the social functions of myth.

In particular, they have suggested that the narrative frameworks that are taken for granted in modern societies perform the indispensable task of conferring social meaning upon relations and practices that hold them together. For instance, sociological studies of institutions often employ the terminology of myth to describe the processes by which social and political norms come to accrue value and stability.[30] A somewhat different argument ascribes a more dynamic function to such narratives that repel criticism, as a force of social change rather than of social reinforcement. This was the widely influential view originally advanced by Georges Sorel, who invented the term "political myth" to argue that collective political action was impossible without the galvanization of such narratives.[31]

Common to both of these conceptions of myth was not only the thought that the unexamined deep myths embedded in contemporary culture cannot be broken down and articulated in a more logical form, but also the view that, should they cease to exist, something essential to the social fabric would be lost—be it the social bonds in a society or the capacity of individuals to come together in social movements to enact meaningful political change. For some, the absence of a distinct expressive venue for these vital frameworks—as non-modern societies found in their literary genre of traditional tales—has accordingly come to signify a deeper crisis in the nature of sociability in the modern world.

These accounts suggest that contemporary societies will not rid themselves of their deep myths so long as their significance as collective communities depends on upholding some level of social cohesion. A different set of arguments comes to a similar conclusion through an alternate path, by pointing to the limitations built into the structures of human psychology and cognition.

One such limitation was suggested by a set of traditions rooted in the belief that humans possessed a universal need to respond expressively to the world in which they live, be it their natural physical environment, or the inner drama of their psyche.[32] Myth, according to these traditions, was the product of that primal expressive impulse in human nature.

Authors who thought of myth in this way certainly did not rule out the possibility that such impulses might be overcome, as children grow out of their childhood habits, and superseded with more sophisticated and reflective forms of interacting with the world. But presenting myth as a product of human nature nonetheless makes a difference to the modernization account, and helps to dampen the optimism with which it is asserted. For a start, it helps to universalize myth across human contexts, by suggesting that the drives responsible for it remain latent in the modern individual and in modern society: should either fall prey to any pathological forms of regression, those tendencies toward myth can be expected to resurface in fairly consistent ways.[33]

A related set of traditions also subscribed to the position that there is something universal to the processes that give rise to myth, but they specifically located this universality in a number of discrete patterns that human cognition tends to follow—patterns reflected in the content of myths. A special point of interest here was the observation that literary myths from disparate cultures often shared striking similarities in the images or motifs they employed: these theories offered by way of explanation the hypothesis that human thought tends to cluster around particular patterns that were universally significant to the human experience, and that frequently recurring mythical elements— like the figure of the trickster, or the story of a great deluge—were ways of representing those patterns. For Carl Jung, who used the term "archetype" to describe the tendency for certain such cognitive patterns to be represented in certain ways, saw in this relation an innate link between the content of myth and universal shapes of thought; for Claude Lévi-Strauss, what was universal was not the particular links between individual elements of myth and what was being expressed in them, but instead the laws governing the structures of cognitive relations, and it was the structure of relationships, rather than their content, that was being replicated in the mythic motif-clusters that he called "mythemes."[34]

When theories locate the origins of myth in universal impulses, patterns, and structures of the human mind, they are put in the position of having to either affirm or find ways around what this implies: namely, that these universal factors are also present in modernity, and that contemporary societies cannot truly rid themselves of all traces of myth.

But the most explicit rebuttal of the modernization thesis was a philosophical one, which was most memorably articulated in Max Horkheimer and Theodor Adorno's thesis in the *Dialectic of Enlightenment*
(1944) that "myth is already enlightenment, and enlightenment reverts
to mythology."[35] This was the diagnosis that modern, enlightened civilization has been hitherto unsuccessful in its efforts to extricate itself
from the mode of thought that generated and sustained the traditional
literary myths of non-modern societies. According to Horkheimer and
Adorno, both myth and the civilizing movement to replace it with scientific content shared a fundamental similarity in the way each approached the world: not just the rational impulse with which both
sought to master nature and render it more familiar, but also the fatalistic tendency with which they regarded their own creations as somehow
immutable. For the modernization thesis, this meant that the rational
achievements of modern society over the course of its historical trajectory have not only failed to provide an antidote to these latter mythic
impulses, but had themselves given way to a veiled version of myth.

A possible explanation as to why exactly this might be the case stems
from a larger debate on the feasibility of divorcing analytic concepts from
the figurative qualities of the language in which they are articulated.
Hans Blumenberg, the foremost philosopher of myth in the second half
of the twentieth century, observed the myriad ways in which language,
including the language of philosophy, is continually drawn to the same
pregnant metaphors and figurative patterns found in mythological expressions.[36] These studies suggest that the content of philosophy cannot
exist in a purely abstract sphere divorced from all traces of myth. Rather,
the deep frameworks underlying ancient literary myths cannot be left
behind because the expressions they generate form the basic fabric of
the language we use to talk about philosophical concepts, which in turn
constrains the way we think, even when we believe ourselves to be reasoning freely and independently.[37]

For Blumenberg, philosophy's reliance on mythological expressions
revealed a deeper need, on the part of philosophy, to impart meaning to
reality through narratives that are reworked, time and again, to frame
the unfamiliar and inexplicable in terms of the familiar and significant.[38] He accordingly downplayed the observation, so central to the

modernizing argument against myth, that contemporary societies lack concrete examples of the kind of literary myths abundant in ancient and otherwise remote civilizations. He suggested, instead, that modernity continues to tell these old stories in new forms—as Goethe and scores of forgotten Romantics did with Faust, or Freud with the Oedipus story—that, in essence, are not radically different from the literary myths of ancient Greece and Germania.

A more general trend, characteristically shared by theorists of myth who reject the modernization thesis, underlies Blumenberg's insistence that contemporary culture continues to generate specifically mythic expressions for deep cultural frames that lack rational foundations. This is the belief that draws a more essential link between mythic frameworks and mythic expressions: there was a reason the former tended to manifest, in modern and non-modern societies alike, in opaque, symbolic, and figurative expressions rather than in reasoned arguments. If, as these authors believed, there are enduring factors built into the structure of sociability or the nature of thought that necessitate the endurance of frameworks that escape rational grounding, then the corresponding expressions are also here to stay, perpetually unable to be reconciled with the language of critical reason.

For authors who opposed the modernization account, the problem of myth was much more nuanced. Because they did not believe that the deep myths persisting in contemporary culture could ever be eradicated or converted into more rational content, lending expression to them could not constitute a barrier to progress. Their position does, however, condemn modern life to a fractured future, in which a separate sphere of cognitive tendencies that can only be expressed figuratively hovers alongside the critical-rational system that forms the bedrock of modern thought and discourse. If it is indeed impossible to reconcile these two spheres, our existing philosophical resources provide no guidance on coping with this dualism, and, in particular, no means of access to those deeply lodged mythic frameworks that continue to wield influence over our worldviews. Thus, when theorists of myth reject a prevailing account that equates political progress with the progressive shedding of myth, they do so without offering an alternate vision of what might constitute progress. In turn, even when one does not malign myth as incompatible with modernity, it remains difficult to wave away the progressive ideals and the optimism entailed in the modernization thesis.

PLATO'S LEGACY AND PLATO'S MYTHS

The thought that our philosophical and political ideals cannot afford a place for commonplaces that are taken for granted is a defining feature of Plato's legacy. It is no novelty to observe that Plato invented an ideal of philosophical citizenship in the figure of Socrates.[39] According to this ideal, the philosopher's contribution to political society is the rational evaluation of convention, whereby the most basic beliefs and customs structuring the city's practices are subjected to critical challenge.[40] And so, Plato depicts a Socrates who, breaking with the convention of his contemporary Athenians of seeking wisdom from poets and traditional sources of authority, relentlessly questions the gatekeepers of received knowledge to expose assumptions that are accepted passively without being grounded in reasons.[41]

There is a way of equating the history of Western philosophy with the legacy that Plato left after him. The foundational position attributed to Plato in the history of philosophy has certainly been overstated,[42] but undeniably philosophy has at several pivotal moments of crisis understood itself, for better or for worse, in relation to an idea of its beginning embodied in this single author.[43] And when Western philosophy is conceived this way, as a tradition with essential roots in Plato, the legacy that is being celebrated is that specifically rational legacy that called for the elimination of unexamined beliefs and frameworks, of unfounded pretenses to knowledge, and of the vague and the mystifying.

For many, that original Platonic accomplishment presented itself specifically as the liberation of philosophy from myth.[44] By this they meant that both the nature and methods of philosophical knowledge as we know it are held to a standard of logical rigor that Plato invented by disassociating it from the influence of myth that had pervaded Greek culture in his time. In a concrete sense, Plato, according to this account, was rejecting a specific body of traditional narratives about the gods as inappropriate, if not pernicious, to the pursuit of true knowledge about the world and our places in it. But tied to the exclusion of a literary genre from the domain of philosophy was also the more significant renunciation of all uncritically upheld cultural frameworks that fall under the broad heading of deep myths. It is often suggested that, prior to Plato, Greek culture had made no systematic distinction between *logos*—the root of "logic"—and *mythos*—myth; both words had synonymously meant "speech."[45] The two terms have since acquired more abstract connotations that point toward two distinct modes of thought: one is active, logical, and objective; the other is passive, imprecise, and impressionistic.[46] And when Plato is credited with the invention of what is now a well-worn opposition between *logos* and *mythos,* he stands for a way of doing philosophy that has not only broken away from the authority of a literary genre of traditional tales, but is guided above all by the demand, prominently displayed in his depiction of Socratic conversation, that beliefs are grounded in rational justifications.

In this regard, a prevailing story told about Plato and his importance aligns with the vision of rational progress that supplies the argument against myth in political theory. Just as striving toward a more rational political society entails the eradication of unconditioned imaginative frameworks, and any avenues of expression that reinforce their opacity, the position of primacy that Plato occupies in the canon of philosophy owes to a reputation for methodological purification, consisting in the rejection of all patterns of thought that do not stand up to critical scrutiny.

Yet Plato famously wrote his own myths, which reworked or otherwise mimicked existing tales of the genre. In Plato's writings, myths burst forth as a respite from the meticulous, detail-oriented arguments comprising the central philosophical investigations.[47] For the most part they are stylistically differentiated from the rest of the work, and to the extent that they are vivid stories, they are accordingly exempt from the standards of argument: they are not logically rigorous, and they posit ideas without grounding them in reasons.[48] They resemble traditional literary myths in that they are imaginative narratives, often featuring supernatural elements, that impart to their audience an impression of the coherence of an idea in its entirety rather than the factual accuracy of the parts that build up to it.[49]

Plato's borrowing from the literary genre of myth and its tropes in his philosophical writings sits oddly against the standard of rigor that he is said to have invented for philosophy.[50] And indeed, readers have alternately criticized them or have felt the need to make excuses for them. Hegel, for instance, saw in Plato's myths a "pollution of thinking through sensory forms," whose use represented Plato's own philosophical limitations, which had prevented him from expressing the same ideas more freely, consciously, or rationally.[51] At the same time, there is no way to deny the deliberate construction of Plato's myths, the overtly philosophical contexts into which they have been placed, and the purposiveness with which Plato appears to be appropriating the trappings of a distinct literary form for his own philosophical ends. Nor is it easy to dismiss their memorability or their cultural influence: surely the most lasting impressions of Plato's *Republic* for the casual contemporary reader are supplied by the Myth of Metals and the Allegory of the Cave; myths like the Atlantis myth in the *Timaeus* and *Critias,* or the Myth of the Charioteer from the *Phaedrus,* were likewise the things for which Plato was best known in popular culture for the greater part of the history of his reception.[52]

The argument against myth had claimed that political society would do well to rid itself of a certain class of deep background frameworks that resist critical examination, and, by extension, also of the amorphous outlets in which they might find expression—modern analogues for an effectively obsolete literary genre of fantastic tales. If we hold on to the argument that these two conceptions of myth are related in such a way that our political ideals are not compatible with either kind, and if we also accept the characterization of the Western philosophical tradition as a Platonic legacy of decoupling philosophy from the uncritical mode of thought particular to myth—then the fact that Plato wrote his own myths becomes problematic.

At one level, it opens up for dispute the exact nature of Plato's accomplishment and, in turn, pushes us to reconsider the prominence of Plato and his legacy in our understanding of the history of Western philosophy. We need only to look to Plato's most famous critics of the last two centuries to appreciate the extent to which the evaluation of Plato's legacy hangs on an evaluation of his relationship to myth. For Nietzsche, Plato inaugurated an entire philosophical tradition devoted to the exclusion of myth: he single-handedly instigated the regrettable separation of philosophy from its mythic, Dionysian past and pioneered its reduction to mere rationality.[53] For Popper, however, writing at the height of the Second World War, Plato and his philosophical successors had to be condemned for the very opposite reasons: Plato was the first and the most influential of the enemies of the open society, an opponent of both democracy and "the critical powers of man."[54] In particular, Plato's political vision relied on the deceptive power of myth to engineer a decidedly nondemocratic social order, arranged around a dogmatic philosophic system. The ease with which Plato can be dressed into either role—a notorious mythmaker, on the one hand, and a champion, on the other, of a demythologized, rational philosophy—speaks to the prevalence of a deep uncertainty about the nature of Plato's legacy, even as he continues to serve as a primary touchstone in arguments about the identity and trajectory of the Western philosophical tradition.

At another level, a reconsideration of Plato's myths and the Platonic legacy reopens the question of the place of myth in political thought. In particular, it should reconcile us to the impossibility of perfectly triangulating the three themes of the foregoing discussion: the argument against myth in political theory, the celebratory identification of Plato's legacy with the history of Western philosophy, and the philosophical significance of Plato's myths. Fully committing to two of these premises will necessarily entail discarding or qualifying the third. Prioritizing the argument against myth and aligning it, in turn, with Plato's rational legacy, leads to what has been the dominant interpretive position on Plato's myths since the Enlightenment: that they are incidental to the rational content of Plato's philosophical accomplishment. Authors who subscribe to this view either ignore the myths entirely, or treat them as rhetorical embellishments to the philosophical arguments, but do not find them consequential to Plato's philosophy or political theory.[55] On the other hand, when one commits to taking Plato's myths seriously while maintaining the position that our philosophical and political ideals cannot afford a place for myth, it becomes impossible not to adopt some version of Popper's indictment: Plato's recourse to myth merits condemnation, and a tradition built on those Platonic foundations can be neither rational nor desirable.[56]

The only way, it seems, to entertain the possibility that Plato's myths were philosophically significant without denying the centrality of reason to our political and philosophical ideals, or the centrality of Plato's contributions to a tradition built around that ideal, would require exploring a third option that adopts a chastened version of the first two premises. Insofar as this position seeks to better appreciate the philosophical intent behind Plato's appropriation of the literary genre of myth, it would offer an interpretation of Plato and his legacy that, without diminishing the distinctiveness of the myths or their influence *as myths* in the history of the reception of Plato, reconciles them against the rational accomplishment for which Plato is known and celebrated. In turn, a revised understanding of Plato's legacy on these terms would also call for a reconsideration of the trajectory of Western philosophy as being merely one of shedding myth, and it would ask anew whether there remains a different role for myth to play in political theory.

Finally, if we can accept, in light of these considerations, that the problem of myth in political theory warrants revisiting, this would also require decoupling the two conceptions of myth with which we began. Myths, as fantastic stories that fall into a literary genre of narrative fiction, and a modern notion of myth, as a designation reserved for a constellation of deeply entrenched imaginative frameworks in culture, both figure in opposite ways in the interpretation of Plato: he made literary use of the former, and is celebrated for rejecting the latter from the province of philosophic inquiry. If reconfiguring our understanding of Plato's accomplishment through the lens of myth is at all going to be relevant for reevaluating the place of myth in political thought more generally, it cannot be enough to take it as given that deep myths and literary myths are necessarily related in such a way that they can be posed as a single problem. Instead, working out these questions will first have to identify what it was that Plato—and, as we will see, his successors—found compelling about the literary genre of myth, and whether they felt that these fantastic stories could bear a more nuanced and constructive relationship to the deeper frameworks undergirding our worldviews.

Three central questions, then, emerge from the friction between Plato's myths and his foundational status in our conception of the Western philosophical tradition:

1. In light of the myths that Plato wrote, how are we to interpret Plato's legacy?
2. What can Plato's legacy teach us about the place of myth in political thought?
3. What is the relationship between literary myths, as traditional tales of a very specific form, and deep myths, those tacit imaginative frameworks that persist even in contemporary society?

THE MYTHIC TRADITION

1. The central aim of this book is to reconstruct an alternate understanding of Plato's legacy that provides an account, on the one hand, of the compatibility of Plato's myths with a philosophically coherent political vision, and, on the other, of the long and significant trajectory that this idea exercised in the history of the reception of Plato. The following chapters will show how, at critical junctures in Plato's modern reception, some of Plato's most devoted readers were imitating Plato's myths in their own philosophical writings, or were otherwise engaged in asking difficult and fundamental questions regarding the place of myth in philosophy and politics. The authors who were part of this tradition were heavily influenced by Plato's philosophy in some way, and were deeply invested in exploring the political and philosophical potential of myth as a narrative medium. As such, it is possible to speak of a coherent, specifically Platonic tradition of writing and thinking about myth.

For contemporary political theorists who are not accustomed to thinking of Plato's legacy in these terms, the reconstruction of this mythic tradition would serve as a reminder of what students of Platonic reception have known for a long time: that the rationalist legacy we attribute to Plato was a relatively late construction, and that, for the greater part of the history of the reception of Plato, he was celebrated not for the rigor of his logical arguments but for some of the more mystic aspects of his work, which were thought to have been divinely inspired.[57] However, the set of authors treated in this study represent a somewhat different approach to Plato. Their interest in myths, Plato's or otherwise, did not stem from a view of myth as a divine medium somehow above human reason. Instead, the authors who participated in this Platonic, mythic tradition were very much wedded to the centrality of reason in philosophy and politics, and were interested in investigating how this distinct literary form could be deployed constructively toward that ideal.

The Plato they were inspired by was a philosopher who viewed the contributions of myth as complementary, rather than antithetical, to the kind of critical reasoning that we tend to celebrate as a defining feature of philosophical activity, including philosophically informed politics. In particular, these authors shared with Plato a sensitivity to the full range of myth's potential to be either harmful *or* salutary for political thought. In that regard this tradition runs alongside, and not against, the traditional and canonical view of Plato's legacy as one primarily defined by the emphasis on critical reason; and to the extent that myths are by definition resistant to critical examination, these authors also held the relationship between myth and critical reason to be delicate and complicated.

2. Where, then, does a reconstruction of the mythic tradition in Plato's legacy leave the larger question of the place that political theory can afford to myth—and especially to those deep, opaque frameworks that carry this designation today?

If Plato served as an influence on a tradition of authors who grappled with the question of myth's role in philosophy and politics, a central feature of this tradition was a shared appreciation for the significance of certain imaginative frameworks that are entrenched into the way we relate to our natural and social environment. These assorted frameworks, which the authors sought to access and rework through literary myths, may not fully cover the expansive range of phenomena that contemporary theorists have associated with the medium—and which I've been calling "deep myths" here—but still share in some of their most characteristic features. Engaging philosophically with them, the authors of this tradition believed, could not just be a matter of picking them apart through criticism, but required something more.

We recall that the argument against both literary and deep myths had grown out of a story of progress and rationalization, and that a countervailing position had rejected the possibility that either could ever be eliminated from modern life. Considered together, the authors who contributed to Plato's mythic legacy suggest a view that leans toward the latter position. To varying degrees, they felt that our reliance on certain deep, unconditioned imaginative frameworks in social and political life was an inevitable consequence of the human condition; and to that extent, they felt that such frameworks would be neither discarded nor rationalized in the foreseeable future.

Accordingly, what this tradition of authors has to offer on the question of the place of myth in political theory is the suggestion that the enduring presence of deep myths in human environments, in some form or another, is something to be acknowledged actively, rather than entrusted to the mechanisms of progress to extinguish. On this view, it is not enough, for example, for political theorists to respond to the mobilization of uncritically held and symbolically charged narratives in politics, especially in mass politics, by lamenting that the rationality of political agents falls short of their philosophical ideals. Furthermore, it is not enough for political theorists to trust that the critical toolkit of philosophy renders them immune from being influenced by myths and their contemporary counterparts. Rather, the authors in the mythic tradition stemming from Plato suggest that there are ways in which philosophy itself relies on some of the functions we have come to associate with myth to navigate territory that cannot be covered by critical reason alone but remains integral to the cultivation of its own projects.

The nature of these cases could vary as much as the authors' own conceptions of philosophy varied, just as they had different motivations driving their shared interest in myth. First, there was the broad understanding of philosophy as a distinct type of theoretical activity that required greater depth of thought, and different objects of thought, than do the demands of ordinary social and political life. If the practice of philosophy constituted a unique enterprise set apart from other occupations, one strand of thinking about myth, as an instrument for social organization, made it an indispensable resource for creating and stabilizing the kinds of political environments that make it possible for philosophers to devote themselves to philosophizing. The instrumental dependence of philosophy on myth, where the latter sustains the external conditions of the former, can be seen in the function of myth in the politics of Plato's *Republic* and the utopias of Thomas More and Francis Bacon, where philosophers make up a separate class and are given a distinct political role in their respective societies.

Such an understanding of the relationship between philosophy and myth may seem superficial at one level, and cynical at another—superficial, because the use of myth to manipulate and to affirm political institutions may, in certain configurations, happen to benefit philosophy without being truly indispensable to it; cynical, because such use risks running dangerously close to being a means of social oppression. However, Plato, More, and Bacon had a deeper and more earnest vision of this relationship—not only because they believed the kind of social stability afforded by myth was an integral condition for philosophical activity, but also because they speculated that philosophers themselves relied on the moral frameworks shaped and sustained by myth to orient their understanding of themselves, and of what it means to be a philosopher. Furthermore, just as they were cognizant of myth's potential for political abuse, they also ascribed to myth a dynamic social power that could not only uphold existing institutions but introduce profound shifts of meaning into the political order without destabilizing it altogether. A radical extension of this thought is to be found in the programmatic vision for a new mythology in German Idealism—which emphasized the capacity of myth to bond individuals together in a social community, but also took myth to be an endlessly dynamic medium that could demolish barriers between philosophers and nonphilosophers, and carry entire peoples through epochs of epistemic change.

A second theme running through the philosophies of the authors in this study is, inevitably, a teleological conception of philosophy informed by Platonic metaphysics. Here, the task of philosophy amounted to the approximate and asymptotic striving for more perfect knowledge—whether that ideal of epistemic perfection was to be conceived in terms of access to the Platonic Forms, or, as in the case of Leibniz, participation in divine reason, or, as in the German Idealist case, the representation of a highest Idea. These conceptions of philosophy tended to emphasize the primacy of a critical faculty of reason, which could properly discriminate between mere semblances of knowledge—as one might encounter in received wisdom, or in the sensuous and emotive—and knowledge that was in fact progressive. However, as long as there remained progress yet to be made in order to bring knowledge closer to a higher ideal, it fell upon faculties associated with myth to furnish an important complement to reason's critical function.

For Plato and for Leibniz, myth could be used, in the service of higher ideas, to convey content that might function as a placeholder for future knowledge that could not yet be secured in reasons that held up to scrutiny—knowledge that demanded acceptance for the time being until it could be replaced with knowledge that could. For the proponents of the program for a new mythology in German Idealism, that order was reversed: they also conceived of myth's philosophical contribution in terms of future knowledge, but it was the work of a purely active and conscious critical reason that was to be succeeded by a more holistic epoch of knowledge ushered in by myth. What bears emphasizing here is that, for philosophies famously arranged around abstract metaphysical ideals, these were all philosophies that did not lose sight of the human endeavor entailed in their pursuit; and the function of myth, for these authors, was not to cordon off esoteric areas of knowledge foreclosed to rational agency—like divine revelation—but instead to supply means of bridging the gap between a very distant ideal and a work eternally in progress toward it. The spirit of this limitation comes to form an important component of the conflicted account of myth in the philosophy of Ernst Cassirer, who, while no proponent of Platonic metaphysics, was committed to a model of the progress of knowledge that saw in myth a unique and necessary stepping stone to the development of more sophisticated forms of thought.

Finally, all these authors advanced, to some degree, a constitutive picture of the relationship between myth and philosophy, where they conceived of philosophy simply as an endeavor to impose meaning on our environment. On this account, myth itself stands for a way of doing philosophy, whereby it furnishes individuals and communities with the stories they tell about themselves and their place in the world. Such stories, in turn, help form the units of meaning on which all our activities rest.

If this recalls Horkheimer and Adorno's bleak vision of a political and philosophical future beholden to myth, the overriding tone running through Plato's mythic legacy, by contrast, is one that cautiously embraces, instead of despairing, the inescapability of myth. Shared between these authors to greater and lesser extents was a sense that we are not so much condemned to myth as we have a need for it, and the appropriate response was not to deny it but to acknowledge it and to make theoretical space for it. In that regard, the authors in this tradition suggest an account of the opaque imaginative frameworks undergirding society that bears comparison to Hans Blumenberg's verdict on myth, as a phenomenon that answers a human need for significance against the absolutism of an indifferent world.[58] Like Blumenberg, they made a cautious case for appreciating the capacity for such passively accepted, criticism-resistant frames to provide a stable ground for both philosophical and political activity.

3. The authors of this mythic tradition were ultimately concerned with the nature of the deeply entrenched imaginative frameworks that are taken for granted in culture, their relationship to critical reason, and how best they might be directed toward desirable ends in our political life. But accompanying their concern for those deep frameworks was also the shared conviction that they could be accessed constructively through literary myths, the peculiar and obsolete genre they saw mimicked and repurposed in Plato's philosophical writings. In confronting the traditional argument against myth in political theory, the authors in this tradition were hence also rethinking the relationship between the two conceptions of myth built into that original problem.

In particular, they were pushing back against an assumption that myth, as a literary form, was necessarily a perpetuating expression of a deeper imaginative mold that rendered it somehow inevitable, natural, and beyond critical challenge. To the extent that they perceived a human need for those deeper frameworks to provide a stable ground for our philosophy and politics, they were cautiously appreciative of the possibility that literary myths and their modern counterparts could help reinforce their stability. This appreciation was limited, because these authors were also keenly aware of the precarious position they were taking up in permitting a place in their political theory for that ossifying effect that myths, as just-so stories, can have on the way reality is imagined.

This meant that, at another level, whenever these authors wrote literary myths in the Platonic vein, or were otherwise thinking theoretically about the importation of the genre in philosophic contexts, they were exploring a distinctively self-conscious, and even playful, use of the literary medium of myth in philosophical writing. It could be said that they were constructing a new genre of philosophic myth that drew attention to the possibilities and limitations of its own form; and this, in turn, was also a way of drawing attention to the contingent epistemic status of the deeper frameworks with which they were concerned.

Finally, their self-conscious approach to myth suggested a further qualification to the orthodox assumptions about the relationship between literary myths and those deeper frameworks entrenched in the background to our worldviews. Even though myths, as a form of expression, had the capacity to mobilize certain implicit narratives about our world that repel critical examination, this did not necessarily mean that such background frameworks were also beyond revision. For the authors in the Platonic mythic tradition, it was important that those imaginative frames fortified by myths were sufficiently authoritative as to provide a stable grounding to our philosophical and political experiences; but it was also important that, their normative authority notwithstanding, they were sufficiently provisional as to be able to be reworked by subsequent myths, should the need arise. The overall vision may point in the direction of Blumenberg's recommendation that myths are taken to be dynamic rather than static, as forms of discourse that demand constant work and reappropriation in shifting historical contexts.[59] The particular approach that these authors took toward it, however, entailed working toward the construction of a distinct class of philosophically tailored myths, aimed at striking the paradoxical balance between the authoritative and the provisional articulation of the tacit narratives framing the way we imagine our world.

What their efforts tell us is that a philosophical interest in the literary genre of myth could ultimately be a vision of hope. Myths did not have to be merely irrational, nor did they have to undermine the central ideals of philosophy and philosophically informed politics; but they offered ways of reconfiguring the deeper substratum to our worldviews in alignment with those ideals. For Plato and the successors to his mythic legacy, the selective philosophical appropriation of myth opened up new avenues of philosophical access, otherwise closed to critical reason, to that which we most take for granted in philosophy and political life.

PART ONE

POLITICAL AND
PHILOSOPHICAL BOUNDARIES

1

NATURE AND MYTH IN PLATO'S *REPUBLIC*

MYTH AS A DYNAMIC MEDIUM FOR
REWORKING FOUNDATIONAL CONCEPTS

READERS OF PLATO'S *REPUBLIC* often respond to the myths in it with a kind of unease that falls somewhere between Karl Popper's condemnation of the Myth of Metals as an "exact counterpart" to Nazi racial policy, and Julia Annas's infamous appraisal of the Myth of Er as a "lame and messy ending" to "an otherwise impressively unified book."[1] At the heart of our discomfort around the myths of the *Republic* is the objection that Plato's resort to the language of myth is in and of itself problematic. At one level, myth seems to be a vague and imprecise medium for conveying philosophical ideas. Much of the confusion and disappointment surrounding the Myth of Er, for instance, has to do with the conspicuous difference between the stylistic conventions of myth from those of logical argumentation. As the complaint goes, the long and careful philosophical argument spanning the breadth of the *Republic* ought to have sufficed on its own to carry out its central task—a defense of justice and the just life—so that capping it off with a myth seems to undermine what had come before. To not only accept the myth as necessary, but to give it the last word, suggests a kind of failure on the part of philosophy to communicate on its own terms with its audience.[2]

Then there are the fantastical literary excesses that lend myth its characteristic inscrutability. Myths, unlike arguments, abound with detailed descriptions that seem to serve no obvious purpose other than to enrich the story somehow. To the extent that they are not as clear or as direct in presenting their message, it is difficult to tell if the myths that Plato wrote into the *Republic* make a distinct philosophical contribution that would not have been better made in a more analytic form.[3] In the case of the Myth of Er, the details of the story are so convoluted that readers, in fact, cannot agree as to whether it is meant to support or to subvert the *Republic*'s main arguments. Either way, the myth remains an awkward puzzle: had Plato written it as supporting material for the dialogue's central ideas, it becomes a redundant iteration, in a different medium, of the preceding lessons, and an unnecessarily confusing one at that.[4] But the alternative interpretation—that we ought to read the myth as a kind of subversive commentary on the rest of the *Republic*—raises more questions than it settles, as it takes on the burden of having to explain why Plato would intimate, in this roundabout manner, the opposite of what he means to say.[5]

There is a further level at which the myths of the *Republic* invite skepticism, and it is that the deliberate deployment of myth, especially for political use, can be seen to be manipulative, deceptive, or dangerous. This is a philosophical betrayal of a different kind, consisting not only in the choice of an inefficient medium of expression, but also in the calculated abuse of myth's obscuring qualities to help close off certain claims from further scrutiny. The Myth of Metals in Book III, for instance, has time and again shocked readers for its seeming cynicism, and for what this might suggest, in turn, about Plato's political thought. One of the more disturbing effects of myths like the Myth of Metals is that they can mislead their audiences into conflating certain social or political arrangements with the natural order of things, so that they seem beyond revision or challenge through critical examination and other philosophical channels. For this reason, myth, employed or tolerated in a political context, is often synonymous with a kind of falsehood told in the service of an end that only alleges to be noble.

Hence, Plato's willingness to use myths in the service of his political vision is routinely taken up by his critics as evidence of his authoritarianism, while his defenders are put in the position of having to excuse his myths by first justifying his greater philosophical agenda.[6] They tend to do so, more often than not, by casting the myths as unfortunate but necessary devices to persuade the unphilosophical: convincing the citizens listening to the Myth of Metals to be content with their assigned stations in the *kallipolis;* coaxing the audience of the Myth of Er into believing in the advantages of justice, even if they might not have followed all of the philosophical arguments Socrates had made for it before launching into this strange story. On this line of interpretation, Plato's use of myth becomes at best a concession to a reality in which not everyone is capable of philosophy in its purest form, and those who are not must instead be reached through an inferior rhetoric.[7]

If these are grounds for being suspicious of the myths interspersed between the arguments of the *Republic,* they are exacerbated by Plato's own seeming dismissal of myth, and his reputation for having inaugurated a distinction between the language of myth and the language of logical argumentation.[8] As we have seen, the canonical position that Plato occupies in the Western intellectual tradition is tied to his groundbreaking efforts to define philosophy as an enterprise that deals in the latter rather than in the former, and demands, in turn, that knowledge is grounded in reasons rather than in unexamined conventions. When Plato critiques the Greek mythological tradition as being morally incoherent and intellectually arbitrary, or, in passing formulations, unfavorably contrasts *mythos* to *logos,* he appears to dismiss the discursive qualities specific to the genre of myth as inadequate, if not counterproductive, to the aims and tasks of this project.[9]

Given so many reasons to find them unsettling, what would constitute a more satisfying reading of the myths of the *Republic?* A defense against these considerations would have to recognize that the myths are an important, integrated part of the *Republic,* rather than pieces of rhetorical ornamentation tacked on as an afterthought: the myths cannot be read separately from the whole, and the whole would be incomplete without the myths.[10] But such a reading would also have to respect the distinctiveness of the myths as *myths,* rather than treat them as passages that are stylistically undifferentiated from the rest of the work: their literary status as myths has something to add to the coherence of the

Republic as a philosophical work.[11] In particular, it would have to answer to the suggestion that the use of myth is at some level antithetical to our commitment to the philosophical ideal that no one view of the world, however deeply entrenched in a society, is immune to criticism and revision.

The aim of this chapter is to present what I believe to be the most promising approach toward meeting these requirements and, in so doing, to shed light on a use Plato makes of the literary genre of myth that is very different from those generally recognized by his readers. A convincing reading of the myths of the *Republic,* I argue, would have to give an account of the larger philosophical project uniting them. My own reading is built around a literary observation: three major myths of the *Republic*—the Myth of Metals, the Allegory of the Cave, and the Myth of Er—share a common plot, which recalls the experience of being delivered from a state of dreaming, underground, to wake up into a new reality aboveground. In each of these myths, the story about dreaming and waking comes to mark a transitional juncture in the educational curriculum of the *kallipolis,* in which citizens who have undergone a certain education are then tested for the qualities of a philosophic nature. Together, they explore a question of existential importance for Plato's purposes in the *Republic:* Can and to what extent does a philosophical education shape the natures of its subjects? Sustained across the myths of the *Republic*, then, is a project that is at once more coherent and more overtly philosophical than commonly acknowledged.

In what follows, I try to make the case that these three myths of the *Republic* are at their most compelling and intelligible when they are read together this way.[12] In so doing, I attempt to give novel reinterpretations of individual myths, especially of the Myth of Er. But I also aim to draw attention to a distinctive philosophical function that the literary genre of myth can fulfill in Plato's political writings. Plato certainly wrote myths in various forms and for different purposes across his dialogues—a practice that scholars have documented extensively—but our understanding of the range of possibilities that he saw in the medium will be significantly expanded by this account of the myths in the *Republic*.[13] This is not only because it is in the context of Plato's most widely read work of political theory that his recourse to myth has attracted the most controversy, but also because these myths instantiate a particularly intriguing use of the genre.

The philosophical inquiry at the core of the *Republic*'s myths is one that relies on the distinctive power of the medium of myth, absent in rational argumentation, to navigate a special kind of tension. A myth, on the one hand, has the unique capacity to ossify concepts in ways that resist critical engagement. In each of the three major myths of the *Republic,* Plato harnesses this function in order to posit an authoritative understanding of the nature of individuals, and with it, of the political reality in which they reside. In so doing, he draws attention to the surprising ways in which the self-understanding of philosophers—and the activities and practices stemming from that understanding—are anchored in conceptual frameworks that are deeply ingrained into our worldviews.

On the other hand, a myth can simultaneously alert us to the provisionality of such understandings and open up the possibility of revising them. This chapter tracks how each myth in the sequence builds on the previous myth's efforts to assert a definitive account of the content of an individual's nature. In so doing, it stresses another aspect of Plato's preoccupation with the genre and its potential: while myths can help mold certain deeply entrenched frameworks in our worldviews, these same frameworks can be further reworked by other, subsequent myths. Read this way, the myths of the *Republic* offer an insight into the capacity of myth to convey both the authority and the provisional status of the unconditioned norms underlying political life.

THE MYTH OF METALS

Myths cushion the *Republic* at its most critical junctures. The question of justice, the dialogue's primary topic of investigation, only enters the discussion with Cephalus's mention of "the tales told about what is in Hades" and their effect on how one might perceive life, both retrospectively and in anticipation of what follows.[14] The decisive challenge that Glaucon poses to Socrates—to defend justice on its own terms, stripped of its rewards—takes the form of a myth about a ring that turns its master invisible.[15] When Socrates answers that challenge, he defines justice in terms of three parts that make up a soul, first introduced to the investigation when the Myth of Metals identifies the corresponding parts that make up his ideal city, *kallipolis.* And the so-called philosophical digression spanning Books V to VII of the *Republic* culminates in what is perhaps the most iconic image of philosophy yet written, the Allegory of the Cave. It is in this way that the famously enigmatic Myth of Er comes to conclude, not only the *Republic,* but also a sequence of philosophically significant myths running through it.

When the myths of the *Republic* are read in conjunction with each other, several new observations come to light. We see, for instance, that at some basic level the Myth of Metals in Book III, the Allegory of the Cave in Book VII, and the Myth of Er at the end of Book X all tell a similar story: the protagonists are underground, asleep, until they ascend to an upper realm and wake up there. The Myth of Metals asks the citizens of the *kallipolis* to think of their early upbringing as something they dreamed up while being fashioned in the earth, and now, fully formed and awake, they have been brought up into the world. The freed prisoner in the Allegory of the Cave makes a famous ascent, also likened to the process of waking up, from an underground cave into the more perfect world above; and in the Myth of Er its eponymous protagonist journeys through the afterlife before he ascends back to the world of the living, and wakes up on his funeral pyre.[16]

Furthermore, at stake in each of these stories about slumber and awakening is the question of how the natures of individuals ought to be reconceptualized following a transformative event. As we shall see, the Myth of Metals and the Allegory of the Cave are explicitly concerned with the effect that particular stages of the *kallipolis's* educational curriculum leave on the natures of their subjects. Er's awakening in the Myth of Er, on the other hand, coincides with the reincarnations of souls who have traveled with him in the afterlife, who are born into new natures that have been determined in part by the patterns of lives they selected at the end of their shared journey.

Why this periodic retelling of the same story? The parallel plots shared between the three myths suggest that they are doing similar work—that each telling of a myth about waking up aboveground marks a new attempt to achieve a similar end. The Myth of Metals and the Allegory of the Cave occur at two pivotal moments in the education of the guardians who are to rule over the *kallipolis:* the former after a basic education in music and gymnastics, and the latter with an elite education in dialectic, the highest level of philosophical training offered to the city's potential philosopher-kings. At these stages, the pool of prospective guardians is periodically purged of its less promising candidates. My hypothesis is that the periodic recurrence of the plot common to the three myths and the periodic sorting of the city's leaders are related, and that this relation will illuminate both the content of the Myth of Er as well as the larger mythic endeavor it concludes. In order, then, to investigate how these observations might come together, we must begin with the Myth of Metals, where Plato first subjects his readers to a tale about waking from an underground slumber.

The Appeal to the Rigidity of Nature

The Myth of Metals is famously a story about the natures of individuals, and about using them as a foundation for organizing a city, by requiring all citizens to practice that role for which they are most naturally equipped. According to the myth, a god has mixed gold into the construction of the rulers, and silver, iron, and bronze into the assistants, farmers, and craftsmen, respectively. The city is to be arranged around these natural aptitudes, so that all its citizens are instated to their rightful places.[17]

At one level, a crucial element of this political vision is an appeal to a rigid conception of individual nature: the myth demands that its audience thinks of these natures as fixed, like pure metals that cannot be transformed from one into another. This fixed understanding of the natures of individuals, in turn, gives the myth the gloss of radicalism for which the *Republic* is so often criticized—most famously by Karl Popper, who found in this myth evidence for the "racialism" that Plato shared with the key ideologues of modern totalitarian politics.[18] Like race, the comparison suggests, the natural dispositions of the citizens cannot be helped and are determined from birth. The view that individuals are naturally one way or another has been ascribed to the Myth of Metals even by commentators who thought much more highly of Plato than Popper did, and remains implicit in most conventional readings of the myth.[19] And when nature is held to be something that is determined and permanent, it is easy to see why appealing to its authority might be a particularly effective political tool: by invoking the idea of a natural order, those propagating the myth to the citizens of the *kallipolis* can claim to restore politics to a state somehow less arbitrary than one offered by existing human institutions.[20]

The Revision of a Rigid Concept

At another level, however, the myth's appeal to the authority of nature is not so straightforward. The Myth of Metals is also known as the Noble Falsehood because Socrates prefaces it as such. The word he picks, γενναῖον, translates to "noble" in the sense of well-born, or of a character befitting one's birth or descent.[21] The falsehood may be γενναῖον, in the sense that it is born out of noble intentions, the deception notwithstanding, but also in the sense that the thing being lied about concerns the circumstances of the citizens' birth: the myth tells them that metals have been mixed into their "genesis [γένεσις]," or their manner of birth.[22] As it happens, the falsehood of the myth consists not only in the claim that the citizens were born with metals in their souls—and that their natures are accordingly fixed in a correspondingly rigid way from birth—but in a total reconceptualization of what it means to be born in the first place. In the myth, birth is essentially redefined as an event that occurs, not at the moment when a citizen is biologically born, but at some point after he has completed the educational curriculum in music and gymnastics described in Books II and III. This is the central lesson of the first half of the myth, which readers often overlook for the later passages about metals and hierarchies for which the myth is better known. It is therefore worth revisiting these lines carefully, though they may already be familiar to us. The myth begins:

> I'll attempt to persuade first the rulers and the soldiers, then the
> rest of the city, that the rearing and education we gave them were

like dreams; they only thought they were undergoing all that was happening to them, while, in truth, at that time they were under the earth within, being fashioned and reared themselves, and their arms and other tools being crafted. When the job had been completely finished, then the earth, which is their mother, sent them up.[23]

According to these opening lines, the citizens of the *kallipolis* have not truly lived until this moment in their lives. Rather, they are told that they have been asleep through the first years of their upbringing, during which they have undergone a basic education in music and gymnastics, and that these years were lived, not really in this world, but inside the womb of their mother, the earth. It is there that their natures were formed. Only upon the completion of this process of gestation were they released aboveground, to wake up into their current reality.

The nature of a citizen, according to the myth, is defined by those qualities with which he is born—*this time around*. It is what comes through at the end of a basic education, and not necessarily the attributes one has at the beginning of his biological life.[24] This is not to claim that biology plays no role in Plato's conception of individual nature; the myth still assumes that members of the several classes in the city will "for the most part" produce offspring like themselves, and poor observation of the city's breeding regulations is to blame for the eventual deterioration of the *kallipolis*.[25] The point of the myth, however, is that the circumstances of biological birth alone are inadequate for determining a citizen's place in society, and that institutions in the city must redefine the measures of a person's nature around a more appropriate standard. What the myth takes care to emphasize is not the norm whereby a child inherits the nature of his parents, but the possibility of exceptions—like the occasional birth of bronze or iron children to golden or silver parents, and vice versa—and the requisite protocols for handling them.[26] For any child whose makeup deviates from that of his parents, the city must restore "the proper value to its nature."[27]

There are, then, two distinct parts to the principal political maneuver of the Myth of Metals. The first is the premise, familiar to the conventional reading of the myth, that the natures of individuals are fixed from "birth" and remain stable thereafter, so that an entire society can be reliably organized around these enduring constants. The second is the fact that the myth makes this appeal to nature as a source of normativity while swapping out its content. Put another way, the radical innovation of the Myth of Metals is the representation of culture as nature: it covers up the fluid character of a much more continuous process of socialization, like education, and takes its product to be a static thing, as though the individual citizens transformed by it had really possessed those qualities all along.[28]

It bears emphasizing that the first part of the myth's work—as the objections of Popper and other readers imply—affects a particularly deep-rooted and uncritical aspect of the citizens' worldviews. In both the traditional conception of nature as the set of attributes with which one is born biologically, and the myth's insistence that it instead refers to those attributes one is left with at the end of a primary education, there is an implicit understanding of nature that stands in for a default prior to the design of the city. It is a set of circumstances that the citizens are to regard as natural, part of the way things are, somehow irreducible or beyond question. One status quo, then, is being replaced with another in the Myth of Metals. If the myth is successful in what it aims to achieve, the citizens of the *kallipolis* will have gone from taking the manner of their lives for granted, to taking as given a different political reality and their places in it.

If our conception of nature is especially foundational to the way we perceive the world, it is through the traditional medium of myth that Plato tries to tap the authority of this fraught concept. When a myth offers a kind of just-so story about the way things are in the world, we might expect this to work differently on the psychology of its audience than would propositions that come up in ordinary arguments. Unlike discourse bound by the expectation of rational justification, a myth might simply present a set of circumstances as part of the natural order of things, as though they already hold the normative status of those deeper aspects of one's worldview that are most taken for granted and rarely come up for critical examination. As Plato was well aware, the psychological effect of such stories is that they influence one's thinking even when they aren't taken entirely seriously.[29] It may be the case that these fanciful stories invite us to let down our critical guard—for what would be the point of taking apart such tales using the rules of logic and fact?—and that the ideas they depict as static, unchanging realities consequently sit all the more easily on our subconscious.

It is in this way that the Myth of Metals can be accused, as it is in Popper's account, of usurping the powers of traditional myths for gains that are political rather than philosophical. Even if it claims to serve philosophical ends, like the rule of philosophers in the city, its selective appropriation of the mythic genre may still remain an obstruction to philosophical thinking: it portrays a certain political arrangement as being fixed into the natural fabric of the world and, in so doing, further removes it from ordinary channels of rational contestation and critique. What this line of interpretation gets right, I think, is that in writing the Myth of Metals, Plato indeed sought to channel something of the ossifying effect that a myth is capable of having on a concept that fundamentally grounds our understanding of ourselves and our world. What such readings miss, however, is that this is only one part of what the myth does. The other feat—a revision of how its audience is meant to understand the content of that concept—is also something that Plato works into a subsequent myth, told at a later juncture of the educational curriculum of the *kallipolis*.

THE ALLEGORY OF THE CAVE

Three books later, a new awakening takes place in the *Republic*.[30] A prisoner who has dwelled in an underground cave all his life is suddenly forced to turn around and scale the path to the world above. Whereas he had known only the darkness of the cave before, now his eyes open to the light of the sun for the first time in this upper realm. These strange prisoners of the cave, Socrates emphasizes, are "like us" to the extent that we, too, have yet to open our eyes to knowledge. A person informed by opinion but not knowledge may be said to be merely "taken in by dreams and slumbering out of his present life," so that he is at no point ever awake: "before waking up here he goes to Hades and falls finally asleep there."[31] It takes a wakeful mind to see past the illusions of the things people tend to believe, and Socrates tells us that the politics of the *kallipolis* or any desirable regime must amount to rule "in a state of waking, not in a dream as the many cities nowadays are governed by men who fight over shadows with one another."[32] Like the earthborn citizens in the Myth of Metals who wake up from the dream of their previous lives, the freed prisoner in the so-called Allegory of the Cave is delivered out of the earth from his state of slumber and into a different reality. To decree, as this story does, that he is to return to the cave and rejoin the community of its denizens, is to envision the possibility of reordering politics around this new reality.

A Dialectical Awakening

The Allegory of the Cave does not tend to attract the kind of controversy with which the Myth of Metals or the Myth of Er is often met; many readers do not even consider it a myth. After all, the story is clearly delivered in the service of a philosophical point that Plato wishes to make about the nature of reality, and it does not so much share in the tropes of existing mythological tradition as it builds on a vocabulary of images that Plato creates and develops himself in the analogies of the Sun and Divided Line spanning Book VI. There are, however, equally compelling reasons to acknowledge those features of the Allegory of the Cave that render it a lot more like a myth than the kinds of argumentation undertaken in the passages surrounding it. It is, prominently, a self-standing narrative told through a set of striking images, which are elaborated using an unusual level of detail. Although the Allegory of the Cave does not feature deities or supernatural elements typically found in traditional myths, the story unfolds in an extraordinary, if not fantastical, setting that—for all its strangeness—conjures a coherent and vivid world.

It may suffice, for now, to set aside thornier questions of categorization for the more modest suggestion that Plato intended to revisit in the Allegory of the Cave the specific literary form in which he wrote the Myth of Metals.[33] Like the Myth of Metals, the Allegory of the Cave tells a story about the experience of coming out of a subterranean slumber. This story is also placed at a critical turning point in the educational curriculum of the *kallipolis,* so that the motifs of dreaming and waking similarly serve as a metaphor for the transformative effect that education can have on the natures of its subjects. Socrates designates the cave as an "image of our nature in its education and want of education"—the light-filled reality of the world aboveground represents educated nature, and the sleepy darkness of the cave its privation.[34] The prisoners' understanding of their own natures is tied to their perception of reality: they have not "seen anything of themselves and one another other than the shadows" they cast on the cave wall, whereas one who has escaped the cave knows his soul to be most truly at home in the upper realm and nowhere else.[35]

The story offers that the nature transformed by a certain education is the more legitimate and true. The Myth of Metals had presented an education in music and gymnastics as capable of forming for the citizen a new and more valid nature to replace the authority of biological nature; the Allegory of the Cave makes an analogous claim about a new, more sophisticated kind of education. Having undergone the preliminary education in music and gymnastics, and having subsequently been sorted on its basis, a select pool of potential guardians now faces a second round of selection, in which they are to be educated in the abstract sciences (arithmetic, geometry, astronomy, and harmony) leading up to the study of dialectic.[36] Progressing through these studies, Socrates tells us, is akin to being led out of the cave in the Allegory, and learning to see in the light of the sun.

The Allegory of the Cave, then, can be read as the continuation of a project begun in the Myth of Metals, whereby a story about an awakening makes a particular kind of assertion regarding the effect of education on the natures of the potential guardians. Those candidates chosen to advance to the next stage of the curriculum are those whose natures had successfully undergone the transformation intended by the relevant education. Both narratives give an account of this transformation by presenting the successfully educated nature as categorically more natural than its uneducated counterpart.

The Progression from a Cultural to a Dialectical Education

How, then, are we to think about the relationship between these parallel assertions about the natures of citizens, repeated at different stages of the educational program of the *kallipolis*? There are two important dis-analogies between the Myth of Metals and the Allegory of the Cave that call for some elaboration. The first concerns a difference in how education is represented in each story. We recall that the Myth of Metals had compared the experience of the citizens' preliminary education to dreams. In the Allegory of the Cave, by contrast, it is only uneducated nature itself that is represented as a dream or a state of diminished reality; the education in dialectic is instead portrayed as a slow and painful awakening, and the nature transformed by this process as the final and desired condition of being awake.

At one level, the discrepancy can be chalked up to the qualitative difference between the types of education at the center of each myth. Gymnastics and music, Socrates tells us, had educated the potential guardians "through habits . . . not knowledge."[37] Dialectic, by contrast, requires its practitioner to look beyond the world of happenstance phenomena to discern the whole containing the particulars, and Socrates accordingly insists that those guardians who now embody this nature learn to see both in the light of the upper realm as well as in the darkness of the cave.[38] In the Myth of Metals, the sum total of the citizens' experiences prior to the completion of their preliminary education is an old reality permanently lost, like a dream one cannot return to, whereas the Allegory of the Cave portrays dialectic as an art that equips its students to traverse dream and reality precisely because they can distinguish between those realms. "But you we have begotten [ἐγεννήσαμεν]," he tells the would-be guardians of the *kallipolis* in a hypothetical speech, to "have been better and more perfectly educated and are more able to participate in both lives."[39] Giving weight to the difference between an education in dialectic and one in music and gymnastics establishes the relative authority of philosophy over habit, and casts the more basic education as a temporary prelude to the definitive transformation of the guardians and their initiation into true reality.[40]

The inauguration of a philosophical education as a definitive pedagogical endpoint to override all prior educations in habit might hardly be a surprising proposal to find in the *Republic*. But here a second point of disanalogy between the Myth of Metals and the Allegory of the Cave suggests a somewhat different reading. Unlike the Myth of Metals, which is presented as a myth intended to be addressed directly to the citizens of the *kallipolis*, the Allegory of the Cave is told just to Socrates's interlocutors, Glaucon and Adeimantus. This means that by the time they have completed the dialectical stage of their education, the guardians of the *kallipolis* would have heard no more than one myth making a claim about what their true natures consist in. Consequently, the central lesson of the Allegory of the Cave—that one's true nature is in fact a nature transformed by a dialectical education—is something that these guardians learn, not from a placeholder myth told during a phase of their upbringing when they could not have known better, but over the long years of a comprehensive dialectical education.

But Glaucon and Adeimantus—and through them, we the readers— encounter this lesson in the form of a story they have heard before. To a reader made familiar with the structure of the Allegory of the Cave through the Myth of Metals, the seeming conclusiveness of the dialectical awakening depicted in it is undercut by the very fact that it deposes an analogous awakening from a previous myth along the way. If the moment of waking in the Allegory of the Cave is meant to help draw a sharp distinction between a discriminating education in dialectic and a blind education in culture—much like the distinction between knowledge and habit—the same myth, by virtue of what it shares with the Myth of Metals, also points to their fundamental similarity. At the end of the day, dialectic remains a form of education that seeks to make knowledge a kind of habit: "steady and strenuous participation in arguments"—the content of dialectical training—is, for Socrates, "a gymnastic that is the antistrophe of the bodily gymnastic."[41]

What the Allegory of the Cave tells us instead is that all practices and institutions taken for granted in the social and political culture of any society are, to some extent, like the Myth of Metals. When the institutional frameworks orienting one's sense of self come to be perceived as natural, they are, in fact, founded on much shiftier ground than they project themselves to be. And although such frameworks might predictably include the accepted norms and practices of Athens that so often bear the brunt of Socrates's critique, and even the content of a preliminary cultural education in the *kallipolis,* they also include some of the tacit premises underpinning the highest philosophical education that the *kallipolis* has to offer to its guardians. If, in the Allegory of the Cave, Plato draws on a familiar narrative template in order to make another revisionary assertion about the content of individual natures, he does so while suggesting, at the same time, that even a philosopher's self-understanding—and the philosophical pursuits framed by this understanding—rest on the scaffolds of ingrained concepts we come to take for granted, and which lend themselves easily to being the subject of myths.

THE MYTH OF ER

Compared to the Myth of Metals and the Allegory of the Cave, the Myth of Er can be especially bewildering to read: it is teeming with opulent literary descriptions of the afterlife, and what purpose it is meant to serve in the larger scheme of the *Republic,* whether political or philosophical, is ambiguous. Read in conjunction with the earlier two myths, however, the Myth of Er begins to make much more sense than it does on its own.

Like the Myth of Metals and the Allegory of the Cave before it, the Myth of Er is structured around an awakening from a dream and a rebirth out of the earth. Its hero-messenger, Er, is killed in a battle but then comes back to life in order to tell the story of what he has seen in the other realm, as though he had merely slept through the ordeal and had "all of a sudden . . . recovered his sight and saw that it was morning and he was lying on the pyre."[42] The journey from the afterworld back to the world of the living is an ascent—a journey that Er makes with the souls sent to be reincarnated as they are carried "up to their birth."[43] The myth in its entirety describes a cycle of reincarnation, and the souls in question face a choice concerning the lives into which they are to be reborn when they next open their eyes. According to the myth, the "ordering of the soul" changes as it makes its way through the life it chooses, and what happens in the afterlife, presented as a thousand-year dream between waking lives, has an effect on the content of that choice.[44]

In both the Myth of Metals and the Allegory of the Cave, such stories of awakening were, explicitly, a metaphor for the transformation of nature by education, and these narrative interludes were accordingly located in places in the *Republic* concerned with the testing and sorting of citizens who have undergone the corresponding stages of the *kallipolis*'s educational curriculum. If we take seriously the observation that the same story is repeated in the Myth of Er, this also encourages us to read it as a myth about these same topics—of education and of testing for its effects.

The Prelude to the Myth

Whether education can make a lasting impact on the natures of individuals is an important question in the *Republic* because the time frame with which it is concerned goes beyond a single lifetime.[45] The Myth of Er is framed as an account of the rewards of justice, both in life and in death.[46] One way of thinking about such a task is to begin by asking whether anything of the complex educational program of the *kallipolis*, geared at creating justice in souls and in the city, matters in the long run. Certainly, Socrates did not leave out considerations about the afterlife when designing the educational curriculum of the *kallipolis*'s guardians. After the preliminary training in music and gymnastics, and a sequence of intermediate studies culminating in an education in dialectic, the guardians descend into the metaphorical cave to apply their lessons to the political affairs of the city. This includes fifteen years of service in the offices related to war, and "the rest of their lives" in a less systematic mix of philosophical engagement, the ruling of the city, and educating the next generation of guardians.[47] But rather than conclude his summary of the guardians' education there, Socrates brings them instead to a curious place: the Isles of the Blessed, where they are to dwell for eternity as they continue to receive public honors from the city.[48] In so doing, Socrates extends the story of the guardians' education and testing into the afterlife—the subject of the myth that concludes the *Republic*.

In his prefatory remarks to the Myth of Er, Socrates raises the question of how individual human nature is to be conceptualized on such a scale.[49] Until this moment in the *Republic*, the discussion had considered the soul only as it is embodied in the material world and, significantly, in political society. The soul, however, being immortal, outlives the conditions of the lives it inhabits. As such, Socrates maintains, its true nature has yet to be revealed. Rather, the embodied soul is not unlike an ancient sea god, who appears to us buried in aquatic debris:

> Just as those who catch sight of the sea god Glaucus would no longer easily see his original nature because some of the old parts of his body have been broken off and the others have been ground down and thoroughly maimed by the waves at the same time as other things have grown on him—shells, seaweed, and rocks—so that he resembles any beast rather than what he was by nature, so, too, we see the soul in such a condition because of countless evils.[50]

To isolate the soul from human life and examine it from an eternal vantage point, like that of the afterlife, would be to draw it "out of the deep ocean in which it is now, and the rocks and shells were hammered off. . . . And then one would see its true nature."[51]

Socrates hypothesizes that the true nature of the uncorrupted soul is a perfectly philosophical soul.[52] Just as philosophy—the love of wisdom—draws the soul toward a realm of eternal truths, the soul in its natural state is a soul stripped of all that is transitory in the world.[53] But Socrates's presentation of both nature and philosophy comes into odds with an understanding sustained throughout the earlier two myths of the *Republic:* that a political education, publically administered in a temporal city, not only shapes a soul's nature but can also make it more philosophical. Are the effects of earthly institutions on the soul—even those geared toward philosophy—mere seashells and rocks grafted onto its nature, ready to fall away when it is lifted out of the social and political settings in which it was embedded during life? Or can the things of this world leave a more lasting mark on that which is immortal?

These, I hope to show, are the questions at the heart of the eschatological myth concluding the *Republic*. The Myth of Er can be read as a response to two demands that have emerged from these prefatory observations: first, that the project of the guardians' education is to be evaluated at the scale of the afterlife; and second, that the nature of the soul in the afterlife and the place of philosophy there have yet to be investigated. On this reading, the Myth of Er becomes a meditation on whether education acquired in a political setting may be conducive to the construction of a genuinely philosophic nature that persists through time, even in the absence of the societal structures that helped cultivate it. The myth thus takes up a coherent line of inquiry, raised in the previous two myths of the *Republic,* on the extent to which the natures of individuals can be formed by the educational apparatuses of the city.

The Thousand-Year Journey: An Education in Cosmic Justice

The first half of the Myth of Er describes the journeys of the souls in the afterlife; a report of how they choose the patterns of their next lives makes up the second. At one level, one half of the myth may seem to follow from the other because the primary purpose of the souls' journeys is judgment and retribution for justices and injustices committed in the previous life.[54] These journeys last a thousand years, and they contain ten lifetimes' worth of pleasures or terrors, for those judged just and unjust, respectively. Only when these moral debts are paid do the souls have a clean ledger from which to begin their next lives.[55] But at another level, the experiences accrued on these thousand-year journeys are more directly connected to *how* the souls make their choices. Significantly, it is this second, rather than the first, connection between the two halves of the myth that accounts for the alarming intricacy of the configuration of its world.

In the Myth of Er, the afterlife boasts a deliberate and convoluted geography. The journeys of the souls begin at a "certain demonic place," with two openings in the ground and two more in the heaven above.[56] There, the souls are judged, and their judgments are attached to them as signs, before they commence their journeys of retribution—the just through one of the heavenly openings toward a path full of pleasures and rewards, and the unjust through an opening in the ground to a path full of terrors and punishments. A thousand years later, a curious thing happens: the journeys loop back to the demonic place of judgment. Two groups of souls, returning from their separate journeys through the second pair of openings in the heaven and the earth, reunite to tell each other about what they have seen on their respective paths. They go together to a meadow, where their numerous stories, too many to recount in the myth, are devoured eagerly.[57] Then they journey to a certain vantage point from which they get a good view of the Spindle of Necessity that holds the cosmos together. Finally, they are taken to Necessity's daughter, Lachesis, where they begin the process of choosing the patterns of their next lives.

If the point of the journey thus far is solely about retribution for the ills and merits of one's life, there is no obvious explanation—on logical grounds or from Greek eschatology currently available to us—as to why the thousand-year journeys must circuit back to the place of judgment, or why the myth emphasizes, to the extent that it does, the exchange of information between the souls who have completed their respective journeys. The signs carried by the souls also figure into the confusion: clearly, they are meant to be read—but by whom, and to what end?[58] Read on its own, the careful construction of these details in the myth can seem excessive, in the way of a pointlessly fanciful story. Commentators have accordingly refrained from ascribing any philosophical purpose to these odd features of the journey.[59]

But when the Myth of Er is considered in light of the educational project of the *Republic,* the oddly elaborate program set out for the souls in the afterlife begins to make more sense. The stranger details of the myth—the convergence of the souls' journeys at the place of judgment, the signs they are made to carry from and back to this place with the strange geography, and the vibrant exchange of stories about each journey—can all be read as contributing pieces to a systematic education in justice and its centrality to the constitution of a harmonious universe. Even when a soul in the myth experiences firsthand the rewards or punishments particular to the conduct of his own life, he does so in a fashion that juxtaposes his subjective journey against those of others, and reveals something about the organizing principles by which they all fit together. This is because the demonic place, where each thousand-year journey begins and ends, is set up in such a way that calls for the commingling of a multiplicity of perspectives (see Table 2).

Table 2. The educational spectacle at the demonic place of judgment

Souls at various stages of their journeys through the afterlife		What they look like to others	What they see
(1) Newly arrived souls awaiting judgment		Unmarked	Signs carried by the souls in (2) and (3) The contrast in the conditions of the souls in (3a) and (3b) [*To the extent that the souls in (1) don't know how they will be judged, both groups of returning souls, (3a) and (3b), should be of equal interest]
(2) Souls who have just been judged, about to depart on their thousand-year journeys	(2a) Just	Signs of the judgments attached in front of them (614c)	The differences between the two halves, (2a) and (2b), of their newly split group A pronounced causal connection between the judgments and deeds indicated in the signs carried by the souls in (2) and (3), and the conditions of the souls in (3) [*As such, the souls in (2a) and (2b) would be particularly interested in those souls returning from the paths designated to them, (3a) and (3b), respectively]
	(2b) Unjust	"Signs of everything they had done" attached behind them (614c–d)	
(3) Souls returning from their thousand-year journeys	(3a) Just	Presumably still carrying signs and looking "as though they had come from a long journey" (614e) Coming down looking "pure from heaven" (614d) Also seen sharing stories of what they had seen on their journey through heaven (615a)	Reminders, in (1) and (2), of the earlier stages of the journey they had just completed The conditions of the souls in either (3b) or (3a), returning from paths they themselves did not take [*The souls in (3a) and (3b) are more explicitly interested in both the appearances and the stories of the souls in the other group, (3b) and (3a), respectively]
	(3b) Unjust	Presumably still carrying signs and looking "as though they had come from a long journey" Coming up "out of the earth, full of dirt and dust" (614e) Also seen "lamenting and crying" as they share stories of what they had seen on their journey under the earth (615a)	

As a consequence of differences in both the time they have spent in the afterlife and the judgments passed on them, souls have differently limited perspectives on the details of how retribution works in this world. Souls who traveled the heavenly path, for instance, have no experience of the underground path, and the souls yet awaiting judgment do not even know which of the paths will be theirs. But their convergence in one place also permits them to access, at the same time, an abundance of information about experiences beyond their own. When, for example, souls return from their journeys, presumably still carrying their telltale signs—appearing "full of dirt and dust" if they had been judged unjust, and "pure from heaven" if they had been just—they are seen, and their stories of terror or pleasure eagerly devoured, not only by other returning souls but by those newly arrived souls, yet to depart on their own thousand-year journeys.[60] Hence, for departing and returning souls alike, the demonic place of judgment offers visual and auditory instruction in the unmistakable advantage of falling in the group that wears signs of justice and travels through the heavenly path.

Of course, the deceptively simple moral lesson that it is better to be just than unjust has been told in less roundabout—though perhaps no less problematic—ways elsewhere. The myth at the end of the *Gorgias* features an overtly educational program, also involving the visible branding of souls with a list of their deeds, in which "everyone who is subject to punishment rightly inflicted by another . . . become[s] better and profit[s] from it, or else [is] made an example for others, so that when they see him suffering whatever it is he suffers, they may be afraid and become better." Those who fall in the latter category are "simply strung up there in the prison in Hades as examples, visible warnings to unjust men who are ever arriving."[61] But it bears emphasizing that instruction in the advantages of justice is not quite so didactic in the Myth of Er.[62] The structure of its eschatological journey mandates that the each of the different paths to the same lesson is always an exercise in drawing connections, in learning where one's own experience and subjective viewpoint fit into the greater scheme of things. At the place of judgment, the souls themselves actively inquire others about journeys that were not their own, and must discern what is relevant in the wealth of information at the crowded site.

Table 3.   The progression of the meaning of justice in the eschatological journey

Location in journey	Quality of perspective	Meaning of justice
Judgment	More subjective	The name given to my deeds in life (or, if I am judged unjust, its opposite)
Retributive thousand-year journey		Retribution for my own deeds, which is an experience I have in common with others on my journey
Return to the demonic place of judgment and the neighboring meadow		The logic that all souls receive the appropriate retribution for their deeds in life, despite the variety of both the lives they led and the journeys they traveled in the afterlife
Gazing upon the Spindle of Necessity	More objective	The harmonious principle holding together the cosmos

Moreover, lessons in the retributive advantages of justice are only one part of the instruction that souls receive in the Myth of Er. The exercises at the demonic place of judgment prepare their subjects, at the end of their thousand-year journeys, for a vision of the coherent universe held together by the Spindle of Necessity. Along the arc of that journey, the perspective that the souls have on their world widens progressively—from the limited gaze they have on their own paths of retribution, to the exchange of information that occurs back at the place of judgment, and to the view of the structure of the universe. Even the passage to the Spindle is approached gradually; the souls at first see it as a column of light, and the intricate stem and nested whorls of the Spindle do not come into visibility until the following day, when the souls move closer.[63] For each soul making this journey, these shifts in perspective correspond to shifts in the meaning of justice. The structure of the souls' journeys tracks a lesson in the unity of cosmic justice as experienced from vantage points that gradually progress from the subjective to the objective: what is at first the retribution for the deeds committed in one's own life develops into a comprehensive system of retribution for all souls in the afterlife, until justice finally corresponds to the harmony of the whole cosmos (see Table 3). In the Myth of Er, then, souls are subjected to an immersive education in cosmic justice before they are sent to choose the patterns of their subsequent lives.

The Choice of the Next Life: The Test of the Educated Soul

The Myth of Metals and the Allegory of the Cave had told stories about waking up into new natures. These stories were told at places in the *Republic* corresponding to major junctures of the *kallipolis*'s educational curriculum, where a program of tests selected for individuals whose natures had been suitably transformed at the relevant stage. The moment when the souls in the Myth of Er choose the patterns of the lives into which they will be reborn can be construed in similar terms. This choice requires "looking off toward the nature of the soul" with special care and—as Socrates interjects in the myth to stress—amounts to the ultimate test of a soul's mastery of "that study by which he might be able to learn and find out who will give him the capacity and the knowledge to distinguish the good and the bad life, and so everywhere and always to choose the better from among those that are possible."[64]

Choosing well would require the capacity to resist packing one's subsequent life with superficial advantages, and to make one's calculations at the scale of the thousand-year journey that follows at the heels of a single lifetime. It would require knowing the shape of a just soul and the ability to discern it when it is embedded in lives as diverse as those belonging to all who traveled the heavenly path. The intricacy of the journey in the afterlife leading up to this moment may be accounted for because its educative agenda prepares the souls for the choice, and the content of the choice itself serves as a test for the effects of that cosmic education.

Readers of the myth might object, at this point, that the souls generally give little consideration to their experiences on that journey when choosing the patterns of their subsequent lives.[65] Rather, for many, those lessons in the rewards of virtue, much less in the harmony of the universe, appear to have been lost, and they make their decisions "according to the habituation of their former life"—a life they had more than a thousand years to forget.[66] Consequently, not many souls in the myth make an informed choice, and it is unclear if any of them chooses a philosophic life. Even Odysseus, who arguably makes a well-considered choice of a quiet life as a private citizen, is said to be reacting to the memories of his previous life.[67] Only those souls who had suffered greatly during their journeys of retribution fare a little better: they make more careful, unhurried choices, not only "because they had labored" themselves but also because they "had seen the labors of others."[68] But there are accompanying dangers to being affected in this way by the experiences and spectacles of only one's own journey, as those souls who had instead traveled along the heavenly path are just as likely to rush their decisions.[69] One such soul hastens to choose the tyrant's life because he had not experienced those labors for himself but was instead "one of those who had come from heaven, having lived in an orderly regime in his former life, participating in virtue by habit, without philosophy."[70] If the choice of a pattern for one's next life is meant to serve as a test of the education acquired on the eschatological journey leading up to this moment, it is, then, a test that nearly all of the souls in the myth appear to fail.

These underwhelming results, however, may raise significant concerns about the test, but do not go so far as to invalidate it. What they do instead is hold to a much higher standard the philosophical qualities for which the souls in the Myth of Er are being tested, and with which the *Republic* is ultimately concerned. At one level, it should be unsurprising that so many of the souls make unphilosophical choices when pressed to put their understanding of a good life to the test: much of the educational curriculum outlined in the *Republic*—and the subject of the Myth of Metals and the Allegory of the Cave—had thus far been devoted to the filtering of natures through increasingly rigorous tests of character, and some routine attrition is to be expected as well at this final round of examination. The need for such vetting becomes clear, for instance, in the case of the soul from the virtuous city who chooses the life of a tyrant: it is not enough, his example tells us, to have been virtuous in one's conduct in life, but it takes another round of education in justice, and the administration of another test, to discern whether one has come to possess a philosophical nature.

But at another level, the ambiguities generated by the difficulty of the test pose a more nuanced philosophical question regarding the relationship between education and the nature of the individual soul. The story of the soul from the virtuous city, in particular, is cause for concern, because it suggests the possibility that even citizenship in a city like the *kallipolis* offers no guarantee of the kind of wisdom required to pass the cosmic test.[71] Whereas education in the *kallipolis,* as depicted in the earlier myths, had been geared toward molding the natures of its citizens as though instilling habits, the true test of a philosophic nature—as the example of the soul from the virtuous city indicates—must be able to distinguish an individual's most deeply ingrained qualities from those habits that merely reflect the character of his city.[72]

That test, then, sets upon itself the task of identifying the soul on whom the educational apparatuses of his city and those of the afterlife have achieved a combined effect of a particular kind. In the worst case, habituation in the norms of a virtuous city can end up hindering one's capacity to choose well, as a thousand years of journeying through heavenly sights and experiences can bring a soul to underestimate the stakes of the choice, and life in a city where virtue is the norm may dull the moral senses.[73] In the correctly aligned nature, however, the educational curriculum of a well-ordered city should serve as a foundation, rather than a liability, for higher levels of instruction and testing that take place in the afterlife—so that a soul trained in the forms of justice in the city and the soul would also be better equipped to recognize it in the cosmos and in the myriad forms of life possible in it.

On Whether the Things of the World Mark Our Immortal Souls

The Myth of Er, then, portrays an extension of the project of education and testing begun in the *kallipolis*—one that seeks to select for the thoroughly philosophical soul who remains so through multiple cycles of reincarnation. This search, we have seen, had proceeded analogically, by returning periodically to a common narrative pattern that was used to denote a shift in the content of individual nature after a certain education: in the Myth of Metals, the citizens of the *kallipolis* wake up into natures that had in fact been fashioned during a prior education in music and gymnastics, just as the freed prisoner in the Allegory of the Cave realizes that his true nature belongs in the realm of the Forms that he encountered through his education in dialectic. To the extent that the Myth of Er echoes the framing of these earlier myths, it appears to illustrate a continuation of the same experiment by which the natures of individuals are educated and then tested for the effects of that education. The ultimate test of the aggregate effect of education on an individual soul, the myth suggests, would occur outside of the particular political context in which the majority of the enterprise was executed.

A reading of the Myth of Er that extrapolates its content from the Myth of Metals and the Allegory of the Cave, in turn, helps us see the extent to which Plato was invested in thinking critically about the effect of the institutions of the city on the soul. Readers of the *Republic* often have a difficult time with the city–soul analogy because they tend to feel pressured to choose which of the two embodiments of justice the book is really about. Justice writ large and small, in the city and in the individual soul, can often seem like two parallel manifestations of the form that do not quite converge.[74] But to ask, as the myth does, whether a philosophical education can leave a lasting effect on the nature of its subjects, is also to raise the question of whether the just city can in fact help make the soul more just.

So can education change one's nature? The answer offered by the Myth of Er is ambiguous at best: because habituation in the ways of a virtuous city is an insufficient guarantee for virtue that endures through the greater scheme of things, the experiences of the afterlife must supplement the education of cities to pick out the possessors of true justice and philosophy, who are few and far between. And yet, even the combination of the education of the city and that of the afterlife seems to have had at most a muted effect on the vast majority of the souls depicted in the myth. The inconclusive ending of the Myth of Er leaves much room to wonder if any soul could or does in fact end up with a nature permanently reformed by the education imposed upon it.

But there is a deeper significance to this answer. It is consistent with the recurrent pattern of education and testing that structures the *Republic*, which hinged on an understanding that education is a continuing, aggregative endeavor that builds over the course of an entire lifetime, if not even longer. At critical junctures in this process, the standard for determining the content of an individual's nature was regularly written over. Even an education culminating in the alignment of one's soul with the harmonious universe, the pattern would suggest, is part of an ongoing mission undertaken in a cosmos eternally in flux. If this is the case, then claiming that our nature is essentially philosophical, as Socrates suggests in his meditation on the sea god Glaucus, is not so simple. While the dream of a truer nature somehow more indelible than one shaped by impermanent institutions may be a crucial philosophical ideal to which to aspire, the myths of the *Republic* seem to imply that there is no essential human nature as such, and that the durability of a philosophical nature depends more on the continual striving toward that ideal than in any possibility of its ultimate realization.[75]

In turn, the myths intimate something of the fragility of Plato's philosophic enterprise, and how closely it is interwoven with the inquiry pursued in its myths. If a central project of the *Republic* concerns the progressive formation of the philosophical soul to whom the stewardship of the *kallipolis* may be entrusted, the conceptual interventions made in the myths play a critical role in how that process is to be understood. We have seen how, in making radical new claims about what individual natures consist in, the myths periodically sought to recalibrate the working understanding of the concept of nature. A distinctive feature of these mythic claims is that they are at once authoritative and provisional. That is, in the myths of the *Republic,* a nature reformed by education is presented as stable, accompanied by a sense of inevitability or destiny. Yet recurring revisions in the sequence of myths, of what gets to be designated as the nature of an individual, bring attention to the provisional character of such claims; a state of the soul equated with an individual's true nature might come up for revision later on in the educational curriculum. This paradoxical combination of authority and provisionality has the effect of demarcating the contours of strict—and yet ultimately elastic—norms and expectations that govern the roles individuals inhabit in their city. In this way the myths accommodate the tension between unconditioned and conditioned thinking—the need to take a certain political reality for granted in order to operate within it, and admitting to its limits without knowing where those limits might be.[76]

THE MYTHIC PROJECT OF THE *REPUBLIC*

When Plato was writing the Myth of Metals, the Allegory of the Cave, and the Myth of Er into the *Republic,* he was tapping into the conventions of an existing genre that had lately come under increased cultural scrutiny. Traditionally, Greek mythology consisted in a loose body of canonical tales, which usually dealt in significant but undemonstrable subject matter—such as the nature and origins of the cosmos, or the deeds of deities and ancient heroes—and which formed a vital part of the fabric of Greek culture. From as early as the seventh century BC, however, pre-Socratic philosophers had begun referring to myths pejoratively, usually as a polemical way of distinguishing their own work from what had formerly passed for conventional wisdom.[77] Plato's immediate predecessors and contemporaries inherited and intensified the practice as they sought to invent new ways of presenting ideas that aspired to a more rigorous standard of truth than the unverifiable, undemonstrable qualities of mythic narratives.[78] Myth and its associated traditions, they were keen to show, were emblematic of an increasingly obsolete orientation to theorizing about the natures of things, which stood in contrast to the approaches that their own work and discourse were better equipped to capture. Myth was understood in opposition, in particular, to the trappings of the kind of critical thinking that would come to be epitomized in the meticulous, detail-oriented arguments that make up the bulk of Plato's work.

In a number of ways, the paradoxical qualities we find in the myths of the *Republic* were features that the ancient critics of myth had begun to pick out to characterize the broader genre of myth, in contradistinction to the superior rigor of the burgeoning norms of argumentative discourse. First, the myths of the *Republic* posit certain claims about the content of the natures of individuals in such a way that these assertions are impervious to further interrogation. Because myths are imagined stories, pressing them for reasons or facts, as one might in an argument, is beside the point. Indeed, Socrates—whose philosophical examinations are otherwise known to revert to a method of relentless questioning—is careful to shield his myths from claims to truth or authorship, that he may not be called to answer for them.[79] Second, the provisional status of the myths' claims about the content of individual nature may be noncommittal, even irresponsible, in a way that claims and reasons given in arguments are not. Socrates's method famously catches interlocutors when they contradict themselves, on the implicit premise that arguments must build on themselves without contradiction.[80] Myths, by contrast, are not held to such standards of consistency, so that each subsequent myth in the *Republic* can supplant the description of individual nature in the myth that came before it.

Given the separate norms that Plato appears to uphold in his argumentative investigations and in the myths that he tells, his readers often attempt to argue for their compatibility in one of two ways. First, they can insist that the myths end up conveying the same conclusions that Plato elsewhere reaches through logical argumentation, and that, by virtue of their appeal as stories, the myths may even communicate these lessons more memorably to a wider audience.[81] This tends to be the line of interpretation favored by readers who wish to emphasize the rhetorical effectiveness of myths as instruments of persuasion—usually for audiences who may be incapable of philosophizing through more rigorous channels, but also for those individuals who, in order to integrate the philosophical lessons of the arguments into their worldviews, require the support of the parts of their souls that are more readily moved by vivid stories and images.[82] Second, Plato's readers can also point to the possibility that the myths were designed to be constructively unsatisfying when ensconced in his philosophical texts. On this view, the most jarring aspects of such myths—their inscrutability, the nature of the claims or the events depicted in them, or any number of seemingly unphilosophical elements that can be engineered to generate a deep sense of dissatisfaction—can ironically direct its audience the other way, jolting them into recognizing unfounded sources of belief and sharpening their faculty for critical judgment.[83]

Myths certainly have the potential to serve philosophical ends in both these capacities, and Plato explicitly acknowledges such functions or takes advantage of them in a number of his other myths. The cosmological myth of the *Laws*, for example, is presented as an effort to persuade a skeptical young man toward piety, just as the myth at the end of the *Phaedo* is introduced in response to an interlocutor's admission to not having been wholly persuaded by the preceding arguments for the immortality of the soul.[84] When applied to the myths of the *Republic*, however, such accounts miss the larger picture. Here, the respite from critical thinking that myth permits is part of the point, not something to be apologized for. Taken together, the myths of the *Republic* demonstrate how myth can create spaces for taking certain foundational concepts—like one's own nature—for granted in ways that are pivotal to Plato's understanding of what it means to be a philosopher. To take a concept, practice, or institution for granted is admittedly dangerous for philosophy, and the pains Plato takes to warn against the temptations of falling into such cognitive habits—even the habits of virtuous cities—are testament to his caution. All the same, the *Republic* also draws attention to his conviction that a philosopher cannot be made overnight, but requires a lifetime or more of practice and habituation into natures like those celebrated in the myths. And so in Book II of the *Republic*, when the discussion of the educational program of the *kallipolis* begins in earnest, Socrates likens the project to the creation of myths: "Come now," he exhorts his interlocutors, "let us educate our guardians as if we were at leisure and telling myths."[85]

Positing, as the myths do, that a particular conception of one's nature is to be taken for granted—that is, at once authoritatively yet provisionally—must be considered a foundational part of how Plato believed philosophers are formed. In the myths of the *Republic*, individuals seem to be told what they are before they are expected to grow into those roles. The coherence of their ideas about themselves and their place in the world is not given, but constructed and reinforced through narratives that already assume an illusion of unity that isn't in fact there.[86] If myths assist in providing such concepts through which a philosophic nature builds its own understanding of itself, they can also ground the philosophic activity of one who thinks of himself in these terms.[87]

The three myths of the *Republic*, then, form a coherent inquiry regarding the political manipulation of individual human nature. They also reveal a paradoxical doubleness to the endeavor, whereby a myth can advance a normative assertion about the nature of the citizens and the political reality they inhabit, while simultaneously admitting to the provisionality of that claim. In so doing, they tell us something more general about the potential of myth. Certainly Plato uses myth across the dialogues in a myriad of ways that are not exhausted by this account, just as he expresses famous misgivings about the way myths are received in his time. But the myths of the *Republic* posit the possibility of a mythic project that is particularly coherent and compelling from the perspective of political theory.

Political myths may appear to be essentially unphilosophical, because they seem to present certain political conditions as being fixed into nature, beyond critical challenge or revision. What Plato's use of myth in the *Republic* demonstrates, at one level, is the extent to which a philosopher's self-understanding and activities rely on the stability of such implicit narratives about reality that are taken for granted. At another level, the unified inquiry pursued in the myths also speaks to the paradoxical plasticity of such narratives and understandings, and their capacity to be revised by subsequent myths.[88] In forging an intimate connection between the myths and the educational curriculum of the philosophical city, the project draws attention to the power of myth to reshape the conceptual frameworks through which its audiences imagine themselves and their political reality. In this instance, myth also comes to bear a more complicated relationship to Plato's philosophy. Plato's myths and his philosophy are neither directly opposed to each other, nor is the former a force to be made merely subservient to the ends of the latter, but the two are very much mutually entwined.

The centrality of Plato's myths to his philosophical project would go on to make a deep impression on some of his most prominent followers in modern philosophy and political thought. The protagonists of the chapters that follow—all astute and important readers of Plato—did not all read the myths of the *Republic* the way I have here. But they each paid close attention to Plato's practice of writing myths into his philosophical works, and they were inspired, in turn, to emulate or to reinvent the practice themselves. Plato, as we have seen, looked to the literary genre of myth as a resource for reworking the basic conceptual building blocks of the philosophical and political imagination. An important contingent of his modern admirers would go on to build on this insight. These authors similarly viewed the literary genre of myth as a medium that could be used to access certain parts of our world-views that are especially thick and deeply ingrained, and especially difficult to parse through more conventional forms of philosophical discourse. Paying attention to this legacy, then, also allows us to see Plato in a different light: as the inaugurator of what we might call a mythic tradition in political thought.

2

THE UTOPIAN FOUNDING MYTHS OF

MORE AND BACON

MYTH AS A STABILIZING FORCE
FOR POLITICS AND KNOWLEDGE

WHEN THOMAS HOBBES sought to distinguish his *Leviathan* from a way of writing about politics that struck him as more wishful thinking than of practical relevance, he cautioned to his readers that his own work was not to be counted among "the Platonic, the Utopian, and Atlantic republics."[1] Such boasts were, by the time Hobbes was writing, something of a knowing wink at an audience already well-acquainted with a burgeoning industry of writing about imagined commonwealths, and who would have been, in particular, predisposed to measure new entries to the field against the canonical works that constituted its most iconic points of reference. Plato's *Republic,* Thomas More's *Utopia* (1516), and Francis Bacon's *New Atlantis* (1626) remain, in our time as much as in Hobbes's, an unsurprising trinity making up the best known, as well as the most influential, exemplars of utopian literature in the history of political thought: the classical model that inspired the genre, the work by More that coined the term, and its most famous imitation.[2]

It is a well-known and oft-repeated observation that utopia, the genre of speculative political fiction invented by More, was partly modeled after Plato's *Republic*.[3] The publication of More's *Utopia* had the effect of recovering, on the one hand, a constellation of Greek—and pointedly Platonic—political ideas, and spawning, on the other, a chain of imitations that similarly reached back to the Greek traditions that had been amplified in More's work.[4] This was true especially on the Continent, where the influence of *Utopia* culminated in such works as Tommaso Campanella's *The City of the Sun* (1602), the theocratic utopia arranged around a natural religion and the community of wives and property familiar to readers of the *Republic*.[5]

But it wasn't until the posthumous publication of *New Atlantis* that utopian writing properly caught on in England, and it was in this later, seventeenth-century English context that the genre thrived and left a lasting, continuous legacy. While the immediate popularity of *Utopia* had resulted in the swift importation of the term "utopia" into the English language, English imitations of it had been notably scarce. Over the course of a seven-decade period following the publication of *New Atlantis*, however, "dozens" of utopias were being written. Numbering among them were James Harrington's *Oceana* (1656), Margaret Cavendish's celebrated work of early science fiction *The Blazing World* (1666), and Henry Neville's *The Isle of Pines* (1668); and it was also during the peak of this productive period that Hobbes published *Leviathan* (1651).[6] *New Atlantis*, it has accordingly been suggested, marks a critical turning point that helped to transform utopia from a concept to a literary genre.[7]

Utopias, if anything, constituted a self-referential genre. New utopias freely embraced the fact that they were imitating something that had come before, often going so far as to insert themselves into the fictional universes created by their predecessors.[8] And if Hobbes, writing at a historic high point for utopian writing, could venture to repudiate the genre by invoking the Platonic, Utopian, and Atlantic commonwealths in the same breath, this was in part possible because the same grouping of these texts had been encouraged by the very authors who defined the genre, and reinforced in their immediate contemporary reception.

Just as *Utopia* was explicitly marketed to its readers as a work continuing in the tradition of Plato's *Republic*, Bacon took care to anchor *New Atlantis* to familiar points of reference supplied by both More and Plato. Notably, *New Atlantis* derived its title from the myths of Atlantis featured in Plato's *Timaeus* and *Critias*—dialogues often read as sequels to the *Republic*.[9] Comparisons to both *Utopia* and the *Republic* were certainly inescapable in the reception of Bacon's work. A pseudonymous publication from the same decade, for example, presented its own project—an endeavor to supply an alternative ending to *New Atlantis*—as "an Atlantic scheme" that hoped to outdo the constitution and laws "of Plato's community, revived by King Utopus or any later Republican."[10]

What features of the *Republic* can we expect to be preserved or discarded when it is reinvented this way? Notwithstanding the abundance of studies on the lineage linking these three works, scant attention has been paid to the continuity between the myths that Plato, More, and Bacon each wrote into them. If myths are an indispensable feature of the *Republic,* both *Utopia* and *New Atlantis* also have their own myths. They are sets of stories about iconic and foundational moments in the history of More's and Bacon's respective utopias, to which presently existing institutions can be traced, and in reference to which they are legitimized. These founding myths, as they might be described, perform the central function of defining not just the institutions of the polities depicted in *Utopia* and *New Atlantis,* but the character of their societies, their values and norms, and their identities as communities. To whatever extent the social arrangements depicted in *Utopia* and *New Atlantis* are intended to represent political ideals, the myths at their center are vital to those visions.

The decisions, on the part of More and Bacon, to invent myths for *Utopia* and *New Atlantis* indicate that both authors regarded such stories to be an important element for inclusion in a sketch of an ideal commonwealth. The aim of this chapter is to unpack why they might have thought so. It argues that the incorporation of founding myths into the texts of *Utopia* and *New Atlantis* represents the elaboration of a Platonic legacy, and in particular the legacy of Plato's myths.

Like Plato, More and Bacon took the traditional literary genre of myth to be a uniquely powerful resource for politics and philosophy. This itself marks the rediscovery of a distinct way of thinking about myth from within a Platonic framework, and a turning point in the traditional reception of Plato's myths. In particular, More and Bacon shared Plato's original investment in the power of myths to shape the norms that end up defining the characters of political communities. They drew an intuitive connection between the medium of myth and the concepts that frame what gets taken for granted in a society. They sought, in turn, to take advantage of this link to stabilize the politics of their respective utopias. By using myths as a stabilizing force, More and Bacon ultimately aimed to create and to sustain political environments conducive to the protection of philosophy as a distinct sphere of intellectual activity with different demands from those of ordinary life.

PLATO'S MYTHS IN THE PLATONIC TRADITION

Before we turn to More's and Bacon's decisions to incorporate myths into their respective reimaginings of Plato's *Republic,* the significance of these gestures must be understood against the background of the reception of Plato and his myths leading up to their time. More, and later Bacon, were heirs to a multifarious and conflicting array of Platonic legacies, across which a number of considerations helped determine the interpretive lenses through which Plato's readers approached his myths. Over centuries, readers found themselves divided on the extent to which Plato could be said to have developed a coherent philosophical system; whether his philosophy was compatible with Christian theology; and to what degree it was necessary to engage directly with his dialogues as literary texts. By the Renaissance, philosophical interest in Plato's myths had been nourished predominantly within the context of a tradition that took an affirmative stance on all three of these points of contention. It was the product, in particular, of a negotiation between strands of interpretation inclined to emphasize the primacy of reason in Platonic philosophy, and those that embraced a theological claim to the superiority of revealed wisdom.

More and Bacon had varying levels of investment in the ancient debates over Plato's philosophical coherence or his compatibility with Christian doctrine. However, they were in agreement in their appreciation of Plato as a stylist, and were, in their own ways, interested in cutting through the veneers of the interpretive traditions in which Plato's texts were often mediated. Consequently, Plato's myths have a rather different legacy in *Utopia* and *New Atlantis* than they do in the frameworks in which they were traditionally received. To locate the significance of Plato's myths in a sociopolitical context, divorced from the language of divine revelation, was to chart out a very different possibility for myth that was human and earthbound in its focus.

The Skeptical Tradition in Platonic Reception: Resisting Philosophical Coherence

The most important question confronting Plato's early interpreters was arguably the issue of whether his writings presented their readers with a coherent system of philosophy. Those inclined to answer in the negative drew on the skeptical spirit of Socrates's inquiries and the aporetic endings of the Socratic dialogues, which, in Plato's depiction, seemed to explore problems of philosophical significance without settling on any conclusive answers.[11] The portrait of a Plato who resisted systems in favor of the critical suspension of judgment was at the center of the interpretive tradition upheld by the central figures associated with the institutional afterlife of Plato's Academy, which adopted this position about three generations after Plato's death and continued to develop it into the first century BC.[12]

For this tradition of so-called Academic Skeptics, Plato's myths appear to have taken on a relatively marginal role for understanding his thought. While some of these early proponents of skepticism followed Socrates's example in writing down nothing of their own philosophies, and the texts of those others who did leave written work did not survive, they would have been largely suspicious of the supernatural motifs in the myths—which often drew from religious images suggestive of dogmatic worldviews—and they would have been especially averse to the myths' characteristic resistance to further inquiry.[13] To the extent that they studied Plato's dialogues, those passages that exhibited the tenacity of Socratic refutation would have received far more attention. The myths would have been considered, at best, as admissions of the impossibility of certain knowledge.

Against the skeptical Platonic tradition centered on the Socratic spirit of critical inquiry, however, a rather different interpretive approach would come to locate a unified philosophical system in Plato's thought by focusing on the metaphysics of the theory of Forms.[14] Being able to thus affirm and defend the coherence of Plato's philosophical system was a defining element of the tradition that would eventually come to be known under the heading of Neoplatonism.[15]

The Neoplatonic Tradition in Platonic Reception: Theological Metaphysics

This rich and varied tradition, which flourished in late antiquity from the third to seventh centuries AD, and which later experienced a dramatic revival in fifteenth-century Renaissance Italy, might be best characterized by reference to a shared metaphysical principle: that the universe was unified around a single highest Form, the goodness of which manifested in varying microcosmic degrees in the diversity of all the things and creatures in existence.

The most comprehensive and influential effort to assert the coherence of Plato's philosophy in such terms appeared in the writings of Plotinus, who crystallized an image of the world that derived its content, not just from a constellation of Forms referenced throughout Plato's corpus, but in particular from a supreme and singularly unifying idea, akin to the Form of the Good discussed in Book VI of the *Republic,* the idea of "the One" in the *Parmenides,* and the anthropomorphic figure of the Demiurge in the *Timaeus.*[16] Plotinus's gloss on Platonic metaphysics had the accidental effect of rendering it more easily compatible with religious trends in late antiquity, but also with monotheistic traditions in Christianity, Judaism, and Islam. This association would in turn prove to be critical to the survival of Plato in late antiquity and beyond.

Assimilating Platonic ideas to a landscape dominated by Christianity in particular did, of course, come with additional hurdles: Plato's Christian defenders first had to find ways of explaining the value of the thought of a pagan thinker who was born before the birth of Christ and who bore no relationship to biblical scripture; and even if it could be granted, along Plotinian lines, that Platonic metaphysics promoted devotion to a single, unifying ideal of goodness vaguely resembling the Christian conception of God, it was still more difficult to reckon with the priority that Plato placed on human reason, rather than on the aid of divine grace, as a sufficient means of accessing that ideal.

Hence, a second question that split the reception of Plato was whether his philosophy was indeed compatible with Christianity. Those who would answer in the negative would condemn the infiltration of Platonic influences in Christian theology as a pagan corruption of true religion.[17] In a well-known early Christian polemic against the authority of pagan philosophers, for instance, Plato is singled out as "a spice-dealer to season all heresies."[18]

But for the heirs and protectors of the intellectual tradition that paid homage to Plato and Plotinus, their essential compatibility with Christian doctrine could yet be defended using a combination of two lines of thought. They could insist that reason, for Plato, had allowed him to arrive at a set of true ideas about the divine during an epoch when the providential guide of Christian religion was yet unavailable; but that these ideas were those that Christians would already know through faith alone.[19] They could also insist that Plato's thought contained religious truths because he had in fact been divinely inspired, as a prophetic instrument of God's design for human history. For this latter account, the descriptions in the *Ion* and *Phaedrus* of divine poetic inspiration acquired special importance, as they seemed to confirm Plato's awareness of his own role as a vessel of a higher power, and, by extension, his writings as records of the esoteric wisdom to which he had been privy. It was in this context that an older designation for the philosopher as "the divine Plato" (ὁ θεῖος Πλάτων)—weaponized, ironically, in Proclus's attempts to assert the superiority of Platonic theology against the growing popularity of Christianity in late antiquity—became newly resonant.[20]

The negotiation of Platonic philosophy with Christianity had important interpretive consequences for how the relationship between Plato's logical arguments and his myths came to be conceived. In contrast to the place of primacy occupied in the skeptical Platonic tradition by the critical spirit of the arguments, later Neoplatonism ended up diminishing both the assumption that reasoning in this vein is the singular—if not sufficient—path toward wisdom, as well as Plato's own agency in writing up a philosophical corpus that lent itself to valuable knowledge. Conversely, in subscribing to the model of the divinely inspired philosopher, the Neoplatonic tradition came to elevate the epistemic status of Plato's myths as a medium that contained revelatory wisdom going beyond knowledge that might be reached through argumentation alone.[21]

Philosophical interest in Plato's myths, then, was overwhelmingly nurtured in the context of Neoplatonism. In contrast to an interpretive approach that emphasized the skepticism at the heart of the Socratic investigations depicted in Plato's dialogues, the path that led to the embrace of Plato's myths was one that chose the radical coherence of Plato's metaphysics over an ethical commitment to the suspension of judgment; the theological extension of that metaphysics over the rejection of dogma; and the model of an inspired philosopher, conversant in the language of divine mysteries, over that of a critical philosopher dealing in the precision and rigor of logical disputation. Approached from this framework, Plato's myths—to the extent that they were taken to be the by-products of the philosopher's encounters with eternal religious truths—were above the ordinary reach of human reason, but were also capable of being deciphered through reason. Rationalized this way, Plato's myths in the Neoplatonic tradition were famously allegorical, so that it was possible to draw exact connections between specific elements in the stories and the deeper religious meanings they represented.[22] As a result, when Plato's opponents in late antiquity—often hailing from rival philosophical schools—took it upon themselves to attack him, it was often on the grounds that his philosophy was incomprehensibly mystical. Colotes, a disciple of Epicurus, famously accused Plato of intellectual hypocrisy in penning the Myth of Er: the myth represented a betrayal of Plato's own principles for rejecting poetry and the Greek mythological tradition in Book II, and it in turn had the effect of turning his entire philosophical work into one such "myth about Hades" that bears no relevance to philosophy.[23]

Two important exceptions in the ancient reception of Plato's myths deserve mention. Whereas the Academic Skeptics were largely uninterested in the myths, and the Neoplatonists gave them special standing as objects of allegorical analysis, only Cicero (106–43 BC) and Plutarch (ca. 45–120 AD) were known to have written philosophical myths themselves after Plato's model.[24] Cicero, in particular, famously concluded his own *Republic* with an overt homage to the Myth of Er: a dream vision of the cosmos beyond mortal existence, illustrating the greater harmony of the universe and its implications for the nature of our earthly duties.[25] The Dream of Scipio, as the passage came to be known, was preserved in a fifth-century commentary by Macrobius, the Roman Neoplatonist, and for centuries it served as an authoritative text on cosmology, and otherwise exercised continuous and significant influence throughout medieval and Renaissance thought, even through long periods in which interest in Plato himself suffered.[26] Despite its distinctiveness and renown, however, the Dream of Scipio does not appear to have had a significant effect on how Plato's myths were received by subsequent generations of philosophers. If anything, Cicero's myth was itself subjected to the same Neoplatonic methods that would predominate the interpretation of Plato's myths into the time of More and Bacon.

Well before this time, however, a third point of contention had begun to gain increased salience in the reception of Plato's philosophy: the question of whether studying Plato's ideas necessarily demanded close engagement with his original texts. It had long been possible, both within and outside of the Neoplatonic framework, to place no particular importance to the texts of the dialogues, and to accept that the ideas they contained were valuable regardless of their form—whether because these ideas were eternal and divine, or, as later readers would suggest, because rationality itself was universal.[27] However, the Italian Renaissance bore witness, on the one hand, to the celebration of eloquence as a virtue in and of itself, and, on the other, to the first complete Latin translation of Plato's works, by Marsilio Ficino (1484).[28] Newly available means of direct access to Plato's prose, and thereby of appreciating its eloquence firsthand, made it not only feasible to devote sustained attention to the literary construction of the dialogues, but methodologically preferable to do so.

In particular, the flourishing of the Neoplatonic tradition in fifteenth-century Italy had the effect of bolstering the special status of Plato's myths and their literary qualities. Collecting together all of the extant dialogues of Plato did little to shift the balance of attention back to the dialogues in which the skeptical spirit of Socratic refutation was fully on display.[29] Instead, Platonic philosophy in the Italian Renaissance supplemented the monotheistic metaphysics derived from the more mystical instantiations of the theory of Forms in the later dialogues with a theory of Christian love, drawn from the accounts of love and beauty in the *Symposium* and *Phaedrus*. Crucially, emphasis on the emotive and aesthetic dimensions of the mania of love served as a counterweight to the rationalism found elsewhere in the Platonic corpus, and elevated the status of poetry as a necessary extension, not only of Plato's philosophy, but also of his politics.[30] In his commentary to the *Republic*, Ficino maintained that the banishment of the poets from the *Republic* is not a total banishment, but merely a partial one: the poets have no place in the city, where they are prone to inflaming the worst passions of the throngs inclined to misinterpret them, but they may remain in exile, outside of the city but still within the bounds of the state itself, so that virtuous philosophers may consult them and discern the true allegorical meaning of their inspired poetry.[31]

More and Bacon: Departures from the Neoplatonic Tradition

The Neoplatonic framework helped form, in different incarnations, the background against which More and Bacon were each reading Plato: More against the intellectual ripples, acutely felt in his own Erasmian circles, of the Renaissance revival of Plato and Plotinus in Italy; Bacon against the background of the popularization of Neoplatonic ideas in English literary culture, and in classical scholarship on the Continent.[32] But although they inherited an intellectual and cultural tradition in which Plato's myths were valued as allegories for revealed wisdom—at once above ordinary human reason and in need of decoding by elite philosophers—More and Bacon approached them somewhat differently. Each held scattered views on the central questions that had been formative in shaping the Neoplatonic approach to Plato's myths. But on the question of whether engaging with Plato's ideas necessarily demanded reading his texts directly, both were committed to answering in the affirmative. More's and Bacon's decisions to emulate the literary construction of the *Republic* attest to a shared appreciation for Plato as a stylist, and their evaluation of Plato's myths must accordingly be understood in this context.[33]

More was an early proponent of reading Plato in the original Greek; he taught himself the language and, alongside Erasmus and the friends they had in common, advocated strongly for Greek education in the university curriculum.[34] Bacon was more explicit in his rejection of the reigning conventions and biases mediating the interpretation of Plato's philosophy. On the one hand, he criticized "Plato and his school"—by which he meant the Neoplatonic tradition and its theologically inflected metaphysics—for their "dangerous and subtle" tendency to mix philosophy with "theology and traditions." Such an approach, he insisted, has produced "fanciful and tumid and half poetical" results, which he alternately called a "false" or "fantastic" philosophy.[35] On the other hand, he was equally critical of the opposite tradition, stemming from what he believed to be a misreading of Plato's skeptical statements, which were surely made "in jest and irony, and in disdain of the older sophists." He charged the skeptical tradition of having "made a dogma" of the disavowal of certain knowledge, and in so doing, "doomed men to perpetual darkness."[36] In advocating instead for a middle path that avoids the extremism of both these rival Platonic traditions, Bacon passed over much of the metaphysical and theological concerns that had grounded the traditional appreciation for Plato's myths.[37] Like More before him, Bacon would find himself largely unencumbered by those Neoplatonic commitments, yet still attentive to the literary features of Plato's writing, when he set out to rework the *Republic* on his own terms.

The founding myths written into *Utopia* and *New Atlantis*, as we shall see, presented a remarkable departure in the reception of Plato's myths—an achievement that had more in common, say, with Cicero's myth-writing than with any traditional institution of Platonism. More and Bacon shared the Neoplatonic premise, absent in the skeptical tradition, that Plato's myths were a significant part of his philosophy. But their versions of the myths would address, not esoteric mysteries, but the norms that underwrite emphatically this-worldly communities.

THE PLATONIC LEGACY OF THE UTOPIAN
FOUNDING MYTHS

The early editions of *Utopia* came encased in supplementary material framing the work as a revival of and improvement upon the *Republic*— one breathing new life into an old work most deserving of resuscitation, but which also brought to completion a project Plato had only just begun.[38] The comparison was even put in verse, attributed to Utopia's purported poet laureate, and included in the front matter of the first edition:

> "No-Place" was once my name, I lay so far;
> But now with Plato's state I can compare
> Perhaps outdo her (for what he only drew
> In empty words I made live anew . . .)[39]

More had not authored all of these notes himself—much of it had been the work of friends called upon to commend the book to its readers—but the self-conscious references to the *Republic* were clearly something of an inside joke he shared with the other philhellenists in his circles.[40] No other author is referenced as often in *Utopia* as Plato. So it was that the tradition of utopian writing that More launched was built on recognizably Platonic foundations, and constituted a renewal and reworking of the *Republic*.

New *Atlantis*, in turn, presents itself as an endeavor to both continue and surpass the legacies of More and Plato. As its title suggests, Bensalem, the utopian island nation at the center of the work, is framed as a novel and superior incarnation of the civilization depicted by Plato in his myths about Atlantis. *New Atlantis* accordingly integrates the history of Bensalem into a chronology laid out in the corresponding passages in Plato's *Timaeus* and *Critias*. *Utopia* makes an appearance in *New Atlantis* as a foreign book familiar to a priest distinguishing the local marriage customs from those in the "Feigned Commonwealth" described by "one of your men."[41]

If More and Bacon self-consciously framed their utopias as landmarks of a coherent genre with Platonic roots, they also invented myths for their imagined commonwealths. Much like the *Republic* itself, *Utopia* and *New Atlantis* each features a distinct set of myths interspersed throughout the text.

The comparison is complicated, of course, by the fact that *Utopia* and *New Atlantis* are unambiguously intended to be read as works of fiction, which make no overt claims to the kind of rational argumentation that had demarcated the myths of the *Republic* from the rest of the dialogue.[42] In utopian writing, the Platonic tension between argumentative and fictional modes of philosophical presentation ceases to be a meaningful distinction, because the genre's ostensible stake in the *Republic* has less to do with Plato's original point of departure—the more abstract question of what justice is—than with the project of envisaging a fictional polity in as much vivid detail as the author's imagination will allow.[43] As such, the myths that More and Bacon created for *Utopia* and *New Atlantis* cannot complement the rest of the exposition in the same distinct way as do the myths of the *Republic*—not when they are part of works that are *already* fanciful fictions. Certainly readers of *Utopia* and *New Atlantis* have described both works in their entirety as being akin to myths in and of themselves, referring to either text as a "fable," a "fairy tale," or, as in Howard White's characterization of *New Atlantis,* as "a rewriting of a Platonic myth."[44]

All the same, these fictions within fictions stand out as a distinct literary feature that endures across the reinvention of the *Republic* into the respective utopias of More and Bacon. They indicate that both authors had a particular interest in the genre of myth, and, above all, that they each felt that an account of an ideal commonwealth called for the incorporation of such stories. What is preserved, then, in their early modern reinterpretation of the *Republic* isn't necessarily the lesson that myth and logical argumentation might be juxtaposed in political philosophical writing to complementary ends. For their purposes, the more salient Platonic insight was the broad conviction that myth had the potential to be a uniquely constructive resource for political thought.

The Founding Myths of Utopia and Bensalem

At the center of the stories told about Utopia's origins is the conquest of the land by one King Utopus, who proceeds to give Utopia its name, its superior culture, and its island geography. References to Utopus occur three times in *Utopia*. The first occurs near the opening of Book II—almost immediately after Hythloday, More's fictional interlocutor, has commenced his descriptive account of Utopia—and recounts Utopus's successful invasion of the land and his subsequent transformation of it from a peninsula into its present island form.[45] Utopus makes a brief reappearance a few pages later, in a description of the design of Utopian houses, where it is revealed that he had drawn up the more foundational aspects of the standardized 1,760-year-old city plans, but had left room for flexibility on smaller matters like ornamentation and the heights of buildings.[46] The third and final mention of the monarch occurs toward the end of the book, in a discussion of Utopian religion: whereas the indigenous population had been deeply divided over religion prior to the conquest, Utopus puts an end to civil strife by setting laws that, within some loose constraints, promote religious freedom and toleration.[47] Additionally, in the contemporary reception of *Utopia,* Utopus appears to have been a popular point of reference for any reader looking for a stylized way of invoking the imaginary island, and references to the republic revived by King Utopus supplied easy synonyms for Utopia itself.[48]

The equivalent figure in *New Atlantis* is a lawgiver named King Solamona, the founder of Bensalem's most important institution, a center for scientific research that bears his name, and whose elusive members hold positions of unparalleled honor in Bensalemite society. The account of Solamona's achievements, however, is only the last in a larger sequence of elaborate stories presented to the shipwrecked European sailors when they first pose questions about the island to a local governor. The first of these stories recounts the miraculous event that prompted the conversion of Bensalem to Christianity, in which a volume containing the Old and New Testaments—universally comprehensible to the entire, multilingual population—floats to the coast of Bensalem beneath a great column of light.[49] Following a brief interruption, the governor returns to the sailors the next day and narrates two episodes from Bensalem's pre-Christian history: Bensalem's bloodless victory, led by one King Altabin, over the mythical Atlantis; and King Solamona's founding of Bensalem's laws and major institutions.[50] The latter event occurs about a millennium after Atlantis is eventually destroyed by a flood, and this span of time tracks the fragmentation of the world from a more connected past—made possible by a distant, golden age of navigational technology—and the retreat of Bensalem from the rest of the world and its shifting fortunes. Together, the governor's stories depict the origins of Bensalem's most defining features: its identity as a Christian nation, and its unique policy of isolationism, combined with an unequivocal commitment to the gathering and protection of knowledge.

There are, of course, important differences separating these two sets of founding narratives, and how they are presented in each work. The origin stories in *Utopia* center just on King Utopus and his founding acts, whereas *New Atlantis* features three such stories, spanning over a millennium, about three separate events from Bensalem's history. The accounts of Utopus barely add up to three paragraphs in the text of *Utopia,* whereas the governor's stories together take up about a third of the extant text of *New Atlantis.* And while the passages concerning Utopus are integrated into descriptions of particular features of Utopia, the governor's stories in *New Atlantis* are—by virtue of being told by a separate narrator—differentiated from the rest of the text.

These differences notwithstanding, both sets of stories are distinct literary elements in *Utopia* and *New Atlantis* that recognizably play into the tropes of a common genre. They are origin stories about significant features of their respective societies that endure into the present. The tone is celebratory, and imbued with the authority of tradition. The stories showcase larger-than-life, if not fantastical, events: the creation of a channel wide enough to transform a peninsula into an island, a grand military victory against a mythical civilization, divine miracles and giant universal floods. They also make reference to preestablished mythological traditions, either by reproducing narrative tropes common to Greek mythology, such as the figure of the lawgiver in the mold of Solon and Lycurgus, or by grafting their own histories onto an existing mythological timeline, like the sequence of events described in Plato's myths about Atlantis. They are, in essence, imitations of classical myths.

Perfect Beginnings and Political Preservation

More and Bacon would not have made these myths occupy such a central place in Utopian and Bensalemite politics had they not shared an intuitive appreciation of the traditional literary genre of myth and its power to shape culture. Certainly, they were echoing a political preoccupation that had been prominently voiced elsewhere—especially in canonical, or soon-to-be-canonical, works that sought to grapple with the political lessons of ancient Rome—for the importance of foundings and founding stories in determining the characters of peoples.[51]

But in particular, they were, like Plato, deploying the literary genre of myth to calibrate certain foundational aspects of the way its audiences might conceptualize the natural order of things in their world. In applying this lesson to the construction of *Utopia* and *New Atlantis*—works that were overtly fashioned after the *Republic*—they were also taking up and amplifying essential themes from the politics of the *kallipolis*. This confluence of Platonic echoes is most evident in how More's and Bacon's invented myths target two particular conceptual frameworks: ways of imagining the end of politics, and the nature of time.

Politics as Preservation

More and Bacon evidently saw myth as a medium capable of helping stabilize politics around a particular status quo. Most conspicuously, they sought to harness this resource by using their myths to construct a thick conception of politics as an essentially preservationist enterprise. As myths of founding, the stories about Utopia's and Bensalem's defining institutions assert a sociopolitical ideal fully realized from the very beginning, designed to remain in its original form for perpetuity. The most central features of Utopia and Bensalem purportedly owe their origins to the events described in these myths; by anchoring present political arrangements in such concrete beginnings, More and Bacon can present them as less arbitrary than those institutions born from unknown or contingent circumstances. At the same time, the founding myths endow the existing political orders in Utopia and Bensalem with exceptional—and in some cases, providential—origins, and present them as structures that have since withstood the test of time. Consequently, the myths end up projecting the message that the institutions they depict are worthy of maintenance. Very little, in fact, has changed in either country since the introduction of the reforms described in their respective myths; we are told, for instance, that all cities in Utopia are more or less identical reproductions of a template first laid down by Utopus.[52] The founding myths, then, are the driving force behind the preservationist ethic that dominates Utopian and Bensalemite politics.

The project should be familiar to students of Plato, not only because its conservationism is a vision espoused and upheld in myths, but because it lends renewed expression to a set of Platonic assumptions about what ideals look like when they are projected onto the sphere of politics. Most importantly, More and Bacon reproduce Plato's presupposition that there exists not only a good but a uniquely correct way of founding a society—so that fidelity to those inaugural conditions is what constitutes political virtue in Utopia and Bensalem. This image of politics echoes, in particular, the perfectionism implicit in an understanding of the *kallipolis* as the best political regime, uniquely superior to all other possibilities. It also reaffirms the *Republic*'s celebration of self-sufficiency as a moral virtue, manifested in the economically self-sufficient city and, most prominently, in the figure of the philosopher who cares for his own soul in a world otherwise vulnerable to corruption.[53]

The conscription of a familiar motif helps reinforce these themes in the utopian founding myths. We recall that, in the central myths of the *Republic,* Plato had employed a recurring image—delivery out of the earth, itself a standard trope in the Greek mythological tradition—whenever he sought to make a revision to the standing conceptualization of individual nature. The image of the earth also carries special meaning in More's and Bacon's founding myths; the accomplishments of Utopus and Solamona are famously stories about the conquest of the natural environment through the conquest of geography. Just as Utopus's first founding act is the digging of a channel that cuts off Utopia from the mainland, the equivalent passage in *New Atlantis* depicts Solamona scanning his island's size, quality of soil, waters, and ports to gauge its agricultural and industrial potential, and, ultimately, its capacity to support itself without further contact with the rest of the world.[54] These are both mythical feats of isolation, which protect the respective lands from potential contamination by external forces that may cause them to deviate from the perfection of their original form. As he contemplates the landscape of his island, Solamona sees that it "might be a thousand ways altered to the worse, but scarce any one way to the better," and this conclusion leads him to lay down a final set of quarantine laws, that they may "give perpetuity to that which was in his time so happily established."[55] In these passages, the earth stands in for a natural prior that only gains validity once it is modified or authorized in alignment with the ideals of perfectionism and self-sufficiency championed by the corresponding founders. We might say that these episodes in the respective founding myths portray moments in which the authority of nature is written over, and endowed with new values.

Time and Degeneration

To the extent that More and Bacon were using the founding myths to shape a deep, default understanding of politics as a practice aimed at preserving a given status quo, part of this effort also entailed reframing a related understanding of the nature of time, as a degenerative force that was essentially antagonistic to the longevity of human creations. The perpetually self-sustaining founding acts celebrated in the myths are presented as extraordinary political achievements precisely because they defy a tacit expectation that institutions, once inaugurated, typically do not preserve their original form for so long. Instead, the picture of time suggested in the myths is essentially cyclical or in flux, so that the feats of their founding figures constitute a triumph against the degenerative effects of the passage of time.[56]

This, too, is a theme of the *Republic,* but with an added twist. Commentators of utopias have often suggested that the Hesiodic core of the Myth of Metals translates easily to a Christian point of departure, whereby humans reside in a fallen world, and the project of early modern utopias had been the restoration of politics to an Edenic state of nature somehow truer than the fallen state in which we find ourselves.[57] Playing on Hesiod's account of the ages of man, Plato charts the eventual decline of the *kallipolis* under the rule of a progressively unimpressive lineage of leaders, each containing less gold and silver in their souls than did the generation that came before.[58] More and Bacon, by contrast, take such trajectories of decline to be the natural course of all civilizations, but they stop short of sharing Plato's view that even the best constitution will eventually cave to the force of its current. The static character of Utopian and Bensalemite politics, then, presents an alternative ending: it suggests that a better constitution than that of Plato's vision is yet possible, one that can stand as a corrective to the default condition of nature.

In *New Atlantis,* in particular, Bensalem's perseverance against the current of time is overtly framed as the amending of a Platonic account. This is dramatized prominently in Bacon's reworked version of Plato's myths of Atlantis, which deserves more sustained treatment. Plato's original myths, spread between the *Timaeus* and the *Critias,* are said to have been passed down from Solon, the legendary lawgiver of Athens, who in turn learned of Atlantis from an Egyptian priest he met on his travels.[59] Notably, Plato introduces the Atlantis myth in the *Timaeus* during a discussion of traditional Greek myths; at stake in the passage is the premise that the myths of a civilization represent the oldest form of historical knowledge available to its people, and are therefore a marker of its age.[60]

The connection that Plato drew between myth and historical longevity is perhaps what made the Atlantis myth especially attractive to Bacon, who develops the theme in his own variation on the myth. When the governor of the House of Strangers tells the story of Bensalem's ancient victory over Atlantis, he presents it as a more accurate account of the "poetical and fabulous" record familiar to the European sailors through the writings of "a great man with you."[61] He begins by dismissing many of the descriptive details about Atlantis laid out in the *Critias,* but sticks closely to the sequence of events narrated in the corresponding myth in the *Timaeus:* in an ancient time predating the memory and records of the Greeks, the world's oceans had been more navigable; Atlantis, one of the great civilizations that flourished in that time, made an attempt to conquer and enslave the rest of the known world, but was eventually put down; and sometime afterward Atlantis was destroyed by a natural disaster. In staying faithful to Plato's outline, Bacon's updated version of the Atlantis myth preserves the overarching message of the original as it is presented in the *Timaeus*—that the trajectories of human civilizations are, by default, governed by cycles of destruction and recovery, so that nations as great as Atlantis at its peak might be destroyed overnight, their cultural achievements lost, and human knowledge left to start over.

There are two places in this history where Bacon has the Bensalemite governor explicitly correct Plato's account. First, he insists that it had not been the ancestors of the Athenians, but instead the forces led by the Bensalemite King Altabin, who stopped the invasion of Atlantis; and second, that the cause of Atlantis's final demise was not an earthquake, but a great flood.[62] In making the latter alteration, Bacon seems to have been motivated by a desire to transpose the more varied cycle of natural disasters in Plato's myth—which goes through floods, earthquakes, and the destruction of the world by fire—onto a streamlined cycle of recurring floods that begins with the biblical flood.[63]

The combined effect of these changes is that the myth told by the Bensalemite governor asserts the singular superiority of Bensalem on a value scale original to Plato's myth, updated with a Christian timeline so as to elevate Bensalem's exceptionalism onto a providential register.[64] The greatness of Bensalem, Bacon's revised myth tells us, had always surpassed that of any other civilization mentioned in Plato's account, and its continued preservation, in turn, is a providential exemption from the natural course of time.[65] It is in this sense, according to the myth, that Bensalem might be considered a new and superior Atlantis: one that saves itself from the fate of the first Atlantis, if not the fate of all other civilizations.[66]

Knowledge, Myth, and Intellectual Aristocracy

There are obvious and intuitive reasons as to why both More and Bacon might have framed the distinguishing virtue of Utopia and Bensalem in terms of their longevity.[67] Through their own involvement in the tumultuous politics of their times, both authors were intimately acquainted with the value and scarcity of lasting political stability. But as Bacon's retelling of the Atlantis myth suggests, one particularly compelling reason for measuring a nation's greatness by its longevity was that the survival of civilizations went hand in hand with the preservation of their repositories of knowledge. A "young people," according to his myth, needs centuries, if not millennia, to rebuild its culture in the wake of the most recent flood to have struck its region, a process that is slowed even further in the absence of the means to leave posterity with "letters, arts and civility."[68] By contrast, the continued survival of Bensalem's own technologies, even through ages in which "navigation did every where decay," equips its envoys to go out in ships to collect knowledge from all the corners of the world, and to sustain dominance over a one-sided "trade, not for gold, silver, or jewels; nor for silks; nor for spices . . . but only for God's first creature, which was *Light*."[69] Similarly, Hythloday draws a clear connection between the long history of Utopia, its superior form of government, and the Utopians' superlative "diligence and zeal to learn," especially from the ideas and inventions of now-bygone empires.[70]

The priority of the status of knowledge in these accounts suggests a certain picture of the relationship between politics and intellectual activity in Utopia and Bensalem, and in turn, between myth and philosophy, broadly construed. More's and Bacon's founding myths uphold an ideal vision of political stasis, which stands in a complementary relationship to a progressive epistemic ideal that champions the advancement of knowledge. Politics, if it is established the right way, does not really ever get better in the worlds of Utopia and Bensalem, but knowledge does. Moreover, the extreme political stability that the founding myths promote is, for More and Bacon, precisely what allows knowledge to build on itself without interruption by external forces.

The thought that political stability might help prop up a protected sphere for the flourishing of knowledge is reflected in the institutional structures of Utopia and Bensalem, which make special provisions for a separate class of elites to devote their time to scholarship. The resulting intellectual aristocracy is perhaps one of the most readily identifiable legacies of the *kallipolis* in Utopian and Bensalemite politics. The respective members of the intellectual classes are, like in the *kallipolis*, selected on the principle that scholarship ought to be pursued by those most suited for the task. They are exempt from other forms of labor, so that they may be employed full-time in intellectual pursuits.[71] In *Utopia*, this arrangement serves as a *kallipolean* rejoinder to a question raised in Book I—in the context of which Plato's name is invoked—of whether philosophers ought to be insulated from politics: all but one of the named public offices in Utopia are filled by individuals elected from the ranks of the scholars.[72] And even though the corresponding class of scholars in Bensalem do not govern, their status and influence in Bensalemite society conspicuously surpass those of its political officers.[73] Bensalem's scholars exercise their own discretion in what information they choose to disclose to the state: the reasons behind their local visits and requests are shrouded in secrecy, and aspects of their research are withheld from the public.[74] Salomon's House, their flagship research institution, is universally understood to be the "eye" and "lanthorn" of the land, if not "the noblest foundation . . . that ever was upon this earth."[75]

Given the centrality of the founding myths to the political culture sustaining these particular institutional arrangements, the function assigned to myth in Utopia and Bensalem might be described as one in which it bears an instrumental relationship to philosophy, here broadly construed as the pursuit of knowledge. The resources of myth, on this view, provide an effective means of stabilizing those political conditions that permit individuals to engage in theoretical activity with special focus. In particular, this approach to myth recalls the professed function of the Myth of Metals from Plato's *Republic,* which recruits the traditional powers associated with the genre of myth in the service of establishing a separate class of intellectuals among the citizenry. Sure enough, Bacon concludes the sequence of myths told by the Bensalemite governor with an account of the creation of Salomon's House.[76]

This is admittedly a conservative, if not a cynical or troubling, way of designating myth's relationship to philosophy. To use myth as a tool for conserving the political conditions of an intellectual aristocracy is to court an array of charges that Karl Popper, writing about the Myth of Metals, had once characterized as a betrayal of the values of philosophy itself. It might be unjust, for example, to exempt the class of intellectual elites from the everyday hardships, demanded of the rest of the citizenry, involved in meeting the basic material needs of the commonwealth. Moreover, there might be something fundamentally deceptive about telling fictitious stories that discourage even these elite scholars from seeking the truth about the origins of their institutions. When myths are deployed to "arrest political change," the character of intellectual inquiry in that community also suffers, resulting in what Popper calls a closed, rather than open, society.[77]

Such concerns may be impossible to shake from More's and Bacon's use of myth in Utopia and Bensalem. As long as the founding myths lie at the crux of the conservationist culture that is so essential to the identities of both commonwealths, which in turn grants special protections to an autonomous sphere set aside for the pursuit of knowledge, More and Bacon can appear to wield myth's powers as a form of social oppression—a convenient shortcut around the need to provide rational justifications of the status quo, or to make room for revisions to it. But this line of interpretation, though warranted in one sense, does not fully capture the deep connection that both authors drew between political stability and the very possibility of cultivating knowledge that lasts, or the suspicion that myth might have something distinctive to offer toward the creation and maintenance of this extraordinary condition. Nor, at the very least, is the most conservative rendering of myth's function in their commonwealths the most subtle or insightful lesson for More and Bacon to have drawn from their engagement with Plato's myths.

In the *Republic,* Plato had shown the literary of genre of myth to be an especially effective tool for molding concepts that are deeply foundational to one's worldviews; but he had availed himself of the resource while also conveying something of philosophy's dependence on these thick frameworks, and of their capacity for revisiting and reworking by subsequent myths. The founding myths of Utopia and Bensalem preserve the nuance of Plato's vision in at least two ways.

First, they are as much an instrument for upholding intellectual aristocracies as they are a claim about the nature and value of scholarship. Intellectual pursuits, as they are represented in Utopia and Bensalem, are set apart as a class of activities with needs and aims that are different from those of other forms of labor in the commonwealth, such that they require their own space and devoted practitioners if they are to be engaged in properly. Giving primacy to this kind of activity, as both commonwealths do, is an enterprise that comes at no insignificant cost for the state, especially when whatever benefits it might confer on the commonwealth or on the formation of its leaders are less tangible and more difficult to isolate, and require longer stretches of time to take effect. It is in turn expedient to have the services of myth at the disposal of this enterprise, because myths that work to normalize the way things are as they stand also end up protecting existing institutions from perennially coming up for renewed justification. Instead the founding myths of Utopia and Bensalem help their respective societies take it for granted that the provisions they make for the autonomy of scholarship are part of a default that is worth preserving. If More and Bacon deemed that the proper practice of this occupation required the aid of myths and their normalizing power, one way of understanding their verdict is that they were also making a broader, practical statement acknowledging the particularity of theoretical activity, the difficulty of translating the value we place on it into instrumental justifications, and its reliance on the external crutches of politics and culture in order to thrive.

Second, while the founding myths lay the groundwork for the preservationist politics of Utopia and Bensalem, they are not themselves monolithic stories. Their open-ended and playful character is easier to appreciate in the context of the more general ambiguity surrounding the presentation of *Utopia* and *New Atlantis*, which perennially leaves readers returning to the question of how earnest More and Bacon were in depicting their ideal commonwealths in the ways that they did. Keeping with the exploratory tone of the larger texts—less wholesale endorsements of the institutions they describe, and more invitations for readers to commit fully to the imaginative exercise without losing their critical distance—the founding myths embrace and advertise the dynamic possibilities of their genre.

For a start, both sets of founding myths are stories of refoundings that depict the introduction of reforms to an existing political community and its circumstances. Utopus integrates his soldiers with an indigenous population, modifies a land that was almost an island already, and establishes laws and institutions that are framed as improvements on what was there before.[78] For all their dramatically lasting repercussions, the events at the center of Bensalem's myths similarly uphold the continuous history of the island nation without causing political rupture. The emphasis on reform, rather than total invention, gives a softer edge to the myths. They advocate the preservation of the status quo because further reform upon it is unnecessary, which is not quite the same thing as being opposed to reform in and of itself. At the very least, their subject matter suggests that More and Bacon held a more dynamic view of myth, as an instrument of radical social change as well as of social preservation, and were keen to remind their readers of both of these functions.

Furthermore, the myths openly draw attention to their constructed status. We see this most clearly in the names that Bacon and More chose for the figures who feature in their myths. Commentaries abound on the names of people, offices, and places invented for *Utopia* and *New Atlantis,* which are famously riddled with wordplay and irony.[79] In the founding myths, however, the protagonists' names have the particular effect of inverting the etymological claims made in association with them. Utopia's founding myth claims that King Utopus gave the island its name, but More's readers—aware of the meaning behind Utopia's Greek name, a pun on οὐ-τόπος ("no-place") and εὐ-τόπος ("good-place")—would know that the name of the commonwealth is in fact prior: More clearly named Utopus after the island, rather than the other way around. A similar kind of reversal is at work in the names of Bensalem's kings. The governor offers two competing etymologies of Salomon's House: some Bensalemites believe it was originally named after its founder (with some of the vowels getting corrupted over time), while he himself thinks that Solamona named it after the biblical King Solomon.[80] The self-referential answer reserved for Bacon's readers, however, is that both Solamona and the house he founded would have been named after the biblical figure. The elaborate suggestion of linguistic corruption in the etymology of Salomon's House, at the same time, may throw new light on the naming of King Altabin. Altabin's name is supposedly intended to evoke the Latin, *bini-alta,* for "twice-lofty," but it also shares its first letters with those of Atlantis itself—as though derived from the same phonetic root, then modified in a similar instance of corruption.[81] By using the names of their characters to nod self-consciously to the process by which the myths had been retrofitted for the utopias they serve, More and Bacon signaled to their readers that they were working with a playful and reflexive genre, even and especially when they were using it toward seemingly orthodox ends.

Thus the conservative character of the Utopian founding myths is simultaneously coated in a layer of open-endedness, self-awareness, and play. If this makes the message of the myths more indeterminate than readers might tend to appreciate, it is an ambiguity that More and Bacon, following Plato, seemed to believe the traditional medium of myth was particularly well suited to accommodate. Myth, on this expansive view, was a genre that could wield its authority to ossify the foundational concepts of a commonwealth's political culture, but its versatile features also allowed room for it to be presented on a note of self-conscious qualification.

It is not clear if the use that More and Bacon made of the genre in the founding myths is the instantiation of a more fully worked-out theory of myth on the part of either author, or if it is just one window into the possibilities of myth preserved in their reimagining of Plato's *Republic*. For More—who penned no small number of fables and "merry tales," eagerly participated in humanist debates on the forms of communication that best serve a community, but otherwise did not leave evidence of having reflected explicitly on the subject of myth—the answer may very well end with the latter interpretation.[82] In Bacon's case, however, the nuanced presentation of the myths of *New Atlantis* also appears to be of a piece with the author's overt investment in the analysis of classical mythology. In particular, the relationship between knowledge and the unique features of myth was a subject of endless fascination for Bacon, and a topic to which he devoted extended, focused study.

"THE CROWNE" OF MYTHOGRAPHERS

A small collection of essays written in late middle age, about a decade and a half before the publication of *New Atlantis,* launched Bacon's reputation among his contemporaries as "the crowne" of mythographers.[83] *Of the Wisdom of the Ancients* (1609), dedicated to Bacon's "nursing-mother the famous University of Cambridge," was a commentary on thirty-one classical myths.[84] The collection presented each myth as an allegorical story about more general truths in the ways of the world: for instance, the myth of the ill-fated flight of Icarus, who fails to heed his father's warning to fly neither too close to the sun nor too close to the sea, was a parable about the virtues of moderation and the dangers of excess in any pursuit. Allegorical analyses of myths in this vein were hardly a novelty at the time.[85] Bacon's collection had a direct antecedent in Natale Conti's celebrated *Mythologiae* (1567), which was a standard source in the Renaissance for the interpretation of Greco-Roman mythology.[86] Nonetheless, Bacon's book was a best seller, even more so than *New Atlantis,* and Bacon took pride in the commercial success it enjoyed across Europe.[87]

Of the Wisdom of the Ancients marked the high point of a prolonged period, lasting nearly two decades, in which Bacon showed conspicuous interest in the study of myths.[88] But if the work secured the coronation of Bacon as an authority on and defender of the hidden wisdom contained in classical mythology, this crown also seems to fit ill against his reputation as the father of the modern scientific method. In the first pages of the *Dialectic of Enlightenment,* for instance, Horkheimer and Adorno prominently hold up Bacon—and his devotion to the ideal of the rational conquest of nature—as the prototypical embodiment of the Enlightenment struggle to escape myth.[89] In this vein, scholars of myth have pointed to Bacon's theory of idols as an early articulation of the modern criticism of myth, as a force that is opposed to intellectual progress: just as Bacon believed the path to scientific knowledge demands that we first clear our minds of the distorting effects of the idols that influence our perception of reality, so must modern thought work to break down and overcome the biases of the deeper mythic frameworks embedded in our worldviews.[90]

Bacon's reverence toward the wisdom of classical myths goes to highlight the extent to which his views on myth resist reduction into more modern categories. As far as the literary genre of myth was concerned, Bacon took a nuanced stance on its ultimate usefulness for the progress of scientific knowledge. On the one hand, he insisted on drawing a distinction between the wisdom at the core of ancient myths and the fabulous expressions in which that wisdom is encased; only the former was worthy of being distilled and preserved by the modern scholar. On the other hand, he did not believe the connection between the valuable content of myths and their form to be entirely arbitrary. Rather, he recognized that mythical expressions can offer communicative resources that are unique to the form. One way of understanding Bacon's general fascination with myth, as well as his particular interest in reworking the genre of Platonic myth, is to see that they were part of an even broader program of literary experimentation. By studying and experimenting with myths, Bacon sought to appropriate their resources toward the development of a richer, more progressive language for scientific inquiry than those available in his time.

The Two-Part Model of Myth

In *Of the Wisdom of the Ancients* and in his other remarks on myth, Bacon advances a model of myth made up of two constituent parts: a core, consisting in a kernel of natural wisdom; and an encasing of corrupted, fabulous expressions that stands as a barrier between a myth's true, ancient meaning and its modern interpreters. Bacon believed that there once existed an ancient time, predating Greek antiquity and written records, when humanity still retained memories of Edenic knowledge, or the natural knowledge that Adam possessed when he had mastery over all nature in the Garden of Eden.[91] The wisdom of this ancient age, otherwise buried in "oblivion and silence," was in turn preserved in the myths of classical Greece—and what written records modern audiences had of these myths were, besides scripture itself, the only remnants available to them of that original state of knowledge from which humanity had fallen away.[92] These slivers of prelapsarian knowledge were exposed to new elements of corruption with each successive phase in the chain of preservation through which they got passed down, all the way to modern times.[93] However, in that golden epoch preceding classical antiquity, a somewhat less corrupted ancient wisdom was encoded in fabulous stories, which their credulous Greek inheritors ended up believing literally and celebrating in their religion.

So it was that, in Bacon's account, "sacred relics and lights airs breathing out of better times" came to be "caught . . . and so received into the flutes and trumpets of the Greeks," forming their mythology.[94] The task of the modern scholar was to devote serious attention to myths, which may seem frivolous on the surface, but which in fact contained lost wisdom in need of recovery. But such study was also to entail extracting what is valuable knowledge from the fabulous expressions encrusted around it. Myth, then, called for a method of interpretation like the kind of allegorical analysis Bacon undertakes in *Of the Wisdom of the Ancients,* whereby the fantastical narrative elements in myths are stripped away to reveal essential lessons about the natural workings and moral order of the universe.

Here, Bacon's method may recall the approach stemming from the Neoplatonic premise that Plato's myths were objects of divine revelation—and the Neoplatonic tradition was indeed a major source of influence for the mythographical conventions that Bacon adopted when he looked for allegorical meaning in classical myths. Just as Bacon sought to apply rational tools to the expressions of myth to unveil their true, hidden meaning, Neoplatonic interpreters of Plato's myths had presumed that they contained divine truths that could only be accessed if they were taken apart in this allegorical vein. A key difference, however, was that for Bacon, the valuable wisdom contained in myths was not dependent on the providence of revelation, which ordinarily fell beyond the scope of human reason. Instead, his theory of myth seems to suggest that the resources of modern reason were in and of themselves sufficient for recovering a body of natural knowledge that had been lost or corrupted over the course of human history.

On this view, mythical expression itself is less the language in which a divinity chose to reveal itself to its chosen vessel, and more an incidental inconvenience for the modern scholar, who is forced to sort through the seeming nonsense in order to retrieve the kernel of true knowledge hidden in its midst. If it were possible to articulate these mythic lessons in a more straightforward and transparent fashion instead, this might seem to be Bacon's preference: translating ancient wisdom into a mode of presentation more readily accessible to reason would then be the corrective that modern scholarship could offer to the imperfection of the mythic form. Bacon alternately describes the myths of antiquity as "a veil . . . of fables" standing between perished wisdom and the reach of extant knowledge, and as "grapes ill-trodden," where "something is squeezed out, but the best parts are left behind and passed over"—as though the task of the modern student of myth were a matter of lifting a veil, or reassessing the grapes of wisdom with fresh eyes and picking one's way through the valuable residue.[95] It would seem, in turn, that many of the characteristic literary features of myths would have to be discarded before their valuable content can be integrated into a modern and progressive body of scientific knowledge. Notably in *New Atlantis*, Salomon's House has a strict prohibition against rhetorical adornment, exaggeration, or "affectation of strangeness" in the description of nature and its workings, which are to be presented by the Fellows "only pure as is."[96]

The Relationship between Myth's Content and Its Form

Bacon's remarks on myth may appear to suggest, then, that the wisdom hidden in myths did not necessarily have to take the form in which they were passed down, and that their core of significance can and ought to be reconstructed in an altogether different mode of expression. Yet Bacon was adamant that the link between mythic content and mythic expression was anything but arbitrary for the ancient creators of myth. At one level, this was merely because he believed that the cognitive capacities of the ancient mind were limited to such expressions.[97] But at another level, Bacon also believed that the expressions of myth were uniquely useful in their own right for their ancient authors, and that their original function could prove instructive even to the modern scientist.

In *Of the Wisdom of the Ancients,* Bacon isolates two "strange" and "contradictory" uses of myth as a device for communication: the first was to "disguise and veil the meaning," and the second was "also to clear and throw light upon it."[98] The clarifying function of myth is largely pedagogical, and Bacon takes it as given that myths can help present complicated ideas in ways that are both simpler and more accessible—much like the way, as he notes with admiration in *The Advancement of Learning* (1605), King Solomon made a practice of teaching through "excellent Parables and Aphorisms."[99] Mythical expressions can, in particular, help clarify meaning, because they allow for inventions and abstract ideas to be cast in "vulgar" images, so that they might "find an easier passage to the understanding."[100] Bacon's point here is not to be confused with the famous Lucretian apology for poetry, as a kind of "honeyed cup" that helps disguise the bitter medicine of philosophy as it is presented to his readers.[101] What Bacon finds special in the form of myth is not so much the ornamental veneer it could lend to otherwise less palatable content, but instead its capacity to introduce new or unfamiliar concepts in terms of the familiar.

Bacon had good reason to be interested in this particular feature of myth, because it potentially held the key to a recurring concern in his thought over the reception of scientific knowledge in society. In much the same way that he fixated on the problem of ensuring the achievements of civilization are not lost to the degenerative effects of time, Bacon feared that the individual scientist, with his scattered discoveries and inventions, could not leave lasting legacies in a society ill-prepared to receive and preserve them. In a confessional preface to *The Great Instauration* (1620), Bacon expresses anxiety regarding "what is now done in the matter of science," which he characterizes with "only a whirling round about, and perpetual agitation, ending where it began." His own work, by contrast, having been built on the correct foundations, has the potential to rise above this lamentable condition, inaugurating an enduring and coherent renewal of the arts and sciences. But the threat of failure is a considerable possibility, and the "solitary" enterprise of his scientific efforts could very well end up meeting the fate of the others, especially given "how hard a thing" his work is "to win faith and credit for."[102] Against the background of these misgivings, it is easy to see the wider appeal that myth and its special pedagogical potential held for Bacon. If classical myths had offered their ancient authors a repository of images that eased the transmission and integration of novel ideas into a familiar cultural landscape, there were valuable lessons to be gained from their study—not only for fostering the understanding of scientific discoveries by a modern audience, but also for promoting their preservation by society at large, so that future generations may continue work on them.

It is far less clear what Bacon means when he also credits myth with the capacity—at least as notable, if not useful, as its potential to clarify ideas—to veil and to disguise meaning. One likely possibility is that he felt an element of mystery was necessary in the presentation of certain ideas. In *Of the Wisdom of the Ancients*, he voices his suspicion that the obscurity of myths was, for the most part, "designed and meditated from the first" by their ancient authors, and "purposely shadowed out."[103] This, he observes, is a feature that myths may have in common with religion, which also "delights in such veils and shadows." In the case of religion, the use of parables and ambiguous metaphors to cloak meaning is a form of "honour" aimed at "communion between divinity and humanity."[104] It has the effect of lending a sense of gravity to religious truths that ought not to be approached lightly. When such truths are cast in terms of the extraordinary and marvelous, they can inspire humility in an audience tasked to work harder to comprehend their sacred subject matter. The same goes, Bacon suggests, for the ancient wisdom contained in myths: their creators may have deliberately made them opaque, in a fashion appropriate to the level of reverence that their subject matter ought to demand of their audience.

The need for humility before that which is not yet understood was an important concern for Bacon's scientific project, and a useful lesson for the modern scholar to try to adapt from the study of ancient myths. To be sure, Bacon was unequivocal in his position that mythical language had no place in natural inquiry.[105] However, he was also uncommonly apprehensive over the limitations of logical argumentation as a discursive medium. Throughout his famous critique of the cognitive "idols" that hamper the progress of human understanding, Bacon takes pains to emphasize that the language of logic is inadequate to the task of freeing the mind from the influence of its idols. So long as such idols—or the various implicit distortions that the human mind imposes on its view of the world—continue to govern our thinking, the work of present scientific methods, no matter how rigorous, would amount at best to "some magnificent structure without any foundation."[106] In particular, when attached to such false starts, logical arguments have the adverse effect of further reinforcing their distortions, and making them all the more difficult to overcome: "that art of logic," when it comes "too late to the rescue, and no way able to set matters right again, has had the effect of fixing errors rather than disclosing truth."[107] On these grounds Bacon calls the "vicious demonstrations" of logic "the strongholds and defenses of Idols," so that their combined effect does "little else than make the world the bond-slave of human thought, and human thought the bond-slave of words."[108]

The proper language of natural inquiry, for Bacon, is one that avoids such risks—a language whose veneer of authority and methodological rigor does not inadvertently cover up its own limitations. Instead, Bacon envisions a scientific mode of presentation that accomplishes several related effects: it ought to be clear, not only with regard to the content it seeks to convey, but also with regard to the epistemic status of that article of knowledge. It ought to be able to signal where that knowledge is incomplete and ripe for further investigation by prosperity; it ought to inspire its audience to examine its claims critically and against evidence, rather than to accept them passively.[109] Bacon does not seem to believe that the resources of any one existing genre or form of expression are adequate to his vision, and this stance is reflected in the stylistic range of his own work. He deliberately constructs *The New Organon* (1620), for instance, not "in the Form of a regular Treatise," but as a collection of aphorisms, whose fragmentary form might leave "room for suspicion that there are many more behind," and encourage readers "to contribute and add something in their turn."[110]

Accompanying Bacon's devotion to scientific experiments, it seems, was a corresponding commitment to literary experimentation. Bacon's studies of myth, as well as his engagement in *New Atlantis* with the model of Plato's myths, have to be understood from within this experimental framework. The expressive form particular to myth—though flawed and inappropriate to modern scientific inquiry—was neither arbitrary nor insignificant, and Bacon felt that its model may offer resources that more conventional modes of presenting knowledge do not. As the founding myths in *New Atlantis* demonstrate, he saw that there was great potential in the genre for reinvention and appropriation toward new ends, and that this insight, in turn, deserved a modern audience.

The founding myths of *Utopia* and *New Atlantis,* then, are at once a conservative and a progressive extension of the possible functions of myth that were brought to light under Plato's use. As More and Bacon took the model of the *Republic* and transposed it into the novel literary genre of utopian writing, they also imported recognizable aspects of the Platonic myth into Utopia and Bensalem—in particular, by channeling the traditional authority of myth into a stabilizing force, in the service of a political vision that reserves a protected space in society for the pursuit of knowledge.

At the same time, the literary construction of the founding myths betrays that they are more dynamic and self-reflexive than might be suggested by their preservationist function. For More and Bacon, the genre of myth is also a site of play, double meanings, self-awareness, refoundings, and reinvention. In turn, the capacious range of myth's possibilities and the richness of its resources help inform Bacon's interest in mythography. Myth is worth studying, for Bacon, because there may be ancient wisdom hidden in it, but also because it is important to experiment with such forms in our literary expressions. Only by applying ourselves diligently to this more ambitious project might we hope to transcend the limitations of existing modes for presenting knowledge.

3

AN ENLIGHTENMENT FABLE

Leibniz and the Boundaries of Reason

MYTH AS A NECESSARY SOLUTION TO THE
DISCONTENTS OF RATIONALISM

CHAPTER 2 HAS SHOWN HOW, when More and Bacon looked to the example of Plato's *Republic* as a model for the genre of utopian litera-ture they developed, they were also confronted with the decision to im-port elements of Plato's myths into their work. The central role played by the founding myths of Utopia and Bensalem suggests that More and Bacon took from Plato's examples an appreciation for the political value of myth—one that distinguished itself, in particular, from the revelation-oriented appreciation for Plato's myths in the Neoplatonic tradition, which had placed the significance of myth in a realm beyond politics and human agency. But what More passed over, and what Bacon was only beginning to intuit, were the philosophical, rather than political, implications of their cautious embrace of myth and its contributions.

In Voltaire's *Zadig* (1747), the eponymous protagonist encounters an angel reading from the "book of destinies," a book that lends its reader privileged knowledge of the future, however improbable its prophesies might seem in the present. Although Zadig himself cannot decipher the strange language in which the book is written, the angel will appeal to its authority in order to justify his increasingly outrageous actions, including the drowning of a child who is otherwise destined to grow up to be a murderer.[1] Voltaire had not yet invented Dr. Pangloss, but nonetheless the unmistakable target of the parody in *Zadig* was Leibnizian theodicy—the insistence on the intelligibility of a universe whose trajectory is ultimately opaque to human cognition. But more specifically, Voltaire's angel and his book of destinies were taking aim at the Petite Fable concluding Leibniz's *Theodicy* (1710).[2]

The Petite Fable is a myth that supplies the most vivid and fanciful illustration of Leibniz's famous doctrine that God had chosen to create only "the best of all possible worlds." Stylistically distinguished from the imposingly dense essays comprising the *Theodicy,* the myth shares obvious similarities with the Myth of Er, as well as with the Dream of Scipio, Cicero's homage to Plato's myth at the end of his own *Republic.* Like its predecessors, the Petite Fable presents a dream vision about the afterlife and the construction of the cosmos, and serves as the conclusion to a philosophical treatise concerning justice—a resemblance that Leibniz chose to underscore by giving the book its conspicuously Hellenizing title. The myth follows the petition of the Roman tyrant Sextus Tarquinius, as he appeals to a pantheon of Greco-Roman deities regarding his fate. Had he been instead given a virtuous nature, he laments, he would not go on to commit the Rape of Lucretia, for which he is destined to be shunned and exiled for the remainder of his life. The myth culminates with the appearance of Pallas Athena in an elaborate dream dreamed by a high priest of Jupiter, who has taken over Sextus's inquiry. There, the goddess of wisdom reveals all the possible worlds that could have been created, including ones in which Sextus does not commit the crime. Each of these worlds constitutes a separate room in the "Palace of Fates," with each room containing a book of the entire history of that world—"the book of its fates," the detail that inspires Voltaire's parody.[3] Upon being presented with such a visualization of all the fates of all the possible worlds in one place, the high priest is able to see that their beauty invariably pales in comparison to that of the world that contains the crime of Sextus, which is also the world we happen to live in. Our world, then, is deemed the best among all possibilities, as only a perfectly rational God could have chosen to create—and the high priest wakes from his dream.

Why did Leibniz conclude the *Theodicy* with such a myth? One way of motivating the question is to begin with the suggestion that what made the Petite Fable an easy target for Voltaire's mockery is related to the antiquarian spirit with which we tend to approach Leibniz's doctrine of theodicy today: as the last breath of a doomed project to defend a holistic way of conceptualizing reason and its place in the world.[4] Leibniz's theodicy essentially consists in a justification for the continuity of reason and faith, or in the position that there exists no boundary separating the realm of philosophy from that of theology. To assign to reason this way the overarching powers of knowledge traditionally attributed to divine revelation was to commit to what Christia Mercer has described as a "radical rationalism": a conception of reason's boundaries that denies any limitations to what humans are capable of knowing through rationality alone.[5]

If this strikes us as naive—the stuff of a philosopher's wishful thinking—we would find ourselves in good company. The reception of the *Theodicy* suggests that some of the fanciful qualities of the closing myth end up being reflected in Leibniz's philosophical system, so that it shares with the myth a certain mysticizing mentality associated with the genre of such stories. The most common critiques of the *Theodicy* tend to converge around the charge of advancing a lofty account of the universe that is removed from the realities of the experienced world: to declare that the created world—just as it is—is the best among all possibilities seems not only to deny all the ways in which it comes up short, but also to falsely designate as intelligible that which is senseless.[6] This was Voltaire's discomfort with the *Theodicy*, immortalized in *Candide* (1759), and it was Hume's when he suggested no philosopher had been so "extravagant" as to claim "so bold and paradoxical an opinion" as Leibniz's apparent denial of meaningless suffering in the world.[7] While his contemporaries and interlocutors in the Enlightenment are celebrated for their mission of wresting reason from intellectual laxity, fable, and superstition, Leibniz himself seems to stand for a misguided departure from these ideals—recalling, for instance, Bertrand Russell's well-known characterization of Leibniz's metaphysics as "a kind of fantastic fairy tale, coherent maybe, but wholly arbitrary."[8]

The aim of this chapter is to explore the relationship between Leibniz's doctrine of theodicy, as a philosophical position on the nature and limitations of human reason, and the decision on the part of its author to compose a myth around this doctrine. I suggest that the two things are indeed related, but not for the reasons one might think. The myth is not, for example, a more palatable way of rearticulating a doctrine that had already been presented in a more rigorous language earlier in the treatise. Nor, more significantly, is the myth an inadvertent admission of a lapse in philosophical rigor, whereby the imprecision of the myth's presentation either reflects or disguises the doctrine's inherent weaknesses. Rather, Leibniz deploys the myth as a deliberate, philosophical solution to the problems generated by his own commitment to rationalism.

Leibniz's unlimited conception of reason envisions a universe that humans have the capacity to know fully using only the power of their own reason—a promise that is as ambitious in theory as it is impossible in practice to meet within human lifetimes. Reconciling the disconcerting gap between what is theoretically intelligible and what is practically knowable leads Leibniz to arrive at a theodicy that is inherently paradoxical, whereby an active and emancipatory vision of reason's activities ultimately rests on an unconditioned story that makes provisions for its suspension in the name of the divine. The Petite Fable can be read as a diagnosis and expression of this paradox. It is, in essence, a philosophical myth in the Platonic tradition, which, in telling a deeper story about the way things are in the world, also tells us why such a story is both provisional and necessary.

LEIBNIZ CONTRA BAYLE IN THE PETITE FABLE

The *Essays on Theodicy* was the only book Leibniz published during his lifetime, and it constituted a response to the work of Pierre Bayle, against whom Leibniz had a long-standing disagreement concerning the boundaries of reason and faith.[9] The book was born out of the conversations he had with his patroness, the Electoress Sophie-Charlotte, over Bayle's *Historical and Critical Dictionary* (1697), and the greater part of the *Theodicy* reads as a point-by-point commentary on passages of interest from

Bayle's oeuvre. The sprawling work is unified, however, by Leibniz's argument for theodicy, a doctrine that is often reduced to the dictum that we live in "the best of all possible worlds." But as a rejoinder to Bayle, Leibniz's theodicy amounts first and foremost to a specific position that he took on the question of reason's boundaries against those of faith.

Bayle had argued for setting limits on reason's realm; Leibniz was against. For both philosophers, reason consisted of an active and critical faculty, independent from the senses, that could help sift truth from untruth through sustained reflection and examination. Bayle turned the full power of this critical faculty against superstition and the unsubstantiated beliefs of his day, relentlessly exposing the absurdities at the heart of so many conventions in the cultural heritage of Europe that were upheld merely for the sake of tradition. But Bayle, unlike Leibniz, spoke of reason as a purely destructive force, which could set its user on the path toward certain knowledge only to the extent that it identifies false or poorly grounded beliefs, but was "too feeble" on its own "to be led back to the truth." Reason, he suggested, "is only proper for raising doubts, and for turning things on all sides to make disputes endless."[10] This meant, at one level, that reason required the guidance of revelation in order to arrive at truth, but it also meant, at another level, that religious doctrine had to be kept at a safe remove from the disruptive capacity of reason for raising endless doubts.[11] Bayle's solution had been to limit the scope of reason so as to decouple it from matters of faith.

Leibniz did not share Bayle's destructive view of reason, but emphasized its constructive function as a faculty engaged in "the linking together of truths."[12] Through the gradual and systematic assembly of its own discoveries, reason would build up knowledge toward those divine truths that are otherwise known through faith.[13] By insisting on the continuity between the realms of reason and faith, Leibniz sought to restore to reason its expansive capacity to know the highest good and everything that fell under its dominion. The doctrine of theodicy supplied this solution: only the best of all possible worlds, and nothing less, would have been selected for creation by a perfectly rational God; and as such, human reason can be said to participate in the same rational laws that govern the divine will, and committing to this conception of divinity is both an act of reason as well as one of faith.[14]

The Petite Fable

Leibniz concludes the *Theodicy* by illustrating this doctrine in the form of a myth. The myth, to which he affectionately refers as a "Petite Fable," is structured around two layered parts: the first half is a faithful reconstruction of an allegorical scene taken from the *Dialogue on Free Will* (ca. 1439) by the fifteenth-century humanist Lorenzo Valla.[15] In the second half, Leibniz supplies an original extension of Valla's story where it breaks off.

Valla's original fable—reproduced in the first half of the Petite Fable—imagines an allegorical conversation between Apollo and the tyrant Sextus Tarquinius. Sextus has come to Apollo for a prophecy regarding his own fate, and Apollo responds by revealing to him the sin that he is destined to commit in the future, and the consequent life of exile and suffering that awaits him. Sextus protests, pointing to the gifts and sacrifices he has brought for the deity, and asks for a better prophecy. To this, Apollo answers that he merely foretells the future, and that Sextus's fate and his sins are his own: if Sextus has any objections, he should instead be making his complaint to Jupiter and to the Fates.

In Valla's dialogue, the imagined exchange between Sextus and Apollo ends here, on an aporetic note, but Leibniz opts to "carry the little fable still further" in the adaptation that forms the second half of the Petite Fable.[16] In his continuation of the story, Sextus goes to Jupiter with his complaint after all. Jupiter ends up offering Sextus a choice: if he agrees to give up his crown in Rome, the Fates will grant him a different future. Sextus rejects the offer and returns to Rome, resigning himself to his doomed fate.

Jupiter's high priest, Theodorus, who has witnessed the encounter, asks the omnipotent deity why he did not simply grant Sextus a nature incapable of sin. Jupiter instructs Theodorus to go to Pallas Athena for his answer, which takes the form of a dream vision presented to the high priest when he falls asleep at the temple of the goddess in Athens. In the dream, Theodorus finds himself transported to the Palace of the Fates. Pallas Athena leads him through halls containing worlds in which Sextus accepts Jupiter's proposal and abandons Rome: in one, he leads a quiet life in Corinth and finds treasure in his garden one day; in another, he moves to Thrace and marries the daughter of the king. When Theodorus enters the most beautiful hall among them all, its splendor is so overwhelming that he briefly loses consciousness, and the goddess has to revive him. He learns from her then that this hall contains the created world as is, whose sinning and suffering Sextus is a mere speckle in the grand vision of a deity who has, quite literally, thought through everything in the process of choosing the best among all the possible worlds. Theodorus wakes from his dream and, satisfied that he now "owns the justice of Jupiter," throws himself into his earthly duties with the utmost zeal and joy.[17]

The Limited and Unlimited Accounts of Reason

Leibniz was clearly pleased with the unusual ending he had put together for the *Theodicy,* which he believed would present "difficult but important truths" to his readers in "an easy and familiar way."[18] But taking this unusual ending as a merely rhetorical recapitulation of the central philosophical doctrine can obscure just how carefully Leibniz had constructed the myth around the debate that had inspired the work in the first place. To the extent that Leibniz had perceived the disagreement between himself and the late Bayle to principally concern the boundaries of reason, he took special pains to ensure that their contrasting positions were reflected in the two-part structure of the Petite Fable.

In the first part of the Petite Fable, Valla's original fable serves as a mouthpiece for Bayle's stance that the boundaries of reason are limited against faith.[19] Valla had written the *Dialogue on Free Will* to protest the growing presence of philosophy in theological disputes, and the passage excerpted in the Petite Fable was intended as an illustration of the limitations of philosophy in settling matters of faith. The hypothetical dialogue it stages between Sextus and Apollo begins to tackle the medieval puzzle of reconciling God's benevolence, the freedom of the human will, and the fact of the presence of evil in the world, but the inquiry ultimately reaches what appears to be a philosophical limit. Here, the clairvoyant Apollo represents God's omniscience, and Sextus the human wrongs and suffering that God knowingly seems to permit in the world. Recasting a problem of Christian theology using pagan deities, with their demarcated realms of dominion, helps to divide up the idea of the Christian God into powers that can and cannot be reconciled with human freedom.[20] Valla's Apollo, accordingly, is able to offer only a partial response to Sextus's protestations, and in turn, to the theological puzzle: just as the deity's own ability to foretell the future does not excuse Sextus from being the source of his own sins, God's foreknowledge of evil has no bearing on human freedom, or on the responsibility that humans bear for their free actions.[21]

Valla's point is that the tools of reason can at best aspire to only a partial resolution to such questions, and that matters of faith must accordingly be separated from those of philosophy.[22] Philosophical inquiry may go so far as to reconcile human freedom with certain attributes of divinity—such as Apollo's foreknowledge—but no rational account exists on "the decrees of Jupiter's will, that is to say, on the orders of providence."[23] The "failure" of philosophers who thought otherwise lay in their having "hearkened more to the answer of philosophy than to that of St. Paul."[24]

If the aporetic ending of Valla's fable is intended to make the Baylean case for limiting the boundaries of reason, Leibniz takes the second half of the Petite Fable to present his countervailing account of a reason that is not limited by faith. He opts to continue Valla's inquiry as a way of demonstrating that philosophy can go yet further in an investigation that had been abandoned prematurely.[25] In the solution that he offers—in the form of the doctrine of theodicy—Jupiter, having made the supremely rational decision to create only the best of all possible worlds, remains a benevolent god, just as Sextus retains his freedom to sin, and both Sextus's crime and his suffering cease to be evils when understood to be necessary parts of this perfectly harmonious universe. The lesson of Theodorus's dream is that God's will is in fact knowable—like a palace of ideas whose rooms are open to visitors—and that this is precisely because God is a rational being.[26] Hearkening to the answer of philosophy, then, cannot be a cause of failure, because faith is not at odds with reason.

The Restrained and Unrestrained Appropriation of Myth

What is striking, however, is that in expanding Valla's fable in order to present a more capacious account of reason's domain, Leibniz also ends up extending the literary possibilities of his medium. Valla's original fable is presented as a dialogue, a form that Leibniz faithfully retains in his reconstruction, restricting himself to reporting only the hypothetical arguments exchanged between Sextus and Apollo.[27] However, in the second half of the Petite Fable, Leibniz shifts to uninterrupted narration, which permits him to indulge in an entirely new level of descriptive detail, going through not only what was said by the expanded cast of characters, but what they did, and what they saw.[28]

As the Petite Fable gains in literary complexity in its second half, this amounts, in particular, to an overt imitation of the genre of myth. Where Valla's half of the fable consists of an allegorical conversation between figures that he happens to borrow from Greco-Roman mythology, Leibniz's extension is, for all intents and purposes, a fully developed eschatological myth. In contrast to the formal sparseness of its first half, the second half of the Petite Fable conspicuously features fantastic and supernatural details, many of them borrowed elements from preexisting mythological tropes—such as the presentation of Jupiter's answer in the form of a dream vision, or the telltale olive branch with which Athena touches the high priest's face in order to enable him to see in the world of his dream. There is more vivid and intricate imagery offering glimpses into a coherent and separate world—as deployed in the detailed description of the Palace of Fates and the various universes contained within it. Above all, there is an overarching sense that the level of narrative elaboration is somehow disproportionate to its stated message.

To be sure, the casting of mythical deities in the original fable was itself a striking decision on Valla's part. Ernst Cassirer, for one, praised the gesture as a reclaiming of the medium of myth for philosophical purposes.[29] But the mythical figures in Valla's fable are little more than mouthpieces for the delivery of arguments, and the use he made of them would not have been unusual in a humanist work in the fifteenth century: borrowing from pagan myth to illustrate arguments of Christian theology was permissible to the extent that the former is employed as a rhetorical device for better communicating the latter to a general readership.[30] Here, being able to justify the use of mythic elements in terms of their rhetorical function was an important limitation. Valla himself cautioned against the danger of taking immoderate comfort in the feelings that myth tends to inspire. In an exchange that occurs later in the *Dialogue on Free Will,* the narrator of Valla's fable suggests that the "ambrosia" and "nectar" of "poetic and fabulous things" offer false promises of resolution on matters that cannot, in fact, be resolved, and he ends with an injunction to "leave this emptiness to the empty and fictitious gods, Jupiter and Apollo."[31] If the first half of the Petite Fable reflects this preference for restraint in the use of mythological materials, it stands in sharp contrast to the second half, whose uninhibited emulation of the mythic genre goes well beyond what would be considered rhetorically instrumental to the delivery of Leibniz's argument.

In deliberately representing the two competing accounts of reason in this way, across the two halves of the Petite Fable, Leibniz suggests a connection between the literary expansion of the medium of myth in his adaptation of Valla's source material, and the philosophical extension of the powers allotted to reason in his account. This raises, then, a further question: What is it about an unlimited—as opposed to a limited—conception of reason's empire that might call for a correspondingly expansive literary representation, and in particular, for recourse to the full range of expressive resources that myth has to offer?

MYTH AND ENLIGHTENMENT

The *Theodicy* was composed at a time when attitudes toward myth were at a critical crossroads, and when the use of myth in philosophical writing, in particular, was no longer innocent. Leibniz and his contemporaries were heirs to a baroque tradition of understanding the significance of myths from within a cultural and aesthetic, rather than theoretical, framework. This approach treated the figures, motifs, and scenes of Greco-Roman mythology as an inherited aesthetic vocabulary with which educated individuals were expected to have familiarized themselves in order to both comprehend and participate in high culture.[32] At the same time, however, shifting trends in the intellectual climate were beginning to draw an unprecedented level of critical attention to the subject of myth. The cultural debates culminating in the Quarrel of the Ancients and the Moderns had brought into question the merits of the mythological repertory that pervaded ancient Greek and Roman literature. The genre of myth itself was also being expanded: where myth had formerly referred almost exclusively to myths from Greco-Roman antiquity, the proliferation of travel narratives from the New World and the Orient also brought an onslaught of new myths into cultural consciousness. These factors helped consolidate the concept of myth as a category of critical study, rather than a timeless component of the cultural heritage of modern Europe.

Myth as an Object of Theoretical Interest

Myth was a favorite topic of intellectual speculation among Leibniz's chief correspondents; even his famous rival, Newton, had written a work of mythography.[33] Crucially, Leibniz's interlocutors were the pioneering force behind the emergence of a recognizably modern conception of myth, conceived not merely as a peculiar genre of narrative fiction but as a distinctly passive and uncritical mode of thinking that is not grounded in knowledge or reasons. A characteristic premise of Enlightenment studies of myth was a pronounced emphasis on the historical distance between enlightened modernity and the cultural epochs, like classical antiquity, in which societies generated myths. If Greek and Roman antiquity had hitherto comprised what modern European society largely knew of its past, and if myths from distant cultures in the New World and elsewhere seemed to resemble Greco-Roman mythology in some essential way, it also seemed to follow that these foreign cultures were in a state of development that was very much like Europe's own past. Cultural progress toward modernity, then, could be understood in terms of a set trajectory by which a society passes from a primitive phase of being imbued with myths, to an advanced phase of having outgrown them. In turn, interest in what separated modernity from the age of myth increasingly drew focus away from the surface content of myths, and instead to the particular modes of thought that might underlie the distinctively fantastical quality of those stories. On this view, myths were stories that reflected the absurd worldviews of their unenlightened creators, which were in turn the products of an insufficiently rigorous, or otherwise erroneous, reasoning about reality.

It is a commonplace that the intellectual climate of the Enlightenment was in large part defined by the effort to liberate philosophy from the influence of myth.[34] But it may be worth pointing out that that the Enlightenment wariness of myth was specifically a wariness about the possibility of cultural regression. If—as suggested by the early mythographers in Leibniz's circles—the essence of myth lay in an uncritical mode of thought, modern culture was not immune to slipping back into the same tendencies that once gave rise to those grotesque stories and beliefs pervading unenlightened societies. The genre of myth, on this account, represented the extreme perils in store for a culture that fails to be sufficiently vigilant in drawing and maintaining hard distinctions between reason and unreason. Both Bayle's and Leibniz's projects to properly define the boundaries of reason against theology can be understood, to some extent, as efforts to answer an Enlightenment question that had been sharpened by the epistemic threats that myth posed to modern thought: How ought reason to be conceptualized, so that the projects of philosophy are genuinely progressive, rather than stagnant or regressive?

Myth between the Error of Reason and the Unreflectiveness of Reason: Bayle

Pierre Bayle, Leibniz's chief interlocutor in the *Theodicy*, voiced what was arguably the most influential view of myth in the late seventeenth century. Bayle advanced and popularized a dismissive account of myth that condemned the grotesque absurdity of its content, but also hinted at the possibility that this characteristic absurdity might be rooted in an underlying inadequacy in reasoning, which continued to present substantive threats to the progress of knowledge. In particular, he emphasized the necessity of separating myths—and intellectual speculation about myths—from the discourse of enlightened culture.

At one level, Bayle merely regarded myths as stories that lacked intelligible content and were of no discernible use to the modern intellectual.

In a section titled "Jupiter" in the *Historical and Critical Dictionary*, Bayle directed his acumen to the most salacious scandals in Greek and Roman mythology and, indulging in particular in an extensive list of the moral crimes of Jupiter, sought to expose the bizarre, nonsensical nature of those ancient stories that depicted deities mating with family members one moment, and devouring them the next—maintaining, all the while, that they were deities worthy of veneration. These heathen tales, Bayle relates, had struck him as "so strange" that further reflection only made them seem "more monstrous."[35] For Bayle, the stories depicted in myths were sufficiently devoid of meaning that continuing to make unreflective references to them in modern culture, or otherwise treating them as though they were somehow profound, did not behoove an enlightened society.[36]

Accordingly, much of Bayle's program to insulate modern discourse from myth was directed specifically at the efforts of philosophers, both ancient and contemporary, who tried to derive allegorical meaning from myths.[37] He ridiculed the intellectual contortions that these authors performed to make sense of myths, and felt they were wasting their energies in attempting to wrest meaning from stories that never contained any to begin with. These efforts "cannot be read," Bayle judged in a dry remark, "without feeling pity for those philosophers who used their time so badly."[38]

But with each rhetorically colorful dismissal of myths as trivial, grotesque, and unworthy of intellectual attention, Bayle was inadvertently helping to construct a theoretical explanation as to why these stories told of such fantastically implausible happenings. Even as he fixates primarily on cataloging the gross absurdities recounted in classical myths, Bayle suggests in the *Dictionary* that ancient belief in such things may have had a distinct cause in an "error" of argumentative reasoning.[39] Bayle goes on to identify two "hypotheses" concerning the nature of material substance and of the soul, mistakenly held by the original creators and audiences of classical mythology, and which he believes essential to myth's underlying logic. Having erroneous beliefs about these matters, he suggests, will lead to the impossible premises of those stories in which material objects seem to have souls, or are inhabited by divinities. From this he concludes that "nothing is more dangerous or more contagious than starting from some false principle. . . . An absurdity once set forth leads to many others. Err only about the nature of the human soul; imagine falsely that it is not a substance distinct from extension; this error is capable of making you believe that there are gods who first sprung from fermentation who afterwards multiplied through marriage."[40] The suggestion that false principles are at the root of myth's absurdities carried significant implications for philosophy. If being wrong about one or two principles was all it took for an entire belief system to unravel into the realm of fantasy, this diagnosis did not so much condemn the errors pervading myths as attest to the fragility of rational systems.

In particular, Bayle drew a link between myths and superstitious thinking, or a timorous susceptibility to beliefs that are not grounded in reasons. In the *Various Thoughts on the Occasion of a Comet* (1682), Bayle had denounced popular superstitions around comets as supernatural harbingers of calamity, and had in turn put forth a more general condemnation of all beliefs that fail to hold up when "examined . . . well on the principles of philosophy."[41] There, he charged myths—as well as their more modern cousins, like fantastical romances—of exacerbating these tendencies toward superstition, by stylistically blending "poetic fictions" with the truth in ways that made it difficult to distinguish one from the other.[42]

It appears that, for Bayle, the kind of credulous mentality with which people believe and spread superstitions instead of subjecting them to more careful examination, was at once a contributing factor to the process by which false principles swell into myths, as well as a psychological effect activated and further perpetuated by myths. Bayle's reasoning seemed to be that stories that told of the affairs of divinities in conjunction with descriptions of observable happenings in our environment, like the changing of seasons or the fact of the world's existence, were stories in which all kinds of information—some grounded in reality, some fantastical and speculative—were left confused and undifferentiated in ways that encouraged indifference to the necessity of sifting truth from untruth.

The myths of antiquity, then, owed their origins to particular erroneous principles of reason, but they were also the products of an unreflective epistemic orientation—which myths in turn fomented—that was incapable of identifying and correcting those principles. As such, Bayle's criticism of philosophers who paid undue attention to myth had not only to do with a concern for their misdirected efforts, but also with a concern for the dangers of ennobling a genre of narrative whose underlying essence presented an obstruction to the progress of human knowledge. Myth was fundamentally regressive, and to pretend otherwise was both misleading and dangerous. The approach to knowledge that was necessary for the advancement of modern enlightened culture, on the other hand, was to be understood in sharp contradistinction to myth and its underlying tendencies: as lucid and questioning rather than inchoate and superstitious, invested in the truth of one's own beliefs rather than indifferent to it, critical rather than resigned to the status quo.

Myth's Psychological Catalysts and the Universality of the Human Psyche: Fontenelle

While Bayle ruled myth a menace to modern reason because it amplified simple errors of reasoning and encouraged them to stand uncorrected, and because it further fostered a passive and uncritical mentality opposed to that of the modern enlightened mind, these arguments against myth were rearticulated in the work of Bernard de Fontenelle, and filled in with a more detailed psychological account of those mechanisms by which chance errors might congeal into myths. But just as Bayle's condemnation of myth turned on a diagnosis of its origins in seemingly innocuous, unmistakably human ways of reasoning, those aggravating psychological factors to which Fontenelle pointed were hardly foreign to modernity. This meant that the authors of the foundational Enlightenment treatments of myth perceived both a surface opposition and an underlying similarity between myth and modern culture. On the one hand, the contents of myth spoke of fantastical beliefs about the world that could not be further from those informed by enlightened reason—beliefs that modern culture was fortunate to have overcome. On the other hand, these myths were also the result of causes and processes that were somehow endemic to human nature. And if a further, self-perpetuating effect of myths was that they made it more difficult for a people to correct for their underlying causes, it seemed to follow that even an enlightened and rational society that had long shed its primordial myths was not immune to the threat of regression.

Fontenelle, perhaps the first great modern theorist of myth, served as the first secretary to the newly established French Royal Academy of Sciences, of which Leibniz was a proud inaugural member.[43] Fontenelle was Leibniz's chief connection to the Academy, and often procured books for him.[44] Although his writings on Greco-Roman and Native American myths were not nearly as immediately influential as Bayle's remarks in the *Dictionary*, Fontenelle, much more so than his predecessor, endeavored to paint a coherent psychological picture of the mind captivated by myths, both as a creator and as a consumer of such stories.[45]

According to Fontenelle, one of the aggravating factors at work in the generation and circulation of myths was a psychological tendency to excuse the absurdities of their contents if one has already accepted the precedent set by the absurdities in another such story.[46] This tendency was not merely a logical fallacy, but was driven by the power of myths to both fulfill and shape psychological needs. At one level, Fontenelle suggested that it is naturally pleasurable to have our "fancy [*esprit*]" tickled by fantastic and marvelous stories. At another level, such stories, to the extent that they were often about common natural phenomena that lacked easy explanations, also provided distractions from the natural discomfort we experience in confronting our ignorance of the unknown.[47] Myths were thus "doubly pleasing" for the universal human psyche, and the production of such stories in a culture dominated by myth was fueled, according to Fontenelle, by the adaptive tastes of their audience, who developed an appetite for the absurd and fanciful narratives the more they were exposed to their pleasures.[48]

At the same time, Fontenelle suggested that the bizarre contents of myths were further perpetuated by a cultural propensity toward the blind respect for tradition. If the pleasures of indulging the absurdity of mythical narratives end up "extend[ing] a stupidity to infinity," the unwillingness to look critically upon inherited stories "preserves it forever."[49] Hence, for Fontenelle, natural facts of human psychology helped casual errors of reasoning grow into myths and ease their way into culture, and the only defense against them was a willingness to criticize rationally that which had come to be taken for granted in a society's cultural inheritance.

The call to modern European societies to turn a critical gaze onto their own culture entailed, in particular, asking difficult questions about what sets the modern mind apart from the mind enthralled by myth, and being prepared to admit that the only reason myth does not take up a greater share of modern life is that Europeans have had the good fortune of being "enlightened by the true religion and . . . by some rays of true philosophy."[50] Like Bayle, Fontenelle was eager to brush myths aside as "nothing but a pile of chimeras, dreams and absurdities," but in so doing, he, too, ended up calling attention to a more general fragility in the human mind and its creations—one that necessitated questioning even the most familiar aspects of one's own culture.[51] Ultimately, the errors of myth served as a warning for his modern readers: "All men are so much alike, that there is no people whose folly shouldn't make us tremble."[52]

The New Critical Vigilance: Religion and Philosophy as Purification from Myth

A consequence of such shifts in the understanding of myth was that philosophy during the Enlightenment was newly tasked with the need to formally and methodologically distinguish itself from both myths and the intellectual passivity associated with them. Running beneath the cavalier dismissiveness of the first Enlightenment tracts on myth was a growing anxiety about what the genre might imply for the status of modernity. On the one hand, efforts to get at the root of myth's pathologies led these authors to discover the universality of those basic impulses within the human psyche, both ancient and modern, that took pleasure in such stories. But on the other hand, these same efforts also ended up exposing the extent to which systems of knowledge and belief seemed to rest on but a few principles, errors about which threatened to topple the whole thing, but whose truth would be genuinely difficult to evaluate from within. The more these authors picked apart the scandals of myth, the more they ended up uncovering an underlying similarity between the mind guided by modern reason and the mind guided by primitive myth and its aggravating impulses. This raised an unsettling suggestion: while myths may seem to belong to a bygone age, the cognitive and psychological tendencies that gave rise to them were still very much a part of modern life.

As such, it became all the more urgent to cling to what truly defines the modern consciousness, and the study of myth hence also gave rise to a new spirit of critical vigilance. The need to guard the modern mind from the same processes that generate myths called for a purification of both philosophy and Christian religion. This movement was importantly defined, in particular, by the conviction that the faculties of reason must be active, rather than passive, at all times in these matters. If myths were the products of common tendencies of the mind and small errors of reasoning that had been left to fester uncorrected for too long, only a sufficiently active reason, willing to shine a critical light on all aspects of society, would be able to catch any potential causes of myth in modern culture before they have had a chance to grow. In religion, this entailed looking askance at unnecessary rituals and superstitious elements in contemporary religious practice, and rejecting those beliefs held merely for the sake of conformity. Religious beliefs and practices, rather, had to come from a state of active affirmation.

The purification of philosophy from the threats represented by myth took the form of a spirited effort to identify and reject all thinking that was not grounded firmly in knowledge. Through constant and active criticism, philosophical endeavors ought to avoid, as much as possible, regarding anything of reality through that state of passivity that lets errors of reasoning stand and grow into larger absurdities.[53] If there was a moral that modern philosophers could take away from studying the myths of ancient and otherwise unenlightened cultures, it was this: in order for reason's activities to be progressive rather than regressive, reason must be conceived in such a way that its endeavors avoid running up against that passive mode of thought that permits the causes of myth to endure, latent, in the modern mind-set.

The Place of Plato in the New Philosophy

Enlightenment efforts toward theological and philosophical purification often boded ill for the status of Plato. A climate of criticism condemning blind respect for antiquity meant that Plato, who was associated with tradition and the ungrounded authority of the ancients, was also regarded with suspicion. The desire to break away from the influence of Plato and other symbolic figures from antiquity, in favor of grounding intellectual culture in modern foundations, resonated in particular with an interpretation of Plato's legacy that portrayed it as a kind of deformed theology.[54] Pitted directly against an older, humanist reverence of Plato as a philosopher inspired by a Christian divinity, this interpretation suggested that a long-standing tradition of applying Neoplatonic frameworks to Christian doctrine in fact constituted the very contamination of religion.[55]

In the influential *Platonism Unveiled* (1700), the Huguenot pastor Matthieu Souverain articulated a specific version of the rising contempt for Greek philosophy, as represented by Plato and Aristotle.[56] Souverain condemned the "deprav'd Platonism" that had introduced extraneous embellishments and complications to an apostolic faith that ought to be simple rather than complex. In Souverain's characterization, Platonism was, in particular, "Absurd as the Theology of the Poets, and as unpolish'd as the Religion of the most superstitious vulgar."[57] A popular argument for the removal of Platonist corruptions from theology, then, explicitly associated Plato's legacy with the absurdity and unpolished vulgarity of a poetic theology, or a superstitious religion—in other words, with those very qualities that Enlightenment readers of myths had found so objectionable about such stories.

It did not help that Plato's own philosophical writings were riddled with myths and other literary flourishes. Plato's myths were familiar to seventeenth-century readers as part of a cultural, and in particular aesthetic, inheritance left over from the ripples of Renaissance humanism and medieval scholasticism.[58] A general audience schooled in humanist rhetoric—even one that wasn't actively reading Plato—would have been acquainted, in some filtered form, with some of the more prominent images from his myths. But in the shifting intellectual culture of the Enlightenment, the growing antipathy toward myth had also begun manifesting in renewed calls for the purification of philosophical writing itself. As early as 1667, a pamphlet issued against the Cambridge Platonists had denounced "Plato and his Followers" specifically for having "communicated their Notions by Emblems, Fables, Symbols, Parables, heaps of Metaphors, Allegories, and all sorts of Mystical Representations (as is vulgarly known). All of which upon the account of their Obscurity and Ambiguity are apparently the unfittest signes in the world to expresse . . . Philosophical Notions and the discoveries of the Natures of things."[59]

The complaint against the "Obscurity and Ambiguity" of Plato's myths was pointedly philosophical: they were unsuitable modes of expressing philosophical notions and scientific discoveries, to the extent that both were better served by clarity and precision. Even those readers who were more favorably disposed toward Plato himself—whose philosophy they believed had been distorted by his Neoplatonic followers—identified Plato's use of myth and poetic language as the source of the misunderstandings that had led to the gradual transformation of Plato's true philosophy into an obscure and mystical Platonism.

As both theology and philosophy were being held to new standards of rigor, then, the Platonic tradition was being associated with myth at two levels: its critics saw it as a pagan theology that had grafted itself onto the true Christian religion; and the indulgence of myths and other imprecise forms of expression, by both Plato and his Neoplatonic interpreters, was deemed deficient against the new ideals of philosophical clarity. Amid these criticisms, the only viable way to salvage Plato's reputation in the eyes of his Enlightenment critics was to emphasize the Socratic spirit valorized in Plato's early dialogues, which seemed to promote skepticism and criticism over credulous belief in the content of contemporary Greek myths. Voltaire, for instance, would come to praise Plato's portrayal of Socrates for "proving that the moon was not a goddess, and that Mercury was not a god."[60]

Not until the mid-eighteenth century, a generation after Leibniz, would a more homogeneously favorable verdict on Plato begin to crystallize.

This was a view that would go on to combine a Voltairean admiration of Socratic skepticism with an appreciation, no doubt aided by Leibniz himself, for the rational content of Plato's theory of Forms. The Plato who would eventually be claimed for the cause of the Enlightenment was thus one who could simultaneously emphasize the critical nature of philosophical reason—so central to the skeptical tradition in his earlier reception—while defending the coherence of his philosophical system, without recourse to the revelation-oriented metaphysics of the Neoplatonic tradition.

In Leibniz's own time, however, the terms of the debate were still being set: interpreters of the Platonic tradition had yet to determine if Plato stood for the absurd and mystical distractions—reminiscent of the vulgarity and obscurity of myths—that had come to infiltrate both religion and philosophy, or whether Plato himself served as the original proponent of a Socratic skepticism specifically targeted at the exposure of ancient Greek mythology in favor of proof-based thinking. As the latter interpretation began to gain currency, it would come to set the stage for a Plato worthy of celebration only insofar as he was understood to be the founder of a rational and critical enterprise of philosophy divorced from myth.

In turn, the shifting debates around the status of Plato illustrate the extent to which he was implicated in the soul-searching of an age. The questions around which Plato's modern reputation was being decided go to show that, as the leading figures of Enlightenment thought endeavored to reinvent philosophy for their times, they were in some part defining their efforts against myths and what they represented. Their philosophical ideals were opposed to myth as a mode of expression, and to the insufficiently critical reasoning they believed to be responsible for it, and both were unambiguously unwelcome in the philosophical projects of modernity.

Myth as an Imperfect Placeholder for More Perfect Knowledge

Leibniz, too, adopted a generally unsympathetic stance toward myth, in alignment with his commitment to securing for philosophy a progressive identity and trajectory. He envisioned historic developments in the progress of philosophy to be accompanied by corresponding improvements in rational expression, so that both the form and the substance of myth would be displaced from the province of human knowledge.

Plato's philosophy, in particular, represented for Leibniz an important turning point in that account of epistemic progress. Unlike many of his contemporaries who were eager to slough off the authority of the ancients, Leibniz affiliated himself with a small group of intellectuals who were committed to the selective and purposeful revival of ancient texts.[61] For this group he translated abridged versions of the *Phaedo* and the *Theaetetus* into Latin, and lobbied for the translation of additional Platonic dialogues into French.[62] Plato was singled out by Leibniz as the only ancient philosopher to have anticipated his own metaphysics. Plato's philosophical system and method therefore had to be regarded as the historical groundwork for a truly rational Christian philosophy.[63] Leibniz unequivocally rejected the thought that Plato's philosophy might represent a pagan corruption of Christian doctrine, and he accordingly strove to disassociate it from the mythic overtones of pagan religion. The core of Plato's philosophy, on Leibniz's account, was a rational metaphysical system that had made it possible for humans to actively pursue knowledge of universal truths using their natural reason, without the aid of divine revelation.

But if Leibniz's celebratory portrait of Plato fit neatly into his own vision of the rational progress of philosophy, his position on myth falls short of being a wholesale rejection of the medium. Rather, the same evolutionary view of epistemic progress through which Leibniz establishes myth's essential backwardness also allows him to make special accommodations for it, as a medium that functions as a rough placeholder for incomplete knowledge, and which provisionally articulates truths that cannot yet be investigated in more complete detail.

This is the account of myth sketched out in Leibniz's Vienna lecture of 1714, "On the Greeks as Founders of Rational Theology," which begins with a comparison of Greek philosophy with the belief systems manifest in pagan mythology.[64] Leibniz sets out to differentiate the "true theology" of the Greeks—by whom he largely means Plato—from the "superstitious, mythological and idolatrous" religion of the "barbarians."[65] Leibniz's argument was that Greek philosophy, like many of the religious beliefs alluded to in pagan myths, contained the seeds of a true natural religion—such as a basic belief in the immortality of the soul, or in the goodness of God—which had been in turn revealed to the relevant cultures by prophets and other vehicles of divine providence. However, it had taken someone like Plato to develop both a rational system of ideas as well as a rigorous language of argumentation in order to inquire into the nature of God with greater subtlety. This way, knowledge of the divine was no longer dependent on the accident of revelation. Plato's efforts had equipped humankind not only to know God and the eternal verities but to know them better: it was thus that the Greeks could be understood to be the founders of a "rational theology" and a "sacred philosophy" that rendered faith continuous with reason.[66]

But if Leibniz's intention in the lecture is to set Greek and Platonic philosophy apart from pagan mythology, he ends up placing their respective contributions to human knowledge on the same epistemic spectrum. Pagan mythology, for Leibniz, is clearly inferior to Plato's philosophy, but still deserves credit as an antecedent to the knowledge of certain divine truths attained by the latter. Leibniz goes through several pagan myths to show that Plato owed to those cultures more or less all that he had gotten right about theology. But where "the wise men in Eastern peoples were accustomed to images" and "were content" to teach just these general truths as a matter of dogma, Plato had refined, through "outstanding arguments" and "certain proofs" that brought on "a greater subtlety of thinking," a philosophical method and rational language that "more distinctly expressed" those truths that otherwise could only have been "described rather obscurely."[67] Compared, then, to the method and language of logical argumentation that Plato invented, myth is flawed to the extent that it is equipped to offer only vague outlines of wisdom and, rather than opening up avenues for more detailed investigation, leads people to be "accustomed" to and passively "content" with incomplete knowledge. But Leibniz's diagnosis also suggests that myth and logical argumentation are illuminated by, and reach for, the same truths. As such, both fall on a shared spectrum—progressing from less to more complete forms of knowledge—that spans the metaphysical gap between the human and the divine. Myth belongs to this broad range of forms, provisional but not invalid, that human knowledge of certain divine truths can historically take.

It is possible for myth, then, to be subsumed into one of the key lessons that Leibniz took away from Plato's system of ideas: that perfect knowledge is an ideal toward which humans strive imperfectly.[68] Leibniz praised Plato for the rigor and precision of his philosophical arguments, and was an early pioneer in arguing for the separation of Plato's philosophy from the mysticism of the Neoplatonic commentary tradition in which his texts were mired at the time. In the interest of reconstructing Plato's philosophy as a coherent, rational system of ideas, he campaigned for the need to read the original dialogues instead of encountering their content through the distortions of commentary and paraphrase.[69] But Leibniz simultaneously took an unusual interest in Plato's myths, even as he continued to fault his Neoplatonic commentators for "throwing themselves upon" these "hyperbolic" expressions to the point of being "weighed down by new illusions."[70] If the Petite Fable—a myth about the cosmos and the afterlife concluding a treatise on justice—constitutes an obvious homage to the Myth of Er, it was also the likely product of a more extended period of experimentation in which Leibniz attempted to write his own version of at least one other Platonic myth. In an extraordinary essay speculatively dated to the early 1690s, Leibniz reworked the Allegory of the Cave into another dream vision, anticipating several of the themes that reappear in the Petite Fable.[71]

Just as Leibniz saw in myth the redemptive potential to lend placeholder expressions to imperfect knowledge, his interest in reworking Plato's myths suggests that he believed the crude and fanciful qualities specific to myth might be harnessed fruitfully in philosophical writing. But to better understand why Leibniz chose this exceptional form for the second half of the Petite Fable, we need to take up a more detailed investigation of what it was about the doctrine of theodicy that required such special resources, and his reasons for believing that his—and not Bayle's—was nonetheless the more progressive account of reason's realm and its project.

REASONING IN AN INTELLIGIBLE WORLD

Two Pathologies of Reason

Prominent throughout Bayle's remarks on the nature and goals of reason are two related themes that can help to explain why he was so intent on separating the realms of reason and faith, and why Leibniz was so intent on uniting them. The first is his concern, so conspicuous in his attacks on superstition, "vain imaginings," and beliefs held merely for the sake of tradition, that it was because people were lazy in their use of critical reason that they were inclined to nourish poorly thought-out ideas in degenerative directions reminiscent of mythical worldviews.[72] Implicit in his diagnosis that a lazy and uncritical reason seemed to be at the root of cultural stagnation was also the prescription for a conversely active reason, the increased use of which would help sort knowledge from misguided beliefs and assumptions that are held for no good reasons. This formed the most basic foundation of Bayle's answer to the question of reason's boundaries, which was also a premise to which Leibniz was fully committed: in order for philosophy to be genuinely progressive, reason first had to be active, assertive, and—within the bounds of its designated sphere—indiscriminating in the objects of its critical scrutiny.

But if Bayle called upon a relentlessly active reason to ward off the pathologies of a lazy reason, this solution did not come without its own set of problems. A second theme that runs through Bayle's work is a skepticism that extended at times to a skepticism directed at reason itself. He considered reason to have the paradoxical powers of "a guide that leads one astray." Philosophy, for him,

> can be compared to some powders that are so corrosive that, after they have eaten away the infected flesh of a wound, they then devour the living flesh, rot the bones, and penetrate to the very marrow. Philosophy at first refutes errors. But if it is not stopped at this point, it goes on to attack truths. *And when it is left on its own, it goes so far that it no longer knows where it is and can find no stopping place.*[73]

Bayle compares philosophy to a strong medical powder used to treat wounds: it will burn through infections, but if used indiscriminately, it will do the same to living tissue. Reason, then, is essentially caustic in its nature, and poses a danger to itself when left to refute and attack whatever is near. Designating separate realms for reason and for faith not only protects religious dogma from its corrosive powers but also sets a "stopping place" for reason so that it doesn't lead itself astray.

Bayle's limited conception of reason's realm, then, can be read as a response to two pathological forms of reason—a remedy to the dangers raised by the solution to another problem. The dual threat of an atrophied reason through insufficient use, on the one hand, and of a freewheeling and self-defeating reason, on the other, was a problem that troubled Leibniz as well.

But for Leibniz, it was a sluggish reason, rather than its corrosive counterpart, that was already causing problems for faith. It was not that Leibniz was unaware or unconcerned for the problems generated by a restless reason in need of guidance. The subject of the *Essays on Theodicy*—the relationship between human freedom, the origin of evil, and the course of events in the world that seem to arise as though by a divinely determined necessity—is famously introduced as a "labyrint[h] where our reason very often goes astray."[74] But Leibniz took on that labyrinth in the *Theodicy,* and rejected Bayle's solution to the problem of a corrosive and restless reason, because he took the opposite threat to be more urgent.

Leibniz believed that limiting the realm of reason would resurrect the pathologies of a lazy reason. For Leibniz, reason could be genuinely active, rather than lazy or passive, only when there exist no constraints on what is and is not within its purview of understanding. Cordoning off matters of faith from those of reason does not result in the freedom of reason from the shackles of religious dogma—as later champions of the Enlightenment might have maintained—but instead does a disservice to both faith and reason. The opposition of the two in the "admirable Dictionary of M. Bayle" is, according to Leibniz's characterization, "where M. Bayle wishes to silence reason after having made it speak too loud: which he calls the triumph of faith."[75]

The Separation of Faith and Reason: Two Deficient
Orientations toward Fate

Leibniz draws a fundamental connection between faith that is separated from reason, and the concept of a "Lazy Reason" that had preoccupied the "the ancients."[76] Lazy reason is the result of a particular attitude toward events that relinquishes human freedom and responsibility, and abandons itself to fatalism. Those who hold this attitude do not question the circumstances in which they find themselves or their future trajectories, because they do not question the will of the divinities or supernatural forces that had brought about these events. Instead, they "will be inclined to evade the difficulty of consideration and abandon themselves to fate or to inclination, as if reason should not be employed except in easy cases."[77] When one refuses, in other words, to think hard and rationally about the course of events in the world, that mind-set of indifference has a tendency to slide into all spheres of life, to detrimental consequences.

Leibniz assigns to this uncritical attitude the unfortunate name "*Fatum Mahometanum,* fate after the Turkish fashion . . . owing to their use of such reasoning as that just recorded," but his point is that most Christians are guilty of "reason in the Turkish fashion" in their dealings, and "will employ the lazy reason, derived from the idea of inevitable fate, to relieve oneself of the need to reason properly."[78] The consequence for faith is that lazy reasoners, whether Christian or pagan, ancient or modern, engage in only the "outward forms of the expression of their religion" diagnosed in the first sentences of the *Theodicy:* in ceremonial practices that only "resemble" virtuous action, and in doctrines or "formularies of belief" that are "like shadows of the truth."[79] Against the hollow state of religion and morality in his own time, Leibniz prescribes a more affirmative vision of faith, and insists that "when virtue is reasonable, when it is related to God, who is the supreme reason of things, it is founded on knowledge."[80] Faith that is not grounded in reason falls short of true faith and virtue, just as it erodes our freedom to reason about the world around us.

Conversely for Leibniz, reason that is not grounded in faith is similarly deficient. What Leibniz calls *Fatum Stoicum* seems to be a way of reasoning that manages to remain active despite subscribing to a weakened form of the same fatalism motivating the *Fatum Mahometanum*. In his characterization of Stoic philosophy, the course of events in the world and the forces behind them are not beyond the domain of reason, but the Stoic who actively reasons about such things does not do so out of faith in a meaningfully ordered universe. Rather, the world, seen through Stoic eyes, runs on an opaque determinism, such that after a certain point it no longer makes sense to ask difficult questions about why things are the way they are. This is not because Leibniz disregards efforts within Stoic thought to grapple with religious questions, but because its gods are thought to be fundamentally inscrutable, if not despotic and thereby "unworthy of veneration."[81] Accordingly, the status of reason in *Fatum Stoicum* is not particular to Stoic philosophy, but is an underlying condition of all approaches to philosophy that are not predicated on the idea of a rational God.

If the *Fatum Mahometanum* consists in a reason that is lazy because of a kind of blind faith, the *Fatum Stoicum* amounts to a reason that is active in spite of it. As far as fatalisms go, Leibniz considers this defiantly active form of reason unequivocally preferable to the alternative, and he reserves admiration for its ability to inspire, in the place of helplessness, "tranquillity in regard to events, through the consideration of necessity, which renders our anxieties and our vexations needless."[82] This tranquility, however, is ultimately deceptive. As long as the happenings that befall humans are understood to be arbitrary rather than rational, even the best efforts of philosophers to make active use of their reason would be "confining" them to a worldview built around the "alleged necessity" of events. Any tranquility one might feel toward a world driven by arbitrariness and mere necessity would therefore in truth be "a forced patience."[83] Reason that lacks faith in the coherence of the world is doomed to be incomplete in its endeavors: it is a reason that manages to resist laziness, but ultimately is not free.

Separating faith and reason, then, renders reason lazy in the worst case, and, even in the best case, imposes limits on reason's freedom. Leibniz saw his theodicy as the rational ground that faith requires, as well as the rational content of faith that will give meaning to reason's activities. The problem of lazy reason, as he conceived it, is resolved rather than aggravated in his system, in which faith and reason are continuous. Unlike the *Fatum Mahometanum,* it allows matters of faith to be deduced rationally, not believed blindly or performed in empty gestures; and because no area of knowledge is beyond its domain, reason accordingly lacks dogmatic hiding places in which to breed lazy habits. Also unlike the *Fatum Stoicum,* Leibniz's system grants reason a genuinely constructive role rather than one resigned to merely defending its projects against the opacity of arbitrary world events. The difference between theodicy and the *Fatum Stoicum* can be conceived as a difference between "joy and patience: for their tranquillity was founded only on necessity, while ours must rest upon the perfection and beauty of things, upon our own happiness."[84] Through "acquaintance with true principles," theodicy grounds the activities of reason in an emancipatory worldview.[85] In turn, reason can assume its true form only when its freedom is unrestricted and all matters of knowledge fall within its comprehensive reach.

The Perfectly Intelligible Universe and the Revenge of Restless Reason

For Leibniz, then, lifting the barrier between the realms of reason and faith is the only genuine way to ensure that reason does not slip into that pathological form that Bayle had presented as a problem of laziness. Much more uncertain, however, is how his theodicy could address the opposite problem of reason that had concerned Bayle. For Bayle, the separation of faith and reason had been necessary because reason required what he called a stopping place; without such restraints, there was no telling what an essentially corrosive form of reason would attack, including itself. At first glance, Leibniz's decision, against Bayle, to grant reason a boundless empire of knowable things may appear straightforwardly emancipatory. But it is not without its own problems. For what would it really mean for reason to know no limits? In a fully intelligible universe, where the objects of reason are infinite, human reason seems to come out empowered and weak at the same time. Only an equivalently infinite reason—that is, God—would be able to comprehend all of it at once. But cast against the vast world of possible knowledge, the finitude of human reason comes to be all the more pronounced.

Insisting on the perfect intelligibility of the universe pushes Leibniz to take up some difficult positions on the relationship between reason and its world. Leibniz can be said to reside in what Hans Blumenberg calls "a meaning-driven world," in which "every event must in principle be open to examination regarding its 'why' and 'whither'—even if it does not willingly provide such information."[86] The smallest details of the universe have been thought through by a perfectly rational creator, and as such, a reason exists behind everything in it, from each strand of hair on our heads, to the imperceptible circumstances that factor into the decision to place a particular foot before the other as we pass through a door.[87] However, not all these reasons and explanations are immediately available to us. These matters are in many cases merely a question of having the patience to apply the sufficient level of scrutiny to that which is in need of explication. Too often are our intellectual endeavors misled simply because we jump too quickly to incomplete answers: we are bound to arrive at the rational explanation to most occurrences in the world, if only we are persistent and rigorous in our efforts.[88] But at other times, certain matters of knowledge are in fact beyond rational comprehension. These "truths" that are "above reason," rather than against it, include God's miracles and the so-called mysteries of religion, in whose ranks Leibniz counts the miracle of Creation itself and the order of the created universe.[89] But even in such cases, Leibniz insists, reason can know something, and ought to continue its pursuit for a greater, however imperfect, understanding of the universe.[90] Leibniz remains, in other words, adamantly committed to reason's capacity to know the world, even as he admits to the presence of matters in nature and theology alike, of which reason is condemned at best to partial knowledge.[91]

However, a familiar problem resurfaces when a finite human reason is left to confront an infinitely knowable world, and in its every crevice, an infinite number of questions waiting to be taken up for examination. If, for Leibniz, the unknown can always be better known through reason's attempts, human reason potentially bears responsibility for every question in the universe it chooses and chooses not to investigate. Among the infinite conundrums yet remaining in the rationally ordered world, which ought a finite reason to take up now? It is here, in

Leibniz's insistence on situating an infinite universe under the purview of a finite human reason, that the second of Bayle's problems creeps back in.

Leibniz had rejected Bayle's conception of reason as essentially destructive, emphasizing that even as it takes down a view held to be knowledge, it then ultimately builds support for the opposite view.[92] But even in its essentially constructive form, Leibniz's conception of reason ends up, if not corrosive, at least restless and easily disoriented. Leibniz, we recall, had defined reason as the "linking together of truths," but truths are often arrived at through a tortuous process full of detours and frustrations.[93] He speaks of the practicality of protecting persons of feeble faith from the potentially "poisonous" effects of rational disputation and, in cases when such protection is impossible, of the importance of providing an "antidote," in the form of rational answers, to the destabilization of beliefs by reason.[94] It seems to Leibniz "a general defect of humanity" that reason is impatient with its own course. Incomplete knowledge is unsatisfying, and people would more readily muddy the matter with sophistry, "to make the most of their wit and learning," than continue on the search for "naked truth." In such situations, reason loses sight of its purpose and gets caught up in chasing minutiae. In this sense, Leibniz observes, "we take pleasure in going astray."[95]

Like Bayle, then, Leibniz thinks reason can lead itself astray. But more damningly, it is in Leibniz's expansive account of reason's realm that reason is especially vulnerable to losing its way. The problem of reason's waywardness, for Bayle, had been one of reason continuing on with its work beyond what would be constructive, like a runner who would run past his mark unless he is told where to stop.[96] A modified version of the same problem emerges in Leibniz's philosophy, in which reason's finite resources might easily be spent on explicating the rational rules underlying every phenomenon it confronts, or worse, on struggling for small advances on questions ultimately beyond total comprehension. Here, reason risks being like a particularly myopic runner, making his way through a vast labyrinth by trying every corner and dead end at random. The larger the labyrinth, and the more limited the runner's time and stamina, the more difficulty he will have finding his way. In Leibniz's philosophy, the threat of a disoriented and restless reason is likewise exacerbated as a result of the gap between the infinity of knowable things in the universe, and the finitude of human reason.

A Third Orientation toward Fate

This is a problem that Leibniz cannot adequately answer except by introducing into his theodicy a passive and uncritical element that serves as a counterpart to Bayle's solution to reason's disorientation. For Bayle, a boundary imposed between the respective realms of faith and reason had served a "stopping place" to prevent reason from losing its way. Because Leibniz is committed to the continuity of reason's domain, he cannot set such definitive limits on the freedom of reason. But by insisting on the intelligibility of the created world while also admitting to the finitude of human rationality, Leibniz's theodicy effectively ends up having to draw a boundary of sorts, albeit a much more fluid and provisional one, between the theoretically intelligible and the practically knowable. This is a boundary between what demands the immediate exercise of our reason, and what can be bracketed off for the time being. The doctrine of theodicy makes such deferral possible under the faith that, to the extent that it belongs in our best of all possible universes, chosen by a perfectly wise deity, an unknown thing can be trusted to make sense, even though we may not be able to comprehend it for some time. This Leibniz calls the *Fatum Christianum:* "It is as if one said to men: Do your duty and be content with that which shall come of it, not only because you cannot resist divine providence, or the nature of things (which may suffice for tranquillity, but not for contentment), but also because you have to do with a good master."[97]

Leibniz uses the term only once in the *Essays on Theodicy,* but it is clear that he equates the establishment of a Christian attitude toward fate with the primary project of his theodicy. The *Fatum Christianum* is conceived in contradistinction to all other positions on fate—that is, those encompassed by the *Fatum Mahometanum* and the *Fatum Stoicum*—that uphold an effective separation between reason and faith.[98] But although it is grounded on the convergence of faith and reason, the *Fatum Christianum* is also like the *Fatum Mahometanum* and the *Fatum Stoicum* in that it retains an uncritical and fatalistic view toward the course of events in the world—namely, the deference of the unknown and the senseless to a deity who knows and comprehends them in our stead. This means that the doctrine of theodicy has both an active and a passive aspect. The active aspect consists in an emancipatory view of reason's relationship to the world, which submits for rational exploration the entirety of the created universe and the questions to be found in it. The passive aspect of theodicy, by contrast, permits a finite human reason not to pursue knowledge of these things at once. It seeks to absolve human rationality of the infinite array of responsibilities it bears in Leibniz's system, in which reason inhabits a perfectly intelligible universe, and is therefore called to account for all that which remains unknown in it.

While Bayle imposed a boundary between a realm of knowledge for the active use of reason, and a realm from which reason was to hold back, Leibniz can be said to resort to a similar solution. On one side of his theodicy, the side that presumes reason's capacity to succeed in understanding all that it takes up for investigation, reason thrives unhampered, in an active mode. However, on the other side of his theodicy, that aligned with the spirit of the *Fatum Christianum,* to have knowledge of the rational nature of God and his creations is a good-enough understanding of the world. And here it becomes permissible, for the time being, for reason to come to rest on the issues it has yet to fully grasp. In excusing what we don't know in terms what we do—that even the greatest and most urgent mysteries of our reality obey the rational design of a perfectly wise God—Leibniz's theodicy effectively draws a boundary beyond which an essentially active reason can assume a passive and uncritical mode.

Reason's Stopping Places

The status of reason on the passive side of that boundary may, however, give a rationalist pause. After all, Leibniz's refusal to delimit the domain of reason had been a way of protecting reason from laziness, and a total rejection of Bayle's solution to the same set of problems. But the passivity of the *Fatum Christianum* itself seems to consist in an evasion of thinking. Faith in the divine, according to Leibniz, "advances beyond the intellect, and takes possession of the will and of the heart, to make us act with zeal and joyfully as the law of God commands. *Then we have no further need to think of reasons or to pause over the difficulties of argument which the mind may anticipate.*"[99]

This, for Leibniz, is reason's stopping place, beyond which the need to keep working at difficult questions is removed. If a primary aim of the doctrine of theodicy is to restore to reason an unbounded freedom to know the world, it would seem a contradiction to Leibniz's vision to allow for rational laxity on any number of difficult matters deemed beyond, though not against, reason. It had been on very similar grounds that Leibniz had rejected Bayle's separation of faith and reason, and all orientations toward fate that failed to reconcile the two domains. Reason, for Leibniz, inevitably suffers when there exists a boundary in the province of knowledge beyond which it is permissible not to reason.

In particular, the atrophy of reason's active and critical function entails giving in to the indulgence of those very superstitions that Bayle fought so hard to expel from our patterns of thinking. Laziness of thought is responsible for a number of contemporary behaviors Leibniz lists with disapproval: the "superstitious" work of fortune tellers, belief in the philosopher's stone, and any tendency to seek "short cuts to the attainment of happiness without trouble."[100] Moreover, when people inhabit a cognitive state that makes them vulnerable to such conduct, this has significant moral consequences. It encourages them to relinquish responsibility for their actions, in the manner of "the pagans of old, who ascribed to the gods the cause of their crimes, as if a divinity drove them to do evil."[101] That is, those who are idle or passive in their use of reason are like primitive peoples of antiquity who, at the expense of their own moral agency, dwelled in a world circumscribed by myth. And, by Leibniz's own reasoning, the admission of a passive and uncritical aspect to his theodicy would appear to invite the same dangers.

If an uncritical orientation toward the world gravitates toward myth, then Leibniz's theodicy, which has such a passive component, can be said to contain those same impulses that drive people to turn to myths. These are unreflective impulses that, in fostering a general reluctance to question the status quo, eventually tend toward a fatalistic belief that the destiny of the moral agent is governed by external forces that are ultimately beyond rational comprehension. Both the generation of myths and belief in them can be conceived as responses to that desire, on the one hand, to do away with the need to reason on certain matters and, on the other, to relinquish one's fate to the unknown. And by committing itself to the *Fatum Christianum,* Leibniz's philosophy creates spaces within reason's domain for an uncritical mode of thought for which myth carries inherent psychological appeal.

At the same time, such potentially myth-prone spaces are also the result of an endeavor to preserve the integrity of reason: the passive component of Leibniz's theodicy functions as a necessary corrective to problems arising from a rationalist premise. That rationalist premise—the unboundedness of reason's realm—was something Bayle had given up on preserving but to which Leibniz was very wedded. Accordingly, even though Bayle and Leibniz had each in his own way prescribed stopping places for reason to serve as a corrective to its waywardness, their solutions differ in one crucial respect. Whereas Bayle sets a precise boundary on what subjects ought to fall within or outside of the purview of reason, Leibniz makes no such commitment. Instead, for Leibniz, it is permissible for human reason to come to rest on just as many matters as it is free to pursue. Furthermore, any such abandonment of an inquiry is treated as provisional, as though progress toward a more perfect understanding of the issue could be resumed anytime. Contained in every intellectual pursuit is an infinity of further questions of which human reason can practically answer only so many, but because these infinite unknowns are held together by the justice of a supremely rational God, knowledge is both stable and buildable. Boundaries between the things that do and do not demand the active use of reason are provisional—and the provisional status of these boundaries in Leibniz's system is at once troubling and redemptive. Troubling, because when no hard metric exists for determining when to cease investigation of a matter, there will always be a danger of postponing thought prematurely and indefinitely. But these provisional boundaries are also an alternative to permanently shuttering off entire realms of knowledge from reason's access, and in that sense they ultimately help redeem his project. For Leibniz, reason's stopping places can be moved, like temporary barricades, as human knowledge incrementally works toward the state of perfection idealized by the divine perspective.

If the doctrine of theodicy makes provisions for the suspension of critical reason, and with it, the ushering in of impulses that give rise to myth, these provisions are also a placeholder for future knowledge, and is therefore subject to philosophical qualification. Given the practical limitations of human inquiry, deferment of rational activity comes to be necessary at some point on all matters of knowledge, but on no subject can the need for further reasoning be permanently foreclosed. Accordingly, any expression of the impulse for myth in the doctrine of theodicy would also have to reflect these reservations. That is, whenever reason assumes a passive mode and submits to sweeping stories unearned by logical argument, such leaps in thinking would have to be interpreted alongside a certain awareness of their own epistemic status, as interim markers of what has yet to be known. Put a different way, Leibniz's theodicy contains a paradoxical tension that requires reason's activities to run two ways, and this paradox in turn calls for a mode of expression that allows it to be accepted and experienced as a tension. This is a tension between the theodicy's suggestion that the entirety of our intelligible universe demands exploration by reason, and the simultaneous concession to the necessity of checking reason from leading itself astray in the capillaries of the unknown.

It is against the background of this tension, and the need for its expression, that the Petite Fable comes to conclude the *Theodicy*. Read in these terms, the Petite Fable takes on new significance as the instantiation of a distinct form of philosophical discourse. As a narrative that takes on the characteristics of the kinds of myths associated with passive or idle reasoning about the unknown, the Petite Fable has the effect of both acknowledging and giving voice to the paradoxical mythic impulse contained within Leibniz's philosophical system. The tropes and conventions of myth become useful for these purposes because one of the ways in which myth, as a form of discourse, distinguishes itself from logical argumentation or even most varieties of fiction is that it does not answer to the rules of logic or, for that matter, of plausibility. Consequently, myth presents tensions and contradictions in a way that allows them to stand unresolved. At the same time, the Petite Fable is a philosophical myth, in that it tries to lend expression to the philosophical concerns delimiting those regions of passivity in reason's domain. The story depicted in the Petite Fable is a response to a philosophical problem concerning what it means to reason in an intelligible universe. And, as such, it is a profession of faith in the coherence of human knowledge and the capacity of rational activity to build on itself. By telling such a story about the nature of reason and its objects, and by doing so in a myth, Leibniz testifies to an important insight about the relationship between world and reason: that being able to take for granted the ultimate intelligibility and goodness of the things that are not yet known is a precondition for reason to operate freely in reality without being led astray.

THE PETITE FABLE AS A PHILOSOPHICAL MYTH

The divine perspective, as Leibniz conceives of it, might be that perfect state of knowledge that humans might hope to approach incrementally, through a progressive shedding of our less precise modes and languages of knowing for more precise ones. However, to the extent that we are finite creatures, our approach toward that divine ideal will always be an ongoing, incomplete process. As we have seen, so long as we are human and not divine, we will always depend on having any number of stopping places for reason, in order to give meaning and direction to those projects that reason does pursue actively. And just as the condition of being human necessitates in Leibniz's philosophy a place for this passive mode of reasoning, the language of myth, too, comes to be an integral part of the continuum of forms that knowledge can assume over the course of its ongoing evolution: as a resource that serves as a placeholder corresponding to those places where reason comes to a pause, and which grants provisional expression to that which is not yet available for further investigation.

If Leibniz sought, in the Petite Fable, to capture the extent to which the passive aspect of his theodicy was in fact a way of preserving the active nature of reason in philosophy, the mythic form in which he chooses to present this insight runs up against some important limitations. He must ensure that his appropriation of the genre of myth into philosophical writing is indeed compatible with the active form of reason that the passive *Fatum Christianum* is intended to protect. His myth is tasked, in particular, to convey that the theological justifications for the stopping places he affords to reason are not permanent substitutes for actual knowledge. It must avoid the danger of perpetuating a narrative about the order of things that snowballs, grows in authority, and eventually stagnates into something no one thinks to challenge—even as it asserts, to paradoxical effect, the flat truth of a theodicy that insists on the absolute goodness of the created world.

The Petite Fable can accordingly be read as a myth that was self-consciously deployed on the part of an author who struggled to present it to his readers on a specifically philosophical register. If the positioning of the myth recalls the Myth of Er and the Dream of Scipio at the end of Plato's and Cicero's respective *Republics,* we are now better equipped to appreciate the significance of this tribute. Tasked to present the doctrine of theodicy in such a way that simultaneously conveys how acceptance of its principles has to be both provisional and necessary for philosophical understanding, Leibniz fashions a myth that takes its cue from an established tradition of writing myths into philosophy.

The gesture suggests that he embraced the writing of a certain kind of philosophical myth to be a distinct element of the Platonic tradition as he understood it, and that he saw himself as a torchbearer to this legacy. In turn, his attempt to reinvigorate a philosophical tradition of myth-writing speaks to a dynamic vision of the potential of the genre and convention of philosophical myth. Just as Leibniz took liberties to refashion Valla's original allegory into the Petite Fable in its final form, he was also updating the Myth of Er for a new philosophy that was continuous with theology, and in so doing, he was attesting to the capacity of such philosophical myths to be reinvented for new philosophical ends.

The Provisionality and Necessity of Theodicy

In the *Republic,* Plato had turned to the literary genre of myth to rework a foundational concept in the web of tacit understandings that form the background to our worldviews. Leibniz was less exercised by the particular political concerns of the *Republic* as he was invested in bringing to completion the more general philosophical inquiry into the nature of justice; and the *Theodicy*'s concluding myth does not so much write over a central concept in one's understanding of the world as provide an account of what it might take for one such understanding to have stability and coherence. Preserved in the Petite Fable, instead, is Plato's hope that the literary genre of myth might grant us special access into the parts of our worldviews that we do not reason actively about, but also his insight into the provisionality of those frameworks that we passively take for granted. Like its traditional forbearer, Leibniz's myth channels the characteristic inscrutability of the genre to present a set of normative claims about the way things are in the world, and, without exactly opening them up for further scrutiny, nonetheless qualifies them in a way that invites recognition of the contingent epistemic status of those very claims.

As such, it is possible to see how, even as the Petite Fable functions as an illustrative restatement of the *Fatum Christianum,* aspects of its literary construction work to advertise the provisionality of this answer. The most prominent instance of this effect can be found in the choice to break up Sextus's inquiry into a relay of appeals made to different gods— Apollo, Jupiter, and finally Pallas Athena—so that the answer of each subsequent deity effectively overrides that of the one that came before. At one level, the myth invites its reader to take notice of the order of the sequence: a place of primacy is reserved for Pallas—wisdom—whose final response to Sextus's complaint ends up supplanting even that of Jupiter, who is diminished to a largely passive role in the myth. At the same time, this progression of responses also gives an open-ended quality to the myth: its revisionary format makes it difficult to take any answer, even that of a god, as the final word on the matter.

This lesson is recapitulated in the climax of the myth, when Pallas guides Theodorus into the hall at the top of the Palace of Fates, which contains the best of all possible worlds—our own. There, the overwhelming beauty of that world leads Theodorus to be "entranced in ecstasy" to the point of temporarily losing consciousness, and having to be revived by the goddess.[102] By denying that final beatific vision of the best possible universe, not only to the reader, but even to the fictional character dreaming about it, Leibniz delivers a point about the inaccessibility of the divine reasoning that can identify the created world as the best among all possibilities. But it is also a reflexive point about the provisional resources that his myth does offer in its stead. Humans may not have the capacity to access a full demonstration of this divine reasoning, but through Pallas's tour of the Palace and its various rooms leading up to this one, the myth has nonetheless equipped its readers with a template for imagining what such a demonstration would entail. To the extent that we can imagine it, that divine demonstration would be akin to the exercises depicted in the myth: of going through the possible universes as though inhabiting different halls in a palace, considering the possible events of each as though watching them play out on a stage (or reading about them in a book), and ultimately evaluating the merits and drawbacks of those possibilities against one another.

But the literary construction of the Petite Fable also offers a deeper lesson about the human standpoint from which we approach and commit to the doctrine of theodicy. A curious twist in the myth is that Jupiter grants Sextus the option to change his doomed fate, on the condition that he relinquishes his political power. It is a moment that recalls the climax of the Myth of Er, in which the souls who have made the thousand-year journey of the afterlife are tasked to choose the fates of their next lives, and an insufficiently philosophical soul finds himself unable to resist the temptation to choose the life of the tyrant.[103] In the Petite Fable, a Sextus who agrees to the proposal—and avoids the miserable end fated to him—exists in any number of alternative futures spread across an infinite number of alternative universes, a couple of which the myth describes in some detail. However, the actual Sextus of our own world cannot bring himself to give up his crown, and he turns down Jupiter's offer in full knowledge of the consequences that await him.

At first blush, getting Sextus to knowingly choose his own downfall may read as an unconvincing effort on Leibniz's part to absolve Jupiter from the sin and suffering in Sextus's lot. But what is more compelling about the portrayal of Sextus's choice may be its underlying moral psychology. In choosing his crown over a happier future, Sextus ends up rejecting the possible universes containing versions of himself that bear an increasingly thin resemblance to his own identity.[104] Part of the point is that particular evils like Sextus's sin, though freely committed, are not matters that can be easily reduced to isolated choices. Rather, human decisions tend to be bound up in intricate tangles of other, often larger and dearer choices, which are guided not so much by impartial reasons as by the things that make up one's sense of self.

The broader point of this moment in the myth, however, is that the limitations that a thick notion of personal identity can impose on an individual's moral choices have a parallel at the level of the universe as well. We might suppose, as detractors of the *Theodicy* often do, that there exists, among the possible universes that God could choose to create, a universe that is better than ours. We might then find ourselves blaming the negligence of a god who ought to have had both the omnipotence and omniscience to create a world with far less evil and suffering than that contained in the world to which we are condemned.[105] But if we were to also suppose that nothing in the idea of this superior universe mandates that we ourselves exist in it—would we then prefer this alternate universe to be the one that God creates over our own? What if this universe lacked not only our own existence, but all of the things and creatures of our world, so that we could not even begin to fathom what it means to have knowledge of that superior universe?

What the Petite Fable tells us is that there is an infinite number of such exercises in speculation, in which we might add or subtract any number of elements to or from the world we inhabit, but real knowledge of any one of these nonexistent universes is closed to us. And so long as that is the case, we might be hard pressed to find a point of reference, outside of our own world, by which to judge one of these universes as being less arbitrary than another. For those skeptics of the *Theodicy* who insist on the possibility of better universes than our own, the lessons of Sextus's choice then offer a partial rejoinder: given a choice between a wholly alien world and one mired in problems and concerns that are relevant to us, we, like Sextus, might be incapacitated to pick the former.

Pallas is careful to emphasize that the created world is the best of all possibilities because it is in fact superior to all other alternatives, not because its familiarity makes us partial to it. But the link that she draws in the myth between Sextus's rejection of Jupiter's offer, and his own rejection of the alternative universes containing more fortunate Sextuses, might be best understood as something of an epistemic qualifier to the doctrine of theodicy. It tells us that the story motivating the Petite Fable—that a divinity chose to create the best of all possible worlds—has as much to do with the rational bounds of God's creative power as with the limited imaginative horizons of the human condition. Though we may think in the abstract that there are aspects of reality we can do without, they are in fact, by however long a chain of relations, tied to the coherent identity of the world. And just as Sextus cannot bring himself to choose a universe containing a sinless but unrecognizable version of himself, there is a truth in insisting that the world that we prefer over all other possibilities is the only one we are in a position to recognize as our own. It is in this sense that Pallas concludes—referring to the alternative Sextuses in the alternative possible universes—that "if Jupiter had placed here a Sextus happy at Corinth or King in Thrace, it would be no longer this world."[106]

In turn, when philosophy commits itself to a deep narrative about the rationality of the created universe, this is a story that is being told from a human rather than a divine perspective, and it is we who are actively choosing our world. By pointing to the ways in which the very structure of meaning is conditioned by human particularity, the Petite Fable shows how the divine justice to which Leibniz surrenders our active reason is a truth that is necessary rather than absolute. Leibniz's philosophical myth, then, offers both an affirmation of the *Fatum Christianum* as well as an insight into the contingent needs that necessitate it. As such, the Petite Fable is to be read, not as a symptom of an uncritical mythic impulse, but instead as a diagnosis of its epistemic and, in turn, human, condition.

Leibniz had made a peculiar choice in closing the *Theodicy* with the Petite Fable: it was strange that such an expansive defense of reason would be rearticulated in such an elaborate myth; and that, too, was strange, because Leibniz was writing in a time when myths were being vilified as a primitive mode of thought and expression that posed a threat to the progress of philosophy. But if philosophy were to aspire to banish from its realm the form of uncritical passivity considered characteristic of the genre of myth, Leibniz tells us that this is an impossible dream. When one commits to preserving both the active nature of human rationality and its freedom to pursue all matters of knowledge, philosophy must necessarily make allowances for reason to assume a passive and uncritical role on any number of matters of inquiry, knowledge of which it is then forced to delegate to a superior, divine rationality. The Petite Fable can be read as a diagnostic expression of these concerns—a fable that distinguishes itself from ordinary myths by following in a Platonic tradition of philosophical myth-writing.

It would be nearly half a century after the publication of the *Theodicy*—three-quarters of a century after the appearance of the Great Comet that occasioned Bayle's first attacks on superstition—that the Great Lisbon Earthquake would shake the philosophical-theological world and put a definitive end to the reign of theodicy. In Voltaire's "Poem on the Lisbon Disaster" (1756), Bayle comes out as "the greatest master of the art of reasoning that ever wrote," whereas Leibniz is attacked as a dispenser of ridiculous lessons:

> From Leibnitz learn we not by what unseen
> Bonds, in this best of all imagined worlds,
> Endless disorder, chaos of distress,
> Must mix our little pleasures thus with pain;
> Nor why the guiltless suffer all this woe
> In common with the most abhorrent guilt.
> 'Tis mockery to tell me all is well.[107]

To point out that Voltaire's attack misses many things would be unhelpfully inadequate, but the real sting of the insult may have been his failure to acknowledge the sheer extent to which Leibniz struggled to rescue reason from blind faith in the determined order. The doctrine of theodicy was Leibniz's best effort to define the boundaries of philosophy in such a way that leaves it entirely free to reason about all matters without losing its way. The Petite Fable, in particular, articulated the central principles of his theodicy while also conveying the constraints, built into the project of philosophy, that necessitate it. The myth placed faith in human reason, but also forgave it for being fragile and finite against the infinity of the knowable universe and its possibilities, with its comets and its earthquakes, and the invisible forces that move the earth and stars.

PART TWO

MYTH AND MODERNITY

4

THE NEW MYTHOLOGY OF GERMAN IDEALISM

MYTH AS A SHARED VOCABULARY FOR RECONCILING
POLITICAL COMMUNITY AND INDIVIDUAL FREEDOM

THERE IS A STORY told about the origins of German Idealism. In the celebrated story, an obscure, "slightly discolored" manuscript of two pages is dug out of the archives by a young academic at work on his first book.[1] Then the young academic (none other than Franz Rosenzweig) declares that the author of the manuscript was not who everyone thought he was (none other than Hegel), and that finding its true author would mean locating the source of the radical ideas motivating the first known attempt to articulate a systematic account of the project of Idealism.[2] For Rosenzweig had recognized in these two pages the outline for a kind of manifesto for the German Idealist movement itself. He called it "The Oldest Systematic Program of German Idealism."

The fragmentary proposals comprising the *Oldest Systematic Program* (1796 / 1797) famously culminate in the call for a radical "new mythology" for the modern age that may unite humanity in universal freedom and equality.[3] The centrality of this idea in the document provides a window into a larger, collaborate project that involved a number of key figures in German Idealism. Over a short-lived period leading up to the turn of the century, a close-knit group of young intellectuals—including Friedrich Schelling, the literary critic Friedrich Schlegel and his brother, the poets Hölderlin and Novalis, among others—began writing both theoretical and literary works developing a program for a new mythology. This fruitful period of experimentation and collaboration, both literary and philosophical, was a watershed in German Idealism, where the various approaches that these disparate authors took to myth came together in an overlapping vision.[4]

Despite Rosenzweig's conviction that the foundations of German Idealism were contained in the *Oldest Systematic Program,* the appeal to mythology in the document's remarkable conclusion tends to get sidelined in most scholarship on German Idealism. Two temptations flank this vacuum of neglect in philosophy and political theory. The first is the temptation to regard the project for the new mythology as part of an apolitical, purely literary movement. The other, opposite temptation is to read the project instead as a philosophically bereft antecedent to the totalitarian politics of the Third Reich.

There are good reasons to be drawn to either camp. Writings on the new mythology were scattered and opaque, and their authors were often better known, both during and after their lifetimes, for their literary achievements. Their fierce devotion to aesthetic freedom often suggested a quietist and reclusive, if not altogether anarchic, outlook on politics. At the same time, their writings easily invite association with a unique German intellectual tradition of thinking about mythology in terms of national identity.[5] Herder's early injunction for a "new use of mythology" comes hand in hand with his famous invention of the *Volk;* and the thesis that mythology was the original repository of a people's creative genius found an enthusiastic reception amid a long and rich line of admirers.[6] As a symptom of the unique energy of a people, myth came to express a common national identity (as Carl Schmitt posited in his critique of fragmented democratic institutions), to be resuscitated for the modern stage under modern conditions (as Wagner endeavored in his operas)— or myth was the stuff of the lost Dionysian, whose unlikely rebirth might have brought unity and vitality to a barren culture (as Nietzsche lamented in his early writings).[7] And when the mythmakers of the Third

Reich paid a terrifying tribute to this legacy, the entire trajectory of German thought on mythology seemed uncomfortably suggestive of crude nationalism, not least of all the German Idealists' prophetic call for a new mythology for a new world order.[8]

But what many conventional takes on the new mythology fail to appreciate is that the project was both a philosophically profound and an explicitly political vision. The new mythology of German Idealism was certainly foundational to a specifically German discourse on mythology, as to a political tradition that placed special import on the unity and cohesion of society. And it was undeniably and unapologetically an aesthetic endeavor. But to consider the project for the new mythology alternately as an anti-philosophical political movement, or as an anti-political aesthetic movement, misses the depth and centrality of political questions to the German Idealists' writings on the new mythology, the coherence of their efforts to answer them, as well as their debt to a long-standing philosophical tradition.

In this chapter I argue that the new mythology of German Idealism was conceived as a solution to a novel problem in modern politics. The proponents of the new mythology identified a tension in modern political life that amounted to a choice between the cohesion of a community and the spiritual freedom of its individual members, which they in turn mapped onto a choice between an ethic founded on rationality and an ethic of poetry. Through the lens of their unique brand of Platonism, the German Idealists believed that the choice between rationality and poetry could be resolved in mythology. They viewed myth as a medium that could supply a community with a common aesthetic vocabulary linking together the creative activities of its members. Reinventing this medium for modernity, they proposed, would be a natural extension of the accomplishments of modern philosophy, as well as a radical new ground from which to reimagine the possibilities of political community. Modern politics, according to this comprehensive vision, need not sacrifice community or individualism to the other. But through a new mythology, it could enable free individuals in a coherent community to flourish together in pursuit of a higher epistemic ideal.

THE OLD MYTHOLOGY

The *Oldest Systematic Program:* Poetry and Rationality in the Modern Age

The call for the new mythology at the end of the *Oldest Systematic Program* is prefaced by an odd claim. The disputed author insists that he is the first to have thought of such a proposal: "I will speak of an idea here that, as far as I know, has still not occurred to anyone else. We must have a new mythology."[9] What exactly was so new about the new mythology? Mythology was hardly a new concept to post-Enlightenment Europe, nor was it particularly novel to take theoretical interest in the potential functions of myth.[10] But before the proposal for a specifically *new* mythology, mythology had been understood as a relic of the past, associated primarily with the ancient Greek mythological tradition.[11]

The period of German Idealism coincides with the peak of German Hellenism, or the onset of what has been coined in the popular imagination as "the tyranny of Greece over Germany."[12] Catapulted into fashion by the aesthetic writings of Johann Joachim Winckelmann in the mid-1700s, glimpses of ancient Greek culture, intimated through the remnants of their art, presented an idealized way of life for a German population that found itself increasingly restless in modernity.[13] The progress of science had brought about technological breakthroughs, industrialization, and rapid urbanization, but also estrangement from nature, displacement, and psychological fragmentation. Through eighteenth-century eyes, the Greeks had led an enviably idyllic existence. The serene poses and expressions of Greek sculpture, conveying the inner composure of their subjects, recalled the calmness of the sea.[14] The beauty of Greek art reflected the beauty of the Greek soul and the beautiful world in which it dwelled. There, life was emotionally coherent, at one with its natural environment, and unified by "noble simplicity and quiet greatness."[15] Mythology entered eighteenth-century discourse primarily in association with the mythic themes expressed in Greek art, and in the context of a more general admiration for antiquity.

The proponents of the new mythology in German Idealism were the immediate heirs to this Hellenism. Ancient Greece provided a foil for the inadequacies of modern existence, and stood in particular for a lost aesthetic disposition toward the world. If Greek art was particularly beautiful, it was because their art was in itself a way of life. The Greeks interacted with their environment through imagination and artistic creation, which accounted for the exceptional harmony of their products: each work of art was part and parcel of a coherent worldview. In this framework, poetry was imbued with a new significance among the arts. Eighteenth-century Hellenists had much to make of the Greek root of the word, *poiesis,* or the act of making or creating. Reality was something that was processed, rather than given, and the notion of poetry, in particular, was strongly associated with the capacity of humans to create and to shape their own world. A generation before the composition of the *Oldest Systematic Program,* for instance, Herder famously drew a connection between poetic language and a people's cognition of its environment, and with it, the formation of its unique way of thinking.[16] Herder's conviction that poetry was a purer form of language, drawn more directly from the original wellspring of creativity, echoed that of his teacher, Johann Georg Hamann, who spoke of poetry as the mother tongue of mankind.[17] In the eighteenth-century cultural landscape, poetry—that particular excellence of the Greeks—was not so much a genre as it was a mode of creativity. It was synonymous with the expression of the special relationship between an individual and his world, and as such, conveyed spiritual wholeness, spontaneity, and emotional immediacy.

The privileged status of poetry was received with enthusiasm by the proponents of the new mythology at the end of the century. The author of the *Oldest Systematic Program* singles out poetry as a medium that is to "become at the end what it was in the beginning—the teacher of humanity."[18] Poetry here is designated—echoing the accounts of Hamann and Herder—as a primeval way of forming knowledge on which humanity had depended from its very beginning. Restoring "a higher dignity" to poetry is imperative in the same way that future thought cannot fail to acknowledge the creative power of the individual subject.[19] It is in this vein that the *Oldest Systematic Program* lays claim to the articulation of "an ethics" of individual freedom: an ethics that begins with "the representation of *myself* as an absolute free being," from whose creative activity "a whole world comes forth from nothing—the only true and thinkable creation from nothing." If the world, and knowledge of that world, is to be constituted so as to "satisfy the creative spirit as ours is or should be," it is poetry that "alone will outlive all other sciences and arts."[20]

The *Oldest Systematic Program* provides a window into the extent to which, for those authors associated with the project for the new mythology, poetry had come to represent the purest expression of the subjective freedom of the individual. But poetry was, in addition, all that remained in the fringes of modernity of the original creative spirit of the ancients. The production of good poetry was important because the quality of a society's poetry said something about the health of its culture. But for all its importance and power, modern poetry was badly in need of resuscitation, and played too marginal a part in contemporary society to have any hand in its transformation. As the proponents of the new mythology saw it, modern society was governed by what they understood to be an all-pervasive culture of rationality. This meant that the triumph of reason in the Age of Enlightenment had made its mark on all aspects of modern existence, from the bureaucratization of social and political institutions, the division of labor and the ubiquity of machinery in the workplace, to the premium on rigor and specialization in intellectual life. In particular, the very concept of political society itself had become inseparable from the rule of rational laws, to the point of rendering any alternative political structure altogether unimaginable.

The dominance of rationality in the modern conception of political community, in particular, resulted in the stifling of that creative individual freedom that the proponents of the new mythology had come to associate with poetry. Their concern was not so much anti-rationalist, or even anti-modern, as it was a worry that modern political thinking had fallen into a rut that fell short of the promise of the Enlightenment. We might recall Kant's famous definition of Enlightenment as a process of emerging from immaturity, where this process of intellectual maturation has to do not so much with "lack of understanding" or the content of knowledge as with the courageous spirit by which the autonomous individual dares to reason for himself, without taking guidance from other people.[21] But in its manifestation in modern life, rationality also ended up confining the product of that individual reasoning to a homogenizing standard of objectivity: after the model of mathematics or scientific thinking, universal agreement on matters of knowledge was not only possible, but expected. In the *Oldest Systematic Program,* intellectual conformism lacking an aesthetic dimension is mocked as characteristic of "philosophers of the letter [*Buchstabenphilosophen*]" entirely dependent on "charts and indices."[22] Crucially, this spirit of conformism has a political counterpart in the modern, rationally organized state. The call for the new mythology in the *Oldest Systematic Program* comes at the heels of a damning diagnosis of the modern state, in which individuals have come to be treated "as if they were cogs in a machine." The natural corollary, the document suggests, of neglecting the creative freedom of the individual subject is "the whole miserable apparatus of state, constitution, government and legislation."[23] The state, it concludes, must be abolished.

The image of the legal and bureaucratic apparatuses of the state as a kind of impersonal machine might strike us as a familiar trope, and it might be tempting to write off the *Oldest Systematic Program*'s call for its abolition as the expression of a romantic longing for re-enchantment, or as an escapist fantasy of a simpler, premodern way of life.[24] But the *Program*'s injunction to "go beyond the state" has to be understood specifically as a claim about the desperate need for modern politics to overcome a very particular impasse generated by the respective spheres allocated to rationality and poetry in contemporary society and culture.[25] A rational conception of politics organized around the uniform application of laws supplied legal and bureaucratic tools to bring individuals together in a modern political community, but it did so at the cost of silencing their individuality. A celebratory idea of poetry, on the other hand, suggested a vision of ethics that gave primacy to the flourishing of individuals as free and creative subjects, but it was silent on the question of how diverse individuals might be organized into a coherent political community in the modern world. The conditions of modernity, it seemed, presented its politics with an unfortunate choice between two foundational values: poetry prioritized the individual, whereas rationality made possible, in the form of the state, a modern understanding of community—and emphasizing one implied sacrificing the other.

The stark opposition that the proponents of the new mythology drew between the rational guarantee of political community and the poetic guarantee of individual freedom, in turn, formed an important structuring framework through which they understood their common project. The *Oldest Systematic Program* begins with a radical condemnation of the rationally organized state, and ends with the call for a new mythology. The connection between the problem of the modern state and the solution of mythology is easy to miss in the two-page document, and the outlines of its logic are more clearly filled out when it is read in context, alongside the theoretical treatments of the new mythology that followed in the intervening years. The *Program*'s proposal for a new mythology, however, is explicitly motivated by the desire to challenge and to overcome a particular status quo in modern political thought. The author of the *Program* effectively imports mythology from its ancient context to answer a modern question, of whether and why a rationally organized political community seems to be incompatible with the freedom of the creative or poetic individual. A different way of formulating the question might be: given the choice that modernity presents between rational community and poetic individuality, is it possible to have a poetic community?

Schlegel's *Dialogue on Poesy:* Myth as the Midpoint of a Poetic Community

Three years after the dating of the *Oldest Systematic Program*, Friedrich Schlegel sketched out an answer to this very question in his *Dialogue on Poesy* (1799), a fictional dialogue in four parts, one of which is devoted to a discussion of a new mythology. In the "Speech on Mythology," the second section of the dialogue, mythology is introduced as a solution to a crisis in the state of modern poetry. The character Ludoviko, who delivers the speech, depicts the modern poet as an individual who works alone, creating each poem anew from scratch. His words might aim at something transcendent, but they ultimately speak to the darkness: they do not inspire what Ludoviko describes as the spirit of love that in turn inspires new creations from other potential poets. Consequently, in modern culture "the power of enthusiasm continue[s] to be splintered *even* in poesy" until it "finally fall[s] silent, alone, when it has fought it-self weary against the hostile element."[26]

The isolation of the individual modern poet constitutes a crisis because, according to Schlegel, this does not in fact reflect the true nature of poetry. The *Dialogue on Poesy* opens with a bold, axiomatic characterization of poetry as a medium that—like modern rationality—has the power to bond individuals to one another. "Poetry," the *Dialogue* begins, "befriends and bonds all those who love it with indissoluble ties."[27] But what is remarkable about the bond forged by poetry is not simply that it brings people together, but that it brings disparate people together. Reason, by contrast, "is unitary and the same in everyone; but just as each person has his own nature and his own love, so too does he carry his own poesy inside himself."[28] The unique power of poetry is its capacity to bond without regulating—a power that reason lacks. The love of poetry connects individuals without in any way compromising their individuality, such that every lover of poetry can and should expand "the expression of his own unique poesy" by coming into contact with the unique poetries of others.[29] Its propagation does not rely on the apparatuses of rationality—"reasonable speeches and teachings [*vernünftige Reden und Lehren*]," much less "punitive laws [*strafende Gesetze*]"—and in fact, "the deadening power of generalization" has a destructive effect on its very nature.[30]

Yet the poetic bond Schlegel deems "indissoluble" in the opening of the dialogue is insufficient for the establishment and maintenance of a functioning community in the modern age. There is something about the modern climate that is stunting the natural capacity of poetry to bond and to befriend, and Schlegel identifies the problem by looking to the model of the ancients. In "The Speech on Mythology," Ludoviko laments: "Our poetry lacks a midpoint [*Mittelpunkt*] as mythology was for the poetry of the ancients, and modern poetic art's inferiority to classical poetic art can be summarized in the words: we have no mythology."[31] If modern poetry alone could not sustain a poetic community, the solution lies in a new, modern mythology—and this is the thesis of Ludoviko's speech. The poetry of the ancients owes its exceptional virtue to their mythology, which is what Schlegel identifies as a "midpoint" for poetry. A new mythology for the modern age, on this diagnosis, can function as a corresponding midpoint for modern poetry; only then will the true, forgotten power of poetry shine through and revitalize modern society and culture.

When Schlegel refers to mythology as a midpoint for poetry, he means it, at one level, in a specific, literary sense: as a kind of shared canonical vocabulary of stories, characters, and motifs supplying the subject matter for the poetry of a coherent culture. Ancient poetry might have had such a midpoint to the extent that its poets sought to give life to the same set of inherited stories about Olympian gods and heroes, and Ludoviko goes so far as to characterize ancient poetry as "a single, indivisible, completed poem."[32]

But both mythology and its status as a midpoint hold a deeper significance for Schlegel. A common mythology might help the poets of an era write better and more coherent poetry, but only insofar as that poetry is the product of the community in which it thrives.[33] As the opening line of the dialogue reminds us, Schlegel's concern with poetry is first and foremost with its capacity to bring people together. In this sense, a midpoint for poetry is also a point of convergence for both individuals and their respective creative pursuits. A poet expands his own poetry, as well as the community formed around it, "if he has found the midpoint through communication with those who have also found it another way, from another direction."[34] What impressed Schlegel about the model of the ancients was that diverse poets not only drew their material from the mythological canon; they also contributed to it. For the ancient poets, mythology was not a dead inheritance but a dynamic medium, where individuals could build on what had come before to make their own contributions to this common cultural project. And if modern culture could be equipped with an equivalent new mythology, individual modern poets would no longer find themselves isolated from one another's work, creating each poem from first principles as though reinventing the wheel. Put another way, the *Dialogue on Poesy* presents a vision of modern society and culture in which the creative activities—or poetry—of free individuals might form the constitutive parts of the common endeavor that binds them together: their mythology.

Hence, Schlegel's claim that mythology supplies a midpoint for poetry amounts not merely to an aesthetic vision concerning the quality and coherence of the poetry generated by a community, but also a social and political vision about the creation of that community itself. By supplying a common core that orients and aligns together the diverse creative projects of individuals, a new mythology could recover those social bonds that he thinks are so natural to poetry: much like the way ancient mythology, "the fair band of community, which linked men and gods," had once found expression in joyous festivities of "poetry, song, dance and sociability."[35] Just as it is unnatural for the poet, "a sociable being," to be isolated from others, poetry is most fully itself when it expresses the individual but is not confined to the individual.[36] Its power to forge human relationships must be allowed to flourish, as it had in antiquity through mythology, or its intrinsic diversity will warp into the atomism that creative agents suffer in modern culture.

The model of ancient mythology, then, suggested for Schlegel the possibility of a genuinely poetic community for the modern era. Mythology, on this account, functions as a midpoint that holds together the poetry of an age and the community formed around it in ways that reason specifically does not. Whereas the laws of reason threaten to impose generalization and uniformity over the creative spirit, mythology unifies without compromising the diverse individuality of both poetry and its poets. In this way, Schlegel envisioned mythology, not only as a midpoint between the poetries of individuals, but also as an optimal point of convergence between the uniformity of reason and the diversity of poetry. Between "the sublation of the course and the laws of reasonably thinking reason" and "the beginning of all poesy"—he has Ludoviko tell us—falls the intermediate stage of "our transportation again into the beautiful confusion of fantasy, the original chaos of human nature for which I have yet to know a more beautiful symbol than the colorful swarm of the ancient gods."[37] Through the proposal of a new mythology, Schlegel sought to navigate the unification of the ideals of individual and community, of poetry and rationality, in what amounted to the vision of a diverse community of free individuals as had once existed in antiquity.

There is, perhaps, a further level at which the aesthetic and sociopolitical dimensions of Schlegel's vision come together. As we have seen, the proponents of the new mythology found themselves in a modern political society so thoroughly dominated by a culture of rationality that it had become impossible to imagine it any other way. Against such circumstances, however, Schlegel calls on the literary genre of myth to serve as a ground from which individuals can begin to imagine different possibilities for what politics and society can look like. Reasoned arguments are unsuited to this task, because they are somehow anchored to the same habits of thought that hold up the rationally organized state as the only conceivable form of modern political community. Schlegel's account of the new mythology, in other words, looks to the mythic genre as a means of breaking out of the established frameworks structuring the modern political imagination.

BREAKING THE ANCIENT MOLD

The Impossibility of Return

If the content and goals of mythology were understood after an ancient model, it remains unclear as to what a new mythology would entail, or how those seeking to resurrect it in modern culture were to situate their project in relation to the more impressive past. Certainly this was a popular dilemma of the mid- and late eighteenth century. Winckelmann's singular esteem for the Greek aesthetic standard had led him to hold up the entirety of Greek culture as a paradigm for imitation. The application of Winckelmann's views to mythological discourse translated into a bizarre conundrum, best articulated in a parenthetical remark by Christian Adolf Klotz in his *Epistolae Homericae* (1764): "To what extent can we, and must we, imitate mythology?" The question was picked up by Herder, who made it the central subject of an early essay, "On the Modern Use of Mythology" (1767), which called for "a new use of mythology."[38] Herder's answer was one of muted enthusiasm. Mythology in its extant form—that is, ancient Greek mythology—was to be an object of study, not for the sake of blind imitation but to harness a certain creative spirit for modernity so that "we may become inventors ourselves."[39] That was the suitable new use of mythology.

Three decades later, a commitment to spontaneity and originality bound the champions of the new mythology to a similar position on the inadequacy of merely imitating ancient mythology in modern times. If their aim was to revive the vitality of the ancient imagination, blindly copying a cultural product rather than its source would have defeated the purpose entirely. An alternate, more tangible solution might have been the importation of themes and motifs from ancient mythology into modern literature: this was an approach to mythology best exemplified in the work of Goethe and Schiller, who generously incorporated elements borrowed from classical mythology into their own poetry. Both were devoted Hellenists who wrote extensively in their philosophical writings about the need to appreciate and revive a more naive, spontaneous, and immediate way of interacting with one's environment, in particular with nature, after the manner of the Greeks.[40] Rather than treat the tropes of classical mythology as mere ornaments to their art, they turned to these motifs as a way of lending expression to a forgotten mode of being in the world.

Yet there is something anemic about an account of a modern mythology consisting only in the appropriation of elements taken from ancient mythology. The incompleteness of such a project is painstakingly self-diagnosed in *Hyperion,* Hölderin's only novel, which was published in two parts in 1797–1799 and was one of the most famous specimens of Hellenism produced in the period of German Idealism. A poet once described as having "clung to Hellenism with all his unbalanced soul," Hölderlin liberally saturated his novel with Greek mythological allusions, divinities, and sacred places.[41] But the eighteenth-century Greek setting of the novel is also riddled with an intense, paralyzing nostalgia: the gods that had once roamed the land have now fled. Hyperion's deep admiration for the splendid past is accompanied by a desire to be free of it. At one point he demands that the unity of the Greek world must be recreated in our own age; at others he believes that the ruins of the past must be destroyed completely before a new world order can be established.[42]

The death of Diotima—Hyperion's love interest, named after the character in Plato's *Symposium*—represents the death of the possibilities of ancient Greek ideals and the unity of man, society, and nature that

Hölderlin and his friends had yearned to rediscover in classical mythology. The epistolary novel dramatizes the impasse by having the
letter on Diotima's death be immediately followed by the letter that
suddenly takes Hyperion away from Greece to Germany.[43] Hence, when
Hyperion mourns his beloved, he also laments the condition of restless-
ness in which he now finds himself in modern Germany, where he
"would be a stranger on earth, and no god would link [him] to the past
anymore.[44] Hyperion is especially fixated on the assurance that Diotima died a "beautiful death."[45] In the wake of the premature death of
an ancient ideal, those left behind in modernity simply have it harder:
"To ward off flies, that is our work in the future; and to gnaw at the
things of the world as children gnaw at the dried iris root, that is our joy
in the end. To grow old among youthful people seems to me a pleasure,
but to grow old where all is old seems to me worse than all else."[46] In
having arrived too late to the scene of history, modern people have been
deprived of the chance to die the beautiful deaths of ancient lore; they
are instead forced to cope with their own inheritance.

To the extent that the vision for the new mythology was a project of
rescuing an idealized way of being from the ruins of the past, its central
theorists were especially attuned to the conundrum at the center of
Hölderin's diagnosis. In order for the new mythology to be a vehicle for
the ideals they associated with the medium, it first had to find a way to
break free of the authoritative grip of past examples. Against the recom-
mendations that accompanied Winckelmann's reverence for antiquity,
then, the theorists of the new mythology agreed, not only that it was
insufficient to imitate the old mythology of the Greeks, but that Greek
mythology could not be simply imported into modernity to serve the
purpose it had in antiquity. This left the proponents of the new mythology in a bind: they wanted an ancient Greek mythology that was
neither ancient nor Greek; a modern mythology that did for their world
what the medium had done for the ancients.

"Why should it not become again as it once was? Obviously, in a different way," goes the lesson that Schlegel immediately draws from the
virtues of ancient mythology. "And why not in a more beautiful, greater
way?"[47] Crucial to the working conception of the new mythology was a
justification of its relevance for modern times: it had to escape regress

into parroting a bygone mythology, and speak instead to the present age. In addition, then, to the promise of lending unity to the diversity of individuals and of their creative pursuits, the new mythology also had to provide a sense of unity with history and one's own time. Thus entailed in this vision was not just the poetic bond that might unify a community of diverse individuals, but also a way of anchoring that community in a harmonious relationship with their modern era. This meant that the German Idealists' thoughts on the new mythology were tied up in the more abstract territory of their philosophical systems at large, especially their philosophy of history.

The Imminent Path to a Modern Mythology

In the *Dialogue on Poesy,* Schlegel prophesies through his mouthpiece, Ludoviko, his conviction that the new mythology was just around the horizon.[48] Modernity was "close to attaining" the mythology that was lacking in the current culture—"or rather," Ludoviko second-guesses, "it is time that we try earnestly to take part in producing one."[49] The difference between the attainment of a mythology and the earnest production of one is a crucial distinction that sets apart the new mythology from its ancient predecessor. Schlegel believes the new mythology "will approach us from an entirely different direction than the old one."[50] There is a sense in Schlegel's characterization of the "old" mythology that it was not so much created as stumbled upon. The Greeks had an effortlessly natural relationship with their mythology, a product of "the first blossom of youthful fantasy immediately joined and accreted to the nearest and most animated part of the sensual world." The new mythology, by contrast, is to be an active creation, "the most artificial of all artworks," and "formed from the deepest depth of the spirit." In order to "be a new bed and vessel for the ancient, eternal well-spring of poesy," it must consciously tap into the unconscious wellspring of creativity.[51]

That Schlegel imagined a conscious endeavor to harness the unconscious in the artificial production of a new mythology reflects the general optimism of German Idealism about the progress of knowledge in the post-Kantian landscape. This meant that, their admiration for the Greek way of life notwithstanding, they forecasted continual progress in the future of humanity. The triumph of Idealism in the wake of Kant, in particular, consisted of a long-awaited convergence of philosophy and modern science, in which the autonomy of the thinking subject could be reconciled with the causal necessity underpinning our experience of reality. The theorists of the new mythology celebrated this starting point. The *Dialogue on Poesy* identifies Idealism as "the great phenomenon of the age" and singles out physics as an example of a science in which "idealism itself actually already erupted before physics was touched by the magic wand of philosophy."[52]

But the proponents of the new mythology also shared the broader assumption underpinning the German Idealist movement that the Kantian system was incomplete, and that its inheritors must take it upon themselves to expand it as they saw necessary. If Kant had made coherent the world of the conscious, thinking subject, it remained to extend this coherence beyond the limits of conscious thinking: to a natural world with its own independent reality (and not merely an object of contemplation), to a unified vision of humanity and its trajectory (and not merely an aggregation of discrete individual units and their actions), and above all, to aesthetic experiences.[53] In store in the immediate future of philosophy was the completion of the system Kant had only begun to build. Hence, Schlegel's claim to the imminence of the new mythology was grounded in the idea that the new mythology was a natural consequence of Idealism.[54]

It is important to emphasize that, for all the criticism that its central theorists levied against the culture of rationality dominating modern politics, the new mythology was never an anti-rationalist project. Instead, as Schlegel's vision suggests, it was conceived as an extension of the accomplishments of modern philosophy. Unlike the old mythology, whose magnificence had never been intended by its unwitting creators, the new mythology was to be the active creation of conscious, thinking minds stepping beyond their own limits. If the new mythology were to be informed by the spirit of its own age, it could not undo the progress of philosophy by trying to recreate the unique path that the Greeks took to arrive at their mythology. Schlegel looks less to the ancients than he does to modern philosophy and the birth of Idealism for a model of how a new mythology might come about. And by incorporating the achievements of modern philosophy and science, the new mythology will be arrived at through Idealism, and in doing so will surpass the old mythology by virtue of its modernity.[55] In "such an age of rejuvenation," Schlegel proposes, the new mythology will connect humanity to both the past and the future: "Gray antiquity will come back to life, and the most distant future of human culture will make itself known by means of omens."[56]

Mythology and Schelling's Philosophy of History

The historical particularity of mythology is most pronounced in the thought of F. W. J. Schelling, who was not only a "philosophical Proteus" whose philosophy spanned the breadth of German Idealism, but also a protean figure in the overlapping social webs of the Idealist movement scattered across late eighteenth- and early nineteenth-century Germany.[57] As a precocious teenager, he roomed with Hölderlin and Hegel at the Tübingen seminary; the disputed authorship of the *Oldest Systematic Program* is alternately attributed to one of these three roommates.[58] He soon found his way into the social circles of the Schlegel brothers in Jena, befriending, in particular, the wife of Friedrich Schlegel's brother, August Wilhelm—Caroline Schlegel—whom Schelling himself married later. At least according to one interpretation, the characters of the *Dialogue on Poesy* are thinly veiled avatars for the core members of the so-called Jena Romantics, with Caroline and Dorothea Schlegel represented in the two female roles, Amalia and Camilla, and Ludoviko from the "Speech on Mythology" standing in for Schelling.[59]

Many of the views that Schlegel attributes to Ludoviko do gesture toward the philosophy articulated in Schelling's *System of Transcendental Idealism* (1800), published within a year of the publication of the *Dialogue on Poesy*, and four years after the dating of the *Oldest Systematic Program*. Both Ludoviko's and Schelling's conceptions of the new mythology are based on an admiration for the unity that the example of ancient mythology lent to Greek society and culture, accompanied by the conviction that the way to arrive at the new mythology is through a distinctly modern, and pointedly philosophical, route in Idealism. Schelling found Greek mythology particularly impressive for both "the harmony whereby everything is united into one great whole" and the lack of "any comprehensive intentionality" in its creation.[60] Even in modernity, he felt, it was important to make a concerted, active effort to capture some of this quality, because the unintended or unconscious is what comprises the "*poetry* in art," which alone can take its audience beyond the limits of the artist's conscious intentions and the rules and skills by which he executes them. The apparatuses of consciousness can be taught and learned, whereas poetry is a "free gift of nature."[61]

Schelling believed, then, that the activity of the conscious mind alone is not the realm of innovation, and knowledge that does not eventually break out of its own system risks stagnation.[62] One could say that, in his idiosyncratic way, he was concerned about the fragmentation of knowledge in the modern sciences, and he saw in the medium of mythology a path to opening up knowledge to the qualities that he associated with poetry. In Schelling's system, the emergence of what is consciously known from what is unconsciously discovered forms a broad arc spanning the history of philosophy. On this account, human knowledge begins in poetry, where, like a vast ocean, it was once a unified, unconscious whole. History has brought aspects of this knowledge into human consciousness by breaking it up, like so many rivulets, into the bounded disciplines of science. But the progress of knowledge, for Schelling, will entail recovering its original unity, and making it whole again:

> Philosophy was born and nourished by poetry in the infancy of knowledge, and with it all those sciences it has guided toward perfection. We may thus expect them, on completion, to flow back like so many individual streams into the universal ocean of poetry from which they took their source. Nor is it in general difficult to say what the medium for this return of science to poetry will be; for in mythology such a medium [*Mittelglied*] existed.[63]

Here Schelling presents poetry and the sciences as two states of human knowledge on opposite poles of its history, and mythology as an intermediary stage between them. Poetry stands in for both an original, oceanic source of knowledge, as well as a final state of knowing in which all of humanity will find itself. Mythology is the medium through which human knowledge passes from poetry to science and back.

Where Schlegel describes mythology as a "midpoint [*Mittelpunkt*]," Schelling, then, also conceives of it as a kind of middle point between poetry and scientific rationality, and he sees the new mythology in particular as a way to future poetry and a higher epoch in the history of knowledge. It may be a forbiddingly abstract vision, but it is guided by a basic insight: that human knowledge takes different forms as it evolves—whether it's poetry or science—and the form that knowledge takes will inevitably help determine the content that gets captured in it. In a modern age of scientific knowledge, a new mythology that extends the achievements of philosophy, and pushes forward the progress of knowledge, becomes a medium through which humans can gain access to certain forms of deep, unconscious knowledge that are not yet available to the toolkits of conscious reason.

Both the focus and scale of Schelling's ambition for a new mythology are, of course, different from Schlegel's. Unlike the account presented in the *Dialogue on Poesy*, Schelling's call for a new mythology is far less interested in the communities localized around individual poets as it is in a temporally conceived stage of culture characterized by poetry. As such, the poetic community that Schlegel's mythology concerns expands, in Schelling's conception, to the level of humanity. In turn, the collective aim of that community also shifts, from drawing together the preexisting creativity of poetic individuals so that their projects could build on each other, to delivering them all to a state of higher knowledge and a new historical epoch. Whereas Schlegel had articulated both an aesthetic and a sociopolitical vision for his proposal for a new mythology, Schelling draws out the historic and epistemic dimensions of their shared project.

These are different points of emphases, but they come together in a remarkably comprehensive program. Just as the main ambition behind Schlegel's new mythology isn't just about the production of better, more coherent poetry, Schelling's concern also isn't just about the creation of a community that preserves the individuality of its members. On top of being both of these things, their combined vision demands that this is a community of free, poetic individuals striving for higher knowledge together. Like the new mythology described in the *Oldest Systematic*

Program, Schlegel's and Schelling's proposals are framed explicitly in terms of a reconciliation of the values represented by poetry and by rationality. Conceived, at one level, as a common cultural bond for a poetic community, and at another level, as a more holistic mode of knowledge occupied by that community, the new mythology is tasked to take the accomplishments of rationality in modern society and extend them toward a poetic ideal: whether by combining the coherence of a rationally organized community with the spiritual freedom that poetry offers to individuals, or by stretching the resources of conscious, scientific reason past its own limitations toward its eventual, poetic destination.

Crucially, the conception of the new mythology as a resource mediating between rationality and poetry is not a compromise between the two modes but an addition to each. Mythology entailed an expanded conception of both poetry and reason. As Schlegel suggests in the *Dialogue on Poesy,* poetry could become more genuinely poetic through mythology—if it expressed the individual but also went beyond the individual by embracing its natural capacity to bind people to each other. Likewise the proponents of the new mythology believed that knowledge itself, conventionally the province of a certain kind of conscious and active rationality, would always prove inadequate in their modern era unless it were to be enhanced by mythology. Of course, the faith that mythology had the unique capacity to broker such a marriage between poetry and rationality is premised on the assumption that mythology entailed a way of thinking that was compatible with both. This particular conception of the nature and capacity of mythology, in turn, is anchored in German Idealism's idiosyncratic debt to Platonism.

PLATO AND THE MYTHOLOGY OF REASON

The call for the new mythology articulated in the *Oldest Systematic Program* is specifically for a "mythology of reason."[64] Admittedly by 1796, the earliest dating of the document, the oxymoronic effect of demanding a new mythology of reason had already been somewhat diluted: a generation ago, Winckelmann had espoused an allegorical theory of myth, which broke myths down into component parts corresponding to familiar moral lessons that were subject to rational analysis. More contemporaneously, Goethe and Schiller were also speaking of myth as a form of rational discourse, in particular as a vehicle for the expression of philosophical ideas.[65] But for the author of the *Oldest Systematic Program,* there was a much more specific sense in which the new mythology had to be rational. According to the document, mythology is capable of being "of reason," so long as it is a mythology "in the service of the ideas."[66] Those ideas, in turn, come together to form a comprehensive system of ethics, whose coherence depends on "the idea that unites all others, the idea of beauty, taking the word in a higher Platonic sense."[67]

The possibility of a mythology of reason in the service of the ideas, then, requires that the ideas served by mythology are understood through a Platonic lens. In the metaphysical system suggested in the *Oldest Systematic Program,* in particular, all ideas are subordinate to one highest Idea of Beauty. This calls for a radical expansion of the traditional scope of reason: if reason is to have access to that highest, overarching idea uniting all others, it must also have the capacity to grasp and to process beauty. It is in this sense that the *Program* insists that "the highest act of reason is an aesthetic act since it comprises all ideas."[68] The aesthetic transformation of reason, through which the philosopher comes to "possess just as much aesthetic power as the poet," is the necessary counterpart to the *Program*'s demand for a rationalization of aesthetics in a mythology of reason.[69]

It was the first major appeal to Plato in German Idealism.[70] In the wake of Winckelmann and the *Graecomania* he had stirred in Germany, classical studies were rapidly on the rise. Late eighteenth-century German intellectuals had inherited the foundations for a largely biblical tradition of systematic and rigorous scholarship, the lessons of which could be easily applied to Greek material.[71] As demand increased for well-edited and accurate texts in the original Greek, several important editions of Plato's works came to be published at this time.[72] Notable among them were widely popular Greek editions of select dialogues, carefully edited and released between 1758 and 1779 by Johann Friedrich Fischer, a philologist and a former roommate of Gotthold Ephraim Lessing at Leipzig; as well as a twelve-volume *Complete Works* by the Bipont Society (1781–1787) as part of a fifty-volume collection of Greek

and Latin classics—the first publication of the entire corpus in the somewhat more portable and easily affordable octavo form.[73]

For the devoted Hellenists among the German Idealists, this meant
that for the first time, they had direct and easy access to Plato's texts,
rather than paraphrase or commentary that had been filtered through
Neoplatonist and Christian traditions.[74] Schelling and Hölderlin were
both avid readers of Plato in the original Greek during their university
studies at the Tübinger Stift. Between 1793 and 1794 Hölderlin abandoned
himself to a literary diet consisting mainly of "Kant and the Greeks,"
among whom Plato figured prominently, while Schelling embarked upon
a deep study of the Platonic dialogues, producing in particular some
short reflections based loosely on the *Ion* (1792) and an extended commentary on the *Timaeus* (1794), both preserved in his notebooks.[75]
Around the same time, Friedrich Schlegel devoted himself to the study
of Greek, having gone through the complete works of Plato in the original Greek by 1788.[76] By 1799 he had determined the need for a German
translation of Plato's complete works and had begun corresponding with
Friedrich Schleiermacher about the project—an endeavor that would
eventually result in German Idealism's most celebrated contribution to
the reception of Plato.[77]

A Rational Platonism of Ideas and a Poetic Platonism of Enthusiasm: Mendelssohn's *Phaedo* and Wolf's *Symposium*

Schleiermacher's translation of Plato's works (1804–1828)—a masterpiece
that would remain the authoritative German translation for decades to
come—must be understood as the culmination of a Platonic renaissance
that gripped Germany in the last decades of the eighteenth century.
Among the new editions and translations of Plato's works that paved the
way for Schleiermacher's magnum opus, two might be worth mentioning
as a way of bringing into relief the major channels of Platonism that
helped form the intellectual background to the aspirations of German
Idealism.

The first is a loose translation of the *Phaedo* by Moses Mendelssohn,
though perhaps the work might be more accurately described as an ad-

aptation.[78] Mendelssohn explicitly intended to write *Phaedo, or on the Immortality of the Soul* (1767)—in the words of his English translator—"in imitation of the Phaedon of Plato" so as to recast Socrates "as a philosopher of the eighteenth century."[79] The work reconstructs the *Phaedo's* arguments for the immortality of the soul, freely blending in Mendelssohn's own proofs, at times to the point of total departure from Plato's text.[80] In a telling moment, Mendelssohn excises from his adaptation the long eschatological myth at the end of the *Phaedo:* his Socrates goes through the motions of acknowledging some of the common tropes in Greek mythology for describing the experiences of the soul in the afterlife, but he ultimately sets them aside as matters of which he has no knowledge, and which "our poets and tellers of fables [*Fabellehrer*]" may know better.[81]

An instant success, the work was received warmly by Kant, who shared Mendelssohn's interest in the *Phaedo,* though not the ability to read it in Greek. Two of the major features of the *Phaedo* must have made an impression on Kant: an argument for the rejection of the senses and a sustained theory of Forms. Although Kant took issue with Plato for "abandon[ing] the world of the senses" and "dar[ing] to go beyond it on the wings of the ideas, in the empty space of pure understanding," he remained thoroughly impressed by Plato's invention of the concept of the Idea as an object of human reason.[82]

What Kant's take on Plato left for those German Idealists who called for a new mythology in the service of a Platonic Idea was a stake in Ideas themselves. "Platonis philosophia genuinus est Idealismus," Schlegel once avowed—*Plato's philosophy is genuine Idealism.*[83] Ideas transcend the bounds of all experience, but are nonetheless real to the human mind, and can be accessed only through reason. Thus for Kant's heirs, paying homage to Plato's Ideas meant contributing to what was for the most part a rational legacy. Just as Mendelssohn found it appropriate to update Socrates's arguments in the *Phaedo* to "offer those arguments which a man like Socrates, who were desirous of founding his belief upon found reason, would find, at the present day," Kant felt he understood Plato's Ideas better than Plato himself did, "since he may not have determined his concept sufficiently and hence sometimes spoke, or even thought, contrary to his own intention."[84] This reception of the *Phaedo* and the theory of Forms reveals that Plato stood for a continuous tradition of knowledge so thoroughly rational that it was a project to be improved upon by any rational agent in a position to reason better.

While Mendelssohn's translation of the *Phaedo* provides a window into the eighteenth-century incarnation of a Platonic legacy centered on the Ideas and their intelligibility to reason, the concerns of a countervailing rival tradition is perhaps best captured in an edition of the *Symposium* by Friedrich August Wolf, the father of modern philology.[85] Wolf's *Symposium* (1782) marked a milestone in the history of a different, vaguely Neoplatonic strand of Platonism that emphasized Plato's thoughts on love and beauty—the topics treated in the *Symposium*—and the poetic mind inspired by such things. Whereas Mendelssohn's interest in the *Phaedo* was obviously motivated more by his own philosophical agenda than in any desire to preserve the original text, Wolf's edition of the *Symposium* was a work of careful philological scholarship, with a Greek text and extensive annotations in German, as well as a lengthy introduction. The work jump-started his career as a philologist before he moved on to his studies of Homer, for which he is better remembered today. Noting the "florid style" of the *Symposium,* Wolf's intent was to pay as much attention to the language of Plato's text as might be due, "for example, to the Latin poet Virgil."[86]

Treating Plato as one would a poet would not have been an alien concept to a tradition of Platonism stemming from the Cambridge School—for whom the special status conferred on the *Symposium* in Renaissance Neoplatonism was a vital influence—and preserved in Shaftesbury's writings on enthusiasm.[87] According to this tradition, eagerly embraced by the champions of the new mythology, enthusiasm was associated with divine inspiration that possessed the individual poet.[88] Wolf describes the dialogues as "sacrifice[s]" that Plato offered to his "philosophical Muse."[89] In contrast to Mendelssohn's and Kant's rational disregard for both the language of Plato's text as well as those ideas deemed outdated in light of modern advances in knowledge, a Platonism of enthusiasm emphasized the poetics of Plato's prose style as well as the individuality of the person of Plato himself as someone who was uniquely inspired by a divine source.

The Platonism of the New Mythology

One of the theoretical achievements of the proponents of the new mythology in German Idealism was combining the two threads of Platonism that they had inherited. A rational tradition based on Plato's Ideas and a poetic tradition of Platonic enthusiasm came together in a conception of mythology that stressed its capacity to lend expression to higher ideas and truths about the nature of the cosmos, as well as the limits of conscious reason to do the same.

The program for the new mythology was first and foremost grounded in a metaphysical system unified by a higher, Platonic idea of beauty. Its proponents believed in the coherence and unity of reality as experienced by the freely thinking subject. In a Platonic vein, they subscribed to the possibility that a single absolute, highest Idea might provide this unity holding together the diversity of the world. A mythology of reason had to express something of this highest Idea. Schelling defines the "character of the true Mythology" as "that which is of the universal, of the infinite," just as Schlegel assigned to the new mythology the task of expressing "something originary and inimitable, which is absolutely indissoluble, which after all transformation still allows the old nature and power to shine through."[90] This means that the unity with which the new mythology promises to hold together diverse individuals is now put to a stricter standard: that unity cannot be a provisional juxtaposition of nonclashing parts, but a coherent system derived from some conception of a higher unifying idea. This was the goal of the new mythology, and as such, mythology itself could not exist without the ideal of the highest.

At the same time, a new mythology was necessary precisely because conscious reason alone was inadequate to the task of accessing this highest ideal. In this way the proponents of the new mythology were sympathetic to the epistemological commitments of a poetic tradition of Platonism, in that they looked to the revelations of the inspired poet as a source of truths that could not be grasped through rational activity. Schelling, for instance, emphasizes in his interpretation of Plato that "in general in the entire investigation of the Platonic theory of ideas, one must keep it always in mind that Plato speaks of them always as ideas of a divine understanding." That is, Plato was a thoroughly "divine" figure, after the enthusiastic tradition of Platonism in which the poet was inspired, as though by a divinity, of his privileged insight. That divine connection to the ideas was "possible in human understanding only through an intellectual communion of man with the origin of all beings."[91] For Schelling, the reach of conscious thought could by no means exhaust the scope of human knowledge. If he had conceived of the new mythology as a medium leading humanity back to a poetic state of knowledge, his image of an original ocean of poetry reemerges in these remarks as a kind of "feeling, longing, the glorious mother of knowledge," whose movement is to be compared to "an undulating, surging sea, similar to Plato's matter."[92] Schelling's point is that aesthetic sensibilities make us intuitively aware of ideas that could not yet be articulated in the language of reason. Imagination, emotion, and the sensory faculties not only provide valuable ways of knowing, but the intuitions they might awaken in us are far more immediate than the things we might think up in the abstract.

It is into these rich resources of cognition that mythology taps. Like Schelling, who characterizes mythology as "sensualized truth" or "sensuous philosophy," Schlegel subscribes to the potential of what he calls the "naïve profundity" of mythology.[93] Mythology presents for Schlegel "one great advantage"—namely, "what otherwise eternally flees consciousness can be seen here sensually-spiritually and held fast, as is the soul in its surrounding body through which it shines in our eye and speaks to our ear."[94] The language of mythology appeals to our sensual and spiritual faculties, which greatly expands the modes in which we receive ideas beyond the boundaries of what can be known through conscious reasoning. Just as knowledge of the soul is possible through the material in which it is embodied, otherwise inaccessible ideas can speak through sensual images. The highest idea, in particular, lies beyond the reach of the conscious mind, such that any hope of access to it is gained only with the recruitment of a sensual-spiritual faculty to augment rational knowledge.[95] Schlegel identifies these alternative paths to knowledge as "actually the point" of mythology: "because of the highest, we do not depend so entirely on our mind alone."[96]

The Platonism of the new mythology, then, consists of a desire to attain a new understanding of the world through the medium of mythology, which could navigate both the appeal of a rational worldview organized around a coherent system of ideas, as well as the poetic longing to transcend what can be known through rational thought. What it emphasized was the possibility of progress toward an ideal by means of gradual and asymptotic approximation. The new mythology promised to lend unity to modern poetry precisely because it would contain in it the highest unifying Idea of beauty. But it would also preserve the diversity inherent to poetry—which comes through in the aggregate approximations of that ideal, through spontaneous, idiosyncratic experimentation on the parts of individual poets. The proponents of the new mythology believed that the modern separation of rationality and poetry could be remedied because their unique Platonism had done just that: their conception of the new mythology took its structure from an interpretation of Plato's philosophy that emphasized the rationality of Ideas as much as the poetic transcendence necessary for accessing them.

Lessons from Plato's Myths

The choice of mythology as the special medium for the convergence of rationality and poetry makes greater sense when we consider how the proponents of the new mythology read Plato's own myths. Much like the giants of Renaissance Neoplatonism, and the later tradition of Platonic enthusiasm they had inspired, proponents of the new mythology were keenly aware of the literary virtues of Plato's writings. Their studied appreciation of the form in which Plato chose to express his ideas remains one of the most significant and lasting contributions to Platonic scholarship from the period associated with German Idealism. Plato's myths struck theorists of the new mythology as entirely consistent with their interpretation of his philosophy at large: the myths were stylistically integrated into what they took to be a thoroughly poetic philosophy; they helped communicate sensual insights beyond the scope of what might be articulated in the language of conscious reason; and above all, they conveyed a commitment to the highest, unifying Idea of beauty.

As we have seen, it was partly Plato's use of myth that had helped to delegitimize his philosophy during the early years of the Enlightenment, when its central figures were eager to shake off the imprecision of poetic language in philosophical discourse and scientific thought. More than a century later, admirers of Plato would still feel the need to defend his myths from their Enlightenment critics. In the celebrated introduction to his translations of Plato, Schleiermacher goes to great pains to show that the myths do not take away from the logical arguments of Plato's philosophy. He insists that the myths in Plato's dialogues serve to reinforce what is argued in the other mode. What "is anticipated mythically," he observes, "more often than not appears later in its scientific form."[97]

Schleiermacher's remark does not quite do justice to his pivotal role in the establishment of Plato as a "philosophical artist," or the efforts taken in his introduction to emphasize the overall coherence of Plato's oeuvre, both within and across individual dialogues, so that together they formed an organic unity, like a living body.[98] Or, it is perhaps all the more astonishing that an author in such a singularly authoritative position to speak about Plato's poetic style would still have to validate his myths by the metric of his "scientific" arguments.[99] As Schleiermacher's comment reveals, mythical elements in philosophical writing would have been read at the time as at best a supplement—if a potentially redundant one—to the language of reason. Such myths might have had either ornamental or allegorical functions: as more pleasant modes of ingesting perfectly rational ideas, or stories capable of being broken down rationally into intelligible units of thought.

By contrast, a decade before Schleiermacher's introduction, the proponents of the new mythology resisted the contemporary pressure to isolate and explain Plato's myths rationally. Schlegel, a onetime (and ultimately unreliable) collaborator on Schleiermacher's translations, lauded Plato's "already thoroughly poetic form" in which "representation and its perfection and beauty are not means, but rather an end in themselves," and featured the Platonic dialogues in an earlier essay on Greek poetry because he couldn't quite decide if they were "poetical philosophemes or philosophical poems."[100] Schelling casually referred to Plato as "the poetic philosopher."[101] Both authors wrote philosophical dialogues after Plato's example: the *Dialogue on Poesy*, which consists of a sequence of speeches on a common theme, with the interludes between speeches filled with dialogue, is self-consciously modeled after the *Symposium,* whereas Schelling's *Bruno* (1802) and the posthumously published *Clara* (1861) are also written in the dialogue form.[102] Against the background of their admiration for Plato's writing, Plato's myths were not a stylistic aberration from the rest of his work. Rather, Schlegel and Schelling seemed eager to downplay the contrast between Plato's myths and the arguments in which they are ensconced—where their distinctiveness was precisely what allowed them to be discrete objects of imitation for More, Bacon, or Leibniz in their respective reimaginings of the *Republic*.[103] Instead, select Platonic myths get an unusually literal reading at the hands of both Schlegel and Schelling. The greater part of *On Diotima* (1795), Schlegel's essay on the central figure from the *Symposium* who delivers the myth on the origin and nature of Love, is devoted to speculation on the person of Diotima on the assumption that she was a historical figure; Schelling's commentary on the *Timaeus* from his student days at the Tübinger Stift treats the "likely myth [εἰκὼς μῦθος]" of the *Timaeus* no differently from the dense ontological discussions of the *Philebus*.[104] For both authors, Plato's myths were simply an extension both of Plato's poetry and of his philosophy, the boundaries of which ought to be similarly collapsed in future knowledge.

What stands out in Schlegel's and Schelling's respective treatments of Plato, however, is the consistency with which they applied to Plato's myths their understanding of the structure of the new mythology. The highest form of mythology was to contain the highest idea, which, though perfectly rational, could not be articulated rationally. Plato's myths were not exempt from the representative function they attributed to mythology, and as such, they were thought to correspond to specific ideas contained in them. The significance of Diotima for Schlegel, for instance, is in her capacity to personify the higher ideals of beauty and wisdom in one coherent and tangible figure who is somehow greater than the sum of her parts.[105] For all the effort Schlegel exerts into joining in on the "antiquarian trifle" of historical speculation on Diotima's person, *On Diotima* builds up to the conclusion that the importance of Diotima hinges on her status as a representative figure, rather than a historical one.[106] Plato's mythic achievement in having created her is in having "immortalized a woman" who "simultaneously satisfied both his tender feeling and the high ideas of reason."[107] She is, as he reiterates elsewhere, "a necessary idea for Socratic philosophy."[108] Similarly, what one commentator calls Schelling's "cosmological use of myth" consists in reading the creation myth of the *Timaeus* as perfectly aligned with Plato's vision of an ordered and coherent cosmos, and as an expression of "the *Idea* of the world."[109]

Schlegel and Schelling described these myths as "images" of the ideas they contained. Diotima's myth about love helps consolidate a single figure who "represents an image of perfected humanity," whereas a cosmos exists in the *Timaeus* myth as "an image of the ideal world."[110] In Plato's philosophy, an image is the material imprint of an idea: the Forms impress them upon the human understanding in much the same way that physical objects might cast shadows.[111] Schlegel and Schelling appear to have drawn on this vocabulary as a way of making a strong claim about the potential of myth to link individual subjects to certain higher ideas. The positing of an ideal in a myth—of humanity, or of the world—leaves behind an image in our psyche, the combination of whose intellectual and sensual faculties can, through that image, reconstruct the idea in it. This reconstruction is a creative act. As much as the ideas expressed in the myths are understood to be somehow dynamic—the person of Diotima, the cosmos as an "ensouled living thing"—the agent doing the reconstructing also interacts dynamically with them, inevitably rediscovering those ideas in his own way, in his own manifestations.[112] An idea of the inner unity of the cosmos can also reflect the unity of an individual soul participating in its motions, and an idea of human perfection the virtues of yet imperfect persons.

If myths have the capacity to contain images of ideas—a quality that Schlegel and Schelling credited to Plato's myths—the proponents of the new mythology had good reason to be specially invested in the relationship between images and the formation of the individual, between *Bild* and *Bildung.* Often translated as "education," *Bildung* was concept that was weighted with special significance at the height of German Idealism, and was closely associated with the process by which an individual subject comes to be formed or shaped.[113] An idea, impressed as an image upon the psyche, may be seen as the beginning of *Bildung,* as it is internalized in an individual as an ideal to approximate in the ongoing cultivation of his own self and his surroundings. The new mythology envisioned in the *Oldest Systematic Program*—a mythology unified around a Platonic idea—had to be able to guide this process of self-formation.

For this same reason, it becomes of particular significance that the highest Platonic idea unifying all ideas in this vision is an idea of beauty. If, as the *Oldest Systematic Program* proposes, the new mythology is to help in the construction of a world for "free, self-conscious being[s]," the idea governing that world has to be one that maximizes the agency of its subjects.[114] Beauty is that idea that communicates with the creative faculty of each individual; what makes humans "capable of understanding the beauty of a poem," according to Schlegel, is that "a part of the poet, a spark of his creative spirit, lives in us as well and never ceases to glow with a mysterious force deep beneath the ashes of self-made unreason."[115] Access to the higher ideas, and through them, to the highest idea of beauty, stimulates the part of us that makes us poets and creators, and it is, for the proponents of the new mythology, our creativity that makes us free.

From the standpoint of the project for the new mythology, then, Plato's myths imparted an important lesson about the nature and potential function of mythology in relation to philosophy. These German Idealists took the myths to be part of Plato's perfectly poetic philosophy, where they represented specific ideas in it that could not be adequately captured in the language of rational thought. In turn, Plato's myths lent insight into the role a mythology unified by the highest idea of beauty might play in a special kind of individual enlightenment: they granted privileged access to rational ideas in a way that preserved the autonomy of the poetic spirit. The Platonism of the new mythology, then, brokers the marriage of rational ideas and poetic freedom in the enlightenment of the individual. But how mythology was to bring an entire community to a corresponding state of knowledge, like the phases of human knowledge envisioned in Schelling's system, is separate question. To answer it, the champions of the new mythology would have to step beyond the Platonic tradition, and extend it.

MYTHOLOGY AND THE ENLIGHTENED COMMUNITY

We recall that the proclamation at the end of the *Oldest Systematic Program* for a new mythology of reason had been accompanied by a confident assertion of its own novelty, as an idea that "has still not occurred to anyone else." In light of the conspicuous admiration that the central theorists of the new mythology reserved for Plato and his thoroughly poetic philosophy, that allegation might now strike us as strange. If the Platonic revival in German Idealism had also brought to light the existence of clear precedents for philosophical myths that were at once rational and poetic, how could the author of the *Program* have insisted, with such certainty, that their project was so new?

One way of understanding the claim is to suggest that the novelty that its champions saw in the new mythology lay not so much in a Platonically inflected reconciliation of poetry and rationality in this medium, but rather in the political application of such a reconciliation. As we have seen, the project for the new mythology had hinged on the premise that contemporary society faced a uniquely modern predicament: one entailing the separation of poetry and rationality, and the corresponding separation of the creative individual from a society bound by bureaucratic and legal institutions. After the model of ancient mythology, a new mythology could bridge this chasm by forging an alternative, voluntary bond between creative individuals in a poetic community. But that mythology would be arrived at, not by seeking to replicate the ancient example, but through an emphatically modern extension of philosophy and science—and specifically of Idealism—whereby conscious reason transcends its own boundaries into the unconscious realm of poetry. The poetic augmentation of reason in mythology was possible through a certain Platonic worldview that combined a rational metaphysics with a poetic epistemology, in which access to the highest ideas of reason depended on poetic channels as well as the rational. This also meant that the spiritual freedom that poetry assured an individual was not merely a lack of inhibition; rather, its content had to be informed by higher Platonic ideas, especially that of beauty. Through its interaction with the higher ideas contained in the new mythology, the soul would be able to form and cultivate its own enlightenment.

Yet this Platonic expansion of rationality and poetry takes place in the psyche of the individual philosopher-poet. For the theorists of the new mythology, this was only the beginning of an answer to their concerns. What, they wanted to know, was the political counterpart to this vision of enlightenment, the realization of which would benefit not just the individual but the entire poetic community that the new mythology was meant to bring together?

The Philosophers and the People: The Limits of Plato's Political Vision

The *Oldest Systematic Program* makes an assumption about the nature of society that should be familiar to readers of Plato's *Republic*. The *Republic* had drawn a "mutually illuminating" analogy between the city and the individual soul: a part of the soul had a corresponding demographic in the larger society that shared its most defining characteristic.[116] The *Oldest Systematic Program* likewise begins from the premise that "the philosophers" and "the people" of a society are separate by virtue of their respective natures: the philosophers are rational, and the people sensuous.[117] Yet the separation between the rational and the sensuous, in societal classes as well as in the faculties of the soul, was something that the new mythology ought to bridge. According to the *Oldest Systematic Program,* the new mythology had to be a mythology of reason precisely because it had to speak to both philosophers and nonphilosophers, and likewise to both the rational and sensuous parts of each person: "Before we make ideas aesthetic, i.e. mythological, they will have no interest for the people. Conversely, before mythology is rational, the philosopher must be ashamed of it. Hence finally the enlightened and unenlightened must shake hands: mythology must become philosophical to make people rational, and philosophy must become mythological to make philosophers sensuous."[118]

As in the Platonic analogy between the city and the soul, the *Program* proposes that political harmony bears a parallel relationship to psychic harmony: the shaking of hands between the enlightened and unenlightened classes also entails the rationalization of the nonphilosophical and the sensualizing of the philosophical. Moreover, this vision revives the more subtle insight from Plato's treatment of myth in the *Republic*, that certain kinds of myth can transform the characters of individuals and how they understand themselves—so that they are more rational, or more sensual, than they might have been otherwise. Like Plato, the author of the *Program* also conceptualizes myth as a force for wide-scale social change that begins with the reformation of individual nature.

But where Plato's political vision sought to preserve a hierarchical relationship between the faculties of the soul and the corresponding classes of society, the ideal such relationship envisaged in the program for the new mythology is one of equality. The proponents of the new mythology would have considered it a shortcoming on Plato's part—one that undermined the potential of his own thought—to have singled out the philosophical class to rule over the others, and the rational faculty to reign in the soul. As they saw it, the real promise of Plato's work was in its capacity to model a genuinely poetic philosophy, and Plato himself embodied the ideal of an individual in whom both rational and aesthetic powers can come together to lend true insight into the ideas. It would have seemed incongruous, then, for Plato to have acknowledged—at the very least—the accessory role that nonrational faculties play in the soul of the ideally constituted individual, but then to have assigned to such philosophical individuals an exclusively rational function in society, with no outlet for the expression of those parts of their souls that had been subordinated to the rational part.[119] What Plato had discounted was the simpler, more consistent solution of giving equal representation to the rational and nonrational faculties in both the soul of the individual as well as in society. That way, each individual would flourish as both a rational and a sensuous being, and society would be so organized to reflect this ideal.

From the standpoint of the new mythology, an equal society of well-rounded individuals was not only the more desirable political outcome; it was also the more genuinely Platonic one that better captured the essence of his philosophy. It was Plato, above all other thinkers, who taught the theorists of the new mythology that the soul of the true philosopher was also poetic.[120] At some level, then, Plato's separation of a class of philosophers from the rest of society suggested, in particular, an admission of the limitations of mythology in its capacity to shape the natures of individuals. For Plato, a philosophical nature might reveal itself in the course of education—a process intimately linked to the myths that frame how individuals in the city understand themselves. But while Plato understood human nature to be malleable, he also took for granted that not everyone becomes a philosopher at the highest level. In assuming that nonphilosophical people must necessarily exist, Plato was also betraying a certain pessimism about what myth can and cannot do in politics: myth might help transform a soul's constitution, but it was to be expected—if not ultimately inevitable—that the ideal balance of faculties might not be realized in most cases.

The proponents of the new mythology thought differently. For the author of the *Oldest Systematic Program,* the existence of two separate intellectual classes in society was not an inevitability, but rather an aberration. In modern society, philosophers and nonphilosophers owed their separate existence to an unnatural imbalance in their psychological development, whereby only one of two faculties in the souls of each, rational and sensual, had been cultivated at the expense of the other. The true ailment of modernity, following a diagnosis Friedrich Schiller made just two years before the *Program,* consisted in "whole classes of men, developing but one part of their potentialities."[121] A man would be just as much "at odds with himself" from the "barbaric" destruction of feelings by rationality as from the "savage" rule of feelings without the guidance of rational principles—two pathological tendencies that exhibited themselves at two opposite ends of modern society.[122]

One of the central objectives of the new mythology was to heal both pathologies, by finding an equal balance of rational and sensual powers in the soul of every individual, and thereby making poetic philosophers of them all. In is in this vein that the author of the *Oldest Systematic Program* insists, not only on making the people more rational through mythology, but that the philosophers had something to gain from being made more sensual as well. The new mythology, as such, was aimed at the "equal development of all powers, of each individual as well as all individuals."[123] Wholeness of character, which would result from reconciling the midpoint of rationality and poetry within the soul of each individual, would also lead to the equivalent collapse in class divisions at the societal level.

If the central theorists of the new mythology in German Idealism disagreed with Plato on the limits of mythology, this ultimately manifested in a sharp divergence in outlook on how they envisioned the eventual direction of politics. Politics arguably trickled downstream for Plato from more noble origins, and much of its work appeared to consist in the preservation of its philosophical beginnings. The project for the new mythology, by contrast, was premised on the hope that politics will progress infinitely. Through it, the bonds between individuals would be strengthened, while the creative activity of those individuals would further the advancement of human knowledge. As the seat of individual innovation, poetry was indispensable to this process. If the poetic Plato—as the champions of the new mythology understood him—had presented a case for the necessity of the aesthetic faculties for accessing the highest ideas, a politics that left no place for the poetic or aesthetic was inadequate to his ultimate vision. At the same time, the happy combination of poetry and reason in a creative mind touched by the higher ideas had to be an attainable ideal for more people, and not just an elite group of philosopher-poets. Political progress, rather, was directed toward the universal enlightenment of all individuals in the community.

The Social Expansion of the New Mythology of Reason

To the extent that the central theorists of the new mythology understood their project in part as a Platonic endeavor, they offered a renewed take on what was admirable about Plato and his myths, updated for the modern age. The new mythology had to bring the separate classes together, and it had to help develop the full potential of every individual. But in addition, the priority that this vision placed on the value of equality over hierarchy as an organizing principle for envisioning the individual and society also extended to how its proponents thought about the authorship of the new mythology, and the process by which it would come about.

For the theorists of the new mythology, restoring the desired balance between the faculties of the soul and the corresponding balance between the divisions of society were two complementary endeavors that had to be pursued simultaneously. As we have seen, cultivating the spirit of the individual poet-philosopher without extending this content to the rest of society was inadequate to the political goals of the new mythology. But introducing political equality to a people that lacked the corresponding equality in their souls, they believed, would lead to disaster. Looming heavily in the background of the political vision of the new mythology was the disappointment experienced by its theorists at the outcome of the French Revolution, which had been matched only by their initial enthusiasm.[124] The years in which the revolution unraveled into the Reign of Terror coincided with those years of remarkable productivity in German Idealism when the central texts of the project for the new mythology were written. In many ways, this common project was an attempt to diagnose and remedy what had gone wrong. It was, in particular, a reckoning with the realization that the ideals of the French Revolution had—in Schiller's words—caught a "generation unprepared."[125] That the revolution had failed to live up to its promise had not so much do with the principles of *liberté, égalité,* and *fraternité,* as with the fact that the people were not ready for them; they did not yet know how to be free. Revolution had, in other words, brought about a new political order without the accompanying reform in human nature. The new mythology, as such, had to do better by targeting both frontiers at the same time, at the level of the individual as well as that of the collective.[126]

Ensuring both forms of equality, however, also translated to a vision in which all individuals in the community acted as poet-philosophers in an equal setting. A mythology of reason handed down from one poet or philosopher to the rest of his community ultimately served this purpose no better than ancient examples of mythology did for modernity. On this dimension the divine Plato had exhausted his usefulness to the new mythology: the poetic inspiration that touched a philosopher of his kind somehow had to touch an entire people as well. Plato had shown a way of writing poetic philosophy and myths of reason, but he was, in the end, one individual. Instead, the proponents of the new mythology agreed that all the members of the community affected by the new mythology would also be its authors. Schelling describes the new mythology as "the creation, not of some individual author, but of a new race, personifying, as it were, one single poet"; for Schlegel, it is the point of convergence of the poetries of all individuals in a poetic community, and for the author of the *Oldest Systematic Program,* the "last and greatest work of humanity."[127] The value of equality, then, was a central precept of their political thought that manifested not only in how they conceived of the ideal relationship of the faculties, both within and between individuals, but also across the authorship of the new mythology. On this account, the new mythology was to be a continuously growing work in which all its participants had equal standing as coauthors, and through the writing of which they encountered the highest idea of beauty and cultivated their creative spirit.

The need for the new mythology to be written collectively by the community as a whole provides a window into how its theorists approached their own literary practice. For all their theoretical enthusiasm for Plato and for the idea of philosophical myth, the early pioneers of German Idealism did not—in the way More, Bacon, or Leibniz had variously done—write myths themselves that might stand as easy correlates to any one of Plato's myths. One reason, as we have seen, had to do with their resistance to drawing a stylistic distinction between philosophy and myth, and their conviction that their convergence was what the future of philosophy would look like. But another factor in play was how they imagined the true focal point of Plato's thought might be realized in modern politics: the equal development of rational and poetic faculties in each member of an equal community of authors. They made brave efforts to put these ideals to practice in their own lives. Schlegel—who had conceived of the new mythology as a shared "midpoint" between poets—advocated for a collaborative model of literary production in which communities of artists, each bound by a common poetry, would seek to spread their message organically outward. Like the young Schelling, who had seen in his circle of friends at Tübingen a "league of free spirits [*Bund freier Geister*]" working toward social change, Schlegel often alluded to the ideal of an "alliance," "league," "eternal union," or "Hansa" of artists.[128]

In turn-of-the-century Jena, the literary groups formed around Schelling, the Schlegel brothers, and the other theorists of the new mythology went through great lengths to ensure that the communality of their association was reflected in both the nature of their writing and its process. If the new mythology was something that had to be actively produced, it made sense for its chief proponents to begin looking for Schlegel's mythological midpoint in literary collaboration. Echoing the language they used to describe a poetic or more organic alternative to the machinery of the modern state, they applied to their conception of the new mythology the same organic—mostly botanical—metaphors that are more famously associated with the German Romantic model of the literary process. Schlegel described mythology as a "bed" for the flowers of poetry and the seeds of their inspiration.[129] It was a telling metaphor, one that captured the way members of his literary circle understood and approached poetic communication and collaboration. Novalis, whose novel prominently featured a "blue flower" that was soon adopted as a symbol of the Romantic movement, contributed a collection of aphoristic fragments titled "Pollen [*Blüthenstaub*]" to the first issue of the *Athenaeum,* the founding journal of Romanticism begun and edited by the Schlegel brothers.[130] He described the fragments as "a literary sowing of the fields" in anticipation of the imminent discovery of a new art of writing books.[131] What art he had in mind is unclear, but the seeds that he understood himself to be sowing in the literary form of the fragment were a statement of the hope of building communities through their creative activities. He and Schlegel conceived of the genre of fragment-writing as an ultimately collaborative project—a harmonious and organic juxtaposition of anonymous fragments written by different authors.[132] Sure enough, in editing *Pollen* for the *Athenaeum,* Schlegel did not shy away from altering Novalis's text and adding his own contributions. More significantly, their process reflects the shared vision of their work as an essentially procreative art: their poetry would create poetry in turn, and draw these emerging poets into their circles.

It is difficult not to draw a deeper parallel between these literary ambitions and the plan for the new mythology. For these central figures of German Idealism, producing the new mythology and waiting for its arrival seemed part of the same process: they had to first sow the modest seeds of their ideas and literary examples, then hope that what sprouts, if anything, will eventually grow together to reveal the unity of their modern culture. But their ideas always ran ahead of their actual achievements. Their years of collaboration peaked between 1796 and 1801, then their literary community fell apart. Novalis died of tuberculosis at the age of twenty-eight. Friedrich Schlegel moved to Paris, his brother August to Berlin, leaving the newly divorced Caroline Schlegel to marry Schelling—the scandal of which necessitated their own departure from Jena. The wedding was the last time Schelling saw his old roommate from Tübingen, Hölderlin, who had already begun to lose his mind. As the giants of German Idealism went their own ways, so did their respective interests in the project for the new mythology.

We have seen how the bonds between poetry and poets afforded by Schlegel's conception of the new mythology had emerged as an alternative to the rational institutions defining the modern bureaucratic state. But the new mythology, its advocates agreed, also had to be a mythology of reason that grew out of the achievements of what had hitherto been a predominantly rational philosophy, and it would open access to the higher Platonic ideas of reason that had not been within reach before. The politics of the new mythology straddles the dual aim of building a coherent community and fostering the development of the individual in it. It sought not only to make better communities, or to make better poet-philosophers, but to create better communities of poet-philosophers approaching the ideal together.

One way of reading the account of the new mythology in German Idealism is that it is a very faithful and thorough interpretation of Plato pushed to its limits, which insists on the holistic fulfillment of both the city and the individual. Plato has been criticized for forcing the philosophers to descend back into the cave from their true home in the upper realm of the Forms. Through its conception of the new mythology, German Idealism had hoped to realize Plato's own unlikely dream of bringing everyone out of the cave together. The resulting vision was admittedly as short-lived as it was optimistic, but its ramifications would linger in European culture for a long time.

5

THE DEMON OF THE CITY

Cassirer on Myth and Plato

MYTH AS AN UNLIKELY RESOURCE FOR MITIGATING THE PATHOLOGIES OF MYTH

IN CHAPTER 4, I examined how the central figures of German Idealism perceived the need for a new mythology for the modern era to fulfill a new political vision. A century and a half later, the heirs of German Idealism looked on with horror as modern Europe fell into the grips of a new breed of political myth.

The rise of fascism in the twentieth century is unthinkable without its weaponized propagation of narratives about racial hierarchies, the destiny of chosen peoples, and kingdoms that were to last a thousand years.[1] They appealed to national mythological traditions, like the images and legends of classical Rome in Mussolini's Italy, or evoked symbols laden with mystical overtones, like the runic symbols that made their way into Nazi iconography.[2] Such narratives, and the symbols and rituals that came with them, were political phenomena that contemporary commentators readily associated with the category of myth. This association was encouraged, in turn, by the effort taken by the principal ideologues of fascism to seek intellectual justification for their project in the ideas of eighteenth- and nineteenth-century thinkers who had called attention to the potential power of myth: the program for the new mythology in German Idealism, Georges Sorel's theory of revolutionary myths, the centrality of mythological material to Wagner's aesthetic vision, Nietzsche's association of myth with a life-affirming vitality lacking in modern culture.[3]

For concerned commentators, what was most striking about the "modern political myths" was their overt anti-rationalism in an age of unparalleled advances in knowledge.[4] Their apparent rejection of the rule of reason in politics and their appeal to extreme passions, the priority they placed on collective experiences over those of the individual, and the complex system of ceremonial rites that enforced them—all seemed radically out of place in the scientifically advanced societies of modern Europe. And they seemed, rather, to have much more in common with the worldviews expressed in the myths of tribal societies in the Amazon, Africa, Australia, and Polynesia, which had fascinated the first generation of modern anthropologists at the turn of the twentieth century. As such, the fascist recourse to the use of myth in politics was bitterly regarded as a "barbaric" and "tribal" betrayal of modern civilization.[5]

The identification of these new political phenomena with myth suggested, on the one hand, that the creation of new mythologies for a modern age was in fact possible. Myths were not merely a relic of the past, nor a characteristic feature of remote, tribal societies on the brink of extinction. Myths also ceased to be harmless, fanciful stories, but proved to have powerful political purchase, and could even drive political action of tremendous scales and stakes. On the other hand, these newfangled myths seemed to make a self-evident case against allowing room for myth to play a role of any kind in modern politics. Even before the world could begin to comprehend the enormity of the atrocities committed in their name, the resort to such myths already seemed to be a wholesale rejection of the very idea that politics ought to be guided by reason. If the horrors of fascism were to be the cost of admitting myth into modern politics, they seemed to supply an unambiguous warning that myth ought to have no business in modernity after all.

Hence, in the time that had elapsed since the composition of the *Oldest Systematic Program of German Idealism,* the political theoretical response to the question of modern myth had shifted entirely. For the proponents of the new mythology in German Idealism, myth had presented a hopeful, if farfetched, solution to the afflictions of modernity. Twentieth-century interest in the place of myth in politics, by contrast, was driven largely by theorists committed to combating what they took to be its very real presence in modern life.

Ernst Cassirer, the foremost philosopher of myth in the first half of the twentieth century, was one such theorist defending the view that modern political thought could not afford a place for myth. This chapter will show that this position, however, is complicated by Cassirer's portrait of Plato and his legacy. In this portrait, Plato epitomizes the rational overcoming of myth in Western political thought, but he is, simultaneously, the author of a set of myths that Cassirer goes to great lengths to celebrate. Cassirer's insistence on claiming Plato for the modern philosophical tradition suggests a deeper ambivalence in his argument against myth. In defending both the philosophical significance of Plato's myths, and the centrality of Plato to the philosophical struggle against myth, Cassirer opens up a space in his philosophy of culture for recognizing a specifically Platonic approach to reconciling myth with a progressive vision of philosophy and politics. On this account, the genre of philosophical myth that Plato invented provides vital guidance in how philosophical discourse can be renewed in creative ways, so that it may be better equipped to take on the pathological forms of myth lurking in modernity.

MYTH IN THE TWENTIETH CENTURY

Cassirer's magnum opus, *The Philosophy of Symbolic Forms* (1923–1929), offers a theory of culture that places myth in a special relationship with philosophy. By isolating myth as an independent "modality" of knowledge, Cassirer takes myth's contributions to the formation of knowledge as both unique and constructive, at once separate from and parallel to other ways of knowing like language, art, or science.[6] Myth is simply one of these different approaches to mediating and understanding reality, or what he calls a "symbolic form."

Take, for instance, how the same natural phenomenon of the changing of seasons might be understood differently in scientific and mythic modes of interpretation. Where modern science might rely on a causal explanation appealing to the relative position of the earth in orbit around the sun, the same phenomenon might be depicted in various myths as the arrival of a figure who personifies some aspect of the season itself—a goddess whose presence allows the crops to grow, a migratory animal whose sojourns are linked to the shedding of the leaves of trees. Cassirer's point is that the difference between the scientific and mythic accounts is not a difference between reason and unreason, but a difference, in this case, stemming from entirely different conceptions of what constitutes causation in the first place.[7] In mythical thought, a single, undifferentiated occasion stands in for the entire chain of visible and invisible events included in the scientific account, such that any one part of the phenomenon serves as an explanation for the whole: "For the mythical view, it is the swallow that *makes* the summer."[8] A story that makes such a claim may seem fantastic, but its internal logic is not unreasonable, but coherent in its own way.

Furthermore, much like science itself, myth is motivated by the same basic human desire to make meaningful sense of the world. Against views that condemn myth to be fundamentally unphilosophical, Cassirer aligns the function of myth with a philosophical task of organizing human experience in meaningful ways. Because mythic approaches to understanding reality obey a logic coherent only to myth, Cassirer's account could recognize myth's difference from other approaches to knowledge, notably empirical science, without dismissing its philosophic content.

At the same time, philosophy, according to Cassirer, is that which ultimately breaks free of myth.[9] Though it is a crucial mode in which humans begin to apprehend the world, myth ultimately remains a rudimentary, primal form of culture at the bottom rung of "a definite systemic gradation" tying together the various spheres of knowledge.[10] As human knowledge evolves, it must also discard its mythic foundations and trade them for more sophisticated modes of thought. Accordingly, Cassirer equates the history of philosophy with a continuous struggle against myth—a struggle dramatized in his final work, *The Myth of the*

State (1946). Completed days before his death and published by his friends at Yale the following year, *The Myth of the State* was Cassirer's only full-length work of political theory, as well as his final statement on the subject of myth. It is only in this book that Cassirer fully confronts the possibility of modern myths, and, in so doing, finds himself taking on a far more critical stance toward myth than ever before.[11] The author of *The Philosophy of Symbolic Forms* would have been reluctant to speak of myth as irrational, because modern standards of rationality simply fell outside the scope of myth. Myth obeyed its own norms and laws; it was not myth's function to be rational in that way.[12] Yet *The Myth of the State* emphatically celebrates the progressive triumph of modern rationality over its mythic origins, and laments the reversal of that trajectory in the fascist trends of contemporary politics.[13] In this light, the reemergence of myth in the twentieth century places Cassirer in a position to condemn myth on a much grander scale: regression to mythic ways of thinking threatens the unraveling of the accomplishments of reason.[14]

And so, *The Myth of the State* calls on all the resources of our higher cognitive faculties to combat the resurgence of myth in modern life. This, in turn, constitutes an unequivocal stance on the place of myth in political thought: Ernst Cassirer, the philosopher of culture who worked tirelessly to underscore myth's inner coherence and complexity, ultimately passed the verdict that modern political thinking cannot afford to tolerate the presence of myth in its midst. But only one part of this verdict, as we shall see, is concerned with the status of myth as a regressive force in modernity—an account that synthesizes certain key paradigms in the predominant approaches to myth in the emergent social sciences. The other component of Cassirer's argument, stemming from his unique diagnoses of both myth and of modernity, shows the conditions of modern culture to be particularly vulnerable to generating the most pernicious chimera of myth mixed up with the apparatuses of modern rationality. Both are reasons for demanding the rejection of myth from politics, but the second, in particular, will come into special tension with his interpretation of Plato and his legacy in the Western intellectual tradition.

Myth and Culture: Aby Warburg

Cassirer's account of myth—as at once a distinct and constructive way of knowing, as well as a properly premodern sphere of thought that urgently demanded replacement with more sophisticated forms—was unique in providing a philosophical synthesis of prevailing ideas about myth from burgeoning contemporary interest in the social sciences, notably in anthropology and psychology, rather than from the literary traditions extending the projects of Romanticism.

However, it bears noting that the overall shape of Cassirer's synthesis had a humanistic aspect; and it shared striking resemblances, in particular, with the vision of culture held by the art historian Aby Warburg, a close friend and the founder of the Warburg Library of Cultural Sciences in Hamburg, where Cassirer was an enthusiastic affiliate.[15] Like Cassirer, Warburg had a deeply sympathetic appreciation for the ways in which human cultures—be they the cultures of classical Greece, the Italian Renaissance, or the indigenous American tribes he encountered during his travels in America—encoded meaning in symbols that manifested in religious rites, ceremonial performances, and iconic motifs in the visual arts.

Two features of Cassirer's approach to myth are worth highlighting in the context of his close association with Aby Warburg and the Warburg Library. The first is the primacy of culture as a subject demanding deep philosophical engagement, and, within it, the singling out of myth as a distinct form of culture—so fundamental to human cultural development and so singular in its internal logic that Cassirer saw fit to devote one of the three volumes of the *Philosophy of Symbolic Forms* to it.[16] Warburg's extensive collection of ethnographic materials—curated with special attention to such themes as pagan religions, magic, and folklore—would have affirmed and deepened Cassirer's conviction that the study of culture was not complete without the study of myth.

A second point of overlap between Cassirer's and Warburg's thought was a shared conception of culture that combined, on the one hand, an appreciation for the plurality of forms that human culture can take, with, on the other hand, a hierarchical organizing principle that took certain forms of cultural expression to be more sophisticated and developed than others.[17] Both of these sensibilities were on display in the famously unorthodox layout of the Warburg Library, which organized its collection according to four themes—"image," "word," "orientation," and "action"—and distributed it over the four floors of the building in an ascending order, so that patrons would move from the sensuous and expressionistic to the more abstract aspects of culture as they made their way through the different levels.[18] The image of culture presented in the Warburg Library resonated with Cassirer's own.[19] In order to do justice to its diversity, its various spheres warranted separation and study on their own unique terms; at the same time, these spheres were connected by an evolutionary logic by which more refined and rigorous forms of cultural expression come to supersede that which is rudimentary and crude.

Cassirer made special efforts, then, to integrate his theory of myth into a more general theory of human culture. But the broadly humanistic appeal of this framework notwithstanding, his insistence on drawing out the nuanced relationship between myth and modernity also translated into a number of important departures from the leading approaches to myth in the social sciences. For instance, Cassirer rejected the premise, common to early twentieth-century anthropological studies of indigenous mythologies, that an impassable distance separated the way of thinking characteristic of myth from the cognitive processes of the modern mind, such that it might be possible to study myth from a privileged position of scientific remove. Throughout *The Philosophy of Symbolic Forms,* he remained intent on demonstrating the coherence and independence of the mythic mode of thinking as a ground of culture—much like science itself, without being a primitive version of it. He went one step further in *The Myth of the State,* suggesting that this mode of thinking remains latent even in a modern culture dominated by more sophisticated forms of thought, so that, when appropriated, it can produce the kinds of modern myths that plagued twentieth-century politics. At the same time, Cassirer also rejected prominent treatments of myth by contemporary psychoanalysts, who accepted that there are latent traces of myth in the modern mind, but either pathologized them or elevated them to the status of universal timelessness. Even in its modern

196 MYTH AND MODERNITY

incarnation, myth had to be understood without undermining either of its most essential characteristics—as an independent and necessary modality of knowledge, and as a way of representing reality that is rendered obsolete at the onset of the higher cultural forms.

Myth in Anthropology: Tylor, Frazer, Lévy-Bruhl

The pioneers of the relatively young discipline of anthropology had set out, among other things, to establish a science for the study of myth. This specifically scientific ambition of the project resulted in two accidental features common to anthropological studies of myth from the late nineteenth and early twentieth centuries.

The first was the treatment of myth as a distinct phenomenon with universal features: it was both possible and instructive to compare myths collected from different peoples and eras. These classic comparative studies—carrying titles like *How Natives Think, Primitive Mentality, Myth in Primitive Psychology,* and *Primitive Culture*—approached myths as the cultural artifacts of a distinctly "primitive" or "savage" way of thinking, into which they sought to gain insight.[20] Cassirer was admittedly cautious about the seemingly "arbitrary" and "incongruous" search for "any bond that connects the most barbaric rites with the world of Homer . . . the orgiastic cults of savage tribes, the magic practices of the shamans of Asia, the delirious whirl of the dancing dervishes with the calmness and the speculative depth of the religion of the Upanishads."[21] Nonetheless, he shared the basic position of the early anthropologists that "the motives of mythical thought and mythical imagination are in a sense always the same."[22] For all the variety of the world's myths, Cassirer endorsed this scientific effort to locate a common mythic consciousness unifying them. Following the early pioneers of anthropology, then, he presumed the existence of an essential relationship linking myths—a traditional genre of oral fiction—to a particular way of thinking about reality that warranted the designation of being "mythic."

More problematic for Cassirer, however, was a second feature of the scientific vision motivating the anthropological approach to myth. Landmark studies of myth from this period endeavored to treat myth as a scientific object—that is, as an external phenomenon removed from the objective standpoint of the scientific observer. To the extent that it was assumed in these studies that a common primitive consciousness was responsible for the diverse content of all myths, this primitive mentality was also taken to be something entirely foreign to the mind of its civilized observer. Consequently in these early anthropological accounts, myth was consistently defined in relation to modern scientific thought. There were two ways of conceptualizing this relation: in the first, endorsed by an earlier generation of anthropologists, myth was a rudimentary form of science stuck at a level of rigor and accuracy that civilization had long outgrown. In response, a subsequent school of thought posed the more radical view that myth and science represented entirely separate realms of thought. For the former camp, myth belonged to a bygone age safely removed from modernity; for the latter, to an alien world separate from our own.

The leading precedent in the former approach to myth was set by E. B. Tylor, whose *Primitive Culture* (1871) proposed a study of the evolution of culture "with especial consideration of the civilization of the lower tribes as related to the civilization of the higher nations."[23] The contrast between the "lower" and "higher" stages of civilization aligned neatly with an opposition between myth and scientific explanation. For Tylor, myth was essentially a crude and inaccurate form of "scientific speculation," born out of "man's craving to know the causes at work in each event he witnesses, the reasons why each state of things he surveys is such as it is and no other."[24] Tylor's account of myth—as a primitive effort at science undertaken from a lower stage of culture—also provided the general framework for James Frazer's encyclopedic masterpiece, *The Golden Bough* (1890–1915).[25] Like Tylor, Frazer collapsed, as much as possible, the qualitative distinction between myth and science, and considered the difference between them to be largely a matter of degree in rigor.[26] At the same time, Frazer expanded upon both Tylor's conception of myth's function as well as the discrete stages of culture through which knowledge passes from myth to science, savagery to civilization. Under this augmented scheme, myth was thought to be aimed not only at explaining worldly phenomena, but also at effecting—through the magical rituals it often legitimized—desired outcomes in the environment as well. It also fell into a more concretely demarcated theory of cultural evolution, separated out into the famous tripartite stages of magic, religion, and science.[27]

Against Tylor's and Frazer's view of myth as an inferior science, later studies of myth in the early twentieth century sought to further separate science from myth. For Tylor's and Frazer's successors in the discipline, the processes of thinking underlying myth differed from those of science, not only in degree but also in kind. Lucien Lévy-Bruhl took a notoriously extreme position in *How Natives Think* (1910), rejecting Tylor's and Frazer's claims to a rational basis of comparison between "the mental processes of 'primitives'" and "those which we are accustomed to describe in men of our own type."[28] As such, myth lacked the rational content and motivation of scientific thought, but was instead the product of an entirely "pre-logical" mind that "perceive[d] nothing in the same way as we do."[29] From the perspective of this alien mind, reality itself was imbued with magic, and myth sought not to explain or explicate the world but to commune with it on an emotional, rather than an intellectual, level.[30]

Cassirer's philosophy of myth owed to its anthropological forbearers a set of assumptions that fell somewhere between the positions taken by Tylor, Frazer, and Lévy-Bruhl. He shared Tylor's and Frazer's desire to dispel a popular view of myth as "motiveless fancy," but not their impulse to judge its contents by the standards of scientific thought.[31] Myth, for Cassirer, was motivated by the same drive toward knowledge as science, but it did not merely consist in brave but mistaken explanations of phenomena to which science provides better answers. In recognizing that myth commands "its own mode of reality," Cassirer aligned himself to a large extent with Lévy-Bruhl's critique of the analogizing of mythic thinking to science, as well as with his thesis that viewing the world through the lens of myth results in a different perception of reality altogether.[32] To wedge myth into the mold of science would be to deny the rich emotional content particular to myth. But far from being the "pre-logical" entity of Lévy-Bruhl's depiction, the mind responsible for myth, on Cassirer's account, "never lacks a definite logical structure."[33] Myth was therefore directed toward a kind of knowledge of the world in the manner of scientific inquiry, but at the same time, it was also an independent mode of thought apart from science. It was akin to science in form but not in content.

Between the conceptions of myth posed by Tylor and Frazer on one side, and by Lévy-Bruhl on the other, Cassirer saw a methodological, rather than a substantive, disagreement, which he in turn sought to arbitrate by appealing to Kant. According to Kant, scientists and scholars were of two kinds. There were those who emphasized the common features in phenomena, and those drawn to the differences—or, people driven by the principle of "homogeneity," and those by that of "specification." Cassirer determined that Tylor and Frazer were of the former mold when it came to myth, and Lévy-Bruhl the latter. Cassirer's point was that the two approaches present "no real contradiction," but merely "the different interests of reason which cause different modes of thought." The diversity of the modes in which scholars operate can be misleading because, "in reality, reason has one interest only, and the conflict of its maxims arises only from a difference and mutual limitation of the methods."[34] A philosophy of myth need not have to choose between recognizing the distinctiveness of myth—especially from other ways of knowing—and the unity of knowledge itself.

Yet in refusing to make that choice, Cassirer also ended up discarding the special standing of the scientific viewpoint assumed in the anthropological studies of myth. By making myth an object of scientific investigation, the early anthropologists had regarded it from a privileged and authoritative vantage point safely removed from the phenomenon they were studying. But because Cassirer insisted on both the separation of myth from science as well as the unity of human knowledge, he could not, like Tylor or Frazer, evaluate myth from the opposite end of a spectrum of scientific advancement; nor could he, like Lévy-Bruhl, deny any common rational ground between myth and science. Instead, Cassirer recognized that scientific methods bring their own interests and limitations to an otherwise unitary and objective world. In this way, he pointed out, the form of science resembles that of myth. Like Lévy-Bruhl, Cassirer believed that reality, as grasped by myth, is but "a world of mere representations," but he denied that any other approach, including science, can claim a more direct, purer way of access to it: "but in its content, its mere *material,* the world of knowledge is nothing else."[35] For Cassirer, the world was always mediated by the form in which we present it to ourselves—in science as in mythic thinking. This condition, by which humans rely on such intermediate systems of representation to interpret reality, made us "symbolic animals" in command of a number of discrete but interrelated "symbolic forms."[36] Deciphering their relationship was the task of a philosophy of culture.[37]

In Cassirer's philosophy, the symbolic forms of myth and science interacted within an evolutionary framework whereby, over the course of history, human knowledge and culture come to depend increasingly less on the lower forms and increasingly more on the higher forms. Eventually, modernity replaces the emotionally charged, expressive order of myth for the formal abstraction of science.[38] On this developmentalist outlook, Cassirer's understanding of the relationship between myth, science, and modernity may not look to differ greatly from that of the early anthropological accounts of myth. Following Tylor's initial move to view myth as diametrically opposed to modern science, it was simply a given in early anthropological thought that science belonged to the moderns in the same way that myth had belonged to their ancestors and, now, to their latter-day "primitive" counterparts in the non-Western world. In particular, Cassirer's belief that myth is transcended in religion then eventually in science, bears a close resemblance to the phases of cultural progress outlined in Frazer's *The Golden Bough.*[39]

Absent in Cassirer's narrative of progress, however, was the simple separation of myth from modernity found in the foundational texts of anthropology. While Tylor, Frazer, and Lévy-Bruhl were quick to assume that modern society had permanently outgrown myth, the lower symbolic forms in Cassirer's philosophy underlie the higher forms, standing as a kind of sedimentary substratum to the modern advancements built on its foundations.[40] "We are always living on volcanic soil," he wrote of modern politics. Myth is "always there, lurking in the dark and waiting for its hour and opportunity."[41] As such, Cassirer took care not to adopt the language of "us" and "them" that pervades so much of early twentieth-century anthropological work. Moreover, in subsuming myth deep beneath the forms of thought that dominate modern existence, he made room in his philosophy for a possibility that did not occur to the anthropologists: the presence of myth in modernity.[42] At moments of cultural crises, according to Cassirer, "the battle which theoretical knowledge thinks it has won for good will keep breaking out afresh. The foe which knowledge has seemingly defeated forever crops up within its own midst."[43]

Myth in Psychoanalysis: Freud and Jung

In the recognition that myth remains latent in modern life, Cassirer's philosophy could be considered a kind of bridge between the anthropological and psychoanalytic approaches to myth in the early twentieth century. Freud had notably turned to myth in *Totem and Taboo* (1913) to illuminate the mental life of the neurotic patient in modern society.[44] Myth functioned for Freud, as it did for the anthropologists, as an artifact of the primitive or savage mind.[45] However, he also observed a structural resemblance between the mind of the savage, who aligns his sexual conduct with the totemic belief systems sustained by the myths of his tribal community, and the mind of the adolescent child, who grapples with his own incestuous desires in the process of growing up. It was "probable," he concluded, that "the totemic system . . . was a product of the conditions involved in the Oedipus complex"; if the neurotic was an adult trapped in the psychosexual traumas of childhood, he was also in some sense a modern individual who had failed to shake off his unconscious savage mentality.[46] For Freud, myths not only lent expression to forbidden, savage desires, but their continuing appeal to modern audiences—our ready and immediate identification, for example, with the myth of Oedipus—was testament to how those same desires prevail in the modern condition. Whatever psychological force that was at work in myth, then, was also latent in the private lives of modern individuals.

While Freud may have correctly broadened the horizon of myth, Cassirer nonetheless faulted him for ultimately mischaracterizing its nature. He pointed out that, when Freud "stood at the sickbed of myth with the same attitude and the same feelings as at the couch of an ordinary patient," he had already committed himself to treating it as a pathology—like so many dismissive theories of myth that failed to recognize its intellectual content.[47] Cassirer was especially put off by Freud's sexualization of myth, which he took as a sign of a propensity for "intellectual reduction," and he played down the suggestive traces of Freud's influence on his own thought.[48]

In some respect, Cassirer's refusal to diagnose myth alongside mental illness might have aligned his account more closely to that of Freud's disciple, Carl Jung, who had brought the study of myth to the forefront of psychoanalysis by proposing that archetypal patterns and symbols, which recur across myths of different cultures, form an unchanging, unconscious substrate to our collective experience of reality.[49] But Cassirer, without ever mentioning Jung by name, was even more resistant to the quest in "psychologism" to find archetypes standing behind the various motifs and narrative elements of myths.[50] Whereas Cassirer found fault with Freud for failing to consider myth a mode of knowledge, he would have felt Jung had overextended the capacity of myth in the other direction, and had failed to acknowledge the comparative sophistication of the higher forms of culture that evolved dialectically over time. In his own diagnosis of the problem of myth's modern presence, Cassirer rejected both of these characterizations—Freud's account of myths as pathologies persisting in modernity, and Jung's account of myths as the concrete manifestations of a timeless and universal ground for all human experience. Instead Cassirer insisted that, even in confronting its modern form, the scholar of myth ought not to lose sight of its status as one of several symbolic forms through which human culture progresses dialectically: it is a legitimate form of thought, but also one that requires hierarchical differentiation against other such forms that belong more properly to modernity.

The Problem of Modern Myth

What, then, was it about the modern presence of myth that Cassirer found so troubling? The easy, albeit partial, answer is that the animation of the mythic forces latent in modern life signified a regressive turn in the trajectory of human culture. This much is suggested by Cassirer's selective synthesis of particular paradigms from the traditions of classical anthropology and psychoanalysis: from the former, the expectation that the advancement of culture consists in the abandonment of myth; and from the latter, the recognition of myth's latent influence in the minds of modern individuals. On this view, Cassirer's diagnosis of the resurgence of myth in contemporary politics may bear resemblances to Freud's later insights in *Civilization and Its Discontents* (1930), where he suggested that the inner drama of the psyche also plays out on the scale of civilization; the neurotic individual had a counterpart in an unhealthy society.[51] If, at the psychic level, the myths of totemic societies expressed an adolescent obsession with incest, modern myths that grip entire nations would constitute a wholesale regression of civilization itself to the degenerate passions of its violent, savage past.

Certainly the understanding of modern myth as a regression is a natural conclusion of the developmentalist account of cultural progress that can seem to be such a pronounced feature of Cassirer's thought, and which helped unfavorably seal his reputation even during his own lifetime. This developmentalist framework was, in particular, a prominent point of disagreement in his highly public debate against his contemporary, Martin Heidegger, which spanned the greater part of the 1920s through the mid-1940s, and came to a climactic standoff in a famous meeting in Davos in 1929. Heidegger took issue, in particular, with the teleological characterization of myth as a symbolic form that eventually had to give way to those higher and more sophisticated forms that, like science, just happened to be those that had proved definitive for modern culture since the Enlightenment. At the heart of Heidegger's critique was a deep skepticism regarding the possibility that humans could truly overcome their need for myth: that need, he maintained, had to arise from a more essential aspect of the human condition than that suggested in Cassirer's account.[52]

The disagreement between the two philosophers may appear to throw into relief the limited nature of Cassirer's attack on the modern myths of his time, which can only be regressive if one subscribes to the teleological premise of his view of culture. Cassirer's account of twentieth-century myths, however, goes beyond a concern for cultural regression.[53] In the critique of "the modern political myths" at the end of *The Myth of the State,* he suggests that it is not merely the case that myth is a comparatively less developed mode of knowledge than those that dominate modern life, but that the very conditions of modernity are not equipped to be compatible with myth. It is a subtle insight, external to the various intellectual traditions synthesized in the broad contours of Cassirer's portrait of myth. In what amounts to a verdict, not only on myth, but on the peculiarities of modern culture, Cassirer observes that the effects of modernity on the human psyche are irreversibly transformative, so that traditional myths by themselves cannot satisfy the cognitive and psychological needs of the collective modern mind.[54] Instead, modern groups and individuals make demands for rational justifications even in the moment that they succumb to the newfangled myths of the twentieth century. "Civilized man" being what he is, "in order to believe he must find some 'reasons' for his belief; he must form a 'theory' to justify his creeds." Modern political myths are thus characterized by "a rational justification for certain conceptions that, in their origin and tendency, were anything but rational."[55] This means, in particular, that these myths are not merely the handiwork of propagandists and political entrepreneurs, but there are contemporary *philosophers*—he singles out Oswald Spengler and, notably, Heidegger—complicit in the machinery of modern myth.[56]

The result is that the myths generated in modern times are not pure myths, but are mixed up with the dressings of modern rationality.[57] This "strange combination," which Cassirer identifies as "one of the most striking features of our political myths," is not just unsettling but catastrophic for modernity itself.[58] First, modern myths, unlike traditional myths, have access to the force wielded by the entire technical apparatus of modern scientific thought, so that it is all the more difficult for their spell to be broken with the conventional tools of reason. These myths not only have their own "technique," but modern, scientific, and rational trappings are precisely what sustain them.[59] Second, they erode a formal boundary that, for Cassirer, is crucial to the self-definition of modernity, and they grant to the modern creators of myths an undifferentiated, double power, "as both a homo magus and a homo faber," simultaneously occupying both the age of myth and the age of technics.[60] At one level this means that the modern politician, freely switching between the two roles, is not constrained by the norms of either mode. At another level the modern citizen, subjected to the new status quo, is left unprepared to recognize myth when confronted with it. Finally, myth, in this incarnation, is not so much a mode of knowledge as it is deployed cynically for some instrumental purpose. Against theorists inclined to patholo-gize it, Cassirer's work repeatedly emphasizes that myth is, in its es-sence, an original and spontaneous creation on the part of humans en-deavoring to understand their world. But the modern myths of the twentieth century, by contrast, lack this earnest motivation, and are instead "artificial things fabricated by very skillful and cunning arti-sans," manufactured en masse "in the same sense and according to the same methods as any other modern weapon—as machine guns or airplanes."[61]

Cassirer's analysis of the modern political myths offers a novel, more urgent reason—different from those suggested in the anthropological or psychoanalytic literature—for the position that myths of any kind cannot be tolerated in modern political thinking. Far from being a safely insu-lated object of scientific inquiry, myth, in Cassirer's account, now proves capable of co-opting the language and tools of scientific rationality. This characterization of modern myth also departs from the psychoanalytic diagnoses that alternately associated myth with a repressed (Freud) or archaic (Jung) unconscious. The modern myths Cassirer attacks are no longer "the result of an unconscious activity" but are consciously and deliberately "made according to plan."[62]

These are not insignificant shifts. To object to the reemergence of myth in modern times because it is regressive, seems to suggest that the event is at worst a pause in the trajectory of human progress, and that Western civilization could be put back on its progressive track using the same scientific resources and methods that had helped end its reliance on myths the first time around. Cassirer's more pointed critique, however, suggests that modern political thought cannot af-ford a place for myth because these very resources may themselves be-come tainted when myth and the trappings of modern reason come together in the paradoxical, vicious combinations described at the end of *The Myth of the State*. But in particular, placing their chimeric na-ture at the center of his criticism of modern myth also presents a con-spicuous problem in Cassirer's interpretation of Plato and the legacy for which he stands.

CASSIRER'S PLATO

Plato occupies a foundational place of importance in Cassirer's account of the endeavor to overcome myth that has, throughout its history, defined the purpose and trajectory of philosophy. Cassirer's Plato was in many ways a celebratory mirror image of the man whom, half a century before, Nietzsche had famously panned as the great antihero of the Western philosophical tradition. Like Nietzsche, Cassirer credited Plato with instigating a great philosophical revolution that decisively set the course of Western thought, which he, like Nietzsche, understood in terms of a grand struggle against myth. But if Nietzsche had despaired the pathologies of an era that he took to be "the result of a Socraticism bent on the extermination of myth," Cassirer could not have been more explicit in his admiration for this same legacy.[63] Plato, in his view, was the quintessential champion of the position that the project of philosophy, and therefore of philosophically informed politics, had to coincide with the continual effort to rid our world of myths and their underlying remnants.

At first glance, the fact that Plato wrote myths might not seem particularly incongruous with either Cassirer's argument against myth in political thought, or with his heroic portrait of Plato and his legacy in these very terms. To the extent that Cassirer depicts the philosophical struggle against myth as a historical unfolding, Plato's indulgence in myths might be excused in light of the premodern time he inhabited: he might have taken the first transitional steps toward setting the project of philosophy into motion, while still living within the all-pervasive influence of the myths from which he endeavored to break away.[64]

However, Plato, in Cassirer's thought, stands in for much more than a historical moment. He consistently serves as a touchstone for characterizing the endeavors of philosophy and of political thought in their most essential forms, and, in particular, an embodiment of the first recognizably modern way of practicing them. He is depicted as an exact and rational figure whose achievements appear to have much more in common with the methods of modern philosophy than those of his predecessors. The Philosophy of Symbolic Forms opens with the assessment that, "compared with the sharpness of Plato's question and the rigor of his approach, all earlier speculation paled to tales or myths about being," so that Plato marks a breaking point, not just in the history of philosophy, but in its normative character: "It was now time to abandon these mythical, cosmological explanations for the true, dialectical explanations of being."[65] Moreover, there is something about Plato's efforts that renders them truer to the task of philosophy than even those of most thinkers who came after him. Had philosophy remained faithful to this original spirit, Cassirer suggests at the end of *The Myth of the State*, it would have been better equipped to prevent the regrettable reemergence of myth in the twentieth century. Notably, "the classical example of Plato alone" should suffice to show that the philosophical struggle against myth was not determined by historical contingencies, but had always required philosophers to "think beyond and against their times."[66]

More conspicuously, Cassirer's critique of modern myth had, as we have seen, emphasized how catastrophic it is for elements of myth and of modern rationality to mix together as they do in the phenomenon of the political myths of the twentieth century. Against this assessment, the interspersing of the languages of myth and of logical argumentation in Plato's philosophy should make him a particularly problematic figurehead for Cassirer's vision of a philosophy and politics committed to the rejection of myth. If it is the recruitment of the devices of rationality that lends modern myths their distinctive malevolence, it is unclear how Plato's philosophical myths can be exempted from this charge. What distinguishes Plato from the ideologues of fascism, so that the latter are mythmakers equipped with the arsenal of modern reason, while Plato remains a philosopher who wrote myths—all the while leading the philosophical struggle against them?

Certainly the contemporary resonance of this convergence of myth and rationalism in Plato's philosophy was not lost on Cassirer's contemporary, Karl Popper.[67] If Cassirer saw in Plato's work the purest model of philosophy's battle against myth, Plato represented for Popper the beginning of totalitarian mythmaking. In making his well-known indictment of Plato as the first and greatest enemy of the open society, Popper looked to the *Republic* and the model of the "arrested state" it had irreversibly released into the stream of Western thought.[68] In particular, he maintained that the alleged beauty of Plato's *kallipolis* could only be sustained by violent repression and deceit that culminate in Plato's "greatest propaganda lie," the Myth of Metals.[69] The resort to myth was a betrayal of the intellectualist principles for which Plato's mentor— Socrates—lived and died, and its total application to all aspects of life in the city was an abuse of the boundary between science and non-science. In a choice invective, Popper posed that "the modern myth of Blood and Soil," the twin determinants of race in Nazi ideology, had "its exact counterpart in Plato's Myth of the Earthborn."[70]

Popper's verdict on Plato and his legacy could not be more different from Cassirer's, but their disagreement is all the more striking because they agreed in so many different respects on the history and proper trajectory of philosophy and political thought. Both cleaved to an account of the Western intellectual tradition as being in large part a legacy stemming from foundations laid by Plato; both conceived of progress in the spheres of philosophy and politics in terms of a liberation from myth.

As such, Popper's Plato represents a conclusion available to, but evaded by, Cassirer as he navigates the tension between these commitments and the fact of Plato's myths. He does not even attempt to ignore or downplay the role of the myths in Plato's philosophy, as others have done in their efforts to either defend or to criticize an unambiguously rationalist Plato.[71] Instead Cassirer speaks of the uniquely "powerful imagination" that enabled Plato to become "one of the greatest myth makers in human history," that "we cannot think of Platonic philosophy without thinking of the Platonic myths."[72] He indicates awareness of the apparent paradox that "the same thinker who admitted mythical concepts and mythical language so easily into his metaphysics and his natural philosophy" was also "the professed enemy of myth" in the spheres of politics and ethics.[73] And in the face of seeming contradiction he goes on to celebrate Plato's myths with unusual ardor, going as far as to place them at the center of Plato's philosophy and political thought. His treatment of the Myth of Er, in particular, demonstrates the extent to which Cassirer is wedded to defending the philosophical value of Plato's myths, even if, as we shall see, this involves qualifying the argument he presents elsewhere against the toleration of myth in political thought.

The Myth of Er in *The Myth of the State*

The Myth of Er at the end of the *Republic* holds special significance for Cassirer. He identifies it as the site of a decisive turning point in the history of philosophy and in particular in the history of political theory's struggle to break free from myth. It is in this myth, Cassirer argues, Plato introduces to ethical and political thought a vital claim to the primacy of freedom in man's encounter with the world.

There are two parts to the argument: the setup of a pun on the word "eudaimonia" and the subsequent application of a microscopic level of focus on a very particular moment in the Myth of Er. Cassirer begins by presenting Plato as the inheritor of what he calls a Socratic definition of happiness as the highest aim of every human soul. The Greek word for happiness, he goes on to explain, is *eudaimonia,* which he translates—literally and idiosyncratically—as the possession of a good demon.[74] This setup in place, Cassirer turns to the climax of the Myth of Er, in which souls who are about to be reincarnated not only choose the pattern of their next lives, but—as Cassirer is eager to point out—also choose a demon that acts both as a guardian and personification of that chosen life.[75] The significance of the moment for the trajectory of political thought is that, in uniquely depicting individual souls as having a choice over their own demons rather than the other way around, Plato effectively inaugurates a new ethic founded on an assumption of individual agency and responsibility.[76] If the highest aim in life is happiness, understood to consist in the possession of a good demon, and if it is also the case—as it is in Plato's myth—that individuals choose their own demons, then it follows that the supreme ends of life are within our grasp, and whether or not we attain them is a matter of the choices we make rather than a matter left to chance.

But for Cassirer, the significance of this moment in the Myth of Er is not only that it placed a new premium on individual freedom in ethical thinking, but that this turning point amounts in particular to a repudiation of an essential element of myth. Cassirer draws a broad association between demons and the myths in which they tend to appear, and suggests that, to the extent that demons are recurring characters in these stories, the relationship they have with humans captures the essence of what constitutes a mythical orientation toward the world. He proposes that "in mythical thought man is possessed by a good or evil demon," and that it is likewise true of mythical thought more generally that it is animated by the presumption that humans are "under the iron grip of a superhuman, divine, or demonic force."[77] Accordingly, the decision, on Plato's part, to depict humans exercising the freedom to choose their own demons in the Myth of Er, effectively inverts a quintessentially mythic trope in order to assert a way of conceiving of man's relationship to his environment that is diametrically opposed to that presupposed in myths. Hence, in that moment in the Myth of Er, "a mythic motive is turned into its very contrary."[78]

In turn, from this same moment in the Myth of Er, Cassirer also draws what he identifies as the most central and valuable principle of Plato's political theory: namely, the rejection of myth from the sphere of politics. The "great revolutionary principle of Plato's *Republic*," for Cassirer, is that "not only the individual man but also the state has to choose its demon," and that "only by choosing a good demon can a state secure its eudaimonia, its real happiness."[79] This entails applying to politics the same lesson of the Myth of Er for the life of the individual, and ensuring that the common welfare of the state is not left to mere chance, but to the kind of rigorous and principled exercise of rationality required of free moral agents made responsible for their own destinies. The distinction, it seems, captures the stakes motivating the greater project of *The Myth of the State*: insofar as he credits Plato with the creation of the "rational theory of the state," Cassirer is committed to making a hard distinction between a politics driven by rational ideals, and a politics that falls victim to myths like the ones he saw in fascist ideology and propaganda.[80] It is in the name of that commitment that Cassirer affirms the banishment of the poets from the *kallipolis* in the *Republic*, which he takes to be a rejection, on Plato's part, not of "poetry in itself, but the myth-making function."[81] To tolerate myths of any kind in politics, Cassirer insists, is to come down on the wrong side of "the choice between an ethical and a mythical conception of the state."[82]

It is a strange, idiosyncratic reading of the Myth of Er. For one thing, it is strange to fixate so much on, and draw out such broad and consequential claims from, what appears to be a relatively minor detail in the Myth of Er. While it would be uncontroversial to locate the climax of the Myth of Er in the souls' choosing the patterns of their next lives, and while the myth presents the selection of a demon as being somehow related to that choice, the exact relationship between these two choices is not immediately clear, and Cassirer could be faulted for being too quick to conflate them. Moreover, it is also strange to read the choice that individual souls have over their demons as an unequivocal claim about the agency of the individual over his own fate, when so much of the eschatological landscape of the myth would appear to complicate, if not undermine, such a claim. In the Myth of Er, as we have seen, the choosing of life patterns takes place before the Spindle of Necessity and the three traditional goddesses of Fate, where the souls' choices are constrained by a number of other factors built into the eschatological apparatus: what patterns are available among the choices to begin with; what lot an individual soul has drawn, which determines the order in which he chooses; the biases each soul brings to the site, formed through his individual experiences in both his former life and the thousand-year journey of the afterlife.[83]

Cassirer may have had special reasons for singling out the demons in the Myth of Er in the way that he did. In addition to the significance he attributes to demons as being somehow emblematic figures of mythical representations, and central to the etymology of *eudaimonia*, Cassirer must have also had on his mind the resonance of the demon famously possessed by Socrates, which is said to have acted as a kind of conscience for the philosopher, or a nondidactic embodiment of a higher calling toward an ethical ideal.[84] But the glaring dissonance in Cassirer's reading of the Myth of Er is that he appears to be rejecting myth in the very same breath in which he celebrates Plato's myths. It is from a myth of Plato's own creation that Cassirer derives both of the following ideas: a paradigmatic claim for the necessity of rejecting myth from the political sphere, and a portrait of Plato as a champion of that endeavor. And what's more, contained in Cassirer's enthusiastic embrace of the myth is an obvious admiration for its literary form. It is clear from the weight that his reading gives to specific, symbolically charged moments in the narrative and fictional landscape of the myth that, for Cassirer, the Myth of Er would not have carried the same philosophical force if it were presented any other way; it had to be written as a myth.

The Enuma Elish

There is another way in which the Myth of Er is significant to Cassirer. Cassirer himself concludes *The Myth of the State* by retelling an ancient Babylonian myth. The Enuma Elish is a myth about the creation of the world: a god slays a great serpentine monster, and uses its limbs and parts to form the heavens and the earth, the constellation and planets, humanity itself. He subdues and binds the other dragons allied with the serpent. He creates order from the forces of chaos.[85]

The story might be read, Cassirer suggests, as an allegory for the status of myth in our world. Modern civilization is the result of a combat against and triumph over myth, and we must continue these struggles lest the monstrous force of myth rise again from its state of subjugation. The final lines of Cassirer's final book are a stern warning against slackening that vigilance: though "the mythical monsters" were defeated and used for the creation of a new world order, "they still survive in this universe. The powers of myth were checked and subdued by superior forces. As long as these forces, intellectual, ethical, and artistic, are in full strength, myth is tamed and subdued. But once they begin to lose their strength chaos is come again. Mythical thought then starts to rise anew to pervade the whole of man's cultural and social life."[86]

The irony of the decision to use a myth to conclude a book dedicated to the criticism of myth was not lost on readers.[87] But although this ending may appear to sound a note of aporia and gloom—does it mean to suggest philosophy will never truly overcome myth?—it also helps recall the lessons of Plato's original example. Even when we set aside his obvious admiration for the Myth of Er, it is impossible to imagine that Cassirer, the great intellectual historian, might have been unaware of the historical resonance of concluding one's great political theoretical treatise with a myth.[88] The ending of *The Myth of the State* falls into a sequence of well-known philosophical myths written in emulation of the Myth of Er—a sequence that includes the Dream of Scipio at the end of Cicero's

Republic, as well as the Petite Fable at the end of the *Theodicy,* whose author was one of Cassirer's great heroes, and the subject of his first book.[89]

More significantly, the features that Cassirer had found most remarkable in the Myth of Er reappear in his rendering of the Enuma Elish. The latter is, first and foremost, a philosophical call to arms against the forces of myth in culture. In particular, Cassirer places the emphasis of that struggle on an ethical ideal of freedom, and an understanding of a disorderly cosmos as capable of being shaped by rational agency. If a soul choosing his own demon in the Myth of Er breaks the spell of fatalism, Marduk, the anthropomorphic god of the Enuma Elish, chooses the shape of his own world as he reassembles the monster he has slain, and imposes his own rule upon the dragons he has defeated. But like his reading of the Myth of Er, Cassirer's Enuma Elish also asserts this ideal by using figures that are in some way quintessentially mythic—monsters, dragons, demons—to make a self-conscious statement on the status of myth itself.

A Compromise on Myth

Both Cassirer's reading of the Myth of Er and his own tribute to it at the end of *The Myth of the State* seem to indicate that he finds nothing particularly problematic about the use of myth as a literary device in philosophical writing. This might be an innocuous position to assume—if not for the strong stance his political theory takes against myth in all its forms, and for the unusually pointed insistence on the unique significance, evidenced in these cases, of the form of myth *as myth* in conveying certain philosophical ideas.

In Cassirer's thought, as we recall, those formal qualities of myth that are characteristic to the traditional literary genre are essentially tied to a particular mode of consciousness, or what he calls mythical thought, in such a way that nothing of myth can be admissible to his vision of politics: to permit the devices of myth to intermix with the achievements of modern rationality would be to introduce unprecedented dangers to the very foundations of our culture, and to risk toppling the entire system. Myth—he explains, in a justification for the banishment of myth in Plato's *Republic*—is characteristically "unbridled and immoderate"; it cannot be tolerated in the political and ethical sphere because it "exceeds and defies all limits."[90] But Cassirer's treatment of the Myth of Er, as well as his more general remarks about Plato's myths, make the mythic representation of these stories indispensable to the philosophical argument itself. Here, Cassirer presents these philosophical myths not only as being congruent with, but as advancing, a vision of political theory committed to combating the influence of myth.

This suggests that, when Cassirer carves out an exceptional place for the literary use of myth in philosophy, his stance on myth also becomes far more ambivalent than what is otherwise his stated position.[91] Effectively, the example of Plato's myths drives a wedge between two of his other claims—the rejection of myth from political thought, and the portrait of Plato as a paradigmatic champion of that cause—and, in defending the genre of the Platonic myth, he softens his commitment to these earlier positions. He ends up, in essence, splitting his conception of myth into parts that are acceptable and parts that are not; under certain conditions, the borrowing of the resources of myth in philosophy can even be salutary. He maintains, on the one hand, that "the famous Platonic myths" belong unambiguously to the genre of myth, just like the traditional stories they sought to imitate. On the other hand, he is also adamant that Plato nonetheless created his myths "in an entirely free spirit," directing them according to "the purposes of dialectical and ethical thought. "Genuine myth," he insists, "does not possess this philosophical freedom, for the images in which it lives are not *known* as images."[92]

WHY MYTH AT ALL?

What does Cassirer mean when he singles out Plato's myths this way? What difference does it make when a myth's images are known as images? Even if Cassirer can defend the distinction as a coherent and meaningful way of setting apart Plato's myths from all other myths, his efforts raise the more puzzling question of why he goes to such lengths to draw the distinction in the first place. Why does he find it important to embrace Plato's myths *as myths,* so that the use that Plato makes of myth in his philosophical writing is not merely an excusable indulgence, but specifically commendable in the way he adapts literary resources particular to the mythic genre?

In order to understand what it is about myth that Cassirer seeks to preserve in its Platonic incarnations, we need a fuller account of the quality of philosophical freedom that Cassirer attributes to Plato's myths. This Platonic account, in turn, allows Cassirer to demarcate a place for myth in his political theory that retains, nonetheless, a progressive and dynamic vision of modern culture and its trajectory.

Innovation and Stabilization in the Symbolic Forms

In Cassirer's philosophy of culture, each of the symbolic forms is caught in a tension between two opposing intellectual inclinations. On the one hand, human intellectual activity is propelled by a spontaneous drive for creative expression, and the symbolic forms are the various modes in which such expression is sought.[93] This expressive drive is an innovative force that continually strives to stretch the boundaries of knowledge beyond the confines of familiar structures of understanding.[94] On the other hand, the products of this expansive process also "have a life of their own" that comes to be at odds with the purely creative impulse. While man constantly creates new constructs of meaning relating himself to his world, he also seeks, at the same time, to "stabilize and propagate his works."[95] As such, the forms of human expression also have a tendency to preserve themselves into stasis, long outlasting the individual circumstances in which they arise. Both of these opposing inclinations govern the dynamics of how all of the various symbolic forms grow, develop, and interlock into a unified system of knowledge:

> In all human activities we find a fundamental polarity, which may be described in various ways. We may speak of a tension between stabilization and evolution, between a tendency that leads to fixed and stable forms of life and another tendency to break up this rigid scheme. Man is torn between these two tendencies, one of which seeks to preserve old forms whereas the

other strives to produce new ones. There is a ceaseless struggle
between tradition and innovation, between reproductive and
creative forces. This dualism is to be found in all the domains
of cultural life.[96]

There are a number of consequences for Cassirer's position on myth
that follow from this. First, his account of the tension between the two
inclinations sheds light on a crucial point of difference that sets apart
his own understanding of the relationship between myth and philosophical knowledge from accounts like that of Popper. Myth was Popper's
name for a "dogmatic attitude" that stood in contrast to the "critical attitude" particular to science, and scientific knowledge progressed from
myth insofar as beliefs previously held true made themselves available
to refutation.[97] Although scientific myths were possible in the form of
dogmatically held axioms or conjectures about scientific content, they
could never pass for scientific knowledge unless their dogmatic character
were to give way to critical awareness; this was the way Popper defined
science. For Cassirer, by contrast, the opposition between dogma and
criticism does not map quite so neatly onto that between myth and science. Dogma is not exclusively the province of myth, just as a certain
discerning attitude toward the provisionality of knowledge is not the exclusive purview of science. Rather, insofar as both myth and science are
symbolic forms, they are both caught in the dialectical tension between
the two tendencies of the intellect. The pathological temptation of the
human spirit "to be imprisoned in its own creations" is hence found not
only "in the images of myth" but also "in the intellectual symbols of cognition."[98] When need be, philosophy must be ready to be critical of the
achievements even of modern science; and one of Cassirer's sharpest
rebukes—anticipating a focal rallying point of the Frankfurt School—
is levied at a purely technical rationality that results from a pathological reliance on the tools of science without this critical capacity.[99]

This also means that, in Cassirer's account, the dialectic governing
the progress of knowledge from myth to science is far more complex.
Precisely because the substantive content of myth and that of science are
not commensurate—as had been assumed by Popper and anthropologists
like Tylor—they do not quite exist on the same continuum of knowledge

in which converting the former into the latter is a matter of criticism and refutation. Instead, in insisting on the distinctiveness of myth and science as separate modalities of knowledge, each pulled in its own way by the two drives, Cassirer implies that innovation that resists cultural inertia may look very different from one symbolic form to another. The overcoming of a myth, for instance, would not take the form of falsification and counterexample, as is common practice in the advancement of scientific knowledge, but would instead require a kind of disruption internal to the mode of myth itself—a breakthrough that pushes mythic conventions from within.

Second, myth is a less progressive symbolic form than its more sophisticated counterparts, not because it is synonymous with the preservationist tendency, but because it is disproportionately inclined toward it. While all forms of knowledge and expression, according to Cassirer, are caught in a tension between the tendency toward stabilization and the tendency toward novelty, they are not equally drawn to either pole, and the proportion by which the counterbalancing forces govern each symbolic form in large part determines its character and "its particular physiognomy."[100] In myth, that proportion is heavily skewed toward the preservationist tendency at the expense of the innovative impulse.

The reason for this appears to stem from myth's incapacity for abstraction, a feature that Cassirer isolates as one of myth's defining characteristics. Unlike science, which can occupy an abstract, disinterested plane from which it can take reality as an object of inquiry, myth commands an undifferentiated empire of intense, immediate impressions of the world, where it "is simply overpowered by the object."[101] It tells stories in which magical forces, demons, idols, and other fantastic elements, originally fabricated by the mythic mind as a means of interpreting reality, easily take on the valence of inevitability. Where the fantastic and the natural are mixed together indistinguishably—any ordinary tree in a myth could very well turn out at any point to be sacred, embody a spirit, carry magical powers, or share its health and fate with a particular hero or the entire cosmos—taboos and rituals upheld by myths can come to dictate life in the same way that natural necessity does. If myth is initially motivated by a drive to create new ways of conferring meaning onto a raw reality that is merely given, that creative process is slowed by the medium's characteristic attachment to particular things in the absence of definition, to a concrete immediacy without abstraction. As such, it is too quick to stabilize around its own creations, which "once again resum[e] the form of the given."[102]

Third, what Cassirer takes to be the task of philosophy is geared not so much at resisting the stabilizing impulse, as at navigating the tension between the two tendencies as they manifest in all of the symbolic forms. For Cassirer, the conservative tendency to preserve and to reproduce old forms is not in and of itself condemnable. It is, at the very least, an unavoidable facet of the "dialectic of bondage and liberation" that "the human spirit experiences with its own self-made image worlds."[103] More significantly, the creative expansion of knowledge requires relatively stable forms to rework and foundations on which to build; a tissue of old knowledge must be comfortably taken for granted in order for new inventions to break out of the established mold, and withstand or be transformed by the scrutiny of criticism.[104] The need to understand the aims of philosophy as a balanced navigation of the two tendencies is always a pressing demand, because the struggle for innovation and the threat of stagnation in fact grow in proportion to each other: "the more richly and energetically the human spirit engages in its formative activity, the farther this activity seems to remove it from the primal source of its own being."[105] The preservationist tendency inevitably accompanies even our most innovative symbolic expressions, so that it takes a discerning art to know what acts are those that consolidate and build progressively on existing cultural forms, and those that replicate them insipidly.

Platonic Dialectic and Platonic Myth

The art of discernment capable of navigating the delicate balance between stabilizing and innovative tendencies within symbolic forms, and in turn, between the diversity of the symbolic forms and the unity of human knowledge, is the art that Cassirer calls "dialectic," after its meaning in Plato's philosophy. It consists of a kind of systematic demarcation, by which parts that make up a whole are put in their proper places. Cassirer believes this organizational endeavor underlies all legitimate efforts toward knowledge, including myth: tying together the various ways of knowing, however undeveloped or rudimentary the form, is "the same capability of analysis and synthesis, of discernment and unification, that, according to Plato, constitute and characterize the dialectic art."[106] Dialectic, so understood, can mark out and delimit discrete realms in which existing forms might stabilize and flourish on their own terms, without stymying the growth of knowledge more generally. Cassirer's stake in Platonic dialectic is hence an answer to his ambition to establish a philosophy of culture that can lend unity to the diversity of the symbolic forms. Our intellectual creations grow in opposite directions, toward stability and the familiar as well as toward dissolution and novelty, and this tension is present, not only across the spectrum of knowledge but within each of its modes, in myth as well as in science. Dialectic steers philosophy through this dynamic, allowing the forms of knowledge and culture to settle without stagnating; it is a way of partaking in the plurality of forms of thought, while also determining the limits of each mode.

It is, in particular, a way of practicing philosophy that requires great vigilance, one that requires philosophers to resist, when necessary, the metastasizing of the most abstract and sophisticated parts of their own systems. In Cassirer's portrait of Plato, the theory of Forms presents at once a monumental achievement in the philosophical struggle against myth, as well as a great temptation toward the danger of intellectual stagnation, to which myth is particularly vulnerable. On the one hand, the abstraction of the Forms introduces "a higher standard . . . that of the 'Idea of Good,'" by which the myths of Plato's *kallipolis* are to be "brought under a strict discipline."[107] On the other hand, the "perfect beauty" of the Form of the Good is also a seductive ideal that inspires in Plato a "deep yearning for the *unio mystica,* for a complete union between the human soul and God."[108] Indeed, some of Plato's followers—Cassirer names Plotinus and other philosophers associated with the Neoplatonic tradition—have fallen into the "mystic" trap suggested by this central element of Plato's philosophy. But Plato himself, Cassirer insists, never gives in to that passion.

> Plato admits no mystical ecstasy by which the human soul can
> reach an immediate union with God. The highest aim, the knowl-
> edge of the idea of the Good . . . cannot be seen in a sudden
> rapture of the human mind. In order to see and understand the
> philosopher must choose "the longer way." The mystical mind
> in Plato was checked both by his logical and by his political
> mind.[109]

Plato's restraint, for Cassirer, is a product of the commitment to balance
that constitutes his dialectical practice: the capacity to simultaneously
assert a philosophical framework for interpreting reality, and to refrain
from pursing it beyond its limits. In Plato's work, this tension is "never
resolved," and the unresolved nature of the struggle is precisely what
characterizes philosophy.[110]

Furthermore, the kind of resistance to intellectual calcification demanded by the balance of dialectic may take surprising forms, and it
may partake in the resources of the plurality of symbolic expression.
Cassirer's deep appreciation for Plato's myths is hence inseparable from
his account of Platonic dialectic. On this reading, Plato's myths function as a creative means of breaking up the inertial pull of familiar
frameworks, both in his philosophy as well as in mythical convention,
all the while without losing sight of the whole, incomplete expanse of
human knowledge, or of the particular limits of its constituent parts.

At one level, the measured quality of self-awareness that Cassirer
claims for Plato's myths is what makes them, despite their hybrid character, radically different from the political myths of the twentieth
century, which lack that sense of limitation. Plato is invoked approvingly
throughout the diagnostic discussion of modern myth concluding *The
Myth of the State,* underscoring Cassirer's efforts to distinguish the
former from the propagators of the latter, and, plausibly, preparing his
readers for the philosophical myth he appends at the very end of the
work. He returns to the Myth of Er once again in an ostensible move to
observe that it has essential identifying features in common with both
traditional myths and their contemporary counterparts—in this case,
the philosophy of Oswald Spengler—but pulls back quickly to emphasize that, the myth's attention to the images of Fate notwithstanding, it

is exceptional all the same. "This is a Platonic myth," he insists, "and Plato always makes a sharp distinction between mythical and philosophical thought. But in some of our modern philosophers this distinction seems to be completely effaced."[111]

But at another level, Platonic myth, as a genre of philosophical myth-writing, is not merely excusable in light of its observance of limits; it is a distinct achievement of philosophical dialectic precisely because it employs its own mythic features to break new ground in philosophical expression. Cassirer's reading of the Myth of Er had located its philosophical force in Plato's inversion of the characteristically mythic figure of the demon, so that it asserted an ethical ideal entirely opposed to that which routinely finds reinforcement in myths. And undoubtedly a similar intention grounds his own decision to adapt a Babylonian creation myth into a somber call to arms against the influence of myth latent in modern culture. He expresses appreciation elsewhere for such moments of reappropriation, whereby elements of mythic convention are directed toward ends other than that to which myth usually defaults. For instance, he praises the allegorical use of Greco-Roman mythological characters in Lorenzo Valla's *Dialogue on Free Will*—in the scene that eventually comes to provide the source material for Leibniz's Petite Fable—as a moment in which "ancient myth . . . receives a new role" and "becomes the vehicle of logical thought."[112] These are moments of innovation that endeavor to test the possibilities of what myths can accomplish, and Cassirer celebrates them because they testify to the creative and dynamic capacity of our symbolic forms of expression to transform themselves from within. They suggest, in particular, the hope that the most durable elements in myth, the ones that are not undone by individual instances of criticism or refutation, might be mitigated more effectively with unexpected forms of expression incorporating resources taken from myth itself.[113]

Myth, Tradition, and Philosophy

Cassirer leaves many questions unanswered when he insists on drawing a fundamental distinction between myth at large and the Platonic genre of myth. He provides little guidance, for instance, on how one might properly recognize myths that are motivated by the spirit of freedom he attributes to Plato's myths, and be certain that they are in fact distinct from myths that—like the modern political myths—are deployed deliberately toward an instrumental end, but still end up binding their authors in the vicious logic of mythical thought. Further complicating such problems of differentiation are the seemingly contradictory claims Cassirer appears to make throughout his investigations, suggesting that myth inherently resists boundaries and limitations, and is inherently impossible to bring fully under control.[114] Moreover, an essential quality that sets apart Plato's myths for Cassirer is that they reinvent mythical conventions in innovative and often unexpected ways, and this makes it particularly difficult to translate into concrete, formal prescriptions the general principles he suggests for separating acceptable and unacceptable categories of philosophical myth.

It may be the case that Cassirer had not fully worked through all of the potential contradictions that arose from defending all three of the positions he held on myth and on Plato. And between his strong indictment of myth, his celebratory portrait of Plato as an emblematic champion of a demythologized philosophy, and his embrace of Plato's myths, he may be accused of having chosen the wrong position on which to compromise. But in reconstructing the progressive capacity of Plato's myths within a theory of myth that is otherwise staunchly opposed to it, Cassirer underscores the incomplete character of the project of modernity: namely, that we inhabit a stage of culture in which, at least for the time being, dense, figurative modes of thought that do not give in to criticism and scrutiny will continue to have purchase in our political and cultural life; and that, so long as this is the case, the literary resources of myth can be incorporated into a dynamic philosophical language seeking to tackle those elusive frameworks of meaning. And in insisting on the foundational importance of Plato for the Western philosophical tradition, he suggests that the identity of modern philosophy is more fragile than we think, and that philosophy, too, relies on founding narratives like the one that Plato represents for us when we try to supply accounts of what philosophy is, where it is now, and how it got there.

In turn, the narrative Cassirer advances of the intellectual tradition stemming from Plato is not one that tracks the legacy of his myths, but it is one that continually reaffirms the ethic of philosophical freedom that had made Plato's myths coherent to him. Throughout his studies of intellectual history Cassirer remains steadfastly bound to affirming the ideal of humanity's progressive self-liberation—from the efforts of the Cambridge Platonists to build on that which they found most worthy of preserving in classical thought, to the commitment on the part of the philosophers of the Enlightenment to the freedom and autonomy of the individual mind.[115] But his celebratory embrace of the progressivist ideal is not so much about rejecting backwardness as it is about first understanding on their own terms those forces and tendencies—mythic or otherwise—that require transcending. He invokes Bacon as a guide, not only for a model of knowledge held to the standards of scientific inquiry, but for the spirit with which he insisted that the understanding of nature must come before its conquest; his work on Leibniz depicts a pioneer who not only dreamed that knowledge might one day be articulated in a universal scientific language, but also took as a central principle of his philosophy that the human mind at thought is, first and foremost, creative and spontaneous in its continual efforts to perfect itself.[116] Even the proponents of the new mythology in German Idealism, whom he charges with having "drunk from the magic cup of myth" and paving an inadvertent path to the political myths of his own time, did so out of deference toward a view of cultural flourishing centered around the ideal of universal freedom.[117]

These historical portraits, in turn, capture Cassirer grappling with a more expansive conception of the role of philosophy in human culture, as an endeavor constantly required to reinvent the forms and modes it inhabits, even as it works toward the same unchanging goals. As he calls on philosophers to stay true, in whatever way they see fit, to the "intellectual and moral courage" of Plato to break out of the default postures of one's own time, Platonic myth also turns into a reminder of the capacity of philosophy to find solutions to its own problems in unexpected places.[118] In that limited and cautious regard, Cassirer looks to the resources of philosophical myth as a disruptive antidote to the danger latent in all legitimate efforts toward making sense of our world—that of falling too hard for one's own intellectual creations, that idolatry of images that constitutes the ultimate Platonic sin.

CONCLUSION

HOW SHOULD THEORISTS UNDERSTAND the legacy of Plato in political thought and its history? I have sought to show that the tradition of philosophy whose beginnings are attributed to Plato is a tradition that goes beyond the reputation it often enjoys in the popular imagination, as well as in accounts that political theorists supply about the identity and trajectory of their discipline. It is, in particular, a tradition that complicates a prevalent portrait of Plato as the figurehead for a movement that casts the category of myth in opposition to that of philosophy, and in turn, as a tangle of opaque and irrational forces whose influence must be removed from the sphere of politics.

The authors we have encountered in this book took Plato's myths to be philosophically significant. They studied them with a careful scrutiny reflective of that premise, imitating them in their own philosophical and political writings, or aspiring to reinvent them anew; and they did so in conjunction with broader reflections on the relationship between myth, critical reason, and the nature and aims of politics. This means that, on their interpretation, Plato's myths represented not only a constructive form of philosophical expression that uniquely complemented logical argumentation, but also a dynamic genre that accommodated perpetual reworking and reevaluation. They attributed this kind of meaning to Plato's myths because they embraced the hypothesis that the literary features particular to the genre of myth can tap into a deeper, figurative process at work in the way humans frame and structure their worldviews. Those dense and opaque stories we tacitly tell about ourselves and our world were, for these authors, an unavoidable facet of philosophy and political life, and they believed it imperative to engage with this thought rather than deny it. The possibilities they discovered in the mythic genre for telling and retelling our stories testify to that conviction and that hope.

A LEGACY RECONSIDERED

A central argument of this book has been a historical claim pointing to the need for a more faithful representation of Plato's legacy in political theory. In the foregoing chapters, I have presented an account of the afterlife of Plato's myths in modern political thought, showing that the philosophical tradition stemming from Plato was not simply a rationalist enterprise, but one in which myths played a special part. This means that, whenever we turn to Plato and his project as a point of reference for talking about the identity of the Western philosophical tradition, we are obliged to get it right: we cannot take the nature of his accomplishment for granted, and we cannot overlook the significance of his myths to his philosophy or his legacy.

Notably, the portrait of the Platonic legacy I have painted stresses the salience of Plato's myths, but not for some of the more familiar reasons that have been given in their defense. It is not the portrait found, for instance, in certain strands of Christian Neoplatonism, which reserves a privileged place for myth as a source of inspired knowledge about topics beyond the reach of philosophy and human reason. Nor is it a portrait—invoked in interpretive approaches to Plato ranging from the humanist to the Straussian—in which the myths serve an important rhetorical function, often in the interest of easing the communication of difficult or otherwise unpalatable philosophical messages to a nonphilosophical audience. Rather, what is distinctive about the Platonic tradition that I have sought to recover is its embrace of the potential that myth could itself be turned into a form of philosophical discourse, for incorporation into philosophical writing alongside argumentative reasoning. As such, it remains a way of understanding Plato's legacy that is consistent with the rational philosophical legacy for which he is conventionally celebrated.

We have seen that, for Plato, the literary medium of myth was a resource that could be used to redraw the contours of certain deep, foundational concepts that are built into the fabric of the philosophical and political imagination. This was, importantly, a way of harnessing myth's constructive features aimed, not at deceiving a credulous citizenry, but at rewriting a conceptual landscape that philosophers in the *Republic* themselves depended on to orient their self-understanding. And if myths had a distinctly philosophical part to play in Plato's writings, this insight was not lost on some of his most astute early modern readers. For More, Bacon, and Leibniz, writing myths for their respective reimaginings of the *Republic* was a means of identifying the frameworks that need to be taken for granted in our thinking before it is possible for us to engage meaningfully in philosophy. More and Bacon invented founding myths for *Utopia* and *New Atlantis* in order to carve out a stable sphere for theoretical activity in their respective utopias; whereas paying homage to the Myth of Er at the end of the *Theodicy* allowed Leibniz both to diagnose and to lend expression to a deep narrative about the rationality of the universe, the fundamental doctrine grounding his emancipatory vision of human reason.

Plato's practice of writing philosophical myths also served as a crucial touchstone for a number of pioneers in the philosophy of myth, even amid mounting anxiety over its ultimate compatibility with modern life and culture. For the central theorists of the new mythology in German Idealism, Plato's myths affirmed a broader conviction underwriting their shared political vision: that myth was an extension of the modern philosophical project as they understood it, and that embracing this would in turn open up new ways of thinking and of living together in society. For Ernst Cassirer, writing at a time when philosophical antipathy toward myth reached new heights, the singular example of Plato's myths exemplified the possibility that the genre might still provide philosophical discourse with the creative resources to revitalize itself against the more pathological forms of myth plaguing modern politics.

Needless to say, the authors in this tradition had different reasons to find the genre of myth fruitful for their projects, just as they did not all read Plato's myths the same way. Binding them together, however, was an uncommonly consistent program built on the principle that the literary genre of myth can be appropriated for philosophical writing to engage a deeper, more figurative dimension of our worldviews—be it the central political concepts from which we draw our identity as individuals and as a community, the shared creative vocabulary that bonds individuals together, or the undemonstrable stories to which philosophy must commit for its activities to hold meaning. The category of myth, for these authors, represented the possibility of better identifying, understanding, and even transforming such frameworks where other philosophical means come up short.

This shared principle, in turn, can help us see the practice of philosophy and its history in a different light. Political theorists need no reminding of the significance of the forms in which ideas are set to text. Nonetheless, the mythic tradition at the center of this book offers a particularly compelling challenge to some of the more persistent preconceptions in the discipline about what the project of philosophy entails, and what it ought to look like. If this tradition undermines a certain image of Plato in the way he has been canonized in political thought—as the champion of a theoretical enterprise built on the exclusion of myth and what it represents—it also helps us to see past an understanding of philosophy that has adopted that particular version of Plato as its founding figure. Philosophy, we are sometimes led to imagine, is a rarefied discipline whose nature is fundamentally bound up in the practice of formulating and refuting arguments. But this narrow image may no more represent the essence of philosophy than it does its history. Many of the authors in this study were canonical, influential figures in their own right, and together they provide—however episodically—a window into significant stretches of the history of Western philosophy. For a start, the remarkable manner in which they brought Plato's influence to bear in their philosophical writing reveals that literary experimentation with the genre of myth was more prevalent in the Western philosophical tradition than commonly recognized.

This is something that tends to get forgotten in approaches to myth in philosophy and political theory today, which continue to have difficulty disentangling the category of myth from its antiphilosophical associations. In the decades during and after Cassirer wrote *The Myth of the State,* theoretical discussions of myth flourished with continued momentum into the 1980s, though Plato was often conspicuously decoupled from many of the mainstream debates. It was the legacy, not of Cassirer, but of his contemporaries, that ended up leaving the more lasting imprint on political theory. Famously in the *Dialectic of Enlightenment,* the founding text of the Frankfurt School, Horkheimer and Adorno embraced a definitional understanding of myth as a kind of fatalistic orientation toward the world, or the perception that the established order of things is beyond change.[1] Though their aim was to expose the false promise of the Enlightenment project, and the ironic extent to which it had ended up getting entangled in those same fatalistic worldviews, Horkheimer and Adorno remained committed to what they took to be its most defining ideal: the liberation of humanity from myths. Their sophisticated but ultimately damning account of myth—as something we ought to conceptualize in opposition to our philosophical and political ideals—continues to resonate with us, especially through the work of Jürgen Habermas and the many theorists of public reason he has come to influence.[2] Although there were significant efforts in the latter half of the twentieth century—notably by the philosopher of myth Hans Blumenberg—to neutralize the concept and to bring out its more specific, literary meaning, they have largely failed to gain a similar level of traction in political theory.[3]

When we pay attention, however, to the constructive use of myth in the writings of Plato and his successors, we can also see that there is something historically misguided about the simple opposition that contemporary political theorists are inclined to draw between myth and philosophy. We see, for a start, that the literary genre of myth has been conflated too quickly and unnecessarily with some of the things it has been made to stand for. It is possible, Plato's mythic tradition has shown us, to write myths for philosophy in conformity with its broader ideals, and without conjuring the unbridled irrationality, delusion, or fatalism that have come to be associated with the medium. Denying this, in fact, consigns theorists to a needlessly narrow vision of both myth and philosophy.

Plato and his successors help us see, at one level, the need for a more nuanced approach to studying myth than those supplied by existing theoretical frameworks. They prescribe that we draw more careful distinctions between the literary genre of myth and the pejorative connotations that have been historically ascribed to it, and that we attend, in turn, to the spectrum of alternate ways it might yet hold significance for us. This task will require us to think beyond the easy and conventional accounts of myth and its broader meaning, and it will involve, as I will elaborate later, redrawing the conceptual terrain of what we can productively draw under the heading of this category today. But in taking such steps, we will be unlocking a rich and vibrant field of study—one that promises to be a fertile ground for better understanding an array of cultural phenomena that often elude our attention and analysis.

At another level, Plato and the mythic tradition he launched also help us embrace a more expansive understanding of philosophy, in particular by encouraging us to take an inclusive stance on what counts as philosophical writing. Calls for inclusiveness in philosophy and its neighboring areas of study can sometimes strike traditionalists as an imperative that has emerged relatively recently, in response to novel pressures and considerations that, though important, are not necessarily internal to the discipline itself. But the writings of Plato and his heirs in the mythic tradition remind us not to overlook, as we so often do, the formal vibrancy of our own canon. When we are more attentive to the richness of this heritage, we are better positioned to both understand and represent philosophy in a more dynamic, imaginative, and inventive light than it is often given credit for. This invites us, in turn, to be open to different styles of philosophical presentation, especially from the margins of our discipline, and to be attuned to the diverse insights we have yet to gain from unconventional forms of knowledge.

THE NARRATIVES OF POLITICAL THEORY

Bound up with my reassessment of Plato's legacy in political thought and its history is a related lesson about the kind of political theory I have done in it. The mythic tradition I have tried to recover in this book is, as we have seen, only one of several overlapping Platonic legacies that have coexisted—some fading in and out of prominence—throughout the history of Plato's reception. These multiple legacies have served to remind us that history is a site of contesting interpretations, but also that navigating them, in turn, is a way of coming to grips with our intellectual heritage and reevaluating our relationship with it. This constitutes, I believe, a relatively overlooked aspect of what it is that political theorists accomplish when they revisit historical authors.

Studies in the history of political thought are often framed in terms of present concerns. They might take up a set of topical or recurring questions in contemporary politics, and show that similar questions have preoccupied authors in the past. On this approach, recovering the work of past authors can be fruitful for political theory because they can teach us older, forgotten ways of thinking about issues that are relevant to us today. Alternately, historians of political thought might hope to learn from past authors whose concerns we might no longer share, but who can still enrich our thinking by showing us alternatives to the questions and solutions we have come to take for granted. Their historically situated insights are valuable, on this view, because they help denaturalize the assumptions undergirding our visions of politics, which can enable us to recognize conceptual blind spots, understand the contingent factors that have shaped the topics at the forefront of our theoretical concern, and bring greater self-awareness to our approach to studying them.

I have sought, in this book, to offer an alternative defense of the history of political thought—one based on the stories that political theory tells about itself. We have seen, in the foregoing chapters, the extent to which the authors in the mythic tradition—as well as their Skeptic, Neoplatonist, and Enlightenment rationalist interlocutors—found themselves at the center of an interpretive battleground as they clashed over what Plato wrote and what he stood for. These disputes are a testament to the variety and range of ways in which readers have drawn meaning and inspiration from Plato over the ages. But they also invite us to take stock of how, for many, these acts of interpretation also became a means of rewriting the narrative of the philosophical tradition as they imagined it.

Political theorists look to authors from the past, and especially to canonical figures, partly as a way of understanding the trajectory, identity, and aims of their discipline. Plato continues to be fought over today, for a range of causes and at a level of intensity that confirm the extent to which he continues to embody a kind of origin story for the discipline, if not, indeed, the Western intellectual tradition.[4] Such stories underscore the tendency on the part of political theorists to organize their thought around inherited traditions and categories. We do not emphasize this enough. Doing so enables us to appreciate the contingency and imperfection of our canon, while also acknowledging the reasons we find these authors—and the narratives formed around them—so attractive.

The history of political thought can be a way of revisiting and reclaiming the narratives that political theory deploys to understand its own project without disavowing our need for them. Rather, it is when we embrace our reliance on such narratives that we can begin to draw out their versatility. By deepening our appreciation for the plurality of interpretative traditions that canonical figures generate, we also guard against monolithic appropriations of them. Their enduring grip on the theoretical imagination should not worry us, but should instead prompt us to remember that they remain available to be claimed by new interpretations.

MYTH AND POLITICS TODAY

Finally, if there is a normative lesson to be learned from the mythic tradition I have recovered in this study, it is that we ought to rethink our conception of myth and, in turn, the way we approach and respond to the figurative dimensions of modern politics.

In the preceding chapters I have largely tried to constrain my use of the term "myth" to the traditional literary genre that fascinated these authors, and have sought, as much as possible, to distinguish it from the modes of thinking, stages of culture, and social phenomena that they and their contemporaries sometimes called by the same name. By drawing out the constructive possibilities that Plato and his readers saw in this genre, however, I have also tried to reclaim a broader concept from its fraught reputation in modern political discourse. Rather than associating the genre with irrationality and obscurity, or with the efforts of a cynical elite to manipulate a gullible, ill-informed public, these authors have shown how myth can also stand for much more: as a resource intimately connected to philosophy and reason; as a vision of organic bottom-up change; as an article of faith in human freedom.

The richness of these connections makes a case for the study of myth as a distinct theoretical category. To the extent that contemporary political theorists take up myth as a subject for investigation, they tend to subsume it under broad headings like ideology or religion, or—in line with the orthodox view—they treat it as a foil for philosophy, primitive and dangerous, as the temptation of irrationality from which we must fight to disentangle our thinking. The things we associate with myth, and in particular the history of theorizing about myth, certainly share substantial overlaps with these spheres, but it would be a mistake to collapse the significance of the concept into any of these topics. For one thing, it would lead us to overlook many of the qualities that are distinct to the constellation of experiences and phenomena that thinkers have tried to conceptualize using the category of myth.

This brings us to the question of the status of myth today. "Myth" has once again become a current term in our politics—a term that is used in a more expansive sense than my own. Today we talk about myths for lack of a more precise way of observing that the widespread assumptions and beliefs that inform our worldviews are littered with stray fantasies, vague and persistent tropes, longings for a past that never quite was, dreams of a future that have no grounding in reality. In recent years, the language of myth has been variously invoked to characterize, for instance, long-standing ideas about how we expect people filling certain roles—victims, heroes, artists, workers, welfare recipients— to look like and to behave; illusory appeals to the concept of a single unified nation, or of a somehow more authentic version of the nation; the nostalgic rhetoric used to romanticize any given part of history as a kind of golden age; creeping echoes of frontier symbols and imagery in American foreign policy.[5]

Designating these things as the myths of our time, in many cases, has been a means of expressing a more general anxiety about the health and future of our politics. The turn to this language comes against the background of a yawning gap between contemporary political developments and the more narrowly rationalist visions that dominated much of twentieth-century liberal thought. In times of mounting disillusionment in the power of facts and reasoned arguments to provide an enduring foundation for politics, worries about the rise of myths in society and culture go beyond a concern about misinformation—though misinformation seems to be a symptom of the deeper problem. At stake instead is the existential threat posed by the growing influence of cultural forces that appear immune to correction altogether—forces that are endemic to our imagination and move us at a more elusive level. Just as writers in the early and mid-twentieth century feared that fascism signaled a resurgence of myth, commentators today are alarmed by the extent to which the worldviews of political actors are governed by grand narratives and symbolic frameworks that resist critical scrutiny.[6]

The array of fantastic narratives percolating in our politics today may not be what Plato and his successors had in mind throughout their investigations into myth and its possibilities. Certainly, if we look for exact counterparts in our society of the mythological tradition to which Plato was responding, or the cultural artifact and literary genre that fascinated his heirs, we are likely to be frustrated in our search. But Plato's philosophical myths, and their continual reinterpretation and reinvention by his readers, remind us that, even in the relatively niche domain of philosophical writing, the genre of myth can assert itself as a medium of fluctuating forms and meanings. It should not surprise us, then, that myth in our world does not look the same: the recognizable stories, motifs, and symbols that we have inherited might be secluded to a more limited sphere; and the narratives of significance that might, in a different cultural context, be expressed mythically, might be articulated today in more scattered and less identifiable forms in our own heterogeneous culture.

More importantly, the preoccupation with myth in the Platonic tradition contains a more general lesson about the powerful role that the figurative aspects of our thinking play in politics, and the importance of engaging these forms of thought in creative ways. By studying and experimenting with a peculiar literary genre, the protagonists of this book also grappled with a set of more deeply ingrained frameworks structuring the way we understand our world. If we take seriously the thought that the worldviews of contemporary political actors are affected by frameworks that similarly activate the imagination, and seem similarly resistant to critical scrutiny, we may then also have to reconsider how we respond to such phenomena.

Political theorists are often reluctant to advocate engaging the contemporary manifestations of what I have earlier called "deep myths." To do so, they feel, would risk reinforcing the crudest, most impulsive parts of our natures rather than demand that we step up to the norms of rationality that our political ideals require of us. Critics often point to the explicit project of Nazi ideologues to present their propaganda as a form of myth—a project that remains a cautionary tale about the catastrophic price of admitting such forces into the domain of politics. Theorists may accordingly conclude that the risks are simply too great, and that, even in their rhetorical capacity, accommodating the seeming incarnations of myth in our politics today ultimately cannot be justified. They might point out, for instance, that Sorel's famous defense of myth—as a catalyst that can mobilize people toward heroic action and progressive ends—ultimately ended up supplying theoretical fodder for Mussolini's fascism. We ought not to involve ourselves with myths at all, they would insist, precisely because they are so consequential and can only trap us in predicaments that will prove all the more difficult to recover from.

Theorists who do feel it is necessary to take on the myths of our times tend to envision a painstaking project of dismantling them, one by one, through facts and arguments. Motivated by a particular, modernizing ideal of rational politics, theorists who take this view are inclined to think that there is nothing of consequence in the content of such myths that isn't better off distilled into a more analytic form, and that we accordingly ought to aspire to leave them behind for more lucid alternatives. The most sophisticated variants of this approach emphasize that the work of debunking and clarifying our myths is necessary in the interest of protecting a fragile public sphere that requires constant, principled maintenance. If we do involve ourselves with myths, such theorists would insist, we ought to do so with the aim of eliminating them in their present form.

There are good reasons to adopt these approaches, both of which are ways of tackling the considerable dangers that the activation and manipulation of deep myths can present in politics. But in focusing too much on the potential hazards of myth, they overlook something fundamental. First, they put us at risk of being in denial about the intractability of certain forces that are very much a part of our political reality and are not about to go away anytime soon. We may consequently approach our present-day myths the wrong way, debunking each one with facts and further scrutiny, only to find them resurfacing in new forms. Or we might be at a loss as to how they might ever fit into our ideas of what a reasonable politics ought to look like, and, lest we inadvertently dignify or legitimize them, might refuse to acknowledge them at all.

But if Plato and his successors were especially attuned to the ways in which our worldviews contain deeply lodged imaginative elements that cannot be translated without loss into more conventionally rational forms, they also suggest to us that there might be something similarly irreducible about the stray myths that seem to drift through contemporary politics and culture. Indeed, a growing body of empirical scholarship suggests that our conceptual systems operate figuratively—in metaphors, symbols, and narratives, rather than in syllogisms or validity claims—and these studies indicate, in turn, that our propensity for myth may be much more ingrained in our thinking than we might care to acknowledge.[7] If this is true, refusing to address the instantiations of myths in our world would not only fail to make their attendant problems go away, but would also shut out an important aspect of political life, if not of human experiences more broadly.

Efforts to dissolve such myths with arguments and facts, however well intended, may not only be misguided, but can backfire. They can paint a misleading picture of a world split between people who are moved by facts and logic, and people who simply need to learn to reason better. To cast groups and individuals into the latter category can be patronizing in a way that proves frustrating on both the side of those seeking to inform and of those who remain unpersuaded. Such impasses, in turn, are easy occasions for breakdowns in political communication and loss of trust, for breeding resentment and aggravating polarization. Efforts to silence our myths altogether by denying them acknowledgment court similar dangers, as they can similarly shut out viewpoints and people from the epistemic mainstream. As long as we resist reconciling ourselves to the possibility that the myths in our environment are more durable than we might like, we will be asking people to relinquish, and alienate themselves from, frameworks of meaning that may still resonate deeply with them.

Second, when we approach our myths as misconceptions to be debunked, or refuse to engage them at all, we also risk overlooking their unique resources, the ones that go beyond their rhetorical function and might still be channeled in constructive alignment with our political values. Plato and his successors believed that, by appropriating the literary genre of myth in philosophical writing, they could gain access to a number of otherwise opaque forms of thought in ways that were consistent with the larger aims of their political theory. Their vision, in turn, raises the possibility that the expression and activation of our own society's deep myths need not necessarily undermine rational politics, but may in fact enhance its practice. In particular, they urge us to pay greater attention to the work that images, symbols, and narratives contribute to the creation of political meaning.

Political discourse can be enriched when its participants work harder to extend recognition to worldviews that do not translate immediately into propositional content, but are more responsive to ambiguous narrative and figurative forms. Expanding our conceptions of appropriate discourse this way can, at one level, point us toward a more inclusive politics that brings together a greater diversity of perspectives.[8] It can be a starting point for opening up, rather than closing off, meaningful inquiry and exchange. But aspiring to such inclusiveness is important, at another level, because its potential advantages are notably bound up with more complex issues of epistemic possibility. In recent decades, scholars of political narrative have been increasingly attuned to a lesson that activists have intuited for a long time: that the value of storytelling has not just a rhetorical but an epistemic dimension.[9] It can help groups and individuals identify, uncover, and make sense of experiences that do not map neatly onto existing categories of what the artist David Wojnarowicz once called "the preinvented world."[10] It has the potential to illuminate intuitions and experiences for which conventionally rational formulations do not exist, chart out new areas of intellectual investigation, and rouse the philosophical imagination.

It would seem, then, that the opaque symbols and template narratives that we call myths today ought not to be approached from a posture of denial about either their persistence or their power. Instead, we ought to be ready to accept a messier political reality in which they may very well be an enduring fixture, and even seek to harness the potential resources they might hold.

But what would engaging our myths this way entail? The response suggested by the protagonists of this book is one that advocates embracing the figurative qualities that make them so opaque to critical scrutiny, while also endeavoring to find creative means of reworking them time and again. Despite mounting pressures to think otherwise, the authors of this mythic tradition related myths to deep frameworks in our worldviews that not only were an important source of meaning and stability but also had the capacity to be reshaped through unconventional means. This tradition underscores the increasing need for us to reckon with both the harmful and the salutary possibilities that our myths might open up for us today. This task will require us to approach them with thoughtfulness and imagination, to dig beneath their surface and draw out the patterns of meaning underpinning them, while also being vigilant to ensure they don't harden into their most pathological forms. Crucially, it asks us to engage dynamically with them, by reframing and reclaiming the symbols and narratives surrounding the ideals we hold dear, and when need be, telling new stories to shake up our perception of the natural order of things.

It is worth emphasizing that engaging our contemporary myths on their own terms brings substantive risks, including the very dangers that have led so many political theorists to be wary of them. Indeed, celebrating our power to create and to revise such myths can paint an overly rosy picture of what they can do for us, and it certainly places us in uncharted theoretical territory. In particular, it raises the problem of having to differentiate, in the absence of a clear framework of guiding principles, between myths that are harmful and those that are not. Many of the authors in the mythic tradition tried to contain this problem by limiting their engagement with myth to the invention of a discrete genre of Platonically inspired philosophical myth. The myths they wrote within these constraints were explicitly allied with philosophy, and were embedded in larger works, where they were often juxtaposed with arguments or other more conventional forms of exposition. They were constructed in a self-conscious fashion that allowed them to signal the dynamism of the medium and the provisional and contingent status of their claims, and this, in turn, helped open them to reinterpretation and revision.

These lessons in reflexivity may be modest, and they may not translate very easily into a neat set of prescriptions for a world and a time in which philosophical writing is at once more sequestered and more specialized than ever before. All the less so in our present age of information, in which the communication of nuance is routinely sacrificed to the demand for simple and distinct—at times sensationalist—sound bites. In such an age, the onus falls harder on the judgment of ordinary citizens to protect what is dynamic and meaningful about our myths without being in thrall to them. As such, making room for them in our politics also places on us a different kind of responsibility. It leaves us with the task of cultivating a culture of vigilance that equips us to be more conscientious consumers and agents of myths. This project demands, for a start, a heightened awareness of our own creative agency in the way we interpret, find expressions for, and reshape our political symbols and narratives. We ought to take them seriously, with epistemic humility and open-mindedness, but without consuming or promulgating them passively. We must take care not to allow the interpretation or creation of myths to be the exclusive purview of the powerful and, as we see fit, must seek to counter them with alternatives.

It may very well transpire that such a prospect raises more difficult questions than we are prepared to answer. But if we decide this is too high a cost to bear, we miss the point. A politics that opens up to its myths demands more of us as we begin to navigate an uncertain balance between their pitfalls and their potential. But it is, ultimately, at once more vulnerable and more ambitious than a politics that aspires to shut them out. In stepping up to the challenge, we recognize that we draw significance, in our everyday lives as well as in times of over-whelming uncertainty, from certain imaginative frameworks for making sense of the world, which, in turn, lend themselves easily to the kinds of metaphorically rich, symbolically fraught expressive structures we find in myths. They can variously equip individuals and communities with momentum and meaning to social movements, alternative accounts to the narratives of those in power, cultural continuity to weather extreme events of abrupt change, or simply the imaginative resources to help us find ourselves at home in our environment.[11]

Whether and to what extent these diverse functions can be construc-tively brought under the same heading is a question that might not be answered definitively, but, in having raised it, the authors in Plato's mythic tradition ask us to take it seriously. In using the genre of myth as a theoretical proxy for exploring the place of these elusive forces in our lives, they deserve credit for their prescient recognition of both the richness and the fragility of the narrative dimensions underwriting human experiences.

NOTES

INTRODUCTION

1. Alix Kirsta, "J'accuse," *Guardian,* April 17, 2004, sec. Guardian Weekend Pages, 34.

2. "The Guilty Party," *Time* 64, no. 23 (December 6, 1954), 43.

3. Rupert Furneaux, "Gaston Dominici, Killer of the Drummonds," in *Famous Criminal Cases,* vol. 2 (London: Wingate, 1955), 113–126.

4. Maitre Rozan, the public prosecutor, repeatedly phrased his account in such terms: "Our charge against Gaston Dominici," he said, "is that for one second in his life he behaved like a monster." Furneaux, "Gaston Dominici," 123.

5. Roland Barthes, "Dominici, ou le triomphe de la littérature," *Les lettres nouvelles* 23 (January 1955): 151–154. By this point Barthes had already published a number of the essays that would come to be collected into *Mythologies* (Paris: Éditions du Seuil, 1957). Like the majority of the other essays that were first published in periodicals, "Dominici" was released as part of an installment that would make up the regular column, "Petite Mythologie du Mois"—*little mythology of the month.*

6. For these examples, see Roland Barthes, *Mythologies,* trans. Richard Howard and Annette Lavers (New York: Hill and Wang, 2012), esp. "Dominici, or the Triumph of Literature" (48–52) and also "The Dupriez Trial" (113–115), "In the Ring" (3–14), "A Few Words from Monsieur Poujade" (92–95), and "Poujade and the Intellectuals" (206–214).

7. Barthes, *Mythologies,* 49, 51.

8. Barthes, *Mythologies,* 51. Barthes estimated that the prosecutor's account was "plausible, as the temple of Sesostris is plausible." Barthes, *Mythologies,* 49.

See also his more elaborate discussion of elemental imagery conjured in the language of Pierre Poujade, the populist politician: the common folk were associated with the earth, and the intellectuals and technocrats with the air. Barthes, *Mythologies*, 206–207, 209.

9. Five years after the infamous trial, Dominici's sentence was commuted to a life sentence with hard labor, and de Gaulle released him on humanitarian grounds in 1960. He was never pardoned. In an interview with the *Guardian* in 2004, Gaston Dominici's grandson testified that the family name is still haunted by superstition. "Many still believe a vice runs in our blood. . . . Listen, even today, some fathers forbid their daughters to go out with anyone called Dominici." Kirsta, "J'accuse."

For an account of the shifting narratives around the reception of the Dominici case in the French popular imagination, as the figure of Dominici transformed in public opinion from the brutish perpetrator of the crimes to the romanticized victim of the modern legal system, see Martin Kitchen, *The Dominici Affair: Murder and Mystery in Provence* (Lincoln: University of Nebraska Press, 2017).

10. Pierre Bourdieu, *Outline of a Theory of Practice* (Cambridge: Cambridge University Press, 1977), 164–172; Ernst Cassirer, *The Philosophy of Symbolic Forms*, trans. Ralph Manheim, vol. 1, *Language* (New Haven, CT: Yale University Press, 1953), e.g., 75–76.

11. Charles Taylor, *Modern Social Imaginaries* (Durham, NC: Duke University Press, 2004), 23–30. See also the forerunner of the term in Cornelius Castoriadis, *The Imaginary Institution of Society*, trans. Kathleen Blamey (Cambridge, MA: Polity Press, 1998). Taylor's own conception of the social imaginary is influenced heavily by Benedict Anderson, *Imagined Communities: Reflections on the Origin and Spread of Nationalism* (London: Verso, 1983).

12. Because Barthes's project in *Mythologies* was the application of structuralist linguistic theory to popular culture, he had a very specific definition of myth, and it should be noted that he himself did not exactly identify these implicit cultural frameworks as myths. Rather, he used the term "myth" to denote a particularly pernicious conflation of both the deep, implicit framework as well as its more explicit expression in the products of culture.

Some theorists of myth have designated specific terms to describe the underlying narrative component of cultural artifacts. These theorists were working from the position that "myth" referred to only the explicit literary manifestations of these deeper cultural frameworks. Instead, the implicit frameworks underlying these stories were given names like *archetype, mytheme,* and *mythologem,* by Carl Jung, Claude Lévi-Strauss, and Hans Blumenberg, respectively. These concepts are set apart, of course, on a number of dimensions, such as the question of whether they are eternal or dynamic, universal or particular to specific cultures and contexts, strictly narrative in nature or consisting in more general clusters of symbolic

NOTES TO PAGES 5-6 **243**

elements. Where they overlap, however, is in that they are understood to be discrete units of an essential substratum to what these theorists accepted as myth.

13. Lincoln, *Discourse;* Mary Midgley, *The Myths We Live By* (London: Routledge, 2003); for politicized instantiations, see Chiara Bottici, *A Philosophy of Political Myth* (Cambridge: Cambridge University Press, 2007); Henry Tudor, *Political Myth* (New York: Praeger, 1972); and Christopher Flood, *Political Myth: A Theoretical Introduction* (New York: Garland, 1996); as well as Georges Sorel, *Reflections on Violence,* trans. Jeremy Jennings (Cambridge: Cambridge University Press, 1999), esp. 21 and 29.

14. Tudor, *Political Myth,* 16, 137–139; W. Lance Bennett, "Myth, Ritual, and Political Control," *Journal of Communication* 30 (1980): 167; Flood, *Political Myth,* 44; Bottici, *A Philosophy of Political Myth,* 7.

Discourse around the definition of myth has produced a number of important fault lines of contention: for instance, whether myth is strictly narrative or more loosely figurative in nature; whether the designation of myth can be used to describe modern phenomena, or whether myths can arise in modern societies to begin with; whether the subject of myth is sacred to the culture in which it arises; whether the significance of myth is specific to its cultural context or more universal in its reach; and whether the audience of myth sincerely believes its content. For a survey of some of these definitional debates, see Percy S. Cohen, "Theories of Myth," *Man* 4, no. 3 (1969): 337–353; and also note 12 above.

15. For Bottici and for Tudor, myth in common usage is characterized by "fictitiousness, unreality, and untruth," and both go on to decouple the criterion of falsehood from the definition of myth. Bottici, *A Philosophy of Political Myth,* 10; Tudor, *Political Myth,* 13, 16–17. The significance of this move on Bottici's part is discussed in Herbert De Vriese, "Political Myth and Sacrifice," *History of European Ideas* 43, no. 7 (2017): 813–815.

16. On myth as false consciousness, see Andrew Von Hendy, *The Modern Construction of Myth* (Bloomington: Indiana University Press, 2002), 51–54.

On the connection between myth and institutions, see G. S. Kirk, *The Nature of Greek Myths* (New York: Penguin, 1974); John W. Meyer and Brian Rowan, "Institutionalized Organizations: Formal Structure as Myth and Ceremony," *American Journal of Sociology* 83, no. 2 (1977): 340–363; Mark C. Suchman and Lauren B. Edelman, "Legal Rational Myths: The New Institutionalism and the Law and Society Tradition," *Law & Social Inquiry* 21, no. 4 (1996): 903–941.

On myth and belief systems, see Émile Durkheim, *The Elementary Forms of Religious Life,* trans. Karen E. Fields (New York: Free Press, 1995); Bronisław Malinowski, "Myth in Primitive Psychology," in *Magic, Science and Religion, and Other Essays* (Garden City, NY: Doubleday, 1954), 72–124; Kirk, *The Nature of Greek Myths,* 32.

On myth and ideology, see Flood, *Political Myth*, 44; Karl Mannheim, *Ideology and Utopia: An Introduction to the Sociology of Knowledge* (London: Routledge, 1991); Louis Althusser, "Ideology and Ideological State Apparatus (Notes towards an Investigation)," in *Lenin and Philosophy, and Other Essays,* trans. Ben Brewster (New York: Monthly Review Press, 2001), 85–126; see also discussions in Von Hendy, *The Modern Construction of Myth*, 278–304; Terry Eagleton, *Ideology: An Introduction* (London: Verso, 1991), 188–192. Barthes also understood his "mythologies" to be ideologically motivated.

On myth and nationalism, see Anthony D. Smith, *The Ethnic Origins of Nations* (Oxford: Blackwell, 1986); Anthony D. Smith, *Myths and Memories of the Nation* (Oxford: Oxford University Press, 1999); Arash Abizadeh, "Historical Truth, National Myths and Liberal Democracy: On the Coherence of Liberal Nationalism," *Journal of Political Philosophy* 12, no. 3 (2004): 291–313; Bruce Lincoln, *Discourse and the Construction of Society: Comparative Studies of Myth, Ritual, and Classification* (Oxford: Oxford University Press, 1989); Duncan S. A. Bell, "Mythscapes: Memory, Mythology, and National Identity," *British Journal of Sociology* 54, no. 1 (2003): 63–81; David Miller, *On Nationality* (Oxford: Oxford University Press, 1995), 35–41; David Archard, "Myths, Lies and Historical Truth: A Defence of Nationalism," *Political Studies* 43, no. 3 (1995): 472–481.

17. Von Hendy, *The Modern Construction of Myth*; Fritz Graf, *Greek Mythology: An Introduction,* trans. Thomas Marier (Baltimore: Johns Hopkins University Press, 1993), 9–56.

18. Bernard de Fontenelle, "Of the Origin of Fables," in *The Rise of Modern Mythology, 1680–1860,* ed. and trans. Burton Feldman and Robert D. Richardson (Bloomington: Indiana University Press, 2000), 18.

19. Graf, *Greek Mythology,* 54.

20. "Thus science must begin with myths, and with the criticism of myths, . . . The scientific tradition is distinguished from the pre-scientific tradition in having two layers. Like the latter, it passes on its theories; but it also passes on a critical attitude towards them. The theories are passed on, not as dogmas, but rather with the challenge to discuss them and improve upon them." Karl Popper, *Conjectures and Refutations: The Growth of Scientific Knowledge* (New York: Basic Books, 1962), 50.

For Habermas, modern rationality similarly requires the shedding of "mythical worldviews," which, "with respect to the conditions for a rational conduct of life . . . present an antithesis to the modern understanding of the world." This is because mythical worldviews make it impossible for a society to achieve the conditions for rational communicative action between its members: they "are not understood by members as interpretive systems that are attached to cultural traditions, constituted by internal interrelations of meaning, symbolically related to reality, and connected with validity claims—and thus exposed to criticism and open to revision." Hence, the modernizing and rationalizing process that Habermas calls the "linguistification of the sacred" entails the conversion of the trappings of myth into norms that invite criticism, whereby the "aura of rapture and terror that emanates from the sacred, the *spellbinding* power of the holy, is sublimated into the *binding/bonding* force of criticizable validity claims." Jürgen Habermas, *The Theory of Communicative Action*, 2 vols., trans. Thomas McCarthy (Boston: Beacon Press, 1984, 1987), 1:44, 1:52–53, and 2:77.

21. See, for example, Alfred Rosenberg, *Der Mythus des zwanzigsten Jahrhunderts: Eine Wertung der seelisch-geistigen Gestaltenkämpfe unserer Zeit* (Munich: Hoheneichen-Verlag, 1933); Arthur Moeller van den Bruck, *Das dritte Reich*, ed. Hans Schwarz (Hamburg: Hanseatische Verlagsanstalt, 1931); Jörg Lanz-Liebenfels, *Theozoologie, oder Die Kunde von den Sodomsäfflingen und dem Götter-elektron* (Vienna: Moderner Verlag, 1905).

22. For instance, Horkheimer and Adorno regarded the ceremonies of Nazism as "imitations of magical practices" with "the *Führer* . . . lead[ing] the dance." Karl Popper likewise accused fascism of having resurrected "the tribal ideal of the Heroic Man" into new forms. Max Horkheimer and Theodor W. Adorno, *Dialectic of Enlightenment: Philosophical Fragments*, ed. Gunzelin Schmid Noerr, trans. Edmund Jephcott (Stanford, CA: Stanford University Press, 2002 [1944]), 152; Karl Popper, *The Open Society and Its Enemies*, vol. 1, *The Spell of Plato* (Princeton, NJ: Princeton University Press, 1966), 277. See also Susan Sontag, "Fascinating Fascism," *New York Review of Books*, February 6, 1975.

23. Frank E. Manuel, *The Eighteenth Century Confronts the Gods* (Cambridge, MA: Harvard University Press, 1959).

24. Wilhelm Nestle, *Vom Mythos zum Logos: Die Selbstentfaltung des griechischen Denkens von Homer bis auf die Sophistik und Sokrates* (Stuttgart: A. Kröner, 1975 [1940]).

25. G. W. F. Hegel, *Vorlesungen über die Geschichte der Philosophie*, vols. 18–20, in Georg Wilhelm Friedrich Hegel, *Werke*, ed. Eva Moldenhauer and Karl Markus Michel, 20 vols. (Frankfurt am Main: Suhrkamp, 1971), 2:29, cited in Michael Rosen, *Hegel's Dialectic and Its Criticism* (Cambridge: Cambridge University Press, 1982), 106.

26. Popper, *Conjectures and Refutations*; Habermas, *The Theory of Communicative Action*, 1:44–53.

27. Abizadeh, "Historical Truth."

28. Elizabeth Markovits, *The Politics of Sincerity: Plato, Frank Speech, and Democratic Judgment* (University Park: Pennsylvania State University Press, 2008), 126–127; Abizadeh, "Historical Truth."

29. On the romantic connection between myth and national character, see Johann Gottfried Herder, "Iduna, oder der Apfel der Verjüngung," in *Sämmtliche Werke,* ed. Bernhard Ludwig Suphan, 33 vols. (Berlin: Weidmann, 1877–1913), 18:483–502; "Von den ältesten Nationalgesängen," in *Sämmtliche Werke,* 23:148–152; "Vom Geist der Ebräischen Poesie," in *Sämmtliche Werke,* 11:213–466 and 12:1–308; "Älteste Urkunde des Menschengeschlechts," in *Sämmtliche Werke,* 6:193–511; Christian Gottlob Heyne, "An Interpretation of the Language of Myths or Symbols Traced to Their Reasons and Causes and Thence to Forms and Rules," in *The Rise of Modern Mythology, 1680–1860,* ed. Burton Feldman and Robert D. Richardson (Bloomington: Indiana University Press, 1972), 220–223; Christian Gottlob Heyne, "Vorrede," in Martin Gottfried Hermann, *Handbuch der Mythologie aus Homer und Hesiod als Grundlage zu einer richtigern Fabellehre des Alterthums* (Berlin: Friedrich Nicolai, 1787).

On the social function of myth in early twentieth-century anthropology, see Durkheim, *The Elementary Forms of Religious Life;* James George Frazer, *The Golden Bough: A Study in Magic and Religion,* abridged ed. (New York: Macmillan, 1960); Jane Ellen Harrison, *Prolegomena to the Study of Greek Religion* (Princeton, NJ: Princeton University Press, 1991); Bronisław Malinowski, *Myth in Primitive Psychology* (New York: W. W. Norton, 1926); Georges Dumézil, *Gods of the Ancient Northmen,* ed. and trans. Einar Haugen (Berkeley: University of California Press, 1973).

30. Meyer and Rowan, "Institutionalized Organizations."

31. Sorel, *Reflections on Violence.*

32. On myth as an expressive response to the natural environment, see, e.g., Giambattista Vico, *New Science,* trans. David Marsh (London: Penguin, 2001); Johann Gottfried Herder, "Fragment of an Essay on Mythology (c. 1782–92)," in *Against Pure Reason: Writings on Religion, Language, and History,* ed. and trans. Marcia Bunge (Minneapolis: Fortress Press, 1993), 80–83.

As a response to the inner drama of the psyche, see Sigmund Freud, *Totem and Taboo: Some Points of Agreement between the Mental Lives of Savages and Neurotics,* ed. and trans. James Strachey (New York: W. W. Norton, 1989).

33. Sigmund Freud, *Civilization and Its Discontents,* ed. and trans. James Strachey (New York: W. W. Norton, 1989); Sigmund Freud, *Moses and Monotheism,* trans. Katherine Jones (New York: Vintage Books, 1967); see also Ernst Cassirer, *The Myth of the State,* ed. Charles William Hendel (New Haven, CT: Yale University Press, 1946), 295–298.

34. Carl Jung, "Approaching the Unconscious," in *Man and His Symbols,* ed. Carl Jung (Garden City, NY: Doubleday, 1964), 1–94; see also Carl Jung, *The Essential Jung,* ed. Anthony Storr (Princeton, NJ: Princeton University Press, 1998), 88–127.

Claude Lévi-Strauss, "The Structural Study of Myth," *Journal of American Folklore* 68, no. 270 (1955): 428–444; Claude Lévi-Strauss, *The Savage Mind* (Chicago: University of Chicago Press, 1966); Claude Lévi-Strauss, *Mythologiques* (Paris: Plon, 2009).

35. Horkheimer and Adorno, *Dialectic of Enlightenment,* xviii.

36. Hans Blumenberg, "Light as a Metaphor for Truth: At the Preliminary Stage of Philosophical Concept Formation," in *Modernity and the Hegemony of Vision,* ed. David Michael Levin (Berkeley: University of California Press, 1993), 30–62; Hans Blumenberg, *Paradigms for a Metaphorology,* trans. Robert Savage (Ithaca, NY: Cornell University Press, 2010); Hans Blumenberg, *Shipwreck with Spectator: Paradigm of a Metaphor for Existence,* trans. Steven Rendall (Cambridge, MA: MIT Press, 1997); Hans Blumenberg, *Care Crosses the River,* trans. Paul Fleming (Stanford, CA: Stanford University Press, 2010).

37. For Derrida, it was itself a brand of myth—or what he called a "white mythology"—to ignore the extent to which the projects of philosophy continued to carry the residual meanings of their borrowed metaphors. Jacques Derrida, "White Mythology: Metaphor in the Text of Philosophy," trans. F. C. T. Moore, *New Literary History* 6, no. 1 (1974): 5–74. Consider also Carl Schmitt's study of the mythical symbol of the leviathan, as appropriated by Hobbes: Schmitt suggests that such symbols will ultimately elude rational attempts to control them for instrumental use. Carl Schmitt, *The Leviathan in the State Theory of Thomas Hobbes: Meaning and Failure of a Political Symbol,* trans. George Schwab and Erna Hilfstein (Chicago: University of Chicago Press, 2008).

38. Hans Blumenberg, *Work on Myth,* trans. Robert M. Wallace (Cambridge, MA: MIT Press, 1990); see also Bernard Yack, "Myth and Modernity: Hans Blumenberg's Reconstruction of Modern Theory," *Political Theory* 15, no. 2 (1987): 244–261; Angus Nicholls, *Myth and the Human Sciences: Hans Blumenberg's Theory of Myth* (London: Routledge, 2014).

39. Dana Villa, *Socratic Citizenship* (Princeton, NJ: Princeton University Press, 2001); see also John R. Wallach, *The Platonic Political Art: A Study of Critical Reason and Democracy* (University Park: Pennsylvania State University Press, 2001); Joel Alden Schlosser, *What Would Socrates Do? Self-Examination, Civic Engagement, and the Politics of Philosophy* (New York: Cambridge University Press, 2014), 21–22, 29–30.

40. John Stuart Mill, "Grote's Plato," in *The Collected Works,* 33 vols., ed. John M. Robson (Toronto: University of Toronto Press, 1963–1991), 18:403–415; see also "On Liberty," in Robson, *The Collected Works,* 18:251; "Inaugural Address Delivered to the University of St. Andrew's," in Robson, *The Collected Works,* 21:229–230.

41. Julia Annas, "Plato the Skeptic," in *Oxford Studies in Ancient Philosophy,* suppl. vol., ed. James C. Klagge and Nicholas D. Smith (1992): 43–72; Hannah Arendt, "Philosophy and Politics," *Social Research* 57, no. 1 (1990): 73–103; Dan Avnon, "Know Thyself: Socratic Companionship and Platonic Community," *Political Theory* 23, no. 2 (1995): 304–329; Ryan Balot, "Socratic Courage and Athenian Democracy," *Ancient Philosophy* 28 (2001): 49–69; J. Peter Euben, *Corrupting Youth: Political Education, Democratic Culture, and Political Theory* (Princeton, NJ: Princeton University Press, 1997); Euben, *Platonic Noise* (Princeton, NJ: Princeton University Press, 2003); S. Sara Monoson, *Plato's Democratic Entanglements: Athenian Politics and the Practice of Philosophy* (Princeton, NJ: Princeton University Press, 2000), 164–165; Mary Nichols, *Socrates and the Political Community* (Albany: State University of New York Press, 1987); Villa, *Socratic Citizenship.*

42. "The safest general characterization of the European philosophical tradition is that it consists of a series of footnotes to Plato." Alfred North Whitehead, *Process and Reality: An Essay in Cosmology,* ed. David Ray Griffin and Donald W. Sherburne (New York: Free Press, 1978), 39.

43. Melissa Lane, *Plato's Progeny: How Socrates and Plato Still Captivate the Modern Mind* (London: Duckworth, 2001); see also Catherine H. Zuckert, *Postmodern Platos* (Chicago: University of Chicago Press, 1996).

44. Cassirer, *The Myth of the State;* Jean-Pierre Vernant, *Myth and Society in Ancient Greece,* trans. Janet Lloyd (Brighton, UK: Harvester, 1980), 221–222. See also Friedrich Nietzsche, *The Birth of Tragedy,* ed. Michael Tanner, trans. Shaun Whiteside (London: Penguin, 2003); Alexander Nehamas, *Virtues of Authenticity: Essays on Plato and Socrates* (Princeton, NJ: Princeton University Press, 1999), 316–318; Martin Luther King Jr., "Letter from Birmingham Jail," in *Why We Can't Wait* (New York: Signet, 1964), 79–80.

45. Kathryn A. Morgan, *Myth and Philosophy: From the Presocratics to Plato* (Cambridge: Cambridge University Press, 2000), 17–24; Bottici, *A Philosophy of Political Myth,* 20–21; Axel Horstmann, "Mythos, Mythologie," in *Historisches Wörterbuch der Philosophie,* 13 vols., ed. Joachim Ritter (Basel: Schwabe, 1971), 6:218–318.

The first known use of the term "mythology" also occurs in Plato, though commentators are divided on the significance of this observation. Morgan, *Myth and Philosophy,* 289n79; G. S. Kirk, *Myth: Its Meaning and Functions in Ancient and Other Cultures* (Berkeley: University of California Press, 1975), 8; see also Robert L. Fowler, "Mythos and Logos," *Journal of Hellenic Studies* 131 (2011): 65.

Famous dismissals of *mythos* prior to Plato occur in Herodotus (2.23.1 and 2.45.1) and in Thucydides (1.21), though the critique is not systematic. For an extensive survey of the mythos–logos dichotomy in antiquity, see Fowler, "Mythos and Logos"; and also Morgan, *Myth and Philosophy.*

46. Nestle, *Vom Mythos zum Logos*, 1, 17.

47. J. A. Stewart, *The Myths of Plato* (London: Macmillan, 1905), 1–2; Seth Benardete, *Socrates' Second Sailing: On Plato's Republic* (Chicago: University of Chicago Press, 1992), 4; see also Penelope Murray, "What Is a Muthos for Plato?," in *From Myth to Reason? Studies in the Development of Greek Thought,* ed. Richard Buxton (Oxford: Oxford University Press, 1999), 254–257.

48. Some scholars have tried to push back against the rigidity of the opposition between myth and dialectic argumentation in Plato's works, by denying that there is much of a stylistic boundary at all between the two. J. N. Findlay, "The Myths of Plato," *Dionysius* 2 (1978): 19–34; Plato, *Dialogues,* 4 vols., ed. and trans. Benjamin Jowett, 4th ed. (Oxford: Clarendon Press, 1953), 3:698, cited in Murray, "What Is a Muthos for Plato?," 151; see also 259–262.

49. Aristotle, *Poetics* 1451a31; Luc Brisson, *Plato the Myth Maker,* trans. Gerard Naddaf (Chicago: University of Chicago Press, 1998), 59–60; Plato, *Gorgias,* ed. E. R. Dodds (Oxford: Clarendon, 1959), 332; Morgan, *Myth and Philosophy,* 179.

50. Bottici, *A Philosophy of Political Myth,* 30–31; Ludwig Edelstein, "The Function of the Myth in Plato's Philosophy," *Journal of the History of Ideas* 10, no. 4 (1949): 463–464.

51. "Die mythische Darstellung, als älter, ist Darstellung, wo der Gedanke noch nicht frei ist: sie ist Verunreinigung des Gedankens durch sinnliche Gestalt." Hegel, *Vorlesungen über die Geschichte der Philosophie,* 2:20.

52. Elizabeth McGrath, "Platonic Myths in Renaissance Iconography," in *Plato's Myths,* ed. Catalin Partenie (Cambridge: Cambridge University Press, 2009), 167–186.

Readers disagree on whether the Allegory of the Myth is a myth. For instance, J. A. Stewart does not include it in his classic study *The Myths of Plato,* though his list is already more conservative than most. For reasons that will become clear in Chapter 1, I follow Jonathan Lear, among many others, in considering the Cave a myth. Jonathan Lear, "Allegory and Myth in Plato's *Republic,*" in *The Blackwell Guide to Plato's Republic,* ed. Gerasimos Xenophon Santas (Oxford: Wiley-Blackwell, 2006), 25–43; see also Bottici, *A Philosophy of Political Myth,* 31.

53. Nietzsche, *The Birth of Tragedy.*

54. Popper, *The Open Society and Its Enemies,* 1:1.

55. For example: Louis Couturat, *De Platonicis Mythis* (Paris: F. Alcan, 1896); G. M. A. Grube, *Plato's Thought* (London: Methuen, 1935); Eric A. Havelock, *Preface to Plato* (Cambridge, MA: Harvard University Press, 1982); see also Kent F. Moors, *Platonic Myth: An Introductory Study* (Washington, DC: University Press of America, 1982), 2–3.

56. E.g., Bertrand Russell, *A History of Western Philosophy* (London: Routledge, 2004), 113; see also Russell, "An Outline of Intellectual Rubbish," in *Basic Writings,* ed.

Robert E. Egner and Lester E. Denonn (London: Routledge, 2009), 59. The extreme counterpart to this position would be one that prioritizes a strand of Neoplatonism in which Plato's myths are taken so seriously as to be considered divinely inspired—that is, of a nature superior to knowledge arrived at through rational channels. See, for example, Joseph Pieper, *Über die platonischen Mythen* (Munich: Kösel Verlag, 1965).

57. Michael J. B. Allen, "Renaissance Neoplatonism," in *The Cambridge History of Literary Criticism,* ed. Glyn P. Norton, vol. 3, *The Renaissance* (Cambridge: Cambridge University Press, 1999), 435–441.

58. Blumenberg, *Work on Myth.*

59. Blumenberg, *Work on Myth.*

1. NATURE AND MYTH IN PLATO'S *REPUBLIC*

1. Karl Popper, *The Open Society and Its Enemies,* vol. 2, *The High Tide of Prophecy: Hegel, Marx, and the Aftermath* (Princeton, NJ: Princeton University Press, 1966), 61; Julia Annas, *An Introduction to Plato's Republic* (Oxford: Oxford University Press, 1981), 353. Though Annas has since withdrawn these notorious remarks, the reasons she gave for her original complaint continue to resonate with Plato's readers. See Julia Annas, "Plato's Myths of Judgment," *Phronesis* 27, no. 2 (1982): 141n25; Ronald R. Johnson, "Does Plato's 'Myth of Er' Contribute to the Argument of the *Republic?*," *Philosophy & Rhetoric* 32, no. 1 (1999): 1–13.

2. For instance, Allan Bloom's essay accompanying his translation of the *Republic* contends that "only the philosopher has no need of the myth," suggesting that the myth is told with a certain reluctance on the part of philosophy, merely for the benefit of nonphilosophers like Glaucon. Allan Bloom, trans., *The Republic of Plato* (New York: Basic Books, 1968), 436.

3. See Perceval Frutiger, *Les mythes de Platon: Étude philosophique et littéraire* (Paris: F. Alcan, 1930), 218–219; Julius A. Elias, *Plato's Defence of Poetry* (London: Macmillan, 1984), 119. For characterizations of Plato's use of myth as a way of eluding rigorous philosophical argument, see W. K. C. Guthrie, *A History of Greek Philosophy,* vol. 1 (Cambridge: Cambridge University Press, 1979), 2.

4. The myth leads Allan Bloom to conclude, for example, that the *Republic* "has taught us nothing other than the necessity of philosophy and its priority and superiority to the political life," where "the myth of Er merely reiterates this message." Bloom, *The Republic of Plato,* 435. Martha Nussbaum echoes the verdict—at least for the myths of the *Republic* and those of other "early / middle works," where myths are "not essential to the philosophical argument" but instead serve to "reinforce" and to "show forth general philosophical truths for which he has already argued." Martha Nussbaum, *The Fragility of Goodness* (Cambridge: Cambridge University Press, 1986), 130.

Julia Annas also takes this position, although unlike Bloom, she finds it deeply disconcerting that "ideas that have powerful expression in the main coherent body of the book are presented at the end in a much cruder form." Part of the crudeness that troubles Annas about the mythic form is a substantive complaint: even though the myth restates the philosophical case for choosing justice over injustice, it paints a severely misleading picture of the reasons for doing so. Readings that take the myth to be coherent with the philosophical argument would have to answer to the open question as to why its moral lessons would be "cast in the most misleading possible form from the point of view of its message." Annas, *An Introduction to Plato's Republic*, 353; see also 349.

5. For instance, Stanley Rosen offers a subversive reading of the myth as a reminder "against taking too seriously the odd proposals that are presented in the main books of the dialogue." Stanley Rosen, *Plato's Republic: A Study* (New Haven, CT: Yale University Press, 2005), 387–388. See also the similarly ironic reading presented in Seth Benardete, *Socrates' Second Sailing* (Chicago: University of Chicago Press, 1989), 225–229.

A related family of interpretations argues that the myths subvert their own surface messages, so that their true intentions are once again aligned with those of the main arguments—e.g., Annas, "Plato's Myths of Judgment," 130–131; Jonathan Lear, "Allegory and Myth in Plato's *Republic*," in *The Blackwell Guide to Plato's Republic*, ed. Gerasimos Xenophon Santas (Oxford: Wiley-Blackwell, 2006), 25–43; Elizabeth Markovits, *The Politics of Sincerity: Plato, Frank Speech, and Democratic Judgment* (University Park: Pennsylvania State University Press, 2008), 130–165; John Evan Seery, "Politics as Ironic Community: On the Themes of Descent and Return in Plato's *Republic*," *Political Theory* 16, no. 2 (1988): 240–248.

6. Popper's depiction of Plato as the original architect of the "closed society" is perhaps the best-known reading of Plato as a proponent of authoritarian politics. A variant of this line of thought is Leo Strauss's response, which, though it unequivocally rejects Popper's reading, nonetheless attributes to Plato a distinctly elitist view of politics that presupposes a distinction between true philosophers and the democratic masses. Popper, *The Open Society and Its Enemies*, vol. 1, *The Spell of Plato* (Princeton, NJ: Princeton University Press, 1966); Leo Strauss, *The City and Man* (Chicago: University of Chicago Press, 1978).

More recent studies that make a case for a specifically democratic Plato are often framed as a response to such charges—e.g., Arlene W. Saxonhouse, "The Socratic Narrative: A Democratic Reading of Plato's Dialogues," *Political Theory* 37, no. 6 (2009): 728–753; see esp. 749n7. See also Peter Euben, *Corrupting Youth: Political Education, Democratic Culture, and Political Theory* (Princeton, NJ: Princeton University Press, 1997); S. Sara Monoson, *Plato's Democratic Entanglements: Athenian Politics and the Practice of Philosophy* (Princeton, NJ: Princeton University Press, 2000).

7. A general dichotomy of this sort between philosophic and nonphilosophic audiences of Plato's myths is common; see, for example, Luc Brisson, *Plato the Myth Maker,* trans. Gerard Naddaf (Chicago: University of Chicago Press, 1998), 11, 87; Janet E. Smith, "Plato's Use of Myth in the Education of Philosophic Man," *Phoenix* 40, no 1 (1986): 20–34; see also Bloom, *The Republic of Plato,* 436; Hannah Arendt, "What Is Authority?," in *Between Past and Future,* ed. Jerome Kohn (London: Penguin, 2006), 108; see also note 2 above.

8. E.g., Lowell Edmunds, introduction to *Approaches to Greek Myth,* ed. Lowell Edmunds (Baltimore: Johns Hopkins University Press, 1990), 1–22; Jean-Pierre Vernant, *Myth and Society in Ancient Greece,* trans. Janet Lloyd (Brighton, UK: Harvester, 1980), 221–222; Glenn W. Most, "Plato's Exoteric Myths," in *Plato and Myth: Studies on the Use and Status of Platonic Myths,* ed. Catherine Collobert, Pierre Destrée, and Francisco J. González (Leiden: Brill, 2012), 13–14; see also the works cited in note 41 of the Introduction.

9. On Plato's critique of the Greek mythological tradition, see, e.g., *Rep.* II 377a–*Rep.* III 392c; *Ap.* 5e–8a; see also *Phaedr.* 229b–230a.

On unfavorable characterizations of *mythos* against *logos* in Plato's language, see, e.g., *Prot.* 320c and 324d; more ambiguously, *Gorg.* 523a and 527a; *Tim.* 22c–d; *Rep.* VII 522a; see also *Soph.* 242c–e; *Phileb.* 14a; *Phaedo* 61b. See also Brisson, *Plato the Myth Maker,* 9–11, 112–115, and the appendixes cataloging instances of *mythos* and its derivatives in the Platonic corpus. Commentators point out that the two words are just as often used interchangeably—for example, in Most, "Plato's Exoteric Myths," 14; Fred D. Miller Jr., "Socrates *Mythologikos,*" in *Socratic, Platonic and Aristotelian Studies: Essays in Honor of Gerasimos Santas,* ed. Georgios Anagnostopoulos (Dordrecht: Springer, 2011), 76–77. Recent scholarship has shown that Plato inherited the trope of the *mythos–logos* distinction from the Sophists. Kathryn A. Morgan, *Myth and Philosophy: From the Presocratics to Plato* (Cambridge: Cambridge University Press, 2000); Robert L. Fowler, "Mythos and Logos," *Journal of Hellenic Studies* 131 (2011): 45–66.

10. See, for instance, Halliwell's proposal that Platonic myths are not to be reduced to literary reiterations of lessons already articulated elsewhere in the philosophic argument. Stephen Halliwell, "The Life-and-Death Journey of the Soul: Interpreting the Myth of Er," in *The Cambridge Companion to Plato's Republic,* ed. G. R. F. Ferrari (Cambridge: Cambridge University Press, 2007), 445–473.

11. See Jonathan Lear, "The Psychic Efficacy of Plato's Cave," in *Wisdom Won from Illness: Essays in Philosophy and Psychoanalysis* (Cambridge, MA: Harvard University Press, 2017), 227–243.

12. A small contingent of scholars has examined the continuity between the myths of the *Republic.* See, for example, Lear, "Allegory and Myth in Plato's *Republic.*" Largely inspired by Lear, Elizabeth Markovits also treats the same three

myths together, even discussing the Allegory of the Cave as a transition between the Myth of Metals and the Myth of Er, notwithstanding her belief that the Allegory of the Cave is not a myth. See Markovits, *The Politics of Sincerity,* 130–165.

13. For an introductory selection to the literature on Plato's myths, see J. A. Stewart, *The Myths of Plato* (London: Macmillan, 1905); Frutiger, *Les mythes de Platon;* Morgan, *Myth and Philosophy,* esp. 155–184; Karl Reinhardt, *Platons Mythen* (Bonn: F. Cohen, 1927); Paul Friedländer, *Plato: An Introduction,* trans. Hans Meyerhoff (New York: Harper and Row, 1958), 171–219; Diskin Clay, "Plato Philomythos," in *The Cambridge Companion to Greek Mythology,* ed. Roger D. Woodard (Cambridge: Cambridge University Press, 2007), 210–237; Ludwig Edelstein, "The Function of the Myth in Plato's Philosophy," *Journal of the History of Ideas* 10, no. 4 (1 October 1949): 463–481; Penelope Murray, "What Is a Muthos for Plato?," in *From Myth to Reason? Studies in the Development of Greek Thought,* ed. Richard Buxton (Oxford: Oxford University Press, 1999), 251–262; Catalin Partenie, ed., *Plato's Myths* (Cambridge: Cambridge University Press, 2009). For a select overview of the history of the study of Plato's myths, see Kent F. Moors, *Platonic Myth: An Introductory Study* (Washington, DC: University Press of America, 1982).

14. *Rep.* I 330d–e and 331c. Unless otherwise indicated, English translations of passages from the *Republic* are taken from Bloom, *The Republic of Plato.*

Many scholars have observed that the Myth of Er, a myth about the afterlife, responds to the very concerns Cephalus raises at the beginning of the *Republic.* See, for example, Rachel Barney, "Platonic Ring-Composition and *Republic* 10," in *Plato's Republic: A Critical Guide,* ed. Mark L. McPherran (Cambridge: Cambridge University Press, 2010), 32–51; Lear, "Allegory and Myth in Plato's *Republic.*"

15. With this challenge, Glaucon is said to have "borrowed" from the argument the external rewards of justice, which must be returned in order for Socrates to tell the Myth of Er. *Rep.* X 612b–614a. G. R. F. Ferrari traces the motif of debt from the first definition of justice in the *Republic,* Glaucon's challenge in Book II to isolate the benefits of justice by itself, and the rewards presented to the just in the Myth of Er. G. R. F. Ferrari, "Glaucon's Reward, Philosophy's Debt," in Partenie, *Plato's Myths,* 123. As for the book-ending effect of the *Republic* at large, Myles Burnyeat also proposes a "ring composition," but one that arcs over Books II to X. In his scheme Book I stands on its own as a "prelude" to the rest of the text, but Burnyeat also reads Book X as a continuation of discussions begun in earlier books. Myles Burnyeat, "Culture and Society in Plato's *Republic,*" in *The Tanner Lectures on Human Values,* vol. 20 (Salt Lake City: University of Utah Press, 1999), 288 and 288n; for the full argument, see 286–319.

16. Several commentators have observed that descent is a recurring motif throughout the *Republic.* It is found in two of the myths identified here (the philosopher's return to the cave and Er's descent into Hades), but it is also thematized in

the book's opening word (κατέβην, or "I went down"), in the Ring of Gyges, and, for some, in the description of the dialectical descent from principles to conclusions in the discussion of the Divided Line at *Rep.* VI 511b (οὕτως ἐπὶ τελευτὴν καταβαίνῃ). Seery, "Politics as Ironic Community"; Eric Voegelin, *Order and History,* vol. 3, *Plato and Aristotle* (Columbia: University of Missouri Press, 2000), 107–116; Rosen, *Plato's Republic,* 19; Diskin Clay, "Plato's First Words," in *Beginnings in Classical Literature,* ed. Francis M. Dunn and Thomas Cole (Cambridge: Cambridge University Press, 1992), 113–130.

The motif of descent is certainly suggestive; however, as I will argue, the similarities between the Myth of Metals, the Allegory of the Cave, and the Myth of Er are even more substantive. First, waking up and being delivered to a new world aboveground are not mere elements found in these myths, but constitute their plot. Second, that plot corresponds—more explicitly in the first two myths—to specific junctures in the educational curriculum of the *kallipolis.* The recurring plot of awakening and ascent can hence be read to progress analogically from one myth to the next in a self-contained series.

17. The Myth of Metals borrows some of its most prominent elements from existing traditional myths, most notably the Hesiodic myth of the races, and the myth of the founding of Thebes by the Phoenician king Cadmus. On the role of such autochthony myths—myths about being generated from the earth—in Athens, see Nicole Loraux, *Born of the Earth: Myth and Politics in Athens,* trans. Selina Stewart (Ithaca, NY: Cornell University Press, 2000). For analyses of the Myth of Metals's debt to Hesiod, as well as to the Cadmean myth of autochthony, see, respectively, Margaret Hartman, "The Hesiodic Roots of Plato's Myth of the Metals," *Helios* 15, no. 2 (1988): 103–114; Kateri Carmola, "Noble Lying: Justice and Intergenerational Tension in Plato's *Republic,*" *Political Theory* 31, no. 1 (2003): 39–62, esp. 53–56.

18. Popper, *The Open Society and Its Enemies,* 1:139–141. See also my discussion, "The Demon of the City," in Chapter 5. Popper's authoritarian reading of the myth is echoed in Daniel Dombrowski, "Plato's 'Noble' Lie," *History of Political Thought* 18, no. 4 (1997): 565–578; C. C. W. Taylor, "Plato's Totalitarianism," in *Plato's Republic: Critical Essays,* ed. Richard Kraut (Lanham, MD: Rowman and Littlefield, 2000), 31–48; Malcolm Schofield, "Fraternité, inégalité, la parole de Dieu: Plato's Authoritarian Myth of Political Legitimation," in Partenie, *Plato's Myths,* 101–115.

19. See, for example, Bloom, *The Republic of Plato,* 366; Monoson, *Plato's Democratic Entanglements,* 128; Arlene Saxonhouse, "Democracy, Equality and Eidê: A Radical View from Book 8 of Plato's *Republic,*" *American Political Science Review* 92, no. 2 (1998): 279.

20. Bloom, *The Republic of Plato,* 365–366.

21. Henry George Liddell, Robert Scott, and Henry Stuart Jones, eds., *A Greek-English Lexicon* (Oxford: Clarendon Press, 1996), s.v. γενναῖος; see also Bloom, *The*

Republic of Plato, 455n65; and Carmola, "Noble Lying," 40; Catherine Rowett, "Why the Philosopher Kings Will Believe the Noble Lie," *Oxford Studies in Ancient Philosophy* 50 (2016): 67.

22. ἀλλ' ὁ θεὸς πλάττων, ὅσοι μὲν ὑμῶν ἱκανοὶ ἄρχειν, χρυσὸν ἐν τῇ γενέσει συνέμειξεν αὐτοῖς, at *Rep.* III 415a; Liddell, Scott, and Jones, *A Greek-English Lexicon,* s.v. γένεσις.

23. *Rep.* III 414d–e. Danielle Allen has brought it to my attention that the opening line of the myth marks a unique moment in the narration. Here, while continuing to talk to Glaucon, Socrates exceptionally projects himself as a narrator into the city to address its hypothetical citizens—something he doesn't do anywhere else in the *Republic.*

24. Also observed in Rowett, "Why the Philosopher Kings Will Believe the Noble Lie," 68–69; and in Edward Andrew, "Equality of Opportunity as the Noble Lie," *History of Political Thought* 10, no. 4 (1989): 581, 589–590; Demetra Kasimis, "Plato's Open Secret," *Contemporary Political Theory* 15, no. 4 (2016): 350.

25. *Rep.* III 415a; *Rep.* VIII 546a–547a.

26. Such hereditary aberrations are to be expected precisely "because [ἅτε]" the citizens "are all related"—because they have undergone the same program of education and testing, and were hence borne out of the same earth-mother. That is, these anomalies occur because the effects of education override the imperfections of biological inheritance. ἅτε οὖν συγγενεῖς ὄντες πάντες τὸ μὲν πολὺ ὁμοίους ἂν ὑμῖν αὐτοῖς γεννῷτε, ἔστι δ' ὅτε ἐκ χρυσοῦ γεννηθείη ἂν ἀργυροῦν καὶ ἐξ ἀργύρου χρυσοῦν ἔκγονον καὶ τἆλλα πάντα οὕτως ἐξ ἀλλήλων, at *Rep.* III 415a–b.

27. τὴν τῇ φύσει προσήκουσαν τιμὴν ἀποδόντες at *Rep.* III. 415c.

28. The educational program outlined in the preceding two books of the *Republic* had in fact hinged on the assumption that political education can change the nature of citizens: that the natures of individuals, especially in youth, are rather malleable. Certain behaviors that are imitated from a young age "become established in habits and nature, in body and sounds and in thought," and the primary education of the citizens must be designed to shape their natures for the best. Once molded, the natures are then tested in various competitions "far more than gold in fire"—by the terms of the myth in question, to sift out those golden souls most suited to be guardians of the city. But after the completion of this basic education and testing—that is, the completion of the earth's work in the myth—the citizens' natures are to be understood as static, as though they had always been that way. *Rep.* III 395d and 413e.

On how the myth "blur[s] the distinction between nature and art and between nature and convention," see Strauss, *The City and Man,* 102; and also Andrew, "Equality of Opportunity as the Noble Lie," 585, and Kasimis, "Plato's Open Secret."

29. *Rep.* I 330d–331b; Lear, "Allegory and Myth in Plato's *Republic*," esp. 28–30; Danielle S. Allen, *Why Plato Wrote* (Malden, MA: Wiley-Blackwell, 2010), 33; Paul Veyne, *Did the Greeks Believe in Their Myths? An Essay on the Constitutive Imagination*, trans. Paula Wissing (Chicago: University of Chicago Press, 1988).

30. The Myth of Metals is told at the end of Book III, the Allegory of the Cave at the beginning of Book VII, and the Myth of Er at the end of book X. Without belaboring the observation, it may be worth noting that the three myths in the sequence are roughly evenly spaced out.

31. *Rep.* VII 515a, 534c. Hence, the process by which such a prisoner will be led "up to the light, just as some men are said to have gone from Hades up to the gods" is like "the turning of a soul around from a day that is like night to the true day," at *Rep.* VII 521c. The metaphor of sleeping through life is used in a similar sense in the *Apology*, where Socrates, famously comparing himself to a gadfly rousing a sleeping horse, warns his audience that killing him would allow them to "sleep on for the rest of [their] days." *Ap.* 31a.

32. *Rep.* VII 520c–d.

33. Jonathan Lear also reads "Socrates's account of the Cave" as "a repetition and re-creation of the Noble Falsehood." Lear, "Allegory and Myth in Plato's *Republic*," 34.

34. ἀπείκασον τοιούτῳ πάθει τὴν ἡμετέραν φύσιν παιδείας τε πέρι καὶ ἀπαιδευσίας, at *Rep.* VII 514a.

35. *Rep.* VII 515a; *Rep.* VII 517c–d; see also the myth of the winged soul in *Phaedr.* 246a–249d.

36. The sorting of citizens following the preliminary education in music and gymnastics is mentioned at *Rep.* VII 521e; the subsequent sorting of candidates through further study is mentioned at *Rep.* VII 537d.

37. *Rep.* VII 522a.

38. *Rep.* VII 537c.

39. *Rep.* VII 520b–c.

40. In this vein, Lear reads the Allegory of the Cave as akin to the punchline of a joke set up earlier in the "proto-philosophical" Myth of Metals: once they have encountered the Forms through a dialectical education, the guardians are positioned to understand the true reason for the dissatisfaction they experienced when they heard the Myth of Metals as children. Lear, "Allegory and Myth in Plato's *Republic*," 34–37.

41. *Rep.* VII 539d.

42. *Rep.* X 621b.

43. φέρεσθαι ἄνω εἰς τὴν γένεσιν, at *Rep.* X 621b. It has been suggested to me that, both in light of the Glaucus image prefacing this myth and the cosmography of the *Phaedo* and *Phaedrus* myths, the world of the Myth of Er is situated above

the mortal realm; this view is held, for example, by Stephen Halliwell. See Plato, *Republic 10: With Translation and Commentary*, ed. Stephen Halliwell (Warminster, UK: Aris and Phillips, 1988), 190. The more popular reading, however, is that Er descends into Hades and ascends back into life when he returns: see Lars Albinus, "The *Katabasis* of Er: Plato's Use of Myths, Exemplified by the Myth of Er," in *Essays on Plato's* Republic, ed. Erik Nis Ostenfeld (Aarhus, Denmark: Aarhus University Press, 1998), 91–105; Seery, "Politics as Ironic Community," 241–242 and 250n11; Voegelin, *Order and History,* 3:108; Rosen, *Plato's Republic,* 19. A way to acknowledge both readings may be to differentiate between an eternal realm imbued with the Forms, and an imperfect afterlife divorced from them. The afterlife in the Myth of Er would then be an instance of the latter.

44. *Rep.* X 618b.

45. A more general conviction framing Plato's thought, according to Kathryn Morgan, is that the "time scale for learning what we need to know about the soul and the world stretches beyond one lifetime." Morgan, *Myth and Philosophy,* 176.

46. *Rep.* X 612c–614b.

47. *Rep.* VII 540a–b.

48. *Rep.* VII 540b.

49. Hence the ensuing myth is framed, not only as an account of the rewards of justice in the afterlife, but also as a reflection on the true nature of the soul.

50. *Rep.* X 611c–d.

51. *Rep.* X 611e–612a. See also the geography of the cosmos in the myth of the *Phaedo,* 107c–115a.

52. *Rep.* X 611e.

53. See the *Phaedrus* myth, where souls are at home in the realm of the Forms. *Phaedr.* 246a–249d.

54. The retributive content of the myth is what, for many commentators, makes it appear inconsistent with the rest of the *Republic,* throughout which Socrates defends justice as a good in and of itself. See Annas, *An Introduction to Plato's Republic,* 349–353; Annas, "Plato's Myths of Judgment," 130–134; Halliwell, "The Life-and-Death Journey of the Soul," 445, 458–465.

55. Lear, "Allegory and Myth in Plato's *Republic,*" 39.

56. *Rep.* X 614c. See James Adam's diagram of the place of judgment in his commentary in *The Republic of Plato, Edited with Critical Notes, Commentary and Appendices,* ed. James Adam (Cambridge: Cambridge University Press, 1902), 435. See also Halliwell, *Republic 10,* 174.

57. There is some controversy regarding the exact geographical relation in the myth between the place of judgment and the meadow, both of which are two distinct tropes in the Greek eschatological tradition. The meadow appears independently, as a place unrelated to judgment, in Homer, Empedocles, Plutarch, and

notably the *Phaedrus* myth. Homer, *Odyssey* XI. 539; Empedocles, *Fragments* B. 121; Plutarch, *De Facie in Orbe Lunae*, 943c; *Phaedr.* 248b.

58. See the discussion of a similar feature in the *Gorgias* myth below.

59. "Socrates seems to complicate the myth needlessly." Benardete, *Socrates' Second Sailing*, 226.

60. *Rep.* X 614d–e.

61. *Gorg.* 525a–c. Exactly how or why the souls benefit or are made better from these lessons is frustratingly unclear, especially given that the *Gorgias* myth lacks an account of resurrection. See Alessandra Fussi, "The Myth of the Last Judgment in the *Gorgias*," *Review of Metaphysics* 54, no. 3 (2001): 529–552.

62. Christina Tarnopolsky believes that the *Gorgias* myth illustrates, all the same, a gradual rather than a didactic education, premised on "the insight that people must be met on their own ground and that the soul must be led not just by turning the eyes, but rather by turning the whole soul" so as to "then slowly lead them to new ways of seeing the world." Tarnopolsky, *Prudes, Perverts, and Tyrants: Plato's* Gorgias *and the Politics of Shame* (Princeton, NJ: Princeton University Press, 2010), 119. The *Phaedo* is the third dialogue that ends with an eschatological myth about judgment in the afterlife. For a comparative study of the three myths, see Annas, "Plato's Myths of Judgment."

63. *Rep.* X 616b–c.

64. *Rep.* X 618c–d.

65. Nicholas P. White, *A Companion to Plato's Republic* (Oxford: Basil Blackwell, 1979), 264–265.

66. *Rep.* X 620a.

67. *Rep.* X 620c–d. Scholars remain divided on the question of how to evaluate Odysseus's choice. In different ways, Seth Benardete, G. R. F. Ferrari, and Nicholas White view Odysseus's example as promising, and potentially preparatory for a philosophic life, without going to far as to exemplify a philosophic choice. Allan Bloom, by contrast, suggests that it does, comparing Odysseus's new life to that of Socrates. David Roochnik likewise takes Odysseus's choice to be both philosophic and prescriptive, but, like Stanley Rosen, believes its private nature undermines the characterization of philosophers in the *kallipolis*. Benardete, *Socrates' Second Sailing*, 299; Ferrari, "Glaucon's Reward, Philosophy's Debt," 129, 132–133; White, *A Companion to Plato's Republic*, 265; Bloom, *The Republic of Plato*, 436; David Roochnik, *Beautiful City: The Dialectical Character of Plato's "Republic"* (Ithaca, NY: Cornell University Press, 2003), 128; Rosen, *Plato's Republic*, 387.

68. *Rep.* X 619d.

69. Michael Inwood suggests that the structure of the myth has an equalizing function. Michael Inwood, "Plato's Eschatological Myths," in Partenie, *Plato's Myths*, 28–50. In a similar vein, Annas suggests that the experiences in the afterlife

end up negating the virtues and vices of the souls' former lives, so that "just and unjust are bound up together on the eternal wheel of reincarnation, and the rewards of justice even in other-worldly terms will only lead to a compensating increase in injustice as a result." Annas, *An Introduction to Plato's Republic*, 351.

70. *Rep.* X 619c–d.

71. Seth Benardete casually identifies the soul who chooses the tyrant's life as a "citizen of Socrates' best city," and an object lesson in the impossibility of "freeing oneself from habit." Benardete, *Socrates' Second Sailing*, 229; see also Leo Strauss, *On Tyranny*, ed. Michael S. Roth and Victor Gourevitch (Chicago: University of Chicago Press, 2013), 182; contra Christopher Bobonich, *Plato's Utopia Recast: His Later Ethics and Politics* (Oxford: Oxford University Press, 2002), 57–58 and 475–476; C. D. C. Reeve, *Philosopher-Kings: The Argument of Plato's Republic* (Princeton, NJ: Princeton University Press, 1988), 319n9.

72. The case of the soul from the virtuous city who chooses the tyrant's life recalls the tale of Themistocles retold by Cephalus in Book I—which maintains that an individual's own merit and the handicap of his birthplace are both important, if not inseparable. *Rep.* I 329e–330a.

73. Consider Kant's insistence on the deeper moral content of moral actions motivated by duty over inclination. Immanuel Kant, *Groundwork for the Metaphysics of Morals,* trans. James W. Ellington (Indianapolis: Hackett, 1981), 12–14 [Ak. 399–401].

74. Bernard Williams's famous critique goes so far as to suggest that the city–soul analogy does not even work as an analogy. Bernard Williams, "The Analogy of City and Soul in Plato's *Republic*," in *Exegesis and Argument: Studies in Greek Philosophy Presented to Gregory Vlastos*, ed. E. N. Lee, Alexander Mourelatos, and Richard Rorty (Assen: Van Gorcum, 1973), 196–206. See also G. R. F. Ferrari, *City and Soul in Plato's Republic* (Chicago: University of Chicago Press, 2005). For a convincing account that does integrate the two forms of justice, see Jonathan Lear, "Inside and Outside the *Republic*," *Phronesis* 37, no. 2 (1992): 184–215.

75. I thank Oded Na'aman for helping me clarify this point.

76. Claude Lévi-Strauss identifies the advantage of myth over science in a similar capacity to withstand and even temper contradictions. Paul Veyne also discusses the ways in which myths open up the possibility of juggling different levels of meaning. Claude Lévi-Strauss, "The Structural Study of Myth," *Journal of American Folklore* 68, no. 270 (1955): 443; Veyne, *Did the Greeks Believe in their Myths?*, 43.

77. Morgan, *Myth and Philosophy*; Marcel Detienne, *The Creation of Mythology,* trans. Margaret Cook (Chicago: University of Chicago Press, 1986).

78. Morgan, *Myth and Philosophy*; see also Brisson, *Plato the Myth Maker,* 87–127. Herodotus and Thucydides have also been credited with a parallel move in

historical writing to reject myth in favor of more rigorous ways of presenting information and ideas. See Herodotus, *The History*, 2.23 and 2.45, and the more famous polemical claim against myth in Thucydides, *History of the Peloponnesian War*, 1.22; see also Luc Brisson, *How Philosophers Saved Myths*, trans. Catherine Tihanyi (Chicago: University of Chicago Press, 2004), 5–14.

79. The Myth of Metals is a "noble lie" and a "Phoenician thing" uttered by poets (*Rep.* III 414c); the Allegory of the Cave is the culmination of a sequence of images that offer an illustration, not of "what the good itself is," but instead of "a child of the good" (*Rep.* VI 506e); and the Myth of Er is not "a story of Alcinous," a Homeric hero, but of a distantly foreign hero from Pamphylia (*Rep.* X 614b). On Plato's practice of distancing himself from the sources of the myths that he narrates, see, e.g., Clay, "Plato Philomythos," 212; Murray, "What Is a Muthos for Plato?," 256. By contrast, the capacity to always question further is often included in the definition of the Socratic *elenchus*. See *Gorg.* 416d; Gregory Vlastos, "The Socratic Elenchus," *Oxford Studies in Ancient Philosophy* 1 (1983): 27–58.

80. See Richard Robinson, *Plato's Earlier Dialectic* (Oxford: Oxford University Press, 1980), 7, 15–17; Thomas C. Brickhouse and Nicholas D. Smith, "Socrates' Elenchic Psychology," *Synthese* 92, no. 1 (1992): 63; Thomas C. Brickhouse and Nicholas D. Smith, *Plato's Socrates* (New York: Oxford University Press, 1994), 10–11; Harold Tarrant, "Elenchus and Exetasis: Capturing the Purpose of Socratic Interrogation," in *Does Socrates Have a Method? Rethinking the Elenchus in Plato's Dialogues and Beyond*, ed. Gary Alan Scott (University Park: Pennsylvania State University Press), 61–63.

81. E.g., Allen, *Why Plato Wrote*.

82. On myth as a device for persuasion, see Brisson, *Plato the Myth Maker*, 75–85; Catalin Partenie, introduction to Partenie, *Plato's Myths*, 5–8; see also Morgan, *Myth and Philosophy*, 162–163, esp. 163n21.

83. E.g., Markovits, *The Politics of Sincerity*, 151–159; Lear, "Allegory and Myth in Plato's *Republic*"; Seery, "Politics as Ironic Community"; see also note 5 above. Jill Frank develops a nuanced variant of this approach, suggesting that Plato does not so much intend for the myths to generate dissatisfaction as a sense of epistemic limitation. Jill Frank, *Poetic Justice: Rereading Plato's "Republic"* (Chicago: University of Chicago Press, 2018).

84. *Laws* X 903b–905b. ἐπῳδῶν γε μὴν προσδεῖσθαί μοι δοκεῖ μύθων ἔτι τινῶν. . . . πείθωμεν τὸν νεανίαν τοῖς λόγοις . . . , at *Laws* X 903b. Notably, the famous "preludes" to certain laws contain elements borrowed from traditional myths. See *Laws* 771c, 804e, 903b, 913c, 927c, 944a, cited in Catalin Partenie and Luc Brisson, "Why Did Plato Write Myths?," in the introduction to Plato, *Selected Myths*, ed. Catalin Partenie (Oxford: Oxford University Press, 2004), xvii–xix, xviiin4.

Phaedo 107c–115a; the myth is introduced to the unconvinced (ἀπιστίαν ἔτι ἔχειν) Simmias and his fellow interlocutors at *Phaedo* 107b. Emphasis on the value of being persuaded (πείθειν) by the myth in question is found in the language of both the Myth of Metals and the Myth of Er, at *Rep.* III 414d and *Rep.* X 621c.

85. ἴθι οὖν, ὥσπερ ἐν μύθῳ μυθολογοῦντές τε καὶ σχολὴν ἄγοντες λόγῳ παιδεύωμεν τοὺς ἄνδρας, at *Rep.* II 376d. For emphasis, I have altered Bloom's translation of *muthoi muthologountes* as "telling a story" to "telling myths." See also Murray, "What Is a Muthos for Plato?," 258.

86. A similar idea might be found in Aristotle's famous connection between virtue and *ethos*—habit—in the proposal that one attains virtue by acting as though he were already a virtuous person. Aristotle, *Nicomachean Ethics,* Book II. See also Tamar Schapiro's discussion of the provisional status of the selves adopted by children. Tamar Schapiro, "What Is a Child?," *Ethics* 109 (July 1999): 715–738, esp. 733. I thank Eric Beerbohm for recommending this article.

87. We may understand such concepts to be examples of what Kwane Anthony Appiah has recently described as an "idealization"—an imperfect representation that, for practical purposes, can be treated as if it were true. Kwame Anthony Appiah, *As If: Idealization and Ideals* (Cambridge, MA: Harvard University Press, 2017).

88. On the plasticity of concepts and their susceptibility to being shaped by symbolic language, including that found in myths, see Danielle S. Allen, "Envisaging the Body of the Condemned: The Power of Platonic Symbols," *Classical Philology* 95, no. 2 (2000): 133–150.

2. THE UTOPIAN FOUNDING MYTHS OF MORE AND BACON

1. Thomas Hobbes, *Latin Works* [Thomae Hobbes Malmesburiensis opera philosophica quae latine scripsit omnia: in unum corpus nunc primum collecta studio et labore], 5 vols., ed. William Molesworth (London: John Bohm, 1839–1845), 3:263–264.

2. *New Atlantis* was appended to the end of *Sylva Sylvarum* (1626), a posthumous collection of essays published within a year of Bacon's death, but the first draft could have been written as early as 1614, and his editor dated the final version to 1624. Alan Stewart and Lisa Jardine, however, push the date of the composition of *New Atlantis* to the end of 1625. Frank E. Manuel and Fritzie P. Manuel, *Utopian Thought in the Western World* (Cambridge, MA: Harvard University Press, 1979), 243, 251; Lisa Jardine and Alan Stewart, *Hostage to Fortune: The Troubled Life of Francis Bacon* (New York: Hill and Wang, 1999), 499–500.

3. James Steintrager, "Plato and More's 'Utopia,'" *Social Research* 36, no. 3 (1969): 357–372; Manuel and Manuel, *Utopian Thought in the Western World*, 118–122;

J. H. Hexter, *More's Utopia: The Biography of an Idea* (Princeton, NJ: Princeton University Press, 1952); Hugh Trevor-Roper, "The Intellectual World of Sir Thomas More," *The American Scholar* 48, no. 1 (1979): 19–32; Lewis Mumford, "Utopia, the City and the Machine," in *Utopias and Utopian Thought,* ed. Frank E. Manuel (Boston: Houghton Mifflin, 1966), 101–115; see also Thomas I. White, "Pride and the Public Good: Thomas More's Use of Plato in *Utopia,*" *Journal of the History of Philosophy* 20, no. 4 (1982): 329–354, esp. 329n1.

4. Eric Nelson, *The Greek Tradition in Republican Thought* (Cambridge: Cambridge University Press, 2004).

5. Notable works of utopian literature after the publication of *Utopia* and prior to Campanella's *City of the Sun* include Anton Francesco Doni's *I Mondi* (1552), Francesco Patrizi da Cherso's *La Città Felice* (1553), and Johann Valentin Andreae's *Christianopolis* [Reipublicae Christianopolitanae descriptio] (1619). See J. C. Davis, "Utopianism," in *The Cambridge History of Political Thought, 1450–1700,* ed. J. H. Burns with Mark Goldie (Cambridge: Cambridge University Press, 1991), 329–344. For the reception of *Utopia* in Renaissance Italy, see Eric Nelson, "Utopia through Italian Eyes: Thomas More and the Critics of Civic Humanism," *Renaissance Quarterly* 59, no. 4 (2006): 1029–1057; Paul F. Grendler, "Utopia in Renaissance Italy: Doni's 'New World,'" *Journal of the History of Ideas* 26, no. 4 (1965): 479–494; see also Eleanor Dickinson Blodgett, "Bacon's *New Atlantis* and Campanella's *Civitas Solis*: A Study in Relationships," *PMLA* 46, no. 3 (1931): 763–780.

6. Amy Boesky, *Founding Fictions: Utopias in Early Modern England* (Athens: University of Georgia Press, 1996), 11. The quotation with which this chapter opened is from the Latin *Leviathan* (1668).

7. Paul Salzman, "Narrative Contexts for Bacon's *New Atlantis,*" in *Francis Bacon's The New Atlantis: New Interdisciplinary Essays,* ed. Bronwen Price (Manchester: Manchester University Press, 2003), 30.

8. For instance, *A Description of the Famous Kingdom of Macaria* (1641) by Samuel Hartlib—one of the central figures associated with the movement to translate the vision of *New Atlantis* into the formation of the Royal Society—is an elaboration on a fictional nation mentioned in *Utopia.* Samuel Hartlib, *A description of the famous Kingdome of Macaria* (London, 1641); see also Thomas More, *Utopia,* ed. George M. Logan and Robert M. Adams (Cambridge: Cambridge University Press, 2002), 34. Such efforts on the part of More's and Bacon's imitators to emulate the tropes, if not the original details, of their antecedents were often complemented by claims to outdo or improve upon them—for instance, in Hume's own "Idea of a Perfect Commonwealth," which Hume claimed was of a more practical nature than "the Republic of Plato, and the Utopia of Sir Thomas More." Many, of course, tried to do both. David Hume, "Idea of a Perfect Commonwealth,"

in *Essays,* ed. Stephen Copley and Andrew Edgar (Oxford: Oxford University Press, 1998), 301.

9. The *Timaeus* famously opens with an allusion to a conversation that purportedly took place the previous day, in which Socrates reports having described an ideal state organized around principles that match those of the *kallipolis. Tim.* 17c–19b. The incomplete *Critias* is generally paired with *Timaeus* for the continuity of their characters and, of course, for the myths that they both tell about Atlantis.

10. "New Atlantis, begun by the Lord Verulam, Viscount St. Albans, and continued by R. H. Esquire" (London, 1660), cited in R. W. Gibson, *St. Thomas More: A Preliminary Bibliography of His Works and of Moreana to the Year 1750* (New Haven, CT: Yale University Press, 1961), 355–356.

11. While Plato was not the only one of Socrates's admirers and followers to write about him, he was the only one to repeatedly draw attention to Socrates's claim that he himself knew nothing and consequently held no epistemic advantage over his interlocutors. A. A. Long, "The Socratic Legacy," in *The Cambridge History of Hellenistic Philosophy,* ed. Keimpe Algra et al. (Cambridge: Cambridge University Press, 1999), 639. For passages of particular interest for the skeptical reading of Plato, see Harold Tarrant, *Plato's First Interpreters* (London: Duckworth, 2000), 10–16.

12. The skeptical phase of the Academy was launched under the leadership of Arcesilaus and lasted for over a century and a half, settling into a softened version under Philo of Larissa, the last known head of the Academy. On the singular contributions of Arcesilaus (ca. 316–241 BC) in allying Socrates with skepticism, see Long, "The Socratic Legacy," 639–640; see also John Dillon, *The Heirs of Plato: A Study of the Old Academy (347–274 B.C.)* (Oxford: Oxford University Press, 2003); and Harold Tarrant, *Scepticism or Platonism: The Philosophy of the Fourth Academy* (Cambridge: Cambridge University Press, 1985), 1–65. For a helpful chronology of Plato's immediate successors in the Academy, see Tiziano Dorandi, "Chronology," in Algra et al., *The Cambridge History of Hellenistic Philosophy,* 31–54.

13. Arcesilaus and Carneades (214–129 BC), perhaps the most radical and most famous figures associated with the skeptical phase of the Academy, did not leave written work.

14. See E. N. Tigerstedt, *The Decline and Fall of the Neoplatonic Interpretation of Plato,* Commentationes Humanarum Litterarum 52 (Helsinki: Societas Scientariarum Fennica, 1974).

15. Plato's most immediate successors had, in fact, been engaged in the effort to further unify Platonic metaphysics, before the Academy took its skeptical turn under Arcesilaus. In many ways what we know of their philosophies anticipates the central themes of the Neoplatonic tradition; though, critically, they did not

fully embrace the theory of Forms, and it is difficult to say if they had had a direct influence on the Neoplatonists. See the passages on the Academy under Speusippus, Xenocrates, Polemon, and, briefly, Crates, in Tarrant, *Plato's First Interpreters*, 44–53; see also Dillon, *The Heirs of Plato*; Philip Merlan, "The Old Academy," and "The Later Academy and Platonism," in *The Cambridge History of Later Greek and Early Medieval Philosophy*, ed. A. H. Armstrong (Cambridge: Cambridge University Press, 1969), 11–38 and 53–83.

Although Plato's successors in the so-called Old Academy wrote both treatises and philosophical dialogues, only Heraclides of Pontus incorporated myths or mythical elements into his writing. John Dillon, "Plato's Myths in the Later Platonist Tradition," in the introduction to Plato, *Selected Myths*, ed. Catalin Partenie (Oxford: Oxford University Press, 2004), xxvi–xxx, xxvi; Partenie, introduction to *Plato's Myths*, ed. Catalin Partenie (Cambridge: Cambridge University Press, 2009), 1–27, 21n20.

16. *Rep.* VI 508e; *Parm.* 129c, 142a; *Tim.* 28a. On the centrality of the *Parmenides* to the Neoplatonic tradition, see Raymond Kiblansky, *Plato's Parmenides in the Middle Ages and the Renaissance: A Chapter in the History of Platonic Studies* (London: Warburg Institute, 1981); Brian P. Copenhaver and John Monfasani, "Platonism," in *The Columbia History of Western Philosophy*, ed. Richard H. Popkin (New York: Columbia University Press, 1998), 305–306. A focus on the absolute and eternal unifying ideas in Plato often drew his early readers to those myths that contained passages on cosmology, eschatology, mystical encounters, and the nature of the soul. Tarrant, *Plato's First Interpreters*, e.g., 85, 95, 136–137, 196, 199.

17. See Tigerstedt, *The Decline and Fall of the Neoplatonic Interpretation of Plato*; and also James Hankins, "Antiplatonism in the Renaissance and the Middle Ages," *Classica et Mediaevalia* 47 (1996): 359–377.

18. "Doleo bona fide, Platonem omnium haereticorum condimentarium factum." Tertullian, *De Anima: Mit Einleitung, Uebersetzung und Kommentar*, trans. J. H. Waszink (Amsterdam: H. J. Paris, 1933), 23.5 [88–89].

19. E.g., Augustine, *City of God*, trans. Henry Bettenson (London: Penguin, 1984), VIII.4–16 [303–321], esp. VIII.10 [313].

20. Carlos Steel, "Proclus," in *The Cambridge History of Philosophy in Late Antiquity*, ed. Lloyd P. Gerson (Cambridge: Cambridge University Press, 2010), 631–634, 648–653. Proclus notably penned an influential commentary on the *Republic*, including lengthy treatments of the Allegory of the Cave and the Myth of Er. Proclus, *In Platonis Rem publicam commentarii*, ed. Wilhelm Kroll, 2 vols. (Leipzig: B. G. Tevbneri, 1901); see also John Dillon, "Proclus on the Myth of Er," *Dionysius* 33 (2015): 132–144. The long legacy of this designation is evident, for instance, in the title under which Marsilio Ficino's celebrated Latin translation of Plato's

oeuvre was published, which attributes the works to a "divine Plato." E.g., Marsilio Ficino, trans., *Omnia divini Platonis opera* (Basel, 1539). This seems to originate from the title page containing Ficino's verses praising the "Divus Plato," found in the 1491 edition, but not in the first printing of 1484. Both editions have been digitized by the Bayerische Staatsbibliothek München at http://daten.digitale-sammlungen.de/~db/0006/bsb00068576/images (1484 ed.) and at http://daten.digitale-sammlungen.de/~db/0005/bsb00059968/images (1491 ed.).

21. Dillon, "Plato's Myths in the Later Platonist Tradition," xxix–xxx.

22. Allegorizing interpretations of specific myths in the ancient Neoplatonic tradition include those by Porphyry, Iamblichus, and Proclus, as well as by Damascius and Olympiodorus. Dillon, "Plato's Myths in the Later Platonist Tradition," xxix–xxx. See also Luc Brisson, *How Philosophers Saved Myths*, trans. Catherine Tihanyi (Chicago: University of Chicago Press, 2004).

23. Colotes's critique survives in Proclus, *In Platonis Rem publicam commentarii*, II: 105–106; cited in František Novotný, *The Posthumous Life of Plato*, trans. Jana Fábryová (Prague: Academia Prague, 1977), 46–47, and Stephen Halliwell, "The Life-and-Death Journey of the Soul: Interpreting the Myth of Er," in *The Cambridge Companion to Plato's Republic*, ed. G. R. F. Ferrari (Cambridge: Cambridge University Press, 2007), 445–473, 460.

24. Dillon, "Plato's Myths in the Later Platonist Tradition," xxvii–xxviii.

25. Cicero, *De Re Publica*, trans. Clinton Walker Keyes, Loeb Classical Library (Cambridge, MA: Harvard University Press, 1928), VI.9–26. For a comparative discussion of the Dream of Scipio and the Myth of Er, see Georg Luck, "Studia Divina in Vita Humana: On Cicero's 'Dream of Scipio' and Its Place in Graeco-Roman Philosophy," *Harvard Theological Review* 49, no. 4 (1956): 208–210. A more through treatment of the Dream of Scipio, as it relates to both the *Republic* as a whole and to Cicero's Platonism, can be found in Jed W. Atkins, *Cicero on Politics and the Limits of Reason: The Republic and Laws* (Cambridge: Cambridge University Press, 2013), 47–80.

26. Macrobius, *Commentary on the Dream of Scipio*, ed. and trans. William Harris Stahl (New York: Columbia University Press, 1952). See, for instance, Juan Luis Vives's sixteenth-century commentary on the Dream of Scipio, which presumes the reader's familiarity with Macrobius's commentary. Juan Luis Vives, *Somnium et Vigilia in Somnium Scipionis: Commentary on the Dream of Scipio*, ed. and trans. Edward V. George (Greenwood, SC: Attic Press, 1989). The extent to which the Dream of Scipio was a long-standing fixture of European cultural vocabulary may be gauged from its prominent appearance in Chaucer's sixteenth-century poem "The Parliament of Fowls," or on the decision on the part of the fifteen-year-old Mozart to use it as the source material for his one-act opera, *Il Sogno di Scipione*, K.126 (1772).

There is much scholarship aimed at dispelling the commonplace narrative that Plato was largely lost in the Middle Ages, but it nonetheless bears remembering that, even after the recovery of Plato's dialogues in the sixteenth century, these developments were not being reflected in Renaissance university curricula, where education in philosophy remained Aristotelian in focus. Sarah Hutton, introduction to *Platonism at the Origins of Modernity: Studies on Platonism and Early Modern Philosophy*, ed. Douglas Hedley and Sarah Hutton (Dordrecht: Springer, 2008), 18. On Plato in the Middle Ages through the Renaissance, see Raymond Klibansky, *Plato's Parmenides in the Middle Ages and the Renaissance* (London: Warburg Institute, 1950).

27. See Gerard Press, "Continuities and Discontinuities in the History of *Republic* Reception," *International Studies in Philosophy* 28, no. 4 (1996): 61–78.

28. Ficino, *Platonis Opera Omnia*; see James Hankins, *Plato in the Italian Renaissance*, 2 vols. (Leiden: Brill, 1991), 1:300–318; Denis J.-J. Robichaud, *Plato's Persona: Marsilio Ficino, Renaissance Humanism, and Platonic Traditions* (Philadelphia: University of Pennsylvania Press, 2018).

29. Copenhaver and Monfasani, "Platonism."

30. Copenhaver and Monfasani, "Platonism," 308–309; Michael J. B. Allen, "Renaissance Neoplatonism," in *The Cambridge History of Literary Criticism*, vol. 3, *The Renaissance*, ed. Glyn P. Norton (Cambridge: Cambridge University Press, 1999), 339.

31. Allen, "Renaissance Neoplatonism," 339.

32. On the English Platonist John Colet, a friend of More and Erasmus, see John B. Gleason, *John Colet* (Berkeley: University of California Press, 1989). Possible links between Ficino and Colet are also outlined in Sears Jayne, "Ficino and the Platonism of the English Renaissance," *Comparative Literature* 4, no. 3 (1952): 216–217. Neoplatonic themes were prominent in, for instance, the poetry of Edward Spenser, and the prose of Sir Walter Raleigh. Elizabeth Jane Bellamy, "Plato," in *The Oxford History of Classical Reception in English Literature*, ed. Patrick Cheney and Philip Hardie, 4 vols. (Oxford: Oxford University Press, 2015), 2:503–516. The bilingual edition of Plato's complete works, published by Henri Estienne and translated into Latin with commentary by Jean de Serres, whose "Stephanus" pagination is still in use today, was published in 1578. It was this Serranus edition of Plato's works that Bacon purchased for five pounds as a gift to St. Albans, deeming it the "best edition" of Plato. Thomas W. Baldwin, *William Shakespere's Small Latine and Lesse Greeke*, 2 vols. (Urbana: University of Illinois Press, 1944), 1:394, cited in Jayne, "Ficino and the Platonism of the English Renaissance," 220–221.

33. Though it had become increasingly common among admirers of Plato to imitate the form of the philosophical dialogue, imitation of the myths remained

rare. Even the aforementioned Dream of Scipio, the conclusion to Cicero's own *Republic,* failed to set a precedent: the political nature of the work notwithstanding, the myth itself was celebrated in its reception as a source of cosmographical information.

34. Nelson, *The Greek Tradition in Republican Thought.* On More's admiration for the combination he likely saw in Plato, of philosophical wisdom and literary eloquence, see White, "Pride and the Public Good," 336.

35. Francis Bacon, *The New Organon,* in *The Works of Francis Bacon,* ed. James Spedding, Robert Leslie Ellis, and Douglas Denon Heath, 14 vols. (Cambridge: Cambridge University Press, 2011), 4:59, 64–66.

36. Bacon, *The New Organon,* 68, 75.

37. This is not to suggest, however, that Bacon's interest in myth at large was unconcerned with philosophy. Nor, as we shall see in the final section of this chapter, was his approach to myth wholly divorced from the legacy of the Neoplatonic models.

38. "Giles to Busleyden," ancillary material from the early editions, in More, *Utopia,* 120. On the significance of the *Republic* for the beginning of English Platonism, and More's direct debt to Plato rather than to Ficino, see Jayne, "Ficino and the Platonism of the English Renaissance," 222, 224; Roberto Weiss, *Humanism in England during the Fifteenth Century* (Oxford: Basil Blackwell, 1941), 54–85. See also note 3 above.

39. "Six Lines on the Island of Utopia," ancillary material, in More, *Utopia,* 117.

40. On the significance of humor to the Philhellenism of More's circles, especially with regard to Plato, see Nelson, *The Greek Tradition in Republican Thought,* 19–28.

41. Francis Bacon, *New Atlantis,* in *The Major Works,* ed. Brian Vickers (Oxford: Oxford University Press, 2002), 478.

42. *Utopia* is split into two books, the first of which does consist in a contemplative conversation that serves to frame the ensuing description of Utopia in the second book. However, there's no question that More fully intended to present *Utopia* as a work of fiction, and to celebrate it as such. According to a Utopian poem inscribed in the first page of the first edition (likely written by Peter Giles), the unique accomplishment of Utopia was in managing, "without philosophy," to portray "the philosophical city"—that is, in bringing such a city to life for its readers without the aid of abstract arguments. "A Quatrain in the Utopian Language," ancillary material, in More, *Utopia,* 119; see also Manuel and Manuel, *Utopian Thought,* 120.

For the suggestion that Book II of *Utopia* was written first, and Book I added later, see Hexter, *More's Utopia,* xv–xiii; George M. Logan, introduction to More,

Utopia, xvi–xvii. The three earliest translations of *Utopia*—into German, Italian, and French—all omitted Book I. J. C. Davis, "Thomas More's *Utopia*: Sources, Legacy, and Interpretation," in *The Cambridge Companion to Utopian Literature,* ed. Gregory Claeys (Cambridge: Cambridge University Press, 2010), 30.

Finally, for a discussion of the significance of the literary status of *New Atlantis* as a work of fiction, see Tobin L. Craig, "On the Significance of the Literary Character of Francis Bacon's 'New Atlantis' for an Understanding of His Political Thought," *Review of Politics* 72, no. 2 (2010): 213–239.

43. This, of course, is not to deny the literary character of the *Republic* as a whole. Nor is it to downplay the centrality of moral questions in utopian writing— as explored thoroughly, for instance, in the rich literature on the nature of and conditions for virtue in *Utopia*. On virtue in *Utopia,* see, e.g., Quentin Skinner, *The Foundations of Modern Political Thought,* 2 vols. (Cambridge: Cambridge University Press, 1978), 1:233–236; Skinner, "Political Philosophy," in *The Cambridge History of Renaissance Philosophy,* ed. Charles B. Schmitt, Quentin Skinner, and Eckhard Kessler (Cambridge: Cambridge University Press, 1988), 389–452; Skinner, "Sir Thomas More's *Utopia* and the Language of Renaissance Humanism," in *The Languages of Political Theory in Early-Modern Europe,* ed. Anthony Pagden (Cambridge: Cambridge University Press, 1987), 123–157; David Wootton, "Friendship Portrayed: A New Account of *Utopia,*" *History Workshop Journal* 45 (1998): 29–48; White, "Pride and the Public Good"; Nelson, *The Greek Tradition in Republican Thought.*

44. William Rawley, Bacon's secretary and editor, who oversaw the posthumous publication of *New Atlantis,* appended a prefatory note to the reader introducing the work as a fable. Similarly, in a famous phrase, J. W. Allen called *Utopia* the "saddest of fairy tales." W. Rawley, "To the Reader," in Spedding, Ellis, and Heath, *The Works of Francis Bacon,* 3:127; J. W. Allen, *A History of Political Thought in the Sixteenth Century* (London: Routledge, 2010), 154; Howard B. White, *Peace among the Willows: The Political Philosophy of Francis Bacon* (The Hague: Martinus Nijhoff, 1968), 112.

45. More, *Utopia,* 42.

46. More, *Utopia,* 46–47.

47. More, *Utopia,* 94–95.

48. E.g., "A Quatrain in the Utopian Language," 119; "New Atlantis, begun by the Lord Verulam" (1660).

49. Bacon, *New Atlantis,* 464–465.

50. Bacon, *New Atlantis,* 467–469, 469–472.

51. Augustine, *City of God,* III.2–3 [65–67], III.4–6 [92–94], III.15 [106–109]; Niccolò Machiavelli, *The Prince,* trans. Harvey Mansfield (Chicago: University of Chicago Press, 1998), 21–25, 103–104; Machiavelli, *The Discourses,* trans. Leslie

Walker, ed. Bernard Crick (London: Penguin, 2003), I.1 [100–104], I.9–I.11 [131–142]. I'm grateful to Sarah Mortimer for suggesting this point. More gave a series of public lectures on the *City of God* in 1501, and though the content of the lectures is lost, scholars have speculated on its significance and possible connection to *Utopia.* See William Roper, *The Life of Sir Thomas More* [1557], in *Two Early Tudor Lives,* ed. Richard S. Sylvester and Davis P. Harding (New Haven, CT: Yale University Press, 1962), 198; Thomas Stapleton, *The Life and Illustrious Martyrdom of Sir Thomas More* [1588], trans. Philip E. Hallett, ed. E. E. Reynolds (London: Burns and Oates, 1966), 7–8; Martin N. Raitiere, "More's *Utopia* and *The City of God,"* *Studies in the Renaissance* 20 (1973): 144–168; Peter Harrison, "Francis Bacon, Natural Philosophy, and the Cultivation of the Mind," *Perspectives on Science* 20, no. 2 (27 April 2012): 139–158.

Although Machiavelli's great works were published well after the publication of *Utopia,* Bacon's familiarity with them is well-documented; he famously cites Machiavelli as an exemplary authority on political writing that describes "what men do, and not what they ought to do." Francis Bacon, *The Advancement of Learning,* in Vickers, *The Major Works,* 254. See B. H. G. Wormald, *Francis Bacon: History, Politics and Science, 1561–1626* (Cambridge: Cambridge University Press, 1993), 190–213. For a speculative account of potential pathways by which Machiavellian ideas might have made their way to More, see William J. Connell, "Machiavelli's Utopia," *Times Literary Supplement,* December 2, 2016, 16.

52. More, *Utopia,* 44, 46.

53. Many identify the longing to preserve the political conditions of a perfect beginning both as something essential to the legacy of the *kallipolis* in utopian writing at large, and as a central element of what has alternately been called utopianism or "the utopian tendency." See, e.g., Northrop Frye, "Varieties of Literary Utopias," in Manuel, *Utopias and Utopian Thought,* 31; Judith Shklar, "The Political Theory of Utopia: From Melancholy to Nostalgia," in Manuel, *Utopias and Utopian Thought,* 105; Manuel and Manuel, *Utopian Thought in the Western World,* 5; Davis, "Utopianism."

54. For a comparison and discussion of a point of contrast between Utopus and Solamona, see Anna-Maria Hartmann, "The Strange Antiquity of Francis Bacon's *New Atlantis,"* *Renaissance Studies* 29, no. 3 (2015): 389–391.

55. Bacon, *New Atlantis,* 470.

56. See also Bacon's reflections on the nature of time, in *Of Innovations* and *Of Vicissitude of Things,* in Vickers, *The Major Works,* 387–388, 451–453.

57. Davis, "Utopianism," 329–330; see also Manuel and Manuel, *Utopian Thought in the Western World.*

58. *Rep.* VIII 546e–547a, see also 546a. The Atlantis myth in the *Critias* features a similarly degenerative lineage of kings.

59. Bacon was particularly fascinated by these myths, and his reflections on the events recounted in them feature in *Of Vicissitude of Things*.

60. Solon goes through some ancient Greek myths as a historical exercise in reconstructing the events of antiquity, and is thereupon told by the Egyptian priest that the "Greeks are ever children," because their knowledge of history goes back only a comparatively short span of years. He proceeds to tell the story of Atlantis, which predates Greek historical memory. The thought here is that a people's repository of knowledge is only as old as its myths, which purport to contain its most ancient wisdom. Among the several levels of irony contained in the framing of the Atlantis myth, the accusation of childishness that the priest levels against the Greeks applies also to the quality of their myths, which, in their failure to provide accounts of earlier events, supply information that is "just like a nursery tale [παίδων . . . μύθων]." *Tim.* 22b, 23b; see also Hartmann, "The Strange Antiquity of Francis Bacon's *New Atlantis*."

61. Bacon, *New Atlantis*, 467. See also Eric Nelson's remarks on a parallel moment in *Utopia*, when its narrator aligns Hythloday's opinions with that of "your friend Plato." Nelson, *The Greek Tradition in Republican Thought*, 38; and More, *Utopia*, 28.

62. Bacon, *New Atlantis*, 468. The *Timaeus* mentions both earthquakes and floods in its description of the fall of Atlantis, and it seems the ancient ancestors of the Athenians are victims of the earthquakes in Plato's actual account, whereas Atlantis is drowned by a flood. This is simplified in the *Critias*, where Atlantis is simply "sunk by earthquakes." *Tim.* 25d and *Crit.* 108e.

63. See *Tim.* 22d–e. See also Brian Vickers's note on this revision, which suggests that the change was informed by Bacon's understanding of the geology of South America, which he read about in Joseph de Acosta's *Naturall and Morall Historie of the East and West Indies* (1590), a major source of the historical and geographical details of *New Atlantis*. Bacon, *New Atlantis*, 793. See also the detailed reconstruction of the chronology of the flood in Hartmann, "The Strange Antiquity of Francis Bacon's *New Atlantis*," 382–389.

64. Bacon further pursues the metaphor, taken from the Egyptian priest's remarks in the *Timaeus*, of the cyclical flooding of the Nile as being akin to the cyclical ebb and flow of human knowledge. Notably, the first of the *New Atlantis* myths, about the miraculous arrival of Christianity to Bensalem, describes the gospels that float their way to the coast of Bensalem as an "ark" that saved the island "from infidelity," just as the "the remain of the old world was [saved] from water" during the biblical flood. Bacon, *New Atlantis*, 465.

65. Hartmann also reads Bacon's use of the Atlantis myth as a celebration of Bensalem's exceptional longevity as a civilization, aligning the Bensalemite governor's claims with the parallel boast made by the Egyptian priest in Plato's original

myth. Hartmann, "The Strange Antiquity of Francis Bacon's *New Atlantis.*" Jerry Weinberger's useful formulation presents Bacon's depiction of Bensalem in these passages as "combin[ing] the deeds of the Athenians (Greeks) and the surviving antiquity of Egypt" highlighted in Plato's original myth. J. Weinberger, "Science and Rule in Bacon's Utopia: An Introduction to the Reading of the New Atlantis," *American Political Science Review* 70, no. 3 (1976): 878.

66. Boesky, *Founding Fictions,* 20.

67. Hythloday's final word on Utopia is his prognosis that it is "likely to last forever." More, *Utopia,* 106.

68. Bacon, *New Atlantis,* 468–469.

69. Bacon, *New Atlantis,* 469, 472.

70. More, *Utopia,* 39–40.

71. In the Utopian context, the scholars' exemption from labor is all the more remarkable given the care More takes to emphasize that Utopia's economic self-sufficiency depends in large part on maximizing the efficiency of the citizen body, in particular by eliminating idleness and putting to work all members of the population capable of it. More, *Utopia,* 48–52. At the same time, in a departure from the principle of specialization around which the *kallipolis* is organized, public lectures in Utopia are attended by both scholars, who are required to be there, and lay citizens, who might volunteer to go at their own leisure without commitment, as it is equally commendable in Utopian society to spend one's free time working at one's trade. More, *Utopia,* 50; see George M. Logan's note at More, *Utopia,* 49n28.

72. Scholars occupy the offices of the "ambassadors, priests, tranibors and the governor himself." The exception are the syphogrants, the elected officials representing groups of households. Admission to the class of scholars is a two-step process: one must first be recommended by the priests, upon which the syphogrants take a secret vote. More, *Utopia,* 52. See also White, "Pride and the Public Good," 349.

73. The Fellows of Salomon's House make regular, if infrequent and unpredictable, circuits of Bensalem's principal cities to give counsel. When one resplendently dressed Fellow makes a rare appearance in the city where the European sailors are stranded, he is met with a parade in which "all the officers and principals of the Companies of the City" trail behind his cushioned chariot. They are also exempt from standard protocol in seating arrangements at feasts. Bacon, *New Atlantis,* 479; see also 475, 478, 486.

74. Bacon, *New Atlantis,* 478, 479, 487.

75. Bacon, *New Atlantis,* 464, 471.

76. More, by contrast, does not include an equivalent origin story for the Utopian class of scholars; nor is the establishment of this class explicitly linked to the

original accomplishments of Utopus at the founding of Utopia. It is the basic equality of the citizens, rather than the difference between kinds of labor, that is emphasized in Utopia's founding myth about the native population and Utopus's soldiers being put to work on digging the same channel.

Nonetheless, More was clearly influenced by the Myth of Metals. Although Hythloday distances himself from the question of "whether it is the business of a philosopher to tell lies," he also borrows directly from the language of Plato's myth when he introduces the Utopian scholar class. See More, *Utopia*, 35; and compare *Rep.* III 415b–c with More, *Utopia*, 52, noting especially the constructions of demotion and promotion to describe mobility between laboring and intellectual classes. Where More diverges from Plato in these passages is a difference in emphasis: if an idiosyncratically defined conception of nature had been Plato's criterion for membership in one class over another in the *kallipolis,* More stresses the value of individual effort; this also means that, unlike in the *kallipolis,* promotion or demotion from the Utopian scholar class can occur at any time, rather than after a particular juncture in the educational curriculum instituted by the state.

77. Karl Popper, *The Open Society and Its Enemies,* vol. 1, *The Spell of Plato* (Princeton, NJ: Princeton University Press, 1966), 122.

78. Tales of Utopus's other deeds emphasize the ways in which he made provisions for flexibility within the enduring institutions he created: although the foundations of the city were laid by Utopus, buildings within the overall design can be adorned and improved to taste. All citizens must believe in the immortality of the soul and in divine providence, but there is religious freedom within these bounds.

79. Nelson, *The Greek Tradition in Republican Thought,* 20–21; James Romm, "More's Strategy of Naming in the *Utopia*," *Sixteenth Century Journal* 22, no. 2 (1991): 173–183; White, *Peace among the Willows,* 144–145; Jerry Weinberger, "On the Miracles in Bacon's *New Atlantis*," in *Francis Bacon's New Atlantis: New Interdisciplinary Essays,* ed. Bronwen Price (Manchester: Manchester University Press, 2002), 107; Weinberger, "Science and Rule in Bacon's Utopia," 875–876.

80. Bacon, *New Atlantis,* 471.

81. The Latin etymology of Altabin is suggested in White, *Peace among the Willows,* 144.

82. A representative selection of More's fables, scattered across his letters and works—including the *Dialogue of Comfort against Tribulation,* which contains the famous "Mother Maud's tale" of the wolf, the fox, and the ass—can be found in Thomas More, *A Thomas More Reader,* ed. Rudolph E. Habenicht (Naalehu, HI: Chelsea Press, 1998), also available at https://www.thomasmorestudies.org /library.html. See also Anne Lake Prescott, "The Ambivalent Heart: Thomas More's Merry Tales," *Criticism* 45, no. 4 (2003): 417–433.

83. George Sandys, *Ovid's Metamorphosis Englished, Mythologiz'd, and Represented in Figures* (London, 1632), 18; cited in Rhodri Lewis, "Francis Bacon, Allegory and the Uses of Myth," *Review of English Studies* 61, no. 250 (2010): 373.

84. Francis Bacon, *Of the Wisdom of the Ancients,* in Spedding, Ellis, and Heath, *The Works of Francis Bacon,* 6:687–764, dedication at 691. There are thirty-one essays in the collection, each devoted to a separate myth. However, the twenty-seventh, on Icarus, also claims to double as an essay on Scylla and Charybdis.

85. See Jean Seznec, *The Survival of the Pagan Gods: The Mythological Tradition and Its Place in Renaissance Humanism and Art* (Princeton, NJ: Princeton University Press, 1995).

86. Natale Conti, *Mythologiae,* trans. John Mulryan and Steven Brown (Tempe, AZ: ACMRS, 2006); Barbara Carman Garner, "Francis Bacon, Natalis Comes and the Mythological Tradition," *Journal of the Warburg and Courtauld Institutes* 33 (1970): 264–291; Charles W. Lemmi, *The Classic Deities in Bacon: A Study in Mythological Symbolism* (Baltimore: Johns Hopkins University Press, 1933); Paolo Rossi, *Francis Bacon: From Magic to Science,* trans. Sacha Rabinovitch (London: Routledge, 1968), 74–75; H. David Brumble, "Let Us Make Gods in Our Image: Greek Myth in Medieval and Renaissance Literature," in *The Cambridge Companion to Greek Mythology,* ed. Roger D. Woodard (Cambridge: Cambridge University Press, 2007), 420–421.

87. "A little work of mine . . . hath begun to pass the world," he wrote to a friend. "They tell me my latin is turned into silver, and become current." Bacon to Matthew, February 17, 1610, cited in Lewis, "Francis Bacon, Allegory and the Uses of Myth," 364.

88. See Lewis, "Francis Bacon, Allegory and the Uses of Myth," 364–365; Rossi, *Francis Bacon;* and Anna-Maria Hartmann, *English Mythography in Its European Context, 1500–1650* (Oxford: Oxford University Press, 2018), 135–163. Bacon's term for myth throughout these studies is "fable." For an overview of the gradual replacement of the word "fable" with "myth" in common usage between the seventeenth and eighteenth centuries, and the implications of this development, see Andrew Von Hendy, *The Modern Construction of Myth* (Bloomington: Indiana University Press, 2002), 1–24, esp. 2–3; Jean Starobinski, "Fable and Mythology in Seventeenth- and Eighteenth-Century Literature and Theoretical Reflection," in *Mythologies,* 2 vols., ed. Yves Bonnefoy, trans. Wendy Doniger (Chicago: University of Chicago Press, 1991), 2:722–732.

89. "Enlightenment's program was the disenchantment of the world. It wanted to dispel myths, to overthrow fantasy with knowledge. Bacon, 'the father of experimental philosophy,' brought these motifs together. He despised the exponents of tradition, who substituted belief for knowledge and were as unwilling to doubt

as they were reckless in supplying answers. All this, he said, stood in the way of 'the happy match between the mind of man and the nature of things,' with the result that humanity was unable to use its knowledge for the betterment of its condition." Max Horkheimer and Theodor W. Adorno, *Dialectic of Enlightenment: Philosophical Fragments,* ed. Gunzelin Schmid Noerr, trans. Edmund Jephcott (Stanford, CA: Stanford University Press, 2002 [1944]), 1.

90. Chiara Bottici, *A Philosophy of Political Myth* (Cambridge: Cambridge University Press, 2007), 67–68; Von Hendy, *The Modern Construction of Myth,* 4. See also Mannheim's claim that the modern criticism of ideology, a concept he relates closely to myth, is anticipated by Bacon's systematic critique of idols. Karl Mannheim, *Ideology and Utopia: An Introduction to the Sociology of Knowledge* (London: Routledge, 1991), 55.

91. See the helpful chart mapping Bacon's conception of the history of knowledge in the appendix to Garner, "Francis Bacon, Natalis Comes and the Mythological Tradition," 291; see also Peter Harrison, *The Fall of Man and the Foundations of Science* (Cambridge: Cambridge University Press, 2007); and Hartmann, *English Mythography in Its European Context.*

92. Bacon, *Of the Wisdom of the Ancients,* 695.

93. Bacon, *Of the Wisdom of the Ancients,* 696–697.

94. Bacon, *Of the Wisdom of the Ancients,* 698.

95. Bacon, *Of the Wisdom of the Ancients,* 695, 762.

96. Bacon, *New Atlantis,* 486.

97. His reasoning seems to attribute to myth not only a historical but a logical primacy. "For as hieroglyphics came before letters, so parables came before arguments." Bacon, *Of the Wisdom of the Ancients,* 698; see also Rossi, *Francis Bacon,* 80–87.

98. Bacon, *Of the Wisdom of the Ancients,* 698; see also Lewis, "Francis Bacon, Allegory and the Uses of Myth," 369.

99. Bacon, *The Advancement of Learning,* 151; Lewis, "Francis Bacon, Allegory and the Uses of Myth,"369.

100. Bacon, *Of the Wisdom of the Ancients,* 698.

101. See Lucretius, *De Rerum Natura,* trans. W. H. D. Rouse and rev. Martin F. Smith, Loeb Classical Library (Cambridge, MA: Harvard University Press, 1924), I.936–950 and IV.11–25.

102. Francis Bacon, *The Great Instauration,* in Spedding, Ellis, and Heath, *The Works of Francis Bacon,* 4:8.

103. Bacon, *Of the Wisdom of the Ancients,* 77.

104. Bacon, *Of the Wisdom of the Ancients,* 76.

105. E.g., Bacon, *The New Organon,* 244.

106. Bacon, *The Great Instauration,* 7.

107. Bacon, *The New Organon,* 40.

108. Bacon, *The New Organon,* 70.

109. Lisa Jardine, *Francis Bacon: Discovery and the Art of Discourse* (Cambridge: Cambridge University Press, 1974), 174–178.

110. Jardine, *Francis Bacon,* 176–177; Bacon, *The New Organon,* 35; Bacon, *Of the Dignity and Advancement of Learning,* in Spedding, Ellis, and Heath, *The Works of Francis Bacon,* 4:470, 451.

3. AN ENLIGHTENMENT FABLE

1. Voltaire, *Zadig,* in *The Portable Voltaire,* ed. Ben Ray Redman (New York: Penguin, 1977), 402–408.

2. Daniel Stempel, "Angels of Reason: Science and Myth in the Enlightenment," *Journal of the History of Ideas* 36, no. 1 (1975): 66–67.

3. English translations of passages from the *Theodicy* are taken from Gottfried Wilhelm Leibniz, *Theodicy: Essays on the Goodness of God, the Freedom of Man, and the Origin of Evil,* trans. Austin Marsden Farrer (La Salle, IL: Open Court, 1985), 371 [§415]. For the original French, see Gottfried Wilhelm Leibniz, *Essais de Théodicée,* in *Die Philosophischen Schriften,* ed. C. I. Gerhardt, 7 vols. (Berlin: Weidmann, 1875–1890), vol. 6.

4. Consider, for instance, Adorno's locating the decisive turning point of the Enlightenment in the Great Lisbon Earthquake, or the occasion in which Voltaire was "cured of his Leibnizian theodicy." Theodor W. Adorno, *Negative Dialectics,* trans. E. B. Ashton (London: Routledge, 1973), 361.

5. Christia Mercer, "Prefacing the Theodicy," in *New Essays on Leibniz's Theodicy,* ed. Larry M. Jorgensen and Samuel Newlands (Oxford: Oxford University Press, 2014), 13–42.

6. Indeed, more than two centuries later, Karl Popper would define myth as an "attempt to rationalize the irrational." Karl Popper, *The Open Society and Its Enemies,* vol. 2, *The High Tide of Prophesy: Hegel, Marx, and the Aftermath* (Princeton, NJ: Princeton University Press, 1963), 245.

7. David Hume, *Dialogues concerning Natural Religion,* ed. Dorothy Coleman (Cambridge: Cambridge University Press, 2007), 69. Consider also Adrian Moore's more contemporary characterization of Leibniz's metaphysics as a "repellent lie about what our actual lives are really like." A. W. Moore, *The Evolution of Modern Metaphysics: Making Sense of Things* (Cambridge: Cambridge University Press, 2012), 70, cited in Paul Lodge, "Theodicy, Metaphysics, and Metaphilosophy in Leibniz," *Philosophical Topics* 43, nos. 1–2 (2015): 27–52.

8. Bertrand Russell, *A Critical Exposition of the Philosophy of Leibniz* (London: Routledge, 1992), xxi.

9. Leibniz's correspondences with Bayle, in the form of private letters as well as published work, extended over two decades, and ended only with Bayle's death. Richard H. Popkin, "Leibniz and the French Sceptics," *Revue Internationale de Philosophie* 20, no. 76/77 (2/3) (1966): 235–238, 245–246.

10. Pierre Bayle, *Historical and Critical Dictionary: Selections,* ed. and trans. Richard H. Popkin (Indianapolis: Hackett, 1991), "Manicheans," remark D, 151.

11. Whether or not Bayle had been sincere in his claims that he was protecting religion from the destructive effects of reason is a matter of some dispute. The reception of Bayle's ideas has pointed in the other direction, and Bayle has often been hailed as a vital contributor to subsequent movements in Enlightenment intellectual culture that shifted authority away from religion. See Richard Popkin's introduction to Bayle, *Historical and Critical Dictionary.*

12. Leibniz, *Theodicy,* 73 [§1].

13. On the special, if complicated, role of divine revelation in Leibniz's account of reason, especially as compared with Bayle's, see Paul Lodge and Benjamin Crowe, "Leibniz, Bayle, and Locke on Faith and Reason," *American Catholic Philosophical Quarterly* 76, no. 4 (2002): 575–600.

14. Leibniz's account of the relationship between human and divine reason does not wholly do away with divine revelation, or with knowledge that is accessible only to God. His point, however, is that humans and God partake in the same reason.

15. Lorenzo Valla, "Dialogue on Free Will," trans. Charles Edward Trinkaus Jr., in *The Renaissance Philosophy of Man,* ed. Ernst Cassirer, Paul Oskar Kristeller, and John Herman Randall (Chicago: University of Chicago Press, 1967), 155–182.

16. Leibniz, *Theodicy,* 369 [§413].

17. Leibniz, *Theodicy,* 373 [§417].

18. Leibniz, Theodicy, 72 [§1].

19. Formally, the structure reproduces a template to which the essays of the *Theodicy* preceding the myth had kept for some time: presenting a lengthy quotation excerpted from Bayle's work, followed by Leibniz's dutiful retort. By more or less quoting Valla at length in the first half, and then continuing to expand the story with original material, the Petite Fable effectively resumes the dialogue Leibniz had set up between himself and Bayle, with Valla cast as a stand-in for Bayle. In so doing, Leibniz frames this debate as part of a long series of historical conversations on the boundaries of reason and faith, aligning Bayle's position with that of "Laurentius Valla against Boethius and . . . that of Luther against Erasmus." Leibniz, *Theodicy,* 365 [§405], 72 [Preface].

The parallel that Leibniz saw between his own debate with Bayle and those of these authors also means that the shadow of Boethius looms like an additional interlocutor over Leibniz's appropriation of Valla in his response to Bayle. For a systematic treatment of Boethius's influence on this passage, see the excellent essay by Margaret Cameron, "Ac Pene Stoicus: Valla and Leibniz on 'The Consolation of Philosophy,'" *History of Philosophy Quarterly* 24, no. 4 (2007): 337–354.

20. Trinkaus, introduction to Valla, "Dialogue on Free Will," 150.

21. Even the interlocutor in Valla's own dialogue is dissatisfied with the answer—likely a reflection of Valla's own dissatisfaction with the limits of philosophy. "It seems to me," the interlocutor observes, "that Apollo in excusing himself accuses Jupiter more than he accuses Sextus." Leibniz, *Theodicy,* 368 [§411]; Valla, "Dialogue on Free Will," 174. On this, see also Valla, "Dialogue on Free Will," 173, and Cameron, "Ac Pene Stoicus,'" 342.

22. In Valla's dialogue, the inquiries of Sextus Tarquinius are to a limited extent also a stand-in for the inquiries of philosophy itself. Valla favorably compares the exile of the sinful Tarquin to the exile of philosophy from the realm of theology during times of "the most pious antiquity." Valla, "Dialogue on Free Will," 156.

23. Leibniz, *Theodicy,* 368 [§411]. Leibniz's paraphrasing of Valla at §§411–412 is freer and more condensed. Compare with Valla, "Dialogue on Free Will," 174.

24. Leibniz, *Theodicy,* 369 [§412]. Valla's objection is more colorful: Boethius, the philosopher in question, had "sail[ed] north instead of south," and "did not bring the fleet laden with wine into the port of the fatherland but dashed it on barbarian coasts and on foreign shores." Valla, "Dialogue on Free Will," 179.

25. Rather, Leibniz considers it a "defect" on the part of Valla that he gives up too soon on the puzzle, and admits prematurely to the limits of philosophy. In continuing to use the fable to find a rational reconciliation of divine benevolence, free will, and the existence of evil, Leibniz writes over Valla's answer in the same fictional medium. Leibniz, *Theodicy,* 365 [§413]; see Cameron, "Ac Pene Stoicus," 349.

26. Pallas Athena, the warden and guide of the Palace of Fates, is meant to embody God's "knowledge of simple intelligence (that embraces all that is possible)," and moving through the halls of the palace is a theoretical exercise in entertaining and analyzing an infinite number of hypothetical scenarios, all brought together "here, that is, in ideas." Leibniz, *Theodicy,* 371 [§414], 373 [§417].

27. See also Leibniz's remarks on "retaining the dialogue form" of Valla's original, in Leibniz, *Theodicy,* 365 [§405].

28. For the most part, Leibniz concentrates his literary efforts on furnishing details that emphasize the rational nature of God's creation, and, by extension, its accessibility to human reason. Notably, the worlds contained in the Palace of Fates are illustrated using a number of evocative images, which, like the image of the book, are taken from a familiar vocabulary of tropes for depicting human knowledge. In particular, geometry figures prominently in representing the relationship between the worlds. See Leibniz, *Theodicy,* 371–372 [§414, §416].

29. "Ancient myth . . . receives a new role; it becomes the vehicle of logical thought." Ernst Cassirer, *The Individual and the Cosmos in Renaissance Philosophy,* trans. Mario Domandi (Chicago: University of Chicago Press, 2010), 80.

30. Trinkaus, introduction to Valla, "Dialogue on Free Will," 147–150.

31. Valla, "Dialogue on Free Will," 175.

32. See the excellent discussions of Charles Rollin, Louis de Jaucourt, and the anonymous author of the *Elementary Encyclopedia* (1775) in Jean Starobinski, "Fable and Mythology in Seventeenth- and Eighteenth-Century Literature and Theoretical Reflection," in *Mythologies,* ed. Yves Bonnefoy, trans. Wendy Doniger, vol. 2 (Chicago: University of Chicago Press, 1991), 722–728. While the use of mythological elements in a range of cultural products—from operas to ceiling decoration—had the effect of ennobling the subject matter on which such ornaments were applied, mythological elements were also used heavily in satire, as a way of parodying the pretensions of a culture that made mythological allusions to signal decorum or grandness. See Starobinski, "Fable and Mythology," 725–727.

33. Isaac Newton, *The Chronology of Ancient Kingdoms Amended* (London, 1728). See discussion in Frank E. Manuel, *The Eighteenth Century Confronts the Gods* (Cambridge, MA: Harvard University Press, 1959), 85–125.

Leibniz was necessarily steeped in these discussions, and he shared with the budding mythographers of his day a fascination with the belief systems and practices of non-Western cultures, genealogy, oral history, and indigenous languages. On Leibniz's deep interest in China and his correspondences with Joachim Bouvet on the topic, see Franklin Perkins, *Leibniz and China: A Commerce of Light* (Cambridge: Cambridge University Press, 2004); Maria Rosa Antognazza, *Leibniz: An Intellectual Biography* (Cambridge: Cambridge University Press, 2011), 433–436. On his research on the history of the Guelf household—Leibniz's primary occupation from 1685 until his death—see Antognazza, *Leibniz,* 230–233, and Justin E. H. Smith, *Nature, Human Nature, and Human Difference: Race in Early Modern Philosophy* (Princeton, NJ: Princeton University Press, 2015), 200. On his study of the languages of indigenous tongues, including that of the mining community at Harz, see Smith, *Nature, Human Nature, and Human Difference,* 194–195; Antognazza, *Leibniz,* 229; on his ambitions to develop a universal symbolic language, see also Antognazza, *Leibniz,* 92–98.

34. Peter Gay, *The Enlightenment: An Interpretation,* 2 vols. (New York: Norton, 1977), 1:145–150; Max Horkheimer and Theodor W. Adorno, *Dialectic of Enlightenment: Philosophical Fragments,* ed. Gunzelin Schmid Noerr, trans. Edmund Jephcott (Stanford, CA: Stanford University Press, 2002 [1944]).

35. Bayle, *Historical and Critical Dictionary,* "Jupiter," 109. The irony, of course, is that Bayle took so much delight in going through the scandalous details

of Greek and Roman myth in the *Dictionary* that his efforts to depict myth as a subject unworthy of interest ended up having the opposite effect. Burton Feldman and Robert D. Richardson, eds., *The Rise of Modern Mythology, 1680–1860* (Bloomington: Indiana University Press, 2000), 19.

36. This account of myth, as being merely absurd and unworthy of philosophical interest, would be passed down in more or less unaltered form to Voltaire, who in turn would become Leibniz's most famous critic. Like Bayle, Voltaire believed myth to be merely foolish, if not immoral, and went on to write mocking and burlesque parodies of mythical material, a practice he extended to his treatment of Christianity. See Feldman and Richardson, *The Rise of Modern Mythology*, 151–156; but also see Starobinski, "Fable and Mythology, 727–778.

37. Manuel, *The Eighteenth Century Confronts the Gods,* 27.

38. Bayle, *Historical and Critical Dictionary,* "Jupiter," note N, 116.

39. Bayle, *Historical and Critical Dictionary,* "Jupiter," 109.

40. Bayle, *Historical and Critical Dictionary,* "Jupiter," note G, 114.

41. Pierre Bayle, *Various Thoughts on the Occasion of a Comet,* trans. Robert C. Bartlett (Albany: State University of New York Press, 2000), 22.

42. The sensationalism around the Comet of 1680 was partly fueled by a claim that the fall of the Roman Republic was linked to a series of comets. Charging poetic sources with having advanced such claims, Bayle vowed that, "so far from believing, on the basis of their word, that the overturning of the Roman Republic was the effect of two or three comets, I would not even believe that any appeared at that time, if there were none other than they to assert it." Bayle, *Various Thoughts on the Occasion of a Comet,* 18–19; "poetic fictions" at 128.

43. Manuel, *The Eighteenth Century Confronts the Gods,* 42; Antognazza, *Leibniz,* 431–432.

44. After Leibniz's death—when academies of sciences elsewhere did nothing to mark the occasion, including the Berlin Academy of Sciences, which Leibniz had helped found—Fontenelle would make a point of delivering his celebrated eulogy before the French Academy. Antognazza, *Leibniz,* 1–2; Gregory Brown, "Leibniz's Endgame and the Ladies of the Courts," *Journal of the History of Ideas* 65, no. 1 (2004): 75–100.

45. Manuel, *The Eighteenth Century Confronts the Gods,* 42.

46. "You already believe the one, why not the other as well?" The result of this fallacious logic, according to Fontenelle, is "an inexhaustible source of prodigies that one cannot call absurd." Bernard de Fontenelle, "Of the Origin of Fables," in Feldman and Richardson, *The Rise of Modern Mythology,* 15. *De l'origine des fables* was published in 1724, but he certainly started work on it much earlier.

47. Fontenelle, "Of the Origin of Fables," 14.

48. Fontenelle, "Of the Origin of Fables," 13–14.

49. "The first, because we are already in error, leads us to become more so, and the second prevents us from extricating ourselves because we have been stuck for some time." Fontenelle, "Of the Origin of Fables," 15.

50. Fontenelle, "Of the Origin of Fables," 15.

51. Fontenelle, "Of the Origin of Fables," 10.

52. Fontenelle, "Of the Origin of Fables," 18.

53. Gay, *The Enlightenment*, 1:145–146.

54. An older tradition attributes the broad term "Platonism" to any sort of theology accused of having been led astray by pagan philosophy. Trinitarianism, for instance, was frequently accused of being Platonist in a pejorative sense. The term was also used synonymously with pagan superstition, as understood in contrast to Christian religion. See Jonathan Z. Smith, *Drudgery Divine: On the Comparison of Early Christianities and the Religions of Late Antiquity* (Chicago: University of Chicago Press, 1990), 15–16.

55. On humanist Neoplatonism, see E. N. Tigerstedt, *The Decline and Fall of the Neoplatonic Interpretation of Plato: An Outline and Some Observations* (Helsinki: Societas Scientariarum Fennica, 1974), 25; Paul Oskar Kristeller, "Renaissance Platonism," in *Facets of the Renaissance,* ed. W. H. Werkmeister (Los Angeles: University of Southern California Press, 1959), 87–107.

56. See Manuel, *The Eighteenth Century Confronts the Gods,* 30. As a Huguenot refugee in England, Souverain came to be linked with two figures with whom Leibniz either corresponded or sought to correspond. Souverain at one point sought employment under Edward Clarke, the father of Samuel Clarke, and through those efforts came to be known to Locke, who appears to have taken an interest in his work. See John Marshall, "Locke, Socinianism, 'Socinianism,' and Unitarianism," in *English Philosophy in the Age of Locke,* ed. Michael Alexander Stewart (Oxford: Oxford University Press, 2000), 126.

57. Matthieu Souverain, *Platonism Unveiled,* English translation (n.p., 1700), 70; Manuel, *The Eighteenth Century Confronts the Gods,* 30; Smith, *Drudgery Divine,* 18.

58. For an overview of the status of Platonism in sixteenth- and seventeenth-century French aesthetics, see Nicholas Cronk, *The Classical Sublime: French Neoclassicism and the Language of Literature* (Charlottesville, VA: Rookwood Press, 2002), 31–50.

59. Samuel Parker, *A Free and Impartial Censure of the Platonick Philosophie, Being a Letter Written to his much Honoured Friend Mr. Nath. Bisbie,* 2nd ed. (Oxford: Oxford University Press, 1667), 71; cited in Robert Edward Norton, *The Beautiful Soul: Aesthetic Morality in the Eighteenth Century* (Ithaca, NY: Cornell University Press, 1995), 102–103.

60. Voltaire, *Philosophical Dictionary,* trans. Peter Gay (New York: Basic Books, 1962); Voltaire, "On Religion," in Feldman and Richardson, *The Rise of*

Modern Mythology, 155. Voltaire's celebratory embrace of the Socratic spirit found its fullest expression in his play *Socrates: A Tragedy in Three Acts* (1759). See Voltaire, *Socrates*, in *The Works of Voltaire: A Contemporary Version*, ed. Tobias Smollett and John Morley, trans. William F. Fleming, 21 vols. (New York: E. R. DuMont, 1901), 8:270–315. On the influence of the play on subsequent "Socrates plays," see Martin Puchner, *The Drama of Ideas: Platonic Provocations in Theater and Philosophy* (Oxford: Oxford University Press, 2010), 57–63. At the same time, Voltaire rejected metaphysics of all kinds, and hence his estimation of Plato ultimately fell on the side of disapproval. Gay, *The Enlightenment*, 1:135.

61. Prior to this period, Leibniz had considerable exposure to Platonic philosophy during his education in Leipzig. Christia Mercer, "The Young Leibniz and His Teachers," in *The Young Leibniz and His Philosophy (1646–76)*, ed. Stuart C. Brown (Dordrecht: Kluwer Academic, 1999), 19–40.

62. Stuart Brown, "Leibniz and Berkeley: Platonic Metaphysics and 'The Mechanical Philosophy,'" in *Platonism at the Origins of Modernity: Studies on Platonism and Early Modern Philosophy*, ed. Douglas Hedley and Sarah Hutton (Dordrecht: Springer, 2008), 245–246. Theodorus in the Petite Fable is quite possibly named after the Theodorus in the *Theaetetus*; see, for instance, the sentiment expressed by Socrates regarding the existence of evil in the mortal world at *Theaet.* 176a.

63. Gottfried Wilhelm Leibniz, "Epistola ad M. Gott. Hanschium, De Enthusiasmo Platonico, 1707," in *Opera omnia, nunc primum collecta . . .* , ed. Ludovici Dutens, 6 vols. (Geneva: Fratres de Tournes, 1768), 2:222–225.

64. The centrality of this short lecture to the coherence of Leibniz's thought, and consequently the Platonic foundations of his monadology, have been argued by Patrick Riley, who published it for the first time in his *Leibniz: Political Writings*. He continued to reflect on the significance of the lecture through the end of his life; one of the last papers he penned presents "On the Greeks as Founders of Rational Theology" as the crucial component completing a "Vienna Trinity" containing the more famous "Monadologie" and the "Principles of Nature and Grace Based on Reason." Patrick Riley, ed., *Leibniz: Political Writings* (Cambridge: Cambridge University Press, 1988), 225–235; Riley, "An Unpublished Lecture by Leibniz on the Greeks as Founders of Rational Theology: Its Relation to His 'Universal Jurisprudence,'" *Journal of the History of Philosophy* 14, no. 2 (1976): 205–216; Riley, "Leibniz' 'Monadologie' 1714–2014," *Leibniz Review* 24 (2014): 1–27. I am grateful that the late Professor Riley persistently pressed this text upon me from the day of our first conversations on Leibniz, and for his having shared with me an early manuscript of the work.

65. Gottfried Wilhelm Leibniz, "On the Greeks as Founders of Rational Theology," in Riley, *Leibniz*, 235.

66. Leibniz, "On the Greeks as Founders of Rational Theology," 240; see also Stuart Brown, "Leibniz and the Classical Tradition," *International Journal of the Classical Tradition* 2, no. 1 (1995): 68–89, esp. 85. Many aspects of the celebratory characterization of Plato's philosophy in the Vienna lecture are anticipated in the 1707 "Letter to Hansch," which Leibniz wrote while finishing the *Theodicy*. Leibniz, "Epistola ad M. Gott. Hanschium, 1707"; see also the discussion of the letter in Novotný, *The Posthumous Life of Plato*, 464–465.

67. Leibniz, "On the Greeks as Founders of Rational Theology," 239–240.

68. One of the cornerstones of Leibniz's Platonism is his embrace of what Christia Mercer calls the "creaturely inferiority complex": the thought that "every product of the supreme being contains all the attributes which constitute the divine essence though the product instantiates each of those attributes in a manner inferior to the way in which they exist in the supreme being," and that the multiplicity of the created world is a product of the diversity of modes and degrees in which creatures participate in the divine. Christia Mercer, "The Platonism at the Core of Leibniz's Philosophy," in Hedley and Hutton, *Platonism at the Origins of Modernity*, 228; Christia Mercer, *Leibniz's Metaphysics: Its Origins and Development* (Cambridge: Cambridge University Press, 2001), esp. 173–205, 243–254. See also Patrick Riley's discussion of the role of perfection in Leibniz's philosophy in his introduction to *Leibniz*, 17–19; and Riley, *Leibniz' Universal Jurisprudence*, 21.

69. Raymond Kiblansky, *Plato's Parmenides in the Middle Ages and the Renaissance* (London: Warburg Institute, 1981), 50.

70. "Ficinus et Patricius ont ensuivi Platon, mais mal, à mon avis, parce qu'ils se son jettés sur les pensées hyperboliques, et ont abandonné ce qui estoit plus simple et en même temps plus solide. Ficinus ne parle partout que d'idées, d'âmes du monde, de nombres mystiques et choses semblables, au lieu de poursuivre les exactes définitions que Platon tâche de donner des notions." Leibniz, Letter to Foucher, 1686, in *Die philosophische Schriften*, ed. C. I. Gerhardt, 7 vols. (Berlin: Weidmann, 1875), 1:380, cited in Kiblansky, *Plato's Parmenides in the Middle Ages and the Renaissance*, 50.

"Weighed down by new illusions" from the following: "Non sine admiratione vanitatis humanae notavi Platonicos posteriores, quae Magister egregia, docta et solida dixit de virtutibus et justitia, de Republica, de definiendi ac dividendi arte, de Scientia veritatum aeternarum, de notitiis Menti nostrae innatis dissimulare, quae vero illi excidere ambigua aut hyperbolica cum forte genio indulsit, et poëtam agere voluit, de Anima Mundi, de ideis subsistentibus extra res . . . a praeclaris illis discipulis avide arripi, in pejus detorqueri et multis novis somniis onerari." Leibniz, Characteristica universalis, fragment, in *Die Philosophische Schriften*, ed. C. I. Gerhardt, 7:147, cited in Kiblansky, *Plato's Parmenides in the Middle Ages and the Renaissance,* 50.

71. The essay is known to us as "Leibniz's Philosopher's Dream." I thank Paul Lodge for introducing me to this fascinating piece. The manuscript, which is forthcoming in the Akademie-Edition (Reihe VI: "Philosophische Schriften," Bd. 5), can be found in *Die Leibniz-Handschriften,* ed. Eduard Bodemann (Hannover: Niedersächsische Landesbibliothek, 1895), LH IV 8 Bl. 51–52. Donald Rutherford's English translation can be found on his website: Gottfried Wilhelm Leibniz, "Leibniz's Philosophical Dream," trans. Donald Rutherford, 2014, http://philosophyfaculty .ucsd.edu/faculty/rutherford/Leibniz/translations/Dream.pdf. See also Paul Lodge's discussion of the "Philosopher's Dream" in Lodge, "Theodicy, Metaphysics, and Metaphilosophy in Leibniz," 43–47.

72. Bayle, *Various Thoughts on the Occasion of a Comet,* 141; Haydn Mason, "Optimism, Progress, and Philosophical History," in *The Cambridge History of Eighteenth-Century Political Thought,* ed. Mark Goldie and Robert Wokler (Cambridge: Cambridge University Press, 2006), 206.

73. Pierre Bayle, *The Dictionary Historical and Critical of Mr. Peter Bayle,* trans. Pierre Des Maizeaux (London: Knapton et al., 1736), entry "Uriel Acosta," remark G; cited in Richard H. Popkin, *The History of Scepticism: From Savonarola to Bayle* (Oxford: Oxford University Press, 2003), 288, emphasis added.

74. Leibniz, *Theodicy,* 53 [Preface]. The topic is one of two such labyrinths, the other being the subject of the *Monadologie.* Leibniz returns to this image several times in *Theodicy,* at 89 [§24–25], 336 [§352], 345 [§367]. The image of the world as a labyrinth that befalls reason to navigate is a trope that can be found in Bacon and Descartes. See Karsten Harries, "Descartes and the Labyrinth of the World," *International Journal of Philosophical Studies* 6, no. 3 (1998): 307–330.

75. Leibniz, *Theodicy,* 63 [Preface].

76. Leibniz, *Theodicy,* 54 [Preface]. "The ancients" probably refers to Cicero; see Cicero, *On Fate,* trans. H. Rackham, Loeb Classical Library (Cambridge, MA: Harvard University Press, 1942), XII. The *ignava ratio* is a long-standing problem in the philosophical tradition: see also Kant's remarks in Kant, *Critique of Pure Reason,* A773 / B801; A689 / B717.

77. Leibniz, *Theodicy,* 55 [Preface].

78. Leibniz, *Theodicy,* 54, 55 [Preface].

79. Leibniz, *Theodicy,* 49 [Preface].

80. Leibniz, *Theodicy,* 52 [Preface].

81. Leibniz's awareness of Stoic approaches to religious questions is evident, for instance, in *Theodicy,* 263 [§217], 342 [§363]. The phrase "unworthy of veneration" is borrowed from Jonathan Israel's description of despotic notions of God in the philosophies of Leibniz's contemporaries, particularly in Bayle. Jonathan Israel,

"Leibniz's Theodicy as a Critique of Spinoza and Bayle—and Blueprint for the Philosophy Wars of the 18th Century," in Jorgensen and Newlands, *New Essays on Leibniz's Theodicy*, 235. The corresponding thought in Leibniz, that an arbitrary and despotic god is "unfitted to be loved and unworthy of being loved," can be found at *Theodicy*, 127 [I.§6], and also 53, 59 [Preface], 95 [§37].

82. Leibniz, *Theodicy*, 54 [Preface].

83. Leibniz, *Theodicy*, 54 [Preface].

84. Leibniz, *Theodicy*, 282–283 [§254].

85. Leibniz, *Theodicy*, 282 [§254].

86. Hans Blumenberg, *Care Crosses the River*, trans. Paul Fleming (Stanford, CA: Stanford University Press, 2010), 54.

87. The example of the hair on our heads occurs at Leibniz, *Theodicy*, 55 [Preface]; that of placing one foot before another, at 143 [I.§31].

88. I.e., Leibniz, *Theodicy*, 92 [§31], 109 [§65], 117 [§77].

89. The "truths" that are "above reason" in this way are listed at Leibniz, *Theodicy*, 88 [§23].

90. Leibniz is not particularly bothered by the existence of things in reason's supposed realm that cannot be fully comprehended: as he points out, "There are a thousand objects in Nature in which we understand something, but which we do not therefore necessarily comprehend." Light, for instance, can be understood to a significant extent through existing ideas, experiments, and demonstrations, but total comprehension of the nature of light is beyond us. *Theodicy*, 114 [§73].

91. "Albeit our mind is finite and cannot comprehend the infinite, of the infinite nevertheless it has proofs whose strength or weakness it comprehends." *Theodicy*, 112 [§69].

92. "M. Bayle also thinks that human reason is a source of destruction and not of edification . . . that it is a runner who knows not where to stop, and who, like another Penelope, herself destroys her own work." Leibniz, *Theodicy*, 99 [§46]. For the argument that it is still a constructive use of reason to disprove a view formerly held to be knowledge, see Leibniz, *Theodicy*, 119 [§80].

93. Leibniz opens the Preliminary Dissertation of the *Theodicy* with this definition, and repeats it throughout the work. *Theodicy*, 73 [§8].

94. Leibniz, *Theodicy*, 97 [§40].

95. Leibniz, *Theodicy*, 92 [§§30–31].

96. Leibniz, *Theodicy*, 99 [§46]. The reference is at Pierre Bayle, "Réponse aux questions d'un provincial," in *Corpus Bayle: Oeuvres complètes,* ed. Antony McKenna and Gianluca Mori (Paris: Classiques Garnier Numérique, 2012), 3:708.

97. Leibniz, *Theodicy*, 55 [Preface].

98. See also the discussion of the *Fatum Mahometanum,* the *Fatum Stoicum,* and the *Fatum Christianum* in Cameron, "Ac Pene Stoicus." Cameron admits to

having difficulty differentiating between the *Fatum Stoicum* and the *Fatum Christianum;* this is an attempt at an answer.

99. Leibniz, *Theodicy,* 91 [§29]; emphasis added.

100. Leibniz, *Theodicy,* 56 [Preface].

101. Leibniz, *Theodicy,* 57 [Preface].

102. Leibniz, *Theodicy,* 372 [§416].

103. *Rep.* X. 615c, 619b-c; see also the discussion of the passage in Chapter 1 above. The figure of the tyrant is also a motif in the Dream of Scipio. Cicero, *De Re Publica,* trans. Clinton Walker Keyes, Loeb Classical Library (Cambridge, MA: Harvard University Press, 1928), 283.

104. The claim that the theme of individual identity lies at the heart of the Petite Fable has also been made in Peter Fenves, "Continuing the Fiction: From Leibniz' 'Petite Fable' to Kafka's 'In Der Strafkolonie,'" *Modern Language Notes* 116, no. 3 (2001): 502–520.

105. Consider also Hans Jonas's claim that the most palatable solution that does not assign blame to God is also one that relinquishes the concept of divine omnipotence. Hans Jonas, "The Concept of God after Auschwitz," *Journal of Religion* 67, no. 1 (1987): 1–13.

106. Leibniz, *Theodicy,* 372 [§416].

107. Voltaire, author's preface to "The Lisbon Earthquake," in Smollett and Morley, *The Works of Voltaire,* 36:57, 7; Voltaire, "Poem on the Lisbon Disaster," in *A Treatise on Toleration and Other Essays,* trans. Joseph McCabe (Buffalo, NY: Prometheus Books, 1994), 17, 6.

> Leibnitz ne m'apprend point par quels nœuds invisibles,
> Dans le mieux ordonné des univers possibles,
> Un désordre éternel, un chaos de malheurs,
> Mêle à nos vains plaisirs de réelles douleurs,
> Ni pourquoi l'innocent, ainsi que le coupable,
> Subit également ce mal inévitable.
> Je ne conçois pas plus comment tout serait bien:
> Je suis comme un docteur; hélas! je ne sais rien.

4. THE NEW MYTHOLOGY OF GERMAN IDEALISM

1. Benjamin Pollock, "Franz Rosenzweig's 'Oldest System-Program,'" *New German Critique* 37, no. 3 (111) (Fall 2010): 59.

2. Franz Rosenzweig, "Das älteste Systemprogramm des deutschen Idealismus," in Franz Rosenzweig, *Der Mensch und sein Werk: Gesammelte Schriften,* ed. Reinhold Mayer and Annemarie Mayer, 6 vols. (Dordrecht: Springer, 1984), 3:109–154.

For a selection of contributions to the still-ongoing debate regarding the authorship of the manuscript, see Otto Pöggeler, "Hegel, der Verfasser des ältesten Systemprogramms des deutschen Idealismus," in *Mythologie der Vernunft: Hegels "Ältestes Systemprogramm des deutschen Idealismus,"* ed. Christoph Jamme and Helmut Schneider (Frankfurt am Main: Suhrkamp, 1984), 126–142; Erkart Förster, "'To Lend Wings to Physics Once Again': Hölderlin and the 'Oldest System-Programme of German Idealism,'" *European Journal of Philosophy* 3, no. 2 (1995): 174–198; and Frank-Peter Hansen, *"Das älteste Systemprogramm des deutschen Idealismus": Rezeptionsgeschichte und Interpretation* (Berlin: De Gruyter, 1989).

3. "Wir müssen eine neue Mythologie haben." English translations of passages from the *Oldest Systematic Program of German Idealism* (hereafter *Oldest Systematic Program*) are from *The Early Political Writings of the German Romantics,* ed. Frederick Beiser (Cambridge: Cambridge University Press, 1997), 1–5.

4. Dieter Sturma, "Politics and the New Mythology: The Turn to Late Romanticism," in *The Cambridge Companion to German Idealism,* ed. Karl Ameriks (Cambridge: Cambridge University Press, 2000), 219–238, 224.

Drawing stricter boundaries between German Romanticism and German Idealism is not part of my argument, but for a better sense of their difference, one might consult Karl Ameriks, "Introduction: Interpreting German Idealism," in Ameriks, *The Cambridge Companion to German Idealism,* 11; and Manfred Frank, *"Unendliche Annäherung": Die Anfänge der philosophischen Frühromantik* (Frankfurt am Main: Suhrkamp, 1997).

5. Philippe Lacoue-Labarthe and Jean-Luc Nancy, "The Nazi Myth," trans. Brian Holmes, *Critical Inquiry* 16, no. 2 (1990): 291–312, esp. 297–299, where the authors present mythology as a problem of identity by turning to Plato's condemnation of myth, in the *Republic,* for its mimetic qualities. On myth and identity, see Chiara Bottici, *A Philosophy of Political Myth* (Cambridge: Cambridge University Press, 2007), 227–245. For the more popular argument that German Romanticism marked the beginning of a specific, ethnocultural brand of nationalism, see Anthony D. Smith, *Nationalism: Theory, Ideology, History* (Cambridge, MA: Polity Press, 2001), esp. 41–42.

The idea that German culture was uniquely preoccupied with myth has been posed, for instance, by Thomas Mann, who suggested that German dedication to the "pure humanity of the mythical age" defined "the essential and characteristic national distinction" between Germany and the West. "With the appreciation of this difference," he offers, "the intricate old question: 'What is German?' perhaps finds its tersest answer." Thomas Mann, *Pro and Contra Wagner,* trans. Allan Blunden (London: Faber and Faber, 1985), 201, cited in George S. Williamson, *The Longing for Myth in Germany: Religion and Aesthetic Culture from Romanticism to Nietzsche* (Chicago: University of Chicago Press, 2004), 1. For a contrast between the German approach to mythology and those of England and France during the Enlightenment era, see Frank E. Manuel, *The Eighteenth Century Confronts the Gods* (Cambridge, MA: Harvard University Press, 1959), esp. 294.

6. Johann Gottfried Herder, "On the Modern Use of Mythology," in *Selected Early Works, 1764–1767,* ed. Ernest A. Menze and Karl Menges, trans. Ernest A. Menze with Michael Palma (University Park: Pennsylvania State University Press, 1992), 215–234; see also Johann Gottfried Herder, "Fragment of an Essay on Mythology (c. 1782–92)," in *Against Pure Reason: Writings on Religion, Language, and History,* ed. and trans. Marcia Bunge (Minneapolis: Fortress Press, 1993), 80–82.

7. Carl Schmitt, *The Crisis of Parliamentary Democracy,* trans. Ellen Kennedy (Cambridge, MA: MIT Press, 1988); *Wagner on Music and Drama,* ed. Albert Harry Goldman and Evert Sprinchorn, trans. H. Ashton Ellis (New York: Da Capo Press, 1981), 85–92, 124–154, 187–199; Friedrich Nietzsche, *The Birth of Tragedy,* ed. Michael Tanner, trans. Shaun Whiteside (London: Penguin, 2003), 109–111. See also Bottici, *A Philosophy of Political Myth,* 227–235; Stewart Spencer, "The 'Romantic Operas' and the Turn to Myth," in *The Cambridge Companion to Wagner,* ed. Thomas S. Grey (Cambridge: Cambridge University Press, 2008), 65–73; Roger Scruton, "Man and Superman," *The Guardian,* April 11, 2003; Cristiano Grottanelli, "Nietzsche and Myth," *History of Religions* 37, no. 1 (1997): 3–20.

8. For the dark shadow that Nazism has cast on the reputation of German Idealism and German Romanticism in particular, see, for example, Peter Viereck, *Metapolitics: From Wagner and the German Romantics to Hitler,* expanded ed. (New Brunswick, NJ: Transaction Publishers, 2003); George L. Mosse, *The Crisis of German Ideology: Intellectual Origins of the Third Reich* (New York: Howard Fertig, 1998); and Georg Lukács, *The Destruction of Reason,* trans. Peter Palmer (Atlantic Highlands, NJ: Humanities Press, 1981).

9. *Oldest Systematic Program,* 5.

10. See Manuel, *The Eighteenth Century Confronts the Gods.*

11. Daniel Greineder depicts the project of the new mythology as oxymoronic, based on the assertion that mythology is by definition something taken from antiquity. Daniel Greineder, *From the Past to the Future: The Role of Mythology from Winckelmann to the Early Schelling* (Oxford: Peter Lang, 2007), 125–127.

12. E. M. Butler, *The Tyranny of Greece over Germany: A Study of the Influence Exercised by Greek Art and Poetry over the Great German Writers of the Eighteenth, Nineteenth and Twentieth Centuries* (Cambridge: Cambridge University Press, 2012); Constanze Güthenke, *Placing Modern Greece: The Dynamics of Romantic Hellenism, 1770–1840* (Oxford: Oxford University Press, 2008); see also Philippe Lacoue-Labarthe and Jean-Luc Nancy, *The Literary Absolute: The Theory of Literature in German Romanticism,* trans. Philip Barnard and Cheryl Lester

(Albany: State University of New York Press, 1988), 10–11; G. L. Hall, "Hellenism in Eighteenth-Century Germany," *The Classical Journal* 51, no. 1 (1955): 35–41.

13. Katherine Harloe, *Winckelmann and the Invention of Antiquity: History and Aesthetics in the Age of Altertumswissenschaft* (Oxford: Oxford University Press, 2013).

14. J. J. Winckelmann, *Gedanken über die Nachahmung der griechischen Werke in der Malerei und Bildhauerkunst*, in *Winckelmanns Werke*, 8 vols., ed. C. L. Fernow (Dresden: Walther, 1808), 1:33–34.

15. "Edle Einfalt und stille Grösse." Winckelmann, *Gedanken über die Nachahmung der griechischen Werke*, 33.

16. Johann Gottfried Herder, "Abhandlung über den Ursprung der Sprache," in *Sämmtliche Werke*, ed. B. Suphan, 33 vols. (Berlin, 1877), 5:1–147.

17. Johann Georg Hamann, *Kreuzzüge des Philologen*, in *Hamann's Schriften*, ed. Friedrich von Roth, 8 vols. (Berlin: Reimer, 1821), 2:258; Johann Gottfried Herder, "Dithyrambische Rhapsodie über die Rhapsodie kabbalistischer Prose," in Suphan, *Sämmtliche Werke*, 1:31.

18. *Oldest Systematic Program*, 4.

19. *Oldest Systematic Program*, 4.

20. *Oldest Systematic Program*, 3, 4.

21. Immanuel Kant, "An Answer to the Question: What Is Enlightenment?," in *Practical Philosophy*, trans. and ed. Mary J. Gregor (Cambridge: Cambridge University Press, 1996), 17.

22. *Oldest Systematic Program*, 4.

23. *Oldest Systematic Program*, 4.

24. In an earlier generation, the model of the state as a rational machine had been idealized as a celebratory image of political order. On the specifically Leibnizian legacy of this model, see Terry Pinkard, *German Philosophy, 1760–1860: The Legacy of Idealism* (Cambridge: Cambridge University Press, 2002), 12. Pinkard also notes Herder's influence on the Jena Romantics in shifting what he calls the "dominant metaphor" for nature from that of the machine to that of "life" (132).

25. *Oldest Systematic Program*, 4.

26. Friedrich Schlegel, "Dialogue on Poesy (1799)," in *Theory as Practice: A Critical Anthology of Early German Romantic Writings*, ed. and trans. Jochen Schulte-Sasse et al. (Minneapolis: University of Minnesota Press, 1997), 182; emphasis added. References to the original text will be to Friedrich Schlegel, *Gespräch über die Poesie*, in *Kritische Friedrich-Schlegel-Ausgabe*, ed. Ernst Behler et al., 33 vols. (Paderborn: F. Schöningh, 1967) (hereafter *KA*), 2:284–351. The characterization of modern poetry as the product of isolated individuals, rather than that of a coherent culture, is also articulated in Schlegel's 1797 essay "On the Study of Greek

Poetry," Friedrich Schlegel, *Über das Studium der griechischen Poesie*, in *KA*, 2:205–367.

27. Schlegel, "Dialogue on Poesy," 180.

28. Schlegel, "Dialogue on Poesy," 180.

29. Schlegel, "Dialogue on Poesy," 181.

30. Schlegel, "Dialogue on Poesy," 181; *KA* 2:285.

31. Schlegel, "Dialogue on Poesy," 182; *KA* 2:312. In Fragment 85 of his *Ideas,* Schlegel also locates the "core, the center of poetry," in mythology and "in the mysteries of the ancients." Friedrich Schlegel, "Ideas," in Beiser, *The Early Political Writings of the German Romantics,* 125–140, §85.

32. Schlegel, "Dialogue on Poesy," 183.

33. This goes against the more common view that Schlegel conceived of the utility of mythology solely in terms of the quality of poetry; see, e.g., Greineder, *From the Past to the Present.*

34. Schlegel, "Dialogue on Poesy," 181.

35. Schlegel, *Über das Studium der griechischen Poesie*, in *KA*, 2:377; my translation.

36. Schlegel, "Dialogue on Poesy," 181.

37. Schlegel, "Dialogue on Poesy," 186–187.

38. Herder, "On the Modern Use of Mythology," 215. J. G. Herder, "Vom neuern Gebrauch der Mythologie" (1767), in Suphan, *Sämmtliche Werke,* 1:444. See also Herder, "Fragment of an Essay on Mythology."

39. Herder, "On the Modern Use of Mythology," 228.

40. Christopher Jamme, "Portraying Myth More Convincingly: Critical Approaches to Myth in the Classical and Romantic Periods," *International Journal of Philosophical Studies* 12, no. 1 (2004): 36–37; Greineder, *From the Past to the Future,* 83–124.

41. Hall, "Hellenism in Eighteenth-Century Germany," 39.

42. Friedrich Hölderlin, *Hyperion, or, The Hermit in Greece,* trans. Ross Benjamin (Brooklyn, NY: Archipelago Books, 2008), 150.

43. Hölderlin, *Hyperion,* 206.

44. Hölderlin, *Hyperion,* 202–203.

45. Hölderlin, *Hyperion,* 203.

46. Hölderlin, *Hyperion,* 201.

47. Schlegel, "Dialogue on Poesy," 183.

48. Greineder believes Ludoviko's faith is in fact ironic and that Schlegel believes the new mythology to be an impossible project. Greineder, *From the Past to the Future.*

49. Schlegel, "Dialogue on Poesy," 183.

50. Schlegel, "Dialogue on Poesy," 183.

51. Schlegel, "Dialogue on Poesy," 183.

52. Schlegel, "Dialogue on Poesy," 183–184.

53. Frederick Beiser, *German Idealism: The Struggle against Subjectivism, 1781–1801* (Cambridge, MA: Harvard University Press, 2009), viii.

54. Schlegel, "Dialogue on Poesy," 184.

55. See also Hamann, *Kreuzzüge des Philologen*, 280.

56. Schlegel, "Dialogue on Poesy," 184.

57. The characterization of Schelling as the Proteus of German Idealism is attributed to Hegel; cited in Bruce Matthews, *Schelling's Organic Form of Philosophy: Life as the Schema of Freedom* (Albany: State University of New York Press, 2011), 218.

58. See note 2 above.

59. Lacoue-Labarthe and Nancy, *The Literary Absolute*, 88–89.

60. Friedrich Wilhelm Joseph von Schelling, *System of Transcendental Idealism (1800)*, trans. Peter Heath (Charlottesville: University Press of Virginia, 1978), 255, substituting Heath's translation of *Absichtlichkeit* as "forethought" for "intentionality"; Schelling, *System des Transzendentalen Idealismus,* ed. Horst D. Brandt and Peter Müller (Hamburg: F. Meiner, 1992), 291.

61. Schelling, *System of Transcendental Idealism*, 224.

62. Bruce Matthews aptly describes the threat as one of philosophy being trapped in a "prison of its own success." Matthews, *Schelling's Organic Form of Philosophy*, 4.

63. Schelling, *System of Transcendental Idealism*, 232.

64. *Oldest Systematic Program*, 4.

65. Jamme, "Portraying Myth More Convincingly," 31–32.

66. *Oldest Systematic Program*, 4.

67. *Oldest Systematic Program*, 4.

68. *Oldest Systematic Program*, 4.

69. *Oldest Systematic Program*, 4.

70. Rüdiger Bubner, *The Innovations of Idealism*, trans. Nicholas Walker (Cambridge: Cambridge University Press, 2003), 7.

71. Suzanne L. Marchand, *Down from Olympus: Archaeology and Philhellenism in Germany, 1750–1970* (Princeton, NJ: Princeton University Press, 2003), 20. Exemplary and influential works of classical scholarship of this kind might be F. A. Wolf's *Prolegomena to Homer* (1795) and *Darstellung der Altertumswissenschaft* (1807).

72. Frank B. Evans, "Platonic Scholarship in Eighteenth-Century England," *Modern Philology* 41, no. 2 (1943): 103–110; see also Frederick C. Beiser, *The Romantic Imperative: The Concept of Early German Romanticism* (Cambridge, MA: Harvard University Press, 2003), 68; Beiser, *German Idealism*, 364–365.

73. Volumes edited by J. F. Fischer: *Axiochus* (Leipzig: Langenheim, 1758); *Platonis Euthyphro, Apologia Socratis, Crito, Phaedo* (Leipzig: Schwickert, 1759); *Platonis Cratylus et Theaetetus* (Leipzig: Langenheim, 1770); *Platonis Sophista, Politicus, Parmenides* (Leipzig: Langenheim, 1774); *Platonis Philebus et Symposium* (Leipzig: Langenheim, 1776); *Platonis Euthyphro, Apologia Socratis, Crito, Phaedo, Cratylus, Theaetetus, Sophista, Politicus, Parmenides, Philebus et Symposium* (Leipzig: Langenheim, 1779). The Bipont edition: *Platonis quae extant*, ed. F. C. Exter and J. V. Embse (Zweibrucken: Bipont, 1781–1787). Schelling drew on the Bipont edition of the *Timaeus* (1786) for his commentary; the Bipont books are also found in Herder's personal library. See also Thomas Frognall Dibdin, *An Introduction to the Knowledge of Rare and Valuable Editions of the Greek and Latin Classics; Including the Scriptores de re Rustica, Greek Romances, and Lexicons and Grammars: To Which Is Added a Complete Index Analyticus: The Whole Preceded by an Account of Polyglot Bibles, and the Best Editions of the Greek Septuagint and Testament* (London: W. Dwyer, 1804), 296.

74. Bubner, *The Innovations of Idealism*, 6.

75. On Hölderlin's literary diet, see Beiser, *German Idealism*, 382–384. Plato's significance for Hölderlin can be glimpsed, for instance, in the much-quoted preface to the penultimate draft of *Hyperion*, which includes a plea to "holy Plato" to "forgive, for we have sinned gravely against you." Friedrich Hölderlin, *Sämtliche Werke: Grosse Stuttgarter Ausgabe*, 8 vols., ed. Friedrich Beissner and Adolf Beck (Stuttgart: J. G. Cottasche, 1943–1985), 3:236–237. Schelling's *Ion* and *Timaeus* studies are part of Schelling's *Berliner Teilnachlaß* at the Akademie-Archive der Berlin-Brandenburgischen Akademie der Wissenschaften, Berlin. The *Timaeus* commentary is published as Friedrich Wilhelm Joseph von Schelling, *"Timaeus" (1794)* (Stuttgart–Bad Cannstatt: Frommann-Holzboog, 1994). K. J. Windischmann, who produced a German translation of the *Timaeus* in 1804, dedicated it to Schelling as a way of acknowledging his "rediscover[y] of the true and most ancient physics" in the *Timaeus*. Bubner, *The Innovations of Idealism*, 11–15, 17. On Schelling's early writings on Plato, see Michael Franz, *Schellings Tübinger Platon-Studien* (Göttingen: Vandenhoeck und Ruprecht, 1996), 153–282. For evidence of Schelling's engagement with Plato before his studies in Tübingen, see Bubner, *The Innovations of Idealism*, 7.

76. Schlegel, *Kritische Friedrich-Schlegel-Ausgabe*, 10:179–180, cited in Beiser, *The Romantic Imperative*, 68–69.

77. Julia A. Lamm, "Schleiermacher as Plato Scholar," *Journal of Religion* 80, no. 2 (2000): 210.

78. Moses Mendelssohn, *Phädon oder über die Unsterblichkeit der Seele*, ed. Anne Pollok (Hamburg: Felix Meiner, 2013). See also Miriam Leonard, *Socrates and the Jews: Hellenism and Hebraism from Moses Mendelssohn to Sigmund Freud* (Chicago: University of Chicago Press, 2012), 33–49.

79. Moses Mendelssohn, *Phaedon; or, the Death of Socrates*, trans. Charles Cullen (London: J. Cooper, 1789), 6. The corresponding thought can be found in Mendelssohn, *Phädon*, 62 and 63.

80. The prominence in some of these additions of Mendelssohn's Leibnizian metaphysics is noted in Leonard, *Socrates and the Jews*, 37–38.

81. Mendelssohn, *Phädon*, 184. On Mendelssohn's treatment of Socrates's daimon, see Leonard, *Socrates and the Jews*, 33–34.

82. Immanuel Kant, *Critique of Pure Reason*, trans. Paul Guyer and Allen W. Wood (Cambridge: Cambridge University Press, 1998), 129 [A5 / B9]; 395 [B369].

83. Schlegel, *Kritische Friedrich-Schlegel-Ausgabe*, 18:xxxvi, cited in Beiser, *The Romantic Imperative*, 70.

84. Mendelssohn, *Phaedon*, 6; Kant, *Critique of Pure* Reason, 396 [B369].

85. Plato, *Platōnos Symposion: Platons Gastmahl; Ein Dialog*, ed. Friedrich August Wolf (Leipzig: Schwickert, 1782).

86. "Wann können wir hoffen, einen Platon oder Aristotles so bearbeitet zu sehen, wie es zum Beispiel unter den lateinischen Dichtern Virgil ist?" Wolf, *Platons Gastmahl*, v. "Der blühenden Schreibart" for "florid style," at vi.

87. Bubner, *The Innovations of Idealism* 4; Ernst Cassirer, *The Platonic Renaissance in England*, trans. James P. Pettergrove (Edinburgh: Nelson, 1953).

88. See *Ion* 533d–534e.

89. "Die *Gesetze*, die wahrscheinlich das letzte Opfer war, das Platon im höhern Alter seiner philosophischen Muse brachte." Wolf, *Platons Gastmahl*, vi. See also Wolf's discussion of the nature of the rhapsode in Friedrich August Wolf, *Prolegomena to Homer* (1795), trans. Anthony Grafton, Glenn W. Most, and James E. G. Zetzel (Princeton, NJ: Princeton University Press, 1985).

90. Friedrich Wilhelm Joseph von Schelling, *Philosophie der Kunst*, in *Sämmtliche Werke*, 14 vols., ed. Karl Friedrich August Schelling (Stuttgart: J. G. Cotta, 1859), 5:413; Schlegel, "Dialogue on Poesy," 186. See also Sturma, "Politics and the New Mythology," 228.

91. Schelling, *"Timaeus" (1794)*, 37; I borrow the translation from John Sallis, "Secluded Nature: The Point of Schelling's Reinscription of the *Timaeus*," *Pli* 8 (1999): 77–78.

92. Friedrich Wilhelm Joseph von Schelling, *Philosophische Untersuchungen über das Wesen der menschlichen Freiheit und die damit zusammenhängenden Gegenstände*, in Schelling, *Sämmtliche Werke*, 7:360. I borrow the translation from Sallis, "Secluded Nature," 74.

93. Friedrich Wilhelm Joseph von Schelling, *Aus Schellings Leben in Briefen*, ed. G. L. Plitt, 3 vols. (Leipzig: S. Hirzel, 1869), 1:37, cited in Matthews, *Schelling's Organic Form of Philosophy*, 10; Schlegel, "Dialogue on Poesy," 186. Schelling's de-

scription of a "sensuous philosophy" is intended as a characterization of "the mythology of the Greeks." Bubner, *The Innovations of Idealism*, 14.

94. Schlegel, "Dialogue on Poesy," 186.

95. Beiser argues for the appreciation of "the deeper current of rationalism within *Frühromantik*, and more specifically its profound debt to the Platonic tradition," in that "the Platonic legacy of *Frühromantik* shows that its aestheticism was itself a form of rationalism." Beiser, *The Romantic Imperative*, 59–60.

96. Schlegel, "Dialogue on Poesy," 186.

97. "Es wäre im Ganzen mit der hier vorgeschlagenen Folge derselbe Fall, indem nach dieser nicht selten mythisch antizipiert wird, was erst später in seiner wissenschaftlichen Gestalt erscheint." Friedrich Schleiermacher, "Einleitung," in Platon, *Werke*, 3 vols., trans. Friedrich Schleiermacher (Berlin: Akademie-Verlag, 1984), 1.1:35. See also Gadamer's celebratory remarks on Schleiermacher's introduction, which Gadamer singles out as a masterpiece of hermeneutic thought. Hans-George Gadamer, "Schleiermacher als Platoniker," in *Kleine Schriften*, vol. 3 (Tübingen: Mohr, 1972), 374–383.

98. Schleiermacher, "Einleitung," 7. See also *Phaedr.* 263c, and Lamm, "Schleiermacher as Plato Scholar," 224.

99. Schleiermacher's remark might betray a larger conception of the function Plato's myths: the comment might also present Plato's myths as anticipating ideas to which the logical arguments often, but not always, catch up. Schleiermacher's attachment to the organic unity of the Platonic corpus as a whole even led him to suggest that the "individual Platonic myths are developed and formed out of one, Platonic Grundmythos." Lamm, "Schleiermacher as Plato Scholar," 226n.

"Ja wer erst tiefer in das Studium des Platon eindringt, dem wird die allmähliche Entwicklung und Ausbildung der Platonischen Mythen aus Einem Grundmythos . . . am deutlichsten wahrnehmen läßt." Schleiermacher, "Einleitung," 35.

100. Schlegel, "Dialogue on Poesy," 190; Schlegel, *Über das Studium der griechischen Poesie*, in *KA*, 1:332, cited in Bubner, *The Innovations of Idealism*, 32. On Schlegel's collaboration with Schleiermacher on the Plato translation, see Lamm, "Schleiermacher as Plato Scholar."

101. Schelling, *"Timaeus" (1794)*, 13.100, cited in Werner Beierwaltes, "The Legacy of Neoplatonism in F. W. J. Schelling's Thought," trans. Peter Adamson, *International Journal of Philosophical Studies* 10, no. 4 (2002): 279n48.

102. It has also been pointed out that the *Dialogue on Poesy* is also a remembered dialogue, mimicking the densely layered narrative structure of the *Symposium*. Lacoue-Labarthe and Nancy, *The Literary Absolute*. Writing Platonic dialogues was

not novel to German Idealists and their immediate predecessors. Besides the aforementioned "translation" of the *Phaedo* by Moses Mendelssohn, an influential dialogue was *Simon, ou des facultés de l'âme* (1787), by Frans Hemsterhuis, the Dutch Platonist. The dialogue recasts Socrates and Diotima from the *Symposium,* and its achievement of bringing Diotima's name "back to life in the most beautiful manner" was highly regarded by Schlegel. Friedrich Schlegel, "On Diotima" (1795), in Schulte-Sasse et al., *Theory as Practice,*401.

103. That the proponents of the new mythology were familiar with the *Republic* is obvious, though they often chose to focus their praise on particular details: having women and property in common, or the philosopher-king's reluctance to rule. For the communality of women and property, see Schlegel, "On Diotima." For the reluctant philosopher-king, see Schlegel, *Ideas,* §54; Second Epoch I, §771; "Philosophical Fragments from the Philosophical Apprenticeship (Excerpts)," in Beiser, *The Early Political Writings of the German Romantics,* 159–168. Schelling also questions the authenticity of the *Timaeus,* noting that its content seems to lack the "highly moral spirit of the more genuine Platonic works" like the *Republic.* Schelling, *"Timaeus" (1794),* 6.36, trans. and cited in Beierwaltes, "The Legacy of Neoplatonism," 276.

104. *Tim.* 29d.

105. Diotima, the figure after whom Hölderlin named Hyperion's idealized love interest, is the central figure in the speech delivered by Socrates in the *Symposium.* She presents both a myth on Love's origin and parentage, as well as a speech likening the discovery of beauty to an ascent up a ladder, with a multiplicity of beautiful things at the lower rungs and the idea of Beauty itself at the highest. (*Symp.* 211c–d.) Both of these lessons are particularly resonant for the proponents of the new mythology: Diotima's ladder anticipates the German Idealists' belief in a highest unifying idea of beauty that is consistent with an appreciation of the diversity of all beautiful things in which that absolute idea is manifested, while the myth representing Love as a child of Resource and Poverty echoes the structure of the new mythology as the union of two ideas producing a third mediating concept.

For an extreme effort at building a complete schematism from mediating concepts, see Friedrich Schlegel, "Philosophical Lectures: Transcendental Philosophy (excerpts), Jena, 1800–1801," in Beiser, *The Early Political Writings of the German Romantics,* 140–158.

106. Schlegel, "On Diotima," 401.

107. Schlegel, "On Diotima," 419.

108. Schlegel, "Philosophical Fragments" (Second Epoch I, §123).

109. Bubner, *The Innovations of Idealism,* 31, 18; Schelling, *Timaeus,* 38.29, cited in Beierwaltes, "The Legacy of Neoplatonism," 271.

110. Schlegel, "On Diotima," 419; Schelling, *Timaeus* 29.18ff, cited in Beierwaltes, "The Legacy of Neoplatonism," 277.

111. See *Rep.* VI. 509d–513e.

112. Schelling, *Timaeus* 29.18ff, cited in Beierwaltes, "The Legacy of Neoplatonism," 277.

113. See Pinkard, *German Philosophy*, 7–8.

114. *Oldest Systematic Program*, 3.

115. Schlegel, "Dialogue on Poesy," 181.

116. Julia Annas, "Politics in Plato's *Republic:* His and Ours," *Apeiron* 33, no. 4
(2000): 303–326. For the city–soul analogy, see *Rep.* 434d–5e.

117. *Oldest Systematic Program*, 5.

118. *Oldest Systematic Program*, 5.

119. See *Rep.* IX 588b–589a.

120. That Plato banishes the poets from his *Republic,* despite his own use of poetic devices, may now be a commonplace observation, but it presented for his
German Idealist readers a more urgent problem that required resolution. Beiser
reads the Romantic emphasis on art as a "reversal of Plato's infamous doctrine in
the *Republic.*" Beiser, *The Romantic Imperative*, 48.

121. Friedrich Schiller, *On the Aesthetic Education of Man in a Series of Letters,*
trans. and ed. Elizabeth M. Wilkinson and L. A. Willoughby (Oxford: Oxford
University Press, 1967), 32–33 [VI.3].

122. Schiller, *On the Aesthetic Education of Man,* 20–21 [IV. 6], 25–27 [V.4–5].

123. *Oldest Systematic Program*, 5.

124. This initial enthusiasm mutated, however, into a residual sense of anticipation saturating their work—the conviction that a purposeful and progressive history was unfolding just over the horizon, though its monumental content had yet
to be revealed. Sturma, "Politics and the New Mythology," 225.

125. Schiller, *On the Aesthetic Education of Man,* 25.

126. Political reform as a choice between revolution and education is a dominant trope in Schiller's *On the Aesthetic Education of Man* and in Hölderlin's
Hyperion.

127. "Eine neue Mythologie, welche nicht Erfindung des einzelnen Dichters,
sondern eines neuen, nur *einen* Dichter gleichsam vorstellenden Geschlechts sein
kann." Schelling, *System of Transcendental Idealism,* 233; Schelling, *System Des
Transzendentalen Idealismus,* 300; *Oldest Systematic Program,* 5.

128. Schelling, *Sämmtliche Werke,* 1:341; and Friedrich Schlegel, *Ideas,* in Beiser,
Early Political Writings of the German Romantics, §§32, 49, and 142, respectively.

129. Schlegel, "Dialogue on Poesy," 183.

130. The "blue flower" is a central motif in Novalis, *Heinrich von Ofterdingen,*
ed. Ursula Ritzenhoff (Stuttgart: P. Reclam, 1988).

131. "The art of writing books is still to be discovered. But it is on the verge of being discovered. Fragments of this kind are a literary sowing of the fields. Of course, there may be many sterile seeds in them. Nevertheless, if only a few would blossom!" Novalis, *Pollen*, in Beiser, *The Early Political Writings of the German Romantics*, 7–31, 31 [§114].

132. See Lacoue-Labarthe and Nancy, *The Literary Absolute*, 40–46, esp. 45.

5. THE DEMON OF THE CITY

1. The millennialist Third Reich purported to realize the Kingdom of the Holy Spirit on earth; *The Myth of the Twentieth Century*, Alfred Rosenberg's notorious pseudo-history of the Aryan race, stressed and celebrated its own mythic overtones. In one instance, Rosenberg attempts to trace the ancestry of the Aryan race to Atlantis. Alfred Rosenberg, *Der Mythus des zwanzigsten Jahrhunderts* (Munich: Hoheneichen-verlag, 1935), 24–25. For a fascinating history of the nationalist afterlife of the Atlantis myth, see Pierre Vidal-Naquet, "Atlantis and the Nations," trans. Janet Lloyd, *Critical Inquiry* 18, no. 2 (1992): 300–326. See also the discussion in Herbert De Vriese, "Political Myth and Sacrifice," *History of European Ideas* 43, no. 7 (2017): 810n8; and Henry Tudor, *Political Myth* (New York: Praeger, 1972), 103–110.

See also Arthur Moeller van den Bruck, *Das Dritte Reich*, ed. Hans Schwarz (Hamburg: Hanseatische Verlagsanstalt, 1931); and also Fritz Stern, *The Politics of Cultural Despair: A Study in the Rise of the Germanic Ideology* (Berkeley: University of California Press, 1989); and George L. Mosse, *Nazi Culture: Intellectual, Cultural and Social Life in the Third Reich* (Madison: University of Wisconsin Press, 2003), 93–128.

2. On myth and Italian fascism, see Guido Bonsaver, "Culture and Intellectuals," in *The Oxford Handbook of Fascism*, ed. R. J. B. Bosworth (Oxford: Oxford University Press, 2010), 113–115; Simonetta Falasca-Zamponi, *Fascist Spectacle: The Aesthetics of Power in Mussolini's Italy* (Berkeley: University of California Press, 1997), 90–118; Emilio Gentile, *The Sacralization of Politics in Fascist Italy*, trans. Keith Botsford (Cambridge, MA: Harvard University Press, 1996); see also Mussolini's Naples Speech of October 24, 1922, in Benito Mussolini, *Opera omnia*, 44 vols., ed. Edoardo Susmel and Duilio Susmel (Florence: La Fenice, 1951), 18:453–438, cited in De Vriese, "Political Myth and Sacrifice," 810n8. On myth in Nazi iconography, see Bernard Mees, "Hitler and *Germanentum*," *Journal of Contemporary History* 39, no. 2 (2004): 255; Nicholas Goodrick-Clarke, *The Occult Roots of Nazism: Secret Aryan Cults and Their Influence on Nazi Ideology; The Ariosophists of Austria and Germany, 1890–1935* (New York: New York University Press, 1992).

3. Jack J. Roth, "The Roots of Italian Fascism: Sorel and Sorelismo," *Journal of Modern History* 39, no. 1 (1967): 30–45; Roth, *The Cult of Violence: Sorel and the Sorelians* (Berkeley: University of California Press, 1980); Pamela M. Potter, "Wagner and the Third Reich: Myths and Realities," in *The Cambridge Companion to Wagner,* ed. Thomas S. Grey (Cambridge: Cambridge University Press, 2008), 235–245.

4. The phrase is Ernst Cassirer's, likely adapted from Sorel's coinage of the term "political myth." Throughout *The Myth of the State,* Cassirer also refers to the phenomenon as "the myth of the twentieth century," a more obvious reference to the work of the same title by Alfred Rosenberg. Ernst Cassirer, "Judaism and the New Political Myths," *Contemporary Jewish Record* 7 (1944): 150–126; Cassirer, *The Myth of the State,* ed. Charles William Hendel (New Haven, CT: Yale University Press, 1946); see also Georges Sorel, *Reflections on Violence,* trans. Jeremy Jennings (Cambridge: Cambridge University Press, 1999).

5. The motivating puzzle driving Horkheimer and Adorno's *Dialectic of Enlightenment* is the question of "why humanity, instead of entering a truly human state, is sinking into a new kind of barbarism." The authors point to twentieth-century racial ideology as a "regression to nature as mere violence" and the integration of the individual into a "barbaric collective," just as they seem especially perturbed by "the barbaric drumming" accompanying the rituals of fascism—or "imitations of magical practices" led by the Führer. Max Horkheimer and Theodor W. Adorno, *Dialectic of Enlightenment: Philosophical Fragments,* ed. Gunzelin Schmid Noerr, trans. Edmund Jephcott (Stanford, CA: Stanford University Press, 2002 [1944]), xiv, 138, 152; see also in the "Editor's Afterword," 232.

Karl Popper consistently describes nationalism as an appeal to "our tribal instincts" and a "myth . . . an irrational, a romantic and Utopian dream, a dream of naturalism and of tribal collectivism." Karl Popper, *The Open Society and Its Enemies,* vol. 2, *The High Tide of Prophecy: Hegel, Marx, and the Aftermath* (Princeton, NJ: Princeton University Press, 1966), 252, 254.

6. Ernst Cassirer, *The Philosophy of Symbolic Forms,* trans. Ralph Manheim, vol. 2, *Mythical Thought* (New Haven, CT: Yale University Press, 1955), 60.

7. Modern empirical science accepts causation as a principle, whereas in Cassirer's account of mythic thinking, causation is much less a principle than it is a kind of magic potency. Ernst Cassirer, *The Philosophy of Symbolic Forms,* trans. Ralph Manheim, vol. 1, *Language* (New Haven, CT: Yale University Press, 1953), 96–97. Cassirer provides more extensive mythic treatments of the other Kantian pure forms of intuition—time and space—in *The Philosophy of Symbolic Forms,* 2:71–151. For a helpful and succinct summary, see Peter E. Gordon, *Continental Divide: Heidegger, Cassirer, Davos* (Cambridge, MA: Harvard University Press, 2010), 234–237.

8. Cassirer, *The Philosophy of Symbolic Forms*, 2:45.

9. This is most explicit in the final volume of the *Philosophy of Symbolic Forms,* in which Cassirer conceives of philosophy as a "concept" that "attains its full power and purity only where the world view expressed in linguistic and mythical concepts is abandoned, where it is in principle overcome": "To achieve its own maturity, philosophy must above all come to grips with the linguistic and mythical worlds and place itself in dialectic opposition to them.... This act of separation marks philosophy's hour of birth." Ernst Cassirer, *The Philosophy of Symbolic Forms*, trans. Ralph Manheim, vol. 3, *The Phenomenology of Knowledge* (New Haven, CT: Yale University Press, 1957), 16, 27.

10. Cassirer, *The Philosophy of Symbolic Forms*, 2:26.

11. Many of the themes of *The Myth of the State* are anticipated in Cassirer's work during the war—for example, the essays collected in Ernst Cassirer, *Symbol, Myth, and Culture: Essays and Lectures of Ernst Cassirer, 1935–1945,* ed. Donald Phillip Verene (New Haven, CT: Yale University Press, 1979).

12. This is one of the major aspects in which Cassirer's philosophy of symbolic forms branches off in a different direction from that of the neo-Kantianism of the Marburg School with which he is associated. Whereas the Marburg School had looked to an idealist conception of a universal reason as providing unity to the diversity of culture, Cassirer shifts that task away from a unified faculty of reason to a faculty for symbolic expression. John Michael Krois, *Cassirer: Symbolic Forms and History* (New Haven, CT: Yale University Press, 1987); Michael Friedman, *A Parting of the Ways: Carnap, Cassirer, and Heidegger* (Chicago: Open Court, 2000), 99–110; Edward Skidelsky, *Ernst Cassirer: The Last Philosopher of Culture* (Princeton, NJ: Princeton University Press, 2008), 23–51; Sebastian Luft, *The Space of Culture: Towards a Neo-Kantian Philosophy of Culture (Cohen, Natorp, and Cassirer)* (Oxford: Oxford University Press, 2015).

13. As Edward Skidelsky notes, it is striking that Cassirer treats Nazi ideology and propaganda very obliquely—not as events specific to their geopolitical context, but as mythic phenomena with more general, abstract features. Skidelsky, *Ernst Cassirer,* 223. For the suggestion that this is deliberately intended to reflect Cassirer's perception of modern myth as a general and persistent threat to contemporary culture, see Luft, *The Space of Culture,* 225–226.

14. On the turn in Cassirer's position on myth between the 1920s and 1940s, see Ursula Renz, "From Philosophy to Criticism of Myth: Cassirer's Concept of Myth," *Synthese* 179, no. 1 (2011): 135–152.

15. For a portrait of Cassirer in the context of his time in Hamburg and his interdisciplinary intellectual circles there, see Emily J. Levine, *Dreamland of Humanists: Warburg, Cassirer, Panofsky, and the Hamburg School* (Chicago: University of Chicago Press, 2013).

16. Skidelsky, *Ernst Cassirer*, 94; Luft, *The Space of Culture*, 133–134.

17. Gordon, *Continental Divide*, 19–22; Jürgen Habermas, "The Liberating Power of Symbols: Ernst Cassirer's Humanistic Legacy and the Warburg Library," in *The Liberating Power of Symbols: Philosophical Essays*, trans. Peter Dews (Cambridge, MA: MIT Press, 2001), 1–29.

18. "Indeed, the entire structure of Cassirer's multi-volume *Philosophy of Symbolic Forms* might be seen as providing a formal conceptual apparatus or transcendental groundwork to the Warburg Library's empirical collection." Gordon, *Continental Divide*, 20.

19. Cassirer, *The Philosophy of Symbolic Forms*, 2:xviii.

20. Lucien Lévy-Bruhl, *How Natives Think*, trans. Lilian A. Clare (Princeton, NJ: Princeton University Press, 1985 [1926]), originally *Les fonctions mentales dans les sociétés inférieures* (1910); Lévy-Bruhl, *Primitive Mentality*, trans. Lilian A. Clare (London: Allen and Unwin, 1923); Bronisław Malinowski, "Myth in Primitive Psychology," in *Magic, Science and Religion, and Other Essays* (Garden City, NY: Doubleday, 1954), 72–124; Edward B. Tylor, *Primitive Culture*, 2 vols. (London: J. Murray, 1920).

The investigation of a distinct "primitive" psychology was one goal of the early studies of the school of thought that came to be known as comparative mythology; another—which fell out of scientific favor by the early twentieth century—was the search for an original "Ur-myth" from which all existing myths might have been derived. A version of the latter approach saw a revival in Joseph Campbell's popular work on hero narratives in the 1950s through 1980s. Joseph Campbell, *The Hero with a Thousand Faces* (New York: Pantheon Books, 1949); Joseph Campbell, *The Masks of God*, 4 vols. (New York: Viking Press, 1959–1968); "Joseph Campbell and the Power of Myth," Bill Moyers and Joseph Campbell, Public Broadcasting Service, June 21–26, 1998.

21. Cassirer, *The Myth of the State*, 37.

22. Cassirer, *The Myth of the State*, 37.

23. Tylor, *Primitive Culture*, 1:1.

24. Tylor, *Primitive Culture*, 1:368–369; see also Cassirer, *The Myth of the State*, 9–10.

25. *The Golden Bough* was published in three separate editions over twenty-five years, acquiring more volumes each time. James G. Frazer, *The Golden Bough: A Study in Comparative Religion*, 2 vols. (London: Macmillan, 1890); 2nd rev. ed., 3 vols. (London: Macmillan, 1900); 3rd rev. ed., 12 vols. (London: Macmillan, 1906–1915).

26. E.g., Frazer, *The Golden Bough: A Study in Magic and Religion*, abridged ed. (New York: Macmillan, 1960), 306–307; see also Cassirer, *The Myth of the State*, 8.

27. Frazer, *The Golden Bough*, abridged ed., 824–825.

28. Lévy-Bruhl, *How Natives Think*, 14.

29. Lévy-Bruhl, *How Natives Think*, 43; see also Cassirer, *The Myth of the State*, 11.

30. Lévy-Bruhl, *How Natives Think*, 45. Bronisław Malinowski also belongs to the camp of anthropologists who responded to Tylor and Frazer by rejecting the view of myth as inferior scientific explanation. However, his understanding of both "primitive psychology" and the function of myth in it diverged greatly from Lévy-Bruhl's. See also Malinowski, "Myth in Primitive Psychology."

31. Tylor, *Primitive Culture*, 1:415; see also Frazer, *The Golden Bough*, abridged ed., 306–307. Cassirer is as critical of the temptation to dismiss myth as an inferior science as he is skeptical of any claim that denies the superior achievements of modern science and thought. "According to [Frazer]'s theory," he writes incredulously, "a man who performs a magic rite does not differ, in principle, from a scientist who in his laboratory makes a physical or chemical experiment." Tylor is guilty of the same fault: "If we accept Tylor's description we must say that between the crudest forms of animism and the most advanced and sophisticated philosophical or theological systems there is only a difference of degree." Cassirer, *The Myth of the State*, 8, 10.

32. Cassirer, *The Philosophy of Symbolic Forms*, 2:4.

33. Cassirer, *The Myth of the State*, 14.

34. Cassirer, *The Myth of the State*, 11.

35. Cassirer, *The Philosophy of Symbolic Forms*, 2:14; see also 1:76.

36. "In what we call the objective reality of things we are thus confronted with a world of self-created signs and images." Ernst Cassirer, "Der Begriff der symbolischen Form im Aufbau der Geisteswissenschaften," in *Vorträge der Bibliothek Warburg, 1921/1922* (Leipzig: B. G. Eubner, 1923), 15, trans. and cited in Gordon, *Continental Divide*, 41.

37. As such, the pluralism of the various symbolic forms is bound together by a holistic understanding of philosophy's task. The "philosophical critique of knowledge" has to "follow the special sciences and survey them as a whole," in the interest of heralding "a universal philosophy of the cultural sciences." Cassirer, *The Philosophy of Symbolic Forms*, 1:77–78.

38. For helpful and concise explanations of the hierarchical structure of the symbolic forms, see Skidelsky, *Ernst Cassirer*, 104, and Gordon, *Continental Divide*, 14–16. On that topic, see also Friedman, *A Parting of the Ways*, 100–110.

39. Cassirer also acknowledges the three phases of cultural development in Comte's positivistic philosophy. Cassirer, *The Philosophy of Symbolic Forms*, 2:236–237.

40. Cassirer, *The Philosophy of Symbolic Forms*, 2:243–245, 248, 251; Cassirer, *The Myth of the State*, 297–298.

41. Cassirer, *The Myth of the State*, 280.

42. More as a consequence of the political events of his day than anything else, Malinowski comes close to providing an exception. See Bronisław Malinowski, "An Anthropological Analysis of War," *American Journal of Sociology* 46, no. 4 (1941): 521–550, esp. 543–550.

43. Cassirer, *The Philosophy of Symbolic Forms*, 2:xvii.

44. Sigmund Freud, *Totem and Taboo: Some Points of Agreement between the Mental Lives of Savages and Neurotics*, ed. and trans. James Strachey (New York: W. W. Norton, 1989).

45. Freud, *Totem and Taboo*, 3.

46. Freud, *Totem and Taboo*, 164.

47. Cassirer, *The Myth of the State*, 29. Cassirer critiques prevailing theories of myth in modern linguistics—for instance, in Max Müller—for a similar tendency to pathologize their subject as "a mere disease." See *The Myth of the State*, 22; see also 16–22.

48. Ernst Cassirer, *An Essay on Man: An Introduction to a Philosophy of Human Culture* (New Haven, CT: Yale University Press, 1944), 75; see also Cassirer, *The Myth of the State*, 33, 35–36; Skidelsky, *Ernst Cassirer*, 262n79; Krois, *Cassirer*, 83–84.

49. E.g., Carl Jung, *The Essential Jung*, ed. Anthony Storr (Princeton, NJ: Princeton University Press, 1998), 91, 118–122, 122–124, 125–127, 274. Paul Bishop brings attention to some of the elements common to the thought of Cassirer and Jung; see Paul Bishop, "Speaking of Symbols: Affinities between Cassirer's and Jung's Theories of Language," in *Symbolic Forms and Cultural Studies*, ed. Cyrus Hamlin and John Michael Krois (New Haven, CT: Yale University Press, 2004), 127–156.

50. Cassirer, *The Philosophy of Symbolic Forms*, 2:11–14. Cassirer continuously criticizes psychoanalysis and all other contemporary approaches to myth for focusing not on the form but on the content of myths, which he believes to be arbitrary.

51. Sigmund Freud, *Civilization and Its Discontents*, ed. and trans. James Strachey (New York: W. W. Norton, 1989), e.g., 104, 110. See also his remarks on religion at 36.

52. Martin Heidegger, "Review of Mythic Thought," in *The Piety of Thinking: Essays by Martin Heidegger*, trans. James Hart and John Maraldo (Bloomington: Indiana University Press, 1976), 32–45; Gordon, *Continental Divide*, esp. 237–245.

53. Skidelsky, *Ernst Cassirer*, 94–95; Gordon, *Continental Divide*, 307–310; Luft, *The Space of Culture*, 224–226.

54. "The personification of a collective wish cannot be satisfied in the same way by a great civilized nation as by a savage tribe." Cassirer, *The Myth of the State*, 280.

55. Cassirer, *The Myth of the State*, 280–281.

56. Cassirer, *The Myth of the State*, 289–293. On Cassirer's naming Heidegger in this role, see Gordon, *Continental Divide*, 309–311.

57. Gordon, *Continental Divide*, 307–308; Skidelsky, *Ernst Cassirer*, 95–96; Habermas, "The Liberating Power of Symbols," 25–26; Luft, *The Space of Culture*, 224–225.

58. Cassirer, *The Myth of the State*, 282.

59. Cassirer, *The Myth of the State*, 277.

60. Cassirer, *The Myth of the State*, 281–282.

61. Cassirer, *The Myth of the State*, 282; see also Ernst Cassirer, *Nachgelassene Manuskripte und Texte* (Hamburg: Felix Meiner, 2008), 9:198, cited in De Vriese, "Political Myth and Sacrifice," 811.

62. Cassirer, *The Myth of the State*, 282.

63. Friedrich Nietzsche, *The Birth of Tragedy*, ed. Michael Tanner, trans. Shaun Whiteside (London: Penguin, 2003), 145–146.

64. See Cassirer, *The Philosophy of Symbolic Forms*, 3:16.

65. Cassirer, *The Philosophy of Symbolic Forms*, 1:74.

66. Cassirer, *The Myth of the State*, 296.

67. Cassirer's and Popper's drastically different evaluations of Plato are particularly striking in light of the parallel trajectories of their careers. Like Cassirer, Popper was a philosopher of science, and a Jewish émigré who had fled the rise of National Socialism in Central Europe. In the popular imagination, both are perhaps best remembered today for their confrontations with other iconic philosophers that later became the stuff of academic lore—Cassirer with Heidegger at Davos in 1929; Popper with Wittgenstein at the Cambridge Moral Sciences Club in 1946. Cassirer began work on *The Myth of the State* in the winter of 1943–1944; an eponymous selection of excerpts was published in July 1944 in *Fortune* magazine. By then Popper had completed *The Open Society and Its Enemies* and was looking for a publisher. In April 1945 Cassirer died, and Routledge published *The Open Society and Its Enemies* that November. The posthumous publication of *The Myth of the State* followed in 1946. *The Open Society and Its Enemies* and *The Myth of the State* were both products of each man's long, undoubtedly personal reflections on the irrationality that took hold of Europe during the Second World War. Both looked for the roots of that irrationality in the entirety of Western thought and its history, and yet each offered a radically different explanation, in which Plato, of course, played very different roles.

On the notorious encounter between Popper and Wittgenstein, see, e.g., David Edmonds and John Eidinow, *Wittgenstein's Poker: The Story of a Ten-Minute Argument between Two Great Philosophers* (London: Faber and Faber, 2001); on Cassirer and Heidegger at Davos, see Gordon, *Continental Divide*, and Friedman,

A Parting of the Ways. On the history of the composition and publication of *The Myth of the State,* see Charles W. Hendel, preface to Cassirer, *The Philosophy of Symbolic Forms,* 1:viii–xiv, xi; see also Gordon, *Continental Divide,* 301.

68. Popper, *The Open Society and Its Enemies,* vol. 1.

69. Popper, *The Open Society and Its Enemies,* 1:122ff.

70. Popper, *The Open Society and Its Enemies,* 2:61. "Myth of the Earthborn" is Popper's name for the Myth of Metals.

71. E.g., Nietzsche, *The Birth of Tragedy.*

72. Cassirer, *The Myth of the State,* 77.

73. Cassirer, *The Myth of the State,* 72.

74. This is, of course, the etymology of the word, though the word would have been so commonplace that its meaning in everyday use would have been somewhat distanced from its original etymology.

75. Cassirer, *The Myth of the State,* 75; see also *Rep.* X, 617d–e, as well as Adam's commentary: *The Republic of Plato, Edited with Critical Notes, Commentary and Appendices,* ed. James Adam (Cambridge: Cambridge University Press, 1902), 617e28.

76. Cassirer's reading of the passage is very close to Adam's; it may be the case that Adam is his source for this line of thought. Halliwell, for instance, does not connect the choosing of a daimon to the notion of eudaimonia in any way; and in particular reads the moment, not as one unequivocally celebrating the freedom to choose one's fate, but instead as one that emphasizes the complexity of the nature of choice, as an interplay between freedom and constraints. Plato, *Republic 10: With Translation and Commentary,* ed. Stephen Halliwell (Warminster, UK: Aris and Phillips, 1988), 184, 191.

77. Cassirer, *The Myth of the State,* 75.

78. Cassirer, *The Myth of the State,* 75.

79. Cassirer, *The Myth of the State,* 76.

80. Cassirer, *The Myth of the State,* 71.

81. Cassirer, *The Myth of the State,* 67; see also 71–74, and the discussion directly following the analysis of the Myth of Er at 77.

82. Cassirer, *The Myth of the State,* 72.

83. Many readers favor a reading of the myth where the fate of the soul ultimately hangs on a combination of the influences of individual choice and external contingencies: for example, in G. R. F. Ferrari, "Glaucon's Reward, Philosophy's Debt," in *Plato's Myths,* ed. Catalin Partenie (Cambridge: Cambridge University Press, 2009), 116–133. In addition to these details internal to the Myth of Er itself, it is also worth noting that, in the eschatological landscape of the *Phaedo* myth, the demon leads the soul to the place of judgment at arrival. *Phaedo* 113d.

84. *Ap.* 31c–d; see also, e.g., *Euthyd.* 273a; *Euthyph.* 3b.

85. See G. S. Kirk, *Myth: Its Meaning and Functions in Ancient and Other Cultures* (Berkeley: University of California Press, 1975), 14; Jean Pierre Vernant, *Myth and Thought among the Greeks,* trans. Janet Lloyd and Jeff Fort (London: Routledge and Kegan Paul, 1983), 345.

86. Cassirer, *The Myth of the State,* 298.

87. E.g., Gordon, *Continental Divide,* 312. The myth in question is, moreover, an especially fraught choice. Not only does Cassirer turn to one of the most ancient myths known to us, but he also tells a creation myth—as though the progress of human culture had barely moved civilization forward in time since the creation of the world.

88. It bears pointing out that the German title of Plato's *Republic* is *Der Staat*— "The State"—adding another layer of resonance to the observation that Cassirer's *The Myth of the State* ends with a myth.

89. Leibniz, according to Cassirer, is the "true originator and founder of the philosophy of the Enlightenment." Ernst Cassirer, "Leibniz, Freiherr von, Gottfried Wilhelm (1646–1716)," in *Encyclopaedia of the Social Sciences,* 15 vols., ed. Edwin R. A. Seligman and Alvin Saunders Johnson (New York: Macmillan, 1930– 1935), 9:402. See Cassirer, *Leibniz' System in seinen wissenschaftlichen Grundlagen,* ed. Marcel Simon, in *Gesammelte Werke,* vol. 1 (Hamburg: F. Meiner, 1998); Cassirer, *The Philosophy of the Enlightenment,* trans. Fritz C. A. Koelln and James P. Pettegrove (Princeton, NJ: Princeton University Press, 1951); see also Gregory B. Moynahan, *Ernst Cassirer and the Critical Science of Germany, 1899–1919* (London: Anthem Press, 2013), 83–120.

90. Cassirer, *The Myth of the State,* 77.

91. In ongoing scholarship on *The Myth of the State,* there is an emergent hypothesis that Cassirer's views on myth have been mischaracterized by Charles Hendel, Frederick W. Lenz, and Brand Blanshar, the editors of the posthumous publication. Whereas Cassirer's condemnation of myth appears unambiguous in the published edition, part 3 of the *Nachlass* version, published in 2008, offers a mixed assessment that is reconciled to the prospect that myth is a permanent feature of culture, and arguably leaves open the possibility that modern political myths might be countered with other, novel myths. Chiara Bottici, "Who Is Afraid of *The Myth of the State?* Remarks on Cassirer's Unpublished Manuscript," *Social Imaginaries* 3, no. 2 (2017): 213–227. See also Ernst Cassirer, "'The Myth of the State: Its Origin and Its Meaning' (Third Part: The Myth of the Twentieth Century)," in *Nachgelassene Manuskripte und Texte,* vol. 9, *Zu Philosophie und Politik,* ed. John Michael Krois and Christian Möckel (Hamburg: Felix Meiner, 2008), 167–224. I thank Angus Nicholls for pointing me to this.

92. Cassirer, *The Myth of the State,* 47.

93. The relationship between the symbolic forms and this central unity of meaning has been described as having a "centrifugal" structure. Krois, *Cassirer,* 78–82; Friedman, *A Parting of the Ways,* 101.

94. See Gordon, *Continental Divide,* 63–64.

95. Cassirer, *An Essay on Man,* 224.

96. Cassirer, *An Essay on Man,* 224.

97. Popper granted that the former was "clearly related to the tendency to verify our laws and schemata by seeking to apply them and to confirm them." The difference was that dogma held on to those laws and schemata "to the point of neglecting refutations, whereas the critical attitude is one of readiness to change them—to test them; to refute them; to falsify them, if possible." Karl Popper, *Conjectures and Refutations: The Growth of Scientific Knowledge* (New York: Basic Books, 1962), 50.

98. Cassirer, *The Philosophy of Symbolic Forms,* 1:113.

99. On the crucial differences between Cassirer and the Frankfurt School on this point, see Gordon, *Continental Divide,* 308–309.

100. Cassirer, *An Essay on Man,* 224.

101. Cassirer, *The Philosophy of Symbolic Forms,* 2:74. Ursula Renz offers the alternative diagnosis that myth is incapable of recognizing pluralism. Renz, "From Philosophy to Criticism of Myth."

102. Cassirer, *The Philosophy of Symbolic Forms,* 2:24.

103. Cassirer, *The Philosophy of Symbolic Forms,* 2:25.

104. Karl Popper might have recognized in this dialectic something akin to the relationship of dependency he perceived between the dogmatic and critical attitudes characteristic of myth and science, respectively: "The critical attitude is not so much opposed to the dogmatic attitude as super-imposed upon it. . . . A critical attitude needs for its raw material, as it were, theories or beliefs which are held more or less dogmatically." Popper, *Conjectures and Refutations,* 50.

105. Cassirer, *The Philosophy of Symbolic Forms,* 1:113; Habermas, "The Liberating Power of Symbols," 25.

106. Cassirer, *The Myth of the State,* 14.

107. Cassirer, *The Myth of the State,* 67.

108. Cassirer, *The Myth of the State,* 65.

109. Cassirer, *The Myth of the State,* 65.

110. Cassirer, *The Myth of the State,* 64.

111. Cassirer, *The Myth of the State,* 291.

112. Ernst Cassirer, *The Individual and the Cosmos in Renaissance Philosophy,* trans. Mario Domandi (Chicago: University of Chicago Press, 2010), 80.

113. For the suggestion that Cassirer imagined a role for religion as a more promising force than scientific reason for taming the modern influence of myth,

see Gordon, *Continental Divide,* 317–322; Habermas, "The Liberating Power of Symbols," 26; Skidelsky, *Ernst Cassirer,* 233–235.

114. See Renz, "From Philosophy to Criticism of Myth," 144–147, 150–151. A similar line of thought is explored in Carl Schmitt's analysis of the mythical symbol of the leviathan in Hobbes's political thought. Schmitt suggests that elements taken from myth necessarily resist rational control and elude the intentions of the authors who attempt to appropriate them for their own purposes. Carl Schmitt, *The Leviathan in the State Theory of Thomas Hobbes: Meaning and Failure of a Political Symbol,* trans. George Schwab and Erna Hilfstein (Chicago: University of Chicago Press, 2008).

115. Ernst Cassirer, *The Platonic Renaissance in England,* trans. James P. Pettergrove (Edinburgh: Nelson, 1953); Cassirer, *The Philosophy of the Enlightenment.*

116. For Cassirer's remarks on Bacon, see Cassirer, *The Myth of the State,* 294; on Leibniz, see Cassirer, *The Philosophy of the Enlightenment,* 124–125; see also Friedman, *A Parting of the Ways,* 107–110.

117. Cassirer, *The Myth of the State,* 5, 183–186.

118. Cassirer, *The Myth of the State,* 296.

CONCLUSION

1. Max Horkheimer and Theodor W. Adorno, *Dialectic of Enlightenment: Philosophical Fragments,* ed. Gunzelin Schmid Noerr, trans. Edmund Jephcott (Stanford, CA: Stanford University Press, 2002 [1944]); see also Adorno, "World-Spirit and Natural History," in *Negative Dialectics,* trans. E. B. Ashton (London: Routledge, 1973), e.g., 117–119, 148, 205, 269, 305, 319, 357, 360, 402; Walter Benjamin, "Critique of Violence," in *Selected Writings,* trans. and ed. Marcus Bullock and Michael W. Jennings, vol. 1, *1913–1926* (Cambridge, MA: Harvard University Press, 1996), 236–252; Benjamin, "The Storyteller," in *Illuminations: Essays and Reflections,* ed. Hannah Arendt, trans. Harry Zohn (New York: Schocken Books, 1968), 83–109.

2. Horkheimer and Adorno helped to launch a critical theory tradition that prescribed a vigilant philosophical practice of "immanent critique" directed at all aspects of society and culture, including contemporary myths in all their forms, broadly understood. The paradoxical entanglement of myth and conventionally rational institutions, like those formed around scientific knowledge, meant that myths may not be immediately recognizable as such prior to being subjected to critique, and consequently called for close, highly contextualized critical engagement. It was a nuanced account that distinguished itself from approaches to myth prescribing that they be countered with isolated facts and arguments that may be foreign to the contexts in which the myths operate and hold meaning. In addition, it seemed to concede that our social world was unlikely to be ever entirely devoid

of myths: but this only made it the perpetual and unending task of the theorist to apply old critical tools to each new myth that comes to harden over society.

But where the Frankfurt School might arguably have left open the question of what an immanent critique of myth "on its own terms" would look like, or what form this would take, Habermas presented a much narrower, teleological vision. His demand that myths, once criticized, must be converted into or replaced with criticizable validity claims effectively closed off the potential open-endedness of the Frankfurt School's approach to myth. See Jürgen Habermas, *The Theory of Communicative Action*, 2 vols., trans. Thomas McCarthy (Boston: Beacon Press, 1984, 1987), 1:44, 1:52–53, 2:77; see also Habermas, "The Entwinement of Myth and Enlightenment: Max Horkheimer and Theodor Adorno," in *The Philosophical Discourse of Modernity*, trans. Frederick Lawrence (Cambridge, MA: MIT Press, 1987), 106–130, esp. 129–130.

3. Hans Blumenberg, *Work on Myth,* trans. Robert M. Wallace (Cambridge, MA: MIT Press, 1990). The political ramifications of Blumenberg's theory of myth are still being worked out—for instance, in Chiara Bottici, *A Philosophy of Political Myth* (Cambridge: Cambridge University Press, 2007); Herbert De Vriese, "Political Myth and Sacrifice," *History of European Ideas* 43, no. 7 (2017): 808–824. Noteworthy philosophers from the same generation to take up the cause of myth also include Leszek Kołakowski: Kołakowski, *The Presence of Myth* (Chicago: University of Chicago Press, 1989).

4. For the range of causes for which Plato's authority has been invoked in the last two centuries, see Melissa Lane, *Plato's Progeny: How Socrates and Plato Still Captivate the Modern Mind* (London: Duckworth, 2001).

5. Olivia Smith and Tina Skinner, "How Rape Myths Are Used and Challenged in Rape and Sexual Assault Trials," *Social & Legal Studies* 26, no. 4 (2017): 441–466; L. Michael Allsep, "The Myth of the Warrior: Martial Masculinity and the End of Don't Ask, Don't Tell," *Journal of Homosexuality* 60, no. 2–3 (2013): 381–400; "Misconceptions: Myth-Busting Common Misconceptions within the Anti-Trafficking Movement," Greater New Orleans Human Trafficking Task Force, http://www.nolatrafficking.org/myths-and-misconceptions; Amanda Hess, "How the Myth of the Artistic Genius Excuses the Abuse of Women," *New York Times,* November 10, 2017, sec. Arts, C1; Alfonso Montuori and Ronald E. Purser, "Deconstructing the Lone Genius Myth: Toward a Contextual View of Creativity," *Journal of Humanistic Psychology* 35, no. 3 (1995): 69–112; Molly Crabapple, "It's Not about Sex," *New York Review of Books* 66, no. 9 (May 23, 2019): 10–12; Josh Levin, *The Queen: The Forgotten Life behind an American Myth* (New York: Little, Brown, 2019); Danielle S. Allen, *Talking to Strangers: Anxieties of Citizenship since Brown v. Board of Education* (Chicago: University of Chicago Press, 2004), 12–20; Rebecca Solnit, "Whose Story (and Country) Is This? On the Myth of a 'Real'

America," in *Whose Story Is This? Old Conflicts, New Chapters* (London: Granta, 2019), 13–21; Richard T. Hughes, *Myths America Lives By: White Supremacy and the Stories That Give Us Meaning* (Urbana: University of Illinois Press, 2018); Andrew R. Murphy, "Longing, Nostalgia, and Golden Age Politics: The American Jeremiad and the Power of the Past," *Perspectives on Politics* 7, no. 1 (2009): 125–141; Greg Grandin, *The End of the Myth: From the Frontier to the Border Wall in the Mind of America* (New York: Metropolitan Books, 2019); Eric Hobsbawm, *Fractured Times: Culture and Society in the Twentieth Century* (London: Little, Brown, 2013), 272–290.

6. For popular commentaries that argue for understanding recent political events through the prism of myth, see, e.g., James Meek, *Dreams of Leaving and Remaining* (London: Verso, 2019); Alex Evans, *The Myth Gap: What Happens When Evidence and Arguments Aren't Enough* (London: Eden Project books, 2017); Kalypso Nicolaïdis, *Exodus, Reckoning, Sacrifice: Three Meanings of Brexit* (London: Unbound, 2019); Grandin, *The End of the Myth*.

7. George Lakoff, *Women, Fire, and Dangerous Things: What Categories Reveal about the Mind* (Chicago: University of Chicago Press, 1987); George Lakoff and Mark Johnson, *Metaphors We Live By* (Chicago: University of Chicago Press, 2003); Jerome S. Bruner, *Actual Minds, Possible Worlds* (Cambridge, MA: Harvard University Press, 1986); Frederick W. Mayer, *Narrative Politics: Stories and Collective Action* (Oxford: Oxford University Press, 2014); William H. Sewell Jr., "Ideologies and Social Revolutions: Reflections on the French Case," in *Social Revolutions in the Modern World*, ed. Theda Skocpol (Cambridge: Cambridge University Press, 1994), 169–198.

8. Richard Delgado, "Storytelling for Oppositionists and Others: A Plea for Narrative," *Michigan Law Review* 87 (1989): 2411–2441; Francesca Polletta, *It Was Like a Fever: Storytelling in Protest and Politics* (Chicago: University of Chicago Press, 2006).

9. Mayer, *Narrative Politics*; Joshua Dienstag, *Dancing in Chains: Narrative and Memory in Political Theory* (Stanford, CA: Stanford University Press, 1997); Molly Patterson and Kristen Renwick Monroe, "Narrative in Political Science," *Annual Review of Political Science* 1 (1998): 315–331; Shaul R. Shenhav, "Political Narratives and Political Reality," *International Political Science Review* 27, no. 3 (2006): 245–262.

10. David Wojnarowicz, *Close to the Knives: A Memoir of Disintegration* (New York: Vintage Books, 1991), 87–88, 117, 121; see also Jonathan Lear, *Radical Hope: Ethics in the Face of Cultural Devastation* (Cambridge, MA: Harvard University Press, 2006).

11. Respectively: Polletta, *It Was Like a Fever*; Delgado, "Storytelling for Oppositionists and Others"; Lear, *Radical Hope*; Blumenberg, *Work on Myth*.

ACKNOWLEDGMENTS

There is a part of me that wants to think of this book as the product of a focused and deliberate process, in which I set out to write a book and did just that. But in truth it feels more like a kind of souvenir, just short of accidental, from a much larger and more nebulous journey of intellectual and personal enrichment. I have been undeservedly lucky in the wealth of companions and mentors I've met during the time this project was gestating. Together, they left a palpable imprint on the foregoing pages, but even more than that, they taught me more than I can say about reading, writing, thinking, myself.

My greatest debt is to Michael Rosen, who supported this project from its very inception to the end. His intellectual generosity, warmth, and good humor have enriched this book in more ways than I can say. Nancy Rosenblum, Eric Nelson, and Danielle Allen also lent their expertise and characteristic acumen to the project at its most formative stages of development. All four have been a constant source of inspiration, and their examples have collectively defined my idea of political theory at its very best.

I have also benefited from the generosity of a number of mentors who have been unrestrained and unwavering in their encouragement over the years. I owe special thanks to Peter Gordon, who read vast portions of this manuscript while it was in various states of disarray. For their friendship and guidance, I am especially grateful to Teresa Bejan, Alex Kuo, and Sophie Smith, and also to Eric Beerbohm, Sarah Mortimer, Cheryl

Welch, and Brian Young. I regret that the late Patrick Riley could not see me complete the book about which he had always been so supportive; I will always treasure the memory of the afternoon I shared with him its first working title: upon hearing it, he looked up to the ceiling, as though to consult the heavens, and, upon having reached a private conclusion on the matter, congratulated me on the idea and shook my hand.

This book conspicuously bears the imprint of conversations I've had with many colleagues and friends. For valuable feedback on individual chapters, I am indebted to Jacob Abolafia, Alex Chadwick, Cécile Laborde, Derin McLeod, Joe Muller, Oded Na'aman, Bernardo Zacka, and Sam Zeitlin. My ideas have been enriched by exchanges with Joshua Bennett, Jonathan Bruno, Charles Clavey, Hansun Hsiung, Jennie Ikuta, Rita Koganzon, Nakul Krishna, Matt Landauer, Charlie Lesch, Paul Lodge, Dan Luban, Kalypso Nicolaïdis, Jennifer Page, Zeynep Pamuk, Al Prescott-Couch, Élise Rouméas, Richard Rutherford, Amia Srinivasan, and Rob Watt. Adriana Alfaro not only supplied comments on several portions of the manuscript, but acted as an indefatigable writing partner as we saw each other through the process of finishing our respective books.

For helping me try out some of the arguments contained in these pages with a friendly audience, I am additionally grateful to Josh Batson, Paul Billingham, Abigail Buglass, Ryan Davis, Oran Doyle, Chihab El Khachab, Mark Hanin, Eddie Keene, Paul Kerry, Gili Kliger, Kit Kowol, Joe La Hausse de Lalouvière, Aline-Florence Manent, Jamie McSpadden, Ruby Shao, and Gabrielle Watson. I would also like to thank the discussants, organizers, and audiences at the various venues in which I presented material from this project.

In the course of researching and writing, I have been fortunate to have had material support from the Harvard Safra Center for Ethics, the Harvard Mahindra Humanities Center, and the American Academy of Arts and Sciences, as well as the Gates-Cambridge Trust, the Deutscher Akademischer Austauschdienst, and the Dan David Foundation. The University of California, Santa Barbara granted me a year's delayed start while I put the finishing touches on this book. A special word of thanks is owed to the Harvard Center for European Studies, where I found something of a sanctuary in a prolonged time of need, and to

Christ Church, Oxford, where I learned the true meaning of community. For giving me a home in these places, I'm grateful to Elizabeth Johnson, Jean-Claude Mondesir, Anna Popiel, Sandy Selesky, and Peter Stevens, and to Ann Barrett, Adam Bailey, and Trevor Jones.

Angus Nicholls and an additional, anonymous reviewer for Harvard University Press provided invaluable feedback on the manuscript, while my patient editor, Ian Malcolm, championed the project through to completion. Portions of Chapter 1 were first published in "Plato's Myth of Er and the Reconfiguration of Nature," *American Political Science Review* 114, no. 1 (2020): 54–67. I thank the journal for giving me the opportunity to first present some of these ideas there.

For the friendships that have sustained me over these years, I owe thanks to Cristina Almendarez, Wilma Bainbridge, Tim Barendt, Josh Ehrlich, Sam Ferguson, Dasha Luchinskaya, Balthasar Müller, Jenny Oliver, Hannah Shepherd, Mike Smith, Brian Spatocco, George Yin, and Irwin Zaid. Augusta Opfermann generously hosted me in Berlin, as did Nick Stone-Villani and Janette Chow in Oxford (until I ended up staying). Through their examples, Agnes Borinsky, Jacob Eigen, Anne Fadiman, and Matt Kozlark held my writing and teaching to a higher standard. For setting me on this path, I am deeply indebted to Norma Thompson, as well as to Carol Jacobs and Tim Robinson. For helping me cross the finish line, and for so much more besides, I thank Jon Templeman.

For the past eleven years and counting, Marianne Bauer has been my interlocutor on all matters of the mind, heart, and soul. So much of what is contained in these pages began as half-formed thoughts written out in emails to her.

Finally, I am grateful to my family: to my inspiring sisters, Bee-Seon and Bo-Won, and to my parents, to whom I never got around to explaining what I was writing about, but who never doubted for a moment that it was something worthwhile. This book was possible because of their quiet support from afar.

INDEX

Valla, Lorenzo, 109, 110–113, 276n19, 277nn21–25; Cassirer on, 112, 221
Various Thoughts on the Occasion of a Comet (Bayle), 117, 146
Voltaire (François-Marie Arouet), 104–106, 146, 275n4; on myths, 279n36; on Socrates, 123–124, 281n60; on Plato, 281n60

Wagner, Richard, 150, 190
Warburg, Aby, 194–196

Warburg Library, 194, 195, 299n18
Weber, Max, 13
Whitehead, Alfred North, 248n42
Winckelmann, Johann Joachim, 152, 160, 162, 168–169
Wittgenstein, Ludwig, 302n67
Wojnarowicz, David, 236–237
Wolf, Friedrich August, 172

Zadig (Voltaire), 104–105